Britain's
Best**B&B**

AA

Typeset by AA Lifestyle Guides

Printed and bound by Graficas Estella, Spain

Editorial contributors: Julia Hynard and Penny Phenix

Cover credits:
Front Cover: Dannah Farm Country House Ltd
Back Cover: (t) Laskill Grange; (c) Blacksmiths Arms; (b) Stockbyte Royalty Free
Spine: AA/N Hicks

A CIP catalogue record for this book is available from the British Library

ISBN: 978-0-7495-6102-4

Published by AA Publishing, which is a trading name of AA Media Limited, whose registered office is:
Fanum House, Basing View, Basingstoke, Hampshire RG21 4EA
Registered number 06112600

www.theAA.com/bookshop

A03911

Britain's
Best**B&B**

Contents

Welcome

Britain's Best B&B is a collection of the finest Guest Houses, Farmhouses, Inns and Restaurants with Rooms offering bed and breakfast accommodation in England, Scotland, Wales, the Isle of Man and the Channel Islands.

A Place to Stay

This fully revised and updated guide makes it easy to find that special place to stay for a weekend or a longer break. There are more than 450 establishments to choose from, including smart town guest houses, contemporary city B&Bs, accessible country farmhouses and undiscovered gems in hidden-away locations.

Best Quality

Establishments in this book have received either a top star or a highly commended star rating following a visit by an AA inspector. This helps to ensure that you have a friendly welcome, comfortable surroundings, excellent food and great value for money. Further details about the AA scheme, inspections, awards and rating system can be found on pages 8–10.

Before You Travel

Some places may offer special breaks and facilities not available at the time of going to press – it might be worth calling the establishment before you book.

Using the Guide

Britain's Best B&B has been created to enable you to find an establishment quickly and efficiently. Each entry provides clear information about the type of accommodation, the facilities available and the local area.

Use page 3 to browse the main gazetteer section by county and the index to find either a location (page 442) or a specific B&B (page 446) by name.

Finding your way

The main section of the guide is divided into five main parts covering England, Channel Islands, Isle of Man, Scotland and Wales.

The counties within each of these sections are ordered alphabetically as are the town or village locations (shown in capital letters as part of the address) within each county. The establishments are then listed alphabetically under each location name. Towns names featured in the guide can also be located in the map section at the back of the guide.

①

The Old Rectory

② ★★★★ 🍴 🛏 🌐 B&B

Address: Ash Lane, WHITCHURCH, Salisbury, SA38 2PP

Tel: 01963 300123

Fax: 01963 300123

③ **Email:** bookings@oldrectory.co.uk

Website: www.oldrectory.co.uk

④ **Map ref:** 3, SZ32

Directions: Next to church at S end of Whitchurch

⑤ **Rooms:** 4 (2 en suite), S £85–120, D £95–£120

⑥ **Parking:** 8 **Notes:** ⊗ on premises 🐾 under 10 **Closed:** 25–26 Dec

⑦
⑧
⑨

Formerly a rectory and now a stylish and comfortable B&B, the perfect place for relaxing and recharging your batteries, whether staying just for a night or a few days. Guests have use of the spa, hot tub and a gym. Beautifully restored, with its character carefully preserved, The Old Rectory features contemporary furnishings that cleverly complements the spacious internal architecture.The comfortable studio bedrooms all have easy chairs, dining table and chairs, mini-fridges with complimentary fresh milk, fruit juice and yoghurt, hairdryers and remote-controlled TVs. Home cooked meals, including breakfast or a pre-booked evening meal, can be served in the public dining room or as room service.

Recommended in the area

Salisbury Cathedral; New Forest National Park; Stonehenge and Salisbury Plain

⑩

❶ Stars and Symbols

All entries in the guide have been inspected by the AA and, at the time of going to press, belong to the AA Guest Accommodation Scheme. Each establishment in the scheme is classified for quality with a grading of one to five stars ★. Each establishment in the Best B&B guide has three, four or five stars and many have a yellow star (highly commended) rating (see page 8 for further details). Establishments with a star rating are given a descriptive category : B&B, GUEST HOUSE, FARMHOUSE, INN, RESTAURANT WITH ROOMS and GUEST ACCOMMODATION. See pages 8–10 for more information on designators and the AA ratings and awards scheme.

continued

5

Egg cups 🍳 and Pies 🥧 – These symbols denote where the breakfast or dinner are really special, and have an emphasis on freshly prepared ingredients.

Rosette ⊚ – This is the AA's food award. See page 9 for further details.

❷ Contact Details

The establishment address includes a locator or place name in capitals (e.g. NORWICH). Within each county, entries are ordered alphabetically first by this place name and then by the name of the establishment.

Telephone and fax numbers, and e-mail and website addresses are given where available. See page 14 for international dialling codes. The telephone and fax numbers are believed correct at the time of going to press but changes may occur. The latest establishment details are on the B&B pages at www.theAA.com.

Website addresses have been supplied by the establishments and lead you to websites that are not under the control of AA Media Limited (AAML). AAML has no control over and accepts no responsibility or liability in respect of the material on any such websites. By including the addresses of third-party websites AAML does not intend to solicit business.

❸ Map reference

Each establishment in this guide is given a map reference for a location which can be found in the atlas section at the back of the guide. It is composed of the map page number (1–13) and two-figure map reference based on the National Grid.

For example: **Map 05 SU48**

05 refers to the page number of the map section at the back of the guide

SU is the National Grid lettered square (representing 100,000sq metres) in which the location will be found

4 is the figure reading across the top and bottom of the map page

8 is the figure reading down each side of the map page

Maps locating each establishment and a route planner are available at www.theAA.com.

❹ Directions

Where possible, directions have been given from the nearest motorway or A road.

❺ Room Information

The number of letting bedrooms with a bath or shower en suite are shown. Bedrooms that have a private bathroom adjacent may be included as

6

en suite. Further details on private bathroom and en suite provision may also be included in the description text (see ❾).

It's a good idea to phone in advance and check that the accommodation has the facilities you require.

Prices: Charges shown are per night except where specified. S denotes bed and breakfast per person (single). D denotes bed and breakfast for two people sharing a room (double).

In some cases prices are also given for twin (T), triple and family rooms, also on a per night basis. Prices are indications only, so do check before booking.

❻ Parking

The number of parking spaces available. Other types of parking (on road or Park and Ride) may also be possible; check the descriptions for further information.

❼ Notes

This section provides specific details relating to:

Smoking policy: Smoking in public areas is now banned in England, Scotland, Wales, Isle of Man and Channel Islands.

The proprietor can designate one or more bedrooms with ventilation systems where the occupants can smoke, but communal areas must be smoke-free.

Dogs: Although some establishments allow dogs, they may be excluded from some areas of the property and some breeds, particularly those requiring an exceptional license, may not be acceptable at all. Under the Disability Discrimination Act 1995 access should be allowed for guide dogs and assistance dogs. Please check the policy when making your booking.

Children: No children (🚼) means children cannot be accommodated, or a minimum age may be specified, e.g. 🚼 under 4 means no children under four years old. The main description may also provide details about facilities available for children.

Establishments with special facilities for children may include additional equipment such as a babysitting service or baby-intercom system and facilities such as a playroom or playground, laundry facilities, drying and ironing facilities, cots, high chairs and special meals. If you have very young children, check before booking.

Other notes: Additional facilities, such as access for the disabled, or notes about other services (e.g. if credit card details are not accepted), may be listed here.

❽ Closed

Details of when the establishment is closed for business. Establishments are open all year unless closed dates/months are shown. Please note that some places are open all year but offer a restricted service in low season.

❾ Description

This is a general overview of the establishment and may include specific information about the various facilities offered in the rooms, a brief history of the establishment, notes about special features and descriptions of the food where an award has been given (see ❶).

Key to symbols

★	Black stars (see page 9)
★	Yellow stars (Highly commended) (see page 9)
◉	AA Rosette Award (see page 9)
🍴	Breakfast Award
🍴	Dinner Award
3, TQ28	Map reference
S	Single room
D	Double room
T	Twin room
Triple	Triple room
⊗	No dogs allowed (guide dogs for the blind and assist dogs should be allowed)
🚼	No children under age specified
Wi-fi	Wireless network connection

7

Best Quality

To achieve one of the highest ratings, an establishment in the AA Guest Accommodation Scheme must provide increased quality standards throughout, with particular emphasis in five key areas: cleanliness, hospitality, food quality, bedrooms and bathrooms.

The AA inspects and classifies more than 4,000 guest houses, farmhouses, inns and restaurants with rooms for its Guest Accommodation Scheme. Establishments recognised by the AA pay an annual fee according to the rating and the number of bedrooms. This rating is not transferable if an establishment changes hands.

Common Standards

A few years ago, the accommodation inspection organisations (The AA, VisitBritain, VisitScotland and VisitWales) undertook extensive consultation with consumers and the hospitality industry which resulted in new quality standards for rating establishments. Guests can now be confident that a star-rated B&B anywhere in the UK and Ireland will offer consistent quality and facilities.

★ Stars

AA Stars classify guest accommodation at five levels of quality, from one at the simplest, to five at the highest level of quality in the scheme. Each rating is also accompanied by a descriptive designator (further explained below).

⋆ Highly Commended

Yellow Stars indicate that an accommodation is in the top ten percent of its star rating. Yellow Stars only apply to 3, 4 or 5 star establishments.

The Inspection Process

Establishments applying for AA recognition are visited by a qualified AA accommodation inspector as a mystery guest. Inspectors stay overnight to make a thorough test of the accommodation, food, and hospitality. After paying the bill the following morning they identify themselves and ask to be shown around the premises. The inspector completes a full report, resulting in a recommendation for the appropriate Star rating. After this first visit, the establishment will receive an annual visit to check that standards are maintained. If it changes hands, the new owners must re-apply for a rating.

Guests can expect to find the following minimum standards at all levels:

- Pleasant and helpful welcome and service, and sound standards of housekeeping and maintenance
- Comfortable accommodation equipped to modern standards
- Bedding and towels changed for each new guest, and at least weekly if the room is taken for a long stay
- Adequate storage, heating, lighting and comfortable seating
- A sufficient hot water supply at reasonable times
- A full cooked breakfast. (If this is not provided, the fact must be advertised and a substantial continental breakfast must be offered.)

There are additional requirements for an establishment to achieve three, four or five Stars:

- Three Stars and above – access to both sides of all beds for double occupancy.
- Three Stars and above – bathrooms/shower rooms cannot be shared by the proprietor.
- Three Stars and above – a washbasin in every guest bedroom (either in the bedroom or the en suite/private facility)
- Four Stars – half of the bedrooms must be en suite or have private facilities.
- Five Stars – all bedrooms must be en suite or have private facilities.

continued

AA Rosette Awards

Out of the many thousands of restaurants in the UK, the AA identifies some 2,000 as the best. The following is an outline of what to expect from restaurants with AA Rosette Awards. For a more detailed explanation of Rosette criteria please see www.theAA.com

◉ Excellent local restaurants serving food prepared with care, understanding and skill, using good quality ingredients.

◉◉ The best local restaurants, which aim for and achieve higher standards, better consistency and where a greater precision is apparent in the cooking. There will be obvious attention to the selection of quality ingredients.

◉◉◉ Outstanding restaurants that demand recognition well beyond their local area.

◉◉◉◉ Amongst the very best restaurants in the British Isles, where the cooking demands national recognition.

◉◉◉◉◉ The finest restaurants in the British Isles, where the cooking stands comparison with the best in the world.

Designators

All guest accommodation inspected by the AA is given one of six descriptive designators to help potential guests understand the different types of accommodation available in Britain. The following are included in this guide:

B&B: B&B accommodation is provided in a private house run by the owner and with no more than six guests. There may be restricted access to the establishment, particularly in the late morning and the afternoon.

GUEST HOUSE: Provides for more than six paying guests and usually offers more services than a B&B, for example dinner, served by staff as well as the owner. London prices tend to be higher than outside the capital, and normally only bed and breakfast is provided, although some establishments do provide a full meal service. Check on the service offered before booking as details may change during the currency of this guide.

FARMHOUSE: A farmhouse usually provides good value B&B or guest house accommodation and excellent home cooking on a working farm or smallholding. Sometimes the land has been sold and only the house remains, but many are working farms and some farmers are happy to allow visitors to look around, or even to help feed the animals. However, you should always take great care and never leave children unsupervised. The farmhouses are listed under towns or villages, but do ask for precise directions when booking.

INN: Traditional inns often have a cosy bar, convivial atmosphere, good beer and pub food. Those listed in the guide will provide breakfast in a suitable room, and should also serve light meals during licensing hours. The character of the properties vary according to whether they are country inns or town establishments. Check arrival times as these may be restricted to opening hours.

RESTAURANT WITH ROOMS: These restaurants offer overnight accommodation with the restaurant being the main business and open to non-residents. The restaurant usually offers a high standard of food and service.

GUEST ACCOMMODATION: This general designator can be chosen by any establishment in the scheme.

Useful Information

There are so many things to remember when embarking on a short trip or weekend break. If you are unsure, always check before you book. Up-to-date information on all B&Bs can be found at the travel section of www.theAA.com

Codes of practice

The AA encourages the use of The Hotel Industry Voluntary Code of Booking Practice in appropriate establishments. The prime objective of the code is to ensure that the customer is clear about the price and the exact services and facilities being purchased, before entering into a contractually binding agreement. If the price has not been previously confirmed in writing, the guest should be handed a card at the time of registration at the establishment, stipulating the total obligatory charge.

The Tourism (Sleeping Accommodation Price Display) Order 1977 compels hotels, motels, guest houses, farmhouses, inns and self-catering accommodation with four or more letting bedrooms to display in entrance halls the minimum and maximum prices charged for each category of room. This order complements the Voluntary Code of Booking Practice.

Fire precautions and safety

Many of the establishments listed in the guide are subject to the requirements of the Fire

www.theAA.com

- Go to www.theAA.com to find more AA listed guest houses, hotels, pubs and restaurants – some 12,000 establishments.
- The AA home page has a link to a route planner. Simply enter your postcode and the establishment postcode given in this guide and click 'Get Route'. Check your details and then click 'Get Route' again and you will have a detailed route plan to take you door-to-door.
- Use the Travel section to search for Hotels & B&Bs or Restaurants & Pubs by location or establishment name. Scroll down the list of finds for the interactive map and local routes.
- Postcode searches can also be made on www.ordnancesurvey.co.uk and www.multimap.com which will also provide useful aerial views of your destination.

Precautions Act 1971. This Act does not apply to the Channel Islands or the Isle of Man, where their own rules are exercised. All establishments should display details of how to summon assistance in the event of an emergency at night.

Licensed premises

Whereas inns hold a licence to sell alcohol, not all guest houses are licensed. Some may have a full liquor licence, or others may have a table licence and wine list. Licensed premises are not obliged to remain open throughout the permitted hours, and they may do so only when they expect reasonable trade.

Children

Restrictions for children may be mentioned in the description. Some establishments may offer free accommodation to children when they share their parents' room. Such conditions are subject to change without notice, therefore always check when booking.

Complaints

Readers who have cause to complain are urged to do so on the spot. This should provide an opportunity for the proprietor to correct matters. If the personal approach fails, readers can inform AA Hotel Services, Fanum House, Basingstoke, Hampshire, RG21 4EA.

The AA may at its sole discretion investigate any complaints received from guide users for the purpose of making any necessary amendments to the guide. The AA will not in any circumstances act as a representative or negotiator or undertake to obtain compensation or enter into any correspondence or deal with the matter in any other way whatsoever. The AA will not guarantee to take any specific action.

Booking

Advance booking is always recommended to avoid disappointment. The peak holiday periods in the UK are Easter, and from June to September; public holidays are also busy times. In some parts of Scotland the winter skiing season is a peak holiday period. Some establishments may only accept weekly bookings from Saturday, and others

require a deposit on booking. Guest houses may not accept credit or debit cards. VAT (Value Added Tax) is payable in the UK and in the Isle of Man, on basic prices and additional services. VAT does not apply in the Channel Islands. Always confirm the current price before booking; the prices in this guide are indications rather than firm quotations. It is a good idea also to confirm exactly what is included in the price when booking. Remember that all details, especially prices, may change without notice during the currency of the guide.

Cancellation

Advise the proprietor immediately if you must cancel a booking. If the room cannot be re-let you may be held legally responsible for partial payment. This could include losing your deposit or being liable for compensation. You should consider taking out cancellation insurance.

Bank and Public Holidays 2009

New Year's Day	1st January
New Year's Holiday	2nd January (Scotland)
Good Friday	10th April
Easter Monday	13th April
May Day Bank Holiday	4th May
Spring Bank Holiday	25th May
August Holiday	3rd August (Scotland)
Late Summer Holiday	31st August
St Andrew's Day	30th November (Scotland)
Christmas Day	25th December
Boxing Day	26th December

International Information

If you're travelling from overseas, the following information will provide some useful guidance to help you enjoy your stay in Britain. The individual entries in this book will also give you information regarding travel and the best routes to take.

Money
Some establishments may not accept travellers' cheques, or credit or debit cards, so ask about payment methods when you book. Most European and American credit and debit cards allow you to withdraw cash from British ATMs.

Driving
In the UK you drive on the left and overtake on the right. Seat belts must be worn by every occupant of the car, whether they sit in the front or the rear. Speed limits are displayed in miles per hour. Visit www.theAA.com for useful motoring advice, travel information and route planning.

Car rental
You will be required to present your driving licence and credit or debit card. You can also provide an International Driving Permit along with your driving licence. Further identification, such as a passport, may also be required. A minimum age limit will apply.

Trains
The UK has an extensive rail network. To find out about routes, special offers or passes, contact National Rail (www.nationalrail.co.uk, tel: 08457 484950; from overseas +44 20 7278 5240, and international rates apply) or a travel agent.

Medical treatment & health insurance
Travellers who normally take medicines or carry an appliance, such as a hypodermic syringe, should ensure that they have sufficient supply for their stay and a doctor's letter describing the condition and treatment required.

Before travelling ensure you have insurance for emergency medical and dental treatment. Many European countries have reciprocal agreements for medical treatment and require EU citizens to obtain a European Health Insurance Card (EHIC) before travel.

Telephones
Many guest houses have direct dial telephones in the rooms. Always check the call rate before dialling. Payphones usually take cash, credit or debit cards, or phonecards. Phonecards can be purchased from newsagents and post offices.

The telephone and fax numbers in this guide show the area code followed by the subscriber number. When dialling from abroad first dial the international network access code, then the country code (44 for the UK). Omit the first digit of the area code then dial the subscriber number. For example:

From Europe	00 44 111 121212
From the US	011 44 111 121212

When dialling from the UK, dial the international network access code, then the country code.

Electrical appliances
The British electrical current is 220–240 volts and appliances have square three-pin plugs. Foreign appliances may require an adaptor for the plug, as well as an electrical voltage converter that will allow, for example, a 110-volt appliance to be powered.

Crown & Garter

★★★★ ⇔ INN

Address: Great Common, Inkpen HUNGERFORD
RG17 9QR
Tel: 01488 668325
Email: gill.hern@btopenworld.com
Website: www.crownandgarter.com
Map ref: 3, SU36
Directions: 4m SE of Hungerford. Off A4 into
Kintbury, opp corner stores onto Inkpen Rd,
straight for 2m
Rooms: 8 en suite (8 GF), **S** £69.50 **D** £99 **Notes:** ⊗ on premises 🌃 under 10yrs **Parking:** 40

Family owned and run, this 16th-century inn set in the beautiful Kennet Valley. The bar and restaurant are in keeping with the character of the building, and real ales, spiced wine and a selection of malt whiskies are available. The restaurant offers an interesting range of country dishes freshly prepared from local produce.The spacious bedrooms are in a courtyard around a tranquil garden. Each room has a bath and power shower, a hairdryer, television and video, and tea and coffee facilities.
Recommended in the area
Newbury Racecourse; Combe Gibbet; Highclere Castle

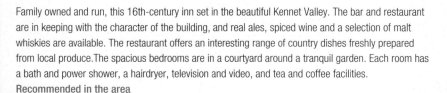

The Swan Inn

★★★★ 🍴 ⇔ INN

Address: Craven Road, Inkpen HUNGERFORD
RG17 9DX
Tel: 01488 668326
Fax: 01488 668306
Email: enquiries@theswaninn-organics.co.uk
Website: www.theswaninn-organics.co.uk
Map ref: 3, SU36
Directions: 3.50m SE of Hungerford. S on
Hungerford High St past railway bridge, left to
Hungerford Common, right signed Inkpen
Rooms: 10 en suite, **S** £60–£70 **D** £80–£95 **Notes:** ⊗ on premises **Parking:** 50 **Closed:** 25–26 Dec

The peaceful north Wessex downs provide an idyllic setting for this 17th-century inn. Inside there are oak beams, open fires and a warm welcome from the Harris family. The owners are organic farmers, and the restaurant and an adjoining farm shop feature superb produce. The spacious en suite bedrooms are firmly rooted in the 21st century, with direct-dial and internet connections.
Recommended in the area
Combe Gibbet; Kennet and Avon Canal; Avebury stone circle; Newbury Racecourse

Windsor Castle across the River Thames

Weir View House

★ ★ ★ ★ GUEST ACCOMMODATION

Address: 9 Shooters Hill, PANGBOURNE RG8 7DZ
Tel: 0118 984 2120
Fax: 0118 984 3777
Email: info@weirview.co.uk
Website: www.weirview.co.uk
Map ref: 3, SU67
Directions: A329 N from Pangbourne, after mini rdbt under rail bridge, opp Swan pub
Rooms: 9 en suite (3 GF), **D** £80–£95
Notes: ⊗ on premises **Parking:** 10 **Closed:** 23 Dec–1 Jan

In an enchanting setting beside the River Thames, this inviting guest house offers spacious en suite bedrooms (many with four-poster beds and river views) equipped with TV with Freeview and DVD, Wi-fi, tea and coffee facilities, telephone, fridge, hairdryer and trouser press. Continental breakfast is served in the bright breakfast room, and cooked meals can be delivered to your room from the pub across the road. During the day coffee and tea are available in the breakfast room.

Recommended in the area

Basildon Park (NT); Child Beale Wildlife Park; The Living Rainforest in Hampstead Norreys

BRISTOL

The Matthew – replica of John Cabot's ship in Bristol

Downlands House

★★★★ GUEST ACCOMMODATION

Address: 33 Henleaze Gardens, Henleaze
BRISTOL BS9 4HH
Tel: 0117 962 1639
Email: info@downlandshouse.co.uk
Website: www.downlandshouse.com
Map ref: 2, ST57
Directions: 2m NW of city centre off A4018. M5 junct 17, signs Westbury-on-Trym/City Centre, pass private girls schools, Henleaze Gdns on left
Rooms: 10 (7 en suite) (3 pri facs) (1 GF), S £40–£55 D £60–£75

This elegant Victorian property, situated between Westbury-on-Trym and Clifton, provides all the charm, atmosphere and comforts of a large family home, in a quiet neighbourhood, and is a welcome relief from the anonymity of some larger establishments. It is conveniently located for enjoying many of the sights in and around Bristol, including walks on the Durdham Downs, shopping in Clifton village and the flora and fauna of Bristol Zoo, and is easily reached from the M4 and M5 motorways, making it a great base for a trip to the area. Inside, most of the attractive, individually decorated bedrooms, have en suite or private facilities, and all come with lots of extra touches to make you feel at home, such as free Wi-fi broadband, TV, hairdryer and hospitality tray. There is a smart lounge with a TV for guests to relax in or, weather permitting, a charming, leafy garden with table and chairs. The tasty cooked breakfasts are served in either the delightful conservatory or the stylish dining room. For evening meals, there are a number of restaurants within walking distance. On-street parking is also available.

Recommended in the area

Clifton Suspension Bridge; SS Great Britain; Harvey Nichols

Westfield House

★ ★ ★ ★ GUEST ACCOMMODATION

Address: 37 Stoke Hill, Stoke Bishop BRISTOL
BS9 1LQ
Tel: 0117 962 6119
Fax: 0117 962 6119
Email: admin@westfieldhouse.net
Website: www.westfieldhouse.net
Map ref: 2, ST57
Directions: 1.8m NW of city centre in Stoke Bishop
Rooms: 3 en suite, **S** £69–£79 **D** £79–£108
Notes: ⊗ on premises 🐾 under 11yrs **Parking:** 5

Set in several acres of private grounds, this large white Georgian-style, family-run guest house makes an ideal retreat from Bristol's city lights. Westfield House is close to Durdham Downs – a vast expanse of open common land, which stretches from Bristol's suburbs to the cliffs of the Avon Gorge – and the Bristol University Halls of Residence. The beautifully decorated and extremely comfortable bedrooms, either single or doubles, are all en suite, and have flat-screen TVs, DVD/CD players, free Wi-fi, fridges and tea- and coffee-making facilities. The living room centres round a cosy fireplace while large bay windows lead onto a large garden terrace. Owner Ann cooks more or less to order using quality local ingredients, and a typical meal may include dishes such as salmon en croûte with puréed spinach and hollandaise sauce accompanied by potatoes dauphinoise, followed by a delicious home-made apple pie – all the better in the summer months when served on the patio overlooking the lovely rear garden. The grounds are also a haven for a variety of wildlife including owls, badgers, newts, falcons, slow worms and hedgehogs. If you still hanker for the bright lights, Westfield House is just a short walk from Bristol city centre. There is ample off-street parking for guests.

Recommended in the area

Clifton Suspension Bridge; SS Great Britain; Bristol Zoo

Ely Cathedral

Rose Bungalow

★★★★ B&B

Address: 68 High Street, Great Wilbraham
CAMBRIDGE CB21 5JD
Tel: 01223 882385
Email: rose.bungalow@btinternet.com
Website: www.rosebungalow.co.uk
Map ref: 3, TL45
Directions: 6m E of Cambridge
Rooms: 2 en suite, (2GF), **S** £35–£40 **D** £55–£60
Notes: ⊗ on premises ⚑ under 12yrs **Parking:** 3

A hidden gem, this attractive bungalow has the advantage of a quiet village location, yet is close to the park and ride for Cambridge with its many attractions. There are two well-equipped rooms, (a twin and a single) each with TV, DVD and video and hospitality tray including fruit and chocolates. There is also free Wi-fi. The full English breakfast is a speciality with Suffolk bacon and sausages, local eggs, home-made bread, fresh fruit and organic apple juice. A continental breakfast can be requested. Other meals can be taken at one of the two local pubs. Please note that credit cards are not accepted.

Recommended in the area

Anglesey Abbey (NT); Wimpole Hall (NT); Cambridge; Duxford Imperial War Museum; Newmarket

The Crown Inn

★★★★★ INN

Address: 8 Duck Street, ELTON PE8 6RQ
Tel: 01832 280232
Email: inncrown@googlemail.com
Website: www.thecrowninn.org
Map: 3, TL09
Directions: A1 junct 17, A605 W. 3.5m right signed Elton, 0.9m left
Rooms: 4 en suite (2 GF), **S** £60–£120 **D** £80–£150
Notes: ⊗ **Parking:** 15 **Closed:** Restaurant 1st wk Jan

Huddling beneath the conker-laden horse chestnut tree in the historic Wold's village of Elton is The Crown, an ancient inn constructed of sandstone and thatch. Guests can enjoy a tranquil night or short break in beautiful, individually appointed bedrooms, with king-size beds, en suite bath and shower, easy chairs, plantation shutters and mini fridges. Some rooms are located upstairs while two nestle in the courtyard on the ground floor. Breakfast is prepared to order by the chef landlord and served in the cosy farmhouse snug. The beamed bar has a huge oak mantel with a roaring fire.

Recommended in the area

Elton Hall; Fothringhay Church & Castle (execution site of Mary Queen of Scots); Burghley House

Arley Hall gardens

Cheshire Cheese Cottage

★ ★ ★ ★ B&B

Address: Burwardsley Road, BURWARDSLEY
CH3 9NS
Tel: 01829 770887
Fax: 01829 770887
Email: r.rosney@yahoo.co.uk
Website: www.cheshirecheesecottage-bb.com
Map ref: 6, SJ55
Directions: Travelling north on A41 to Chester,
follow signs to Tattenhall and Burwardsley.
Situated between the two villages
Rooms: 2 en suite (2 GF), D £75–£85
Notes: ⊗ on premises **Parking:** 4

Rose and Roy Rosney extend a warm welcome to guests at their delightful little cottage set in its own extensive grounds and colourful gardens on the outskirts of the village of Burwardsley. It is right in the heart of the Cheshire countryside and ideally located for visiting the ancient Roman City of Chester and the many heritage sites in the area. This friendly, family-run establishment provides two en suite garden suites. One has a double bed and the other a king size and each has a private lounge area. The rooms here are tastefully decorated and well equipped and come with free Wi-fi access, central heating, flat-screen TV with Freeview, CD and DVD players, hairdryer and tea- and coffee-making facilities. Breakfasts, full English or lighter options, are freshly cooked and hearty, and vegetarians can be catered for. On-site parking is available, and guests are welcome to make use of the patio and half acre of gardens.

Recommended in the area

Sandstone trail; Chester; Beeston Castle

Sandhollow Farm B&B

★★★★ B&B

Address: Harthill Road, BURWARDSLEY, Tattenhall,
Chester CH3 9NU
Tel: 01829 770894
Email: paul.kickdrum@tiscali.co.uk
Website: www.sandhollow.co.uk
Map ref: 6, SJ55
Directions: A41, exit to Tattenhall, follow signs to
Burwardsley. After post office, 0.25m on right
Rooms: 3 en suite (1 GF), S £60–£80 D £85–£120
Notes: ⊗ on premises ⋇ under 12yrs **Parking:** 4 **Closed:** Annual holiday

Commanding spectacular views of the Cheshire Plain and Welsh hills, this lovely converted farmhouse is set in the sandstone ridge of the Peckforton Hills, on the Sandstone Trail, midway between Frodsham and Whitchurch. It provides an idyllic base for visiting Chester, Liverpool and Manchester, suiting leisure guests, who might be interested in the wealth of attractions the area has to offer, and business travellers alike. Sandhollow Farm is family run by Elise and Paul Stafford, who were recent finalists in the AA Landlady of the Year Award. The carefully renovated bedrooms offer beautiful views, and each has en suite facilities. Expect exceptional comfort from the goosedown pillows and duvets, Egytian cotton bed linens and towels, Molton Brown toiletries and tea- and coffee-making facilities. Home-made treats and chocolates add a welcoming touch. (Elise's complimentary home-made damson or sloe gin is not for the faint hearted.) Public areas are comfortable and inviting, including a lounge with a log fire. Substantial breakfasts, using organic, home-made and local produce, are served in the adjoining dining room with views across the garden and surrounding countryside. Outside, guests can explore the 2 acres of well-kept grounds. There are several good local restaurants and pubs for meals.
Recommended in the area
Beston Castle; Oulton Park; Chester

Lavender Lodge

★ ★ ★ ★ GUEST ACCOMMODATION
Address: 46 Hoole Road, CHESTER CH2 3NL
Tel: 01244 323204
Fax: 01244 329821
Email: bockings@lavenderlodgechester.co.uk
Website: www.lavenderlodgechester.co.uk
Map ref: 5, SJ46
Directions: 1m NE of city centre on A56, opp All Saints church
Rooms: 5 en suite, S £35–£50 D £65–£80
Parking: 7 **Closed:** 24 Dec–2 Jan

Built towards the end of the 20th century, Lavender Lodge is a friendly, family-run establishment occupying a smart Edwardian property. Set back from the road, just off the A56, it is a peaceful place to stay with free on-site parking available. There is a quiet garden that gets the afternoon sun and makes a lovely place to sit and relax. Hoole village is an interesting part of Chester; a self-contained area with a traditional high street and lots of smaller shops. It is a pleasant place to explore, with good places to eat, all just a stroll from the house. The entrance hall at the Lodge leads to a large and impressive staircase sweeping up to the guest bedrooms, which have views over the garden or the grounds of the church opposite. Double, triple and family bedrooms are available, with tea, coffee, herbal and fruit infusions, hot chocolate, mineral water and biscuits provided. Rooms are also equipped with hairdryers, colour televisions and wireless broadband. The en suite bathrooms feature luxury toiletries and plenty of large fluffy towels. A freshly cooked full English breakfast, using local produce where possible, is served at separate tables in the attractive dining room.

Recommended in the area

Blue Planet Aquarium; Chester Zoo; Chester's Roman walls

CORNWALL

Porthcurno, The Minack Theatre

Cotswold House

★★★★ GUEST HOUSE
Address: 49 Melvill Road, FALMOUTH TR11 4DF
Tel: 01326 312077
Email: info@cotswoldhousehotel.com
Website: www.cotswoldhousehotel.com
Map ref: 1, SW82
Directions: On A39 near town centre & docks
Rooms: 10 en suite (1 GF) Notes: ⊗ on premises
Parking: 10 Closed: Xmas

With Falmouth's superb sandy Gyllyngvase Beach and the busy estuary, harbour and yachting marina just a short walk away, this small family-run hotel is ideal for both a holiday or a short break. The smart Victorian property is also close to the picturesque, cobbled town centre with its historic buildings and range of specialist shops. All the bedrooms have a bath or shower room en suite and hospitality trays; and many have lovely views of the sea and the River Fal. Well-cooked traditional cuisine is a feature of a stay here, and the friendly owners offer attentive service. The convivial bar is another plus at this relaxed house, and a popular place for socialising in the evening.

Recommended in the area
Falmouth National Maritime Museum; The Eden Project; Trebah and Glendurgan gardens

Rosemullion

★★★★ GUEST ACCOMMODATION
Address: Gyllyngvase Hill, FALMOUTH TR11 4DF
Tel: 01326 314690
Fax: 01326 210098
Email: gail@rosemullionhotel.demon.co.uk
Map ref: 1, SW82
Rooms: 13 (11 en suite) (2 pri facs) (3 GF), S £35–£40
D £68–£76 Notes: ⊗ on premises Parking: 18
Closed: 23–29 Dec

This striking mock-Tudor property, close to Gyllyngvase Beach and handy for the town and harbour, caters for the discerning guest and its peaceful atmosphere draws people back again and again. Bedrooms, including ground floor rooms, are beautifully decorated and furnished, and some have balconies and glorious views of the sea. Breakfast is served in a smart wood-panelled dining room, and the guest lounge is delightful for relaxing. There is free Wi-fi and a large car park.

Recommended in the area
Gyllyngvase Beach and Pendennis Castle; Helford River and Trebah Garden; The Eden Project

Penleen

★★★ GUEST ACCOMMODATION
Address: South Road, GOLDSITHNEY TR20 9LF
Tel: 01736 710633
Email: jimblain@penleen.com
Website: www.penleen.com
Map ref: 1, SW53
Directions: Off main street in village
Rooms: 2 (1 en suite) (1 pri facs), D £55–£60
Notes: ⊗ on premises ⚑ under 8yrs **Parking:** 2
Closed: 19 Dec–5 Jan

The character of this 18th-century miners' cob cottage has been carefully maintained. Original features include beams and an inglenook fireplace. The twin room has garden views and an en suite shower, while the double room has period charm and an adjoining private bathroom. Both bedrooms are equipped with televisions, DVD/CD players and easy chairs. Delicious breakfasts are served in a relaxed, informal atmosphere and varied diets can be catered for. Evening meals are available at the two village pubs, and off-road parking is provided within the grounds.

Recommended in the area

St Michael's Mount; The Minack Theatre; Tate Gallery at St Ives

Tregerrick Farm B & B

★★★★ ⌂ FARMHOUSE
Address: GORRAN, St Austell, PL26 6NF
Tel/Fax: 01726 843418
Email: fandc.thomas@btconnect.com
Website: www.tregerrickfarm.co.uk
Map ref: 1, SW94
Directions: 1m NW of Gorran. B3273 S from St
Austell, right after Pentewan Sands campsite to The
Lost Gardens of Heligan, continue 3m, farm on left
Rooms: 4 (2 en suite) (2 pri facs) (2 GF), D £60–£70
Notes: ⊗ on premises ⚑ under 4yrs **Parking:** 4 **Closed:** Nov–Jan

This is an interesting place to stay for anyone who is enthusiastic about ecological issues, as it is a working farm where sustainability and biodiversity are paramount. The varied and imaginative breakfasts, based on locally produced food, are served in the dining room or conservatory. The bedrooms, are tastefully furnished in keeping with the age of the property and there's wireless internet in the main house. A delightful garden annexe can sleep up to five.

Recommended in the area

Lost Gardens of Heligan; South West Coast Path; The Eden Project

Zennor, Land's End

Calize Country House

★ ★ ★ ★ 🛏 GUEST ACCOMMODATION

Address: Prosper Hill, Gwithian HAYLE TR27 5BW
Tel/Fax: 01736 753268
Email: jilly@calize.co.uk
Website: www.calize.co.uk
Map ref: 1, SW54
Directions: 2m NE of Hayle. B3301 in Gwithian at
Red River Inn, house 350yds up hill on left
Rooms: 4 en suite, **S** £50–£60 **D** £80–£90
Notes: ⊗ on premises 🚸 under 12yrs **Parking:** 6

Calize has superb views of the sea and countryside, and is close to the beaches and coves of West
Penwith. The Whitakers are naturally friendly and their hospitality is outstanding (home-made cake
and tea are offered on arrival). The comfortable lounge has a log-burning fire during colder months.
Memorable breakfasts are served around a communal table, with treats including home-made seeded
bread and blackberry jelly, fresh fruit, creamy scrambled eggs and fresh smoked salmon, and a full
English breakfast made with locally produced ingredients. The local seals are also an attraction.
Recommended in the area
South West Coast Path; St Ives Bay; St Michael's Mount (NT); National Seal Sanctuary

Hurdon

★ ★ ★ ★ 🖛 FARMHOUSE
Address: LAUNCESTON PL15 9LS
Tel: 01566 772955
Map ref: 1, SX38
Directions: A30 onto A388 to Launceston, at rdbt
exit for hospital, 2nd right signed Trebullett, premises
1st on right
Rooms: 6 en suite (1 GF), **S** £30–£34 **D** £50–£66
Notes: ⊗ on premises **Parking:** 10
Closed: Nov–Apr

Situated just south of the historic Cornish capital of Launceston, Hurdon is a 400-acre working farm with cows, sheep and pigs, where guests are welcome to wander around and enjoy the countryside. Quietly located at the end of a tree-lined drive, the elegant 18th-century stone and granite farmhouse has retained many original features, especially in the kitchen, with its open granite fireplace, original Dutch oven and collection of old jacks and trivets. Bedrooms, including one ground-floor family room with adjoining children's room, are all en suite and individually furnished. They come with many thoughtful extras such as electric blankets and hot-water bottles, bathrobes, colour TV, hairdryer, playing cards, magazines and tea and coffee-making facilities. Breakfasts, and delicious dinners by prior arrangement, make use of produce from the farm whenever possible, and the home-made clotted cream is a special treat. Meals are served in the dining room, with its sash windows, original panelled shutters, built-in dressers and tables overlooking the garden, while the lounge features a log stove and has large, comfortable chairs, colour TV and a selection of books, magazines and games. Hurdon Farm makes an ideal base for exploring Cornwall and its coastlines.

Recommended in the area

The Eden Project; South West Coast Path; Dartmoor and Bodmin Moor

Primrose Cottage

★★★★★ 🏠 B&B

Address: Lawhitton, LAUNCESTON PL15 9PE
Tel: 01566 773645
Email: enquiry@primrosecottagesuites.co.uk
Website: www.primrosecottagesuites.co.uk
Map ref: 1, SX38
Directions: Exit A30 Tavistock, follow A388 through Launceston for Plymouth then B3362, Tavistock 2.50m
Rooms: 3 en suite (1 GF), **S** £70–£90 **D** £80–£130
Notes: ⊗ on premises 👶 under 12yrs
Parking: 5

Set in 4 acres of gardens and ancient woodland on the banks of the River Tamar, Primrose Cottage is located between Dartmoor and Bodmin Moor, and within easy reach of both the north and south coasts. The three luxury suites – The Stable, Tamar View and The Garden Room all enjoy beautiful views across the Tamar valley, and all have their own private entrance, sitting room and en suite facilities. Furnished with designer fabrics, antiques and thoughtful extra touches, every luxury is provided. A bottle of chilled white wine will be waiting to welcome you on your arrival. Sip your wine admiring the stunning views from your sitting room or choose one of the secluded corners of the garden. Once settled you can stroll down through the woods to the river to watch the salmon jump or wait quietly for a kingfisher to dive. Each season brings its own delights; the woodland is an untouched natural haven where wildlife lives undisturbed. After a day out exploring this beautiful undiscovered part of the South West return to Primrose Cottage and enjoy afternoon tea in the garden or by the log fire on a colder day.

Recommended in the area

Dartmoor: Tavistock; North Coast

Mevagissey harbour

Redgate Smithy

★★★★ B&B

Address: Redgate, St Cleer LISKEARD PL14 6RU
Tel: 01579 321578
Email: enquiries@redgatesmithy.co.uk
Website: www.redgatesmithy.co.uk
Map ref: 1, SW26
Directions: 3m NW of Liskeard. Off A30 at
Bolventor/Jamaica Inn onto St Cleer Rd for 7m,
B&B just past x-rds
Rooms: 3 (2 en suite) (1 pri facs), S £45 D £70
Notes: 🐾 under 12yrs Parking: 3 Closed: Xmas & New Year

Redgate Smithy, situated just above Golitha Falls on the southern edge of rugged Bodmin Moor, was built around 200 years ago and is great for walkers and less energetic holidaymakers alike. Guests can relax in the comfortable cottage-style bedrooms, which come with digital TV, hairdryer, local food guide, and tea and coffee-making facilities. A full breakfast using local produce offers a range of options, including full Cornish, continental and Redgate Eggs Royale. Garden and patio available.
Recommended in the area
Golitha Falls; The Eden Project; Bodmin Moor and The Cheesewring

Barclay House

★ ★ ★ ★ ◉ GUEST ACCOMMODATION
Address: St Martin's Road, LOOE PL13 1LP
Tel: 01503 262929
Fax: 01503 262632
Email: reception@barclayhouse.co.uk
Website: www.barclayhouse.co.uk
Map ref: 1, SX25
Directions: 1st house on left on entering Looe
from A38
Rooms: 11 en suite (1 GF), S £65–£110
D £100–£160 **Notes:** ⊗ on premises **Parking:** 25

Perched on the hillside overlooking the harbour of historic Looe, but within walking distance of the town, Barclay House has captivating views over the water and countryside beyond. Originally a Victorian family home set in 6 acres of grounds, the house is now family-run guest accommodation with a spacious elegance and relaxed air about it. On the ground floor are a large lounge bar and a sitting room offering light meals, snacks and cream teas, and there is a panoramic terrace where you can enjoy an aperitif in summer. Enjoyable, freshly-made dinners prepared by head chef Ben Palmer, including fish caught locally that day, are also served most evenings in the light and airy restaurant, which is popular with tourists and locals alike and has French doors opening out onto views of the East Looe river valley. The bedrooms, including one on the ground floor and a family room, have modern facilities and are decorated in pastel shades. All have been thoughtfully provided with extras such as Cornish bottled water, Sky TV, backlit bathrooms with make-up mirrors and hairdryers. Guests who wish to take a break from the abundant sightseeing the area has to offer can choose to relax beside the outdoor heated pool or sauna, work out in the gym, or explore the peaceful gardens and woodland.

Recommended in the area

Lost Gardens of Heligan; The Eden Project; Lanhydrock (NT)

Bay View Farm

★★★★ 🍴 FARMHOUSE

Address: St Martins, LOOE PL13 1NZ
Tel: 01503 265922
Fax: 01503 265922
Email: mike@looebaycaravans.co.uk
Website: www.looedirectory.co.uk/bay-view-farm.
htm
Map ref: 1, SX25
Directions: 2m NE of Looe. Off B3253 for Monkey
Sanctuary, farm signed

Rooms: 3 en suite (3 GF), **S** £35–£40 **D** £60–£65 **Notes:** ⊗ on premises 🚼 under 5yrs **Parking:** 3

A genuine warm Cornish welcome, an air of tranquillity and great food are the hallmarks of Bay View Farm, which is home to a team of prize-winning shire horses. Mrs Elford is a delightful host and it's easy to see why her guests are drawn back to this special place again and again. The renovated and extended bungalow is situated in a truly spectacular spot with ever-changing views across Looe Bay, and is beautifully decorated and furnished throughout to give a light, spacious feel. The three en suite bedrooms each have their own very individual character – one is huge with comfy sofas and a spectacular view, the others smaller but still very inviting. Two of the rooms also have spacious private conservatories. Guests can relax at the end of the day either in the lounge or on the lovely patio and watch the sun set over Looe. Breakfasts at Bay View Farm are substantial and the evening meals feature home-made desserts accompanied by clotted cream. If you do choose to eat out there are numerous restaurants and pubs nearby. The old town of East Looe is a delight of tall buildings, narrow streets and passageways and the fishing industry brings a maritime bustle to the harbour and quayside. West Looe, the smaller settlement, has a lovely outlook across the harbour to East Looe.

Recommended in the area

Lost Gardens of Heligan; The Eden Project; Looe

The Beach House

★★★★★ ⚐ GUEST ACCOMMODATION

Address: Marine Drive, Hannafore LOOE PL13 2DH
Tel: 01503 262598
Fax: 01503 262298
Email: enquiries@thebeachhouselooe.co.uk
Website: www.thebeachhouselooe.co.uk
Map ref: 1, SX25
Directions: From Looe W over bridge, left to Hannafore & Marine Dr, on right after Tom Sawyer Tavern

Rooms: 5 en suite (4 GF), S £60–£70 D £80–£120 **Notes:** ⊗ on premises ✸ under 16yrs **Parking:** 6

This big, white-painted house is on the seafront at Hannafore, with the South West Coastal Path running past the front gate. Huge windows make the most of the stunning views and create a lovely bright interior. The bedrooms are equally light and many enjoy the sea views; the ground-floor rooms have the use of the garden room. All rooms have quality linens, luxury towels and bathrobes, toiletries and TV. Breakfast is served in the balcony dining room. A particularly relaxing place to stay.

Recommended in the area

The Eden Project; Lost Gardens of Heligan; walking the South West Coastal Path to Polperro

Bucklawren Farm

★★★★ GUEST ACCOMMODATION

Address: St Martin-by-Looe, LOOE PL13 1NZ
Tel: 01503 240738
Fax: 01503 240481
Email: bucklawren@btopenworld.com
Website: www.bucklawren.co.uk
Map ref: 1, SX25
Directions: 2m NE of Looe. Off B3253 to Monkey Sanctuary, 0.50m right to Bucklawren, farmhouse 0.50m on left

Rooms: 6 en suite (1 GF), S £35–£50 D £58–£70 **Notes:** ⊗ on premises ✸ under 5yrs **Parking:** 6
Closed: Nov–Feb

With a lovely beach just a mile away, this spacious 19th-century farmhouse, set in 500 acres, is the perfect place for a holiday. Front-facing rooms have sea views, and all bedrooms are attractively furnished; one room is on the ground floor. The Granary restaurant in an adjacent converted barn is the setting for evening meals prepared from fresh local produce. Jean Henly is a charming hostess.

Recommended in the area

The Eden Project; fishing villages of Looe and Polperro; Lanhydrock (NT)

Trehaven Manor

★★★★ 🛏 ☕ GUEST ACCOMMODATION
Address: Station Road, LOOE PL13 1HN
Tel: 01503 262028
Fax: 01503 265613
Email: enquiries@trehavenhotel.co.uk
Website: www.trehavenhotel.co.uk
Map ref: 1, SX25
Directions: In East Looe between railway station &
bridge. Trehaven drive adjacent to The Globe PH
Rooms: 7 en suite (1 GF), **D Notes:** ⊗ on premises
Parking: 8

Neil and Ella Hipkiss, the enthusiastic owners of Trehaven Manor, are committed to providing the best
service. Bedrooms provide a high level of comfort and style, with quality furnishings and thoughtful
extras such as clocks and hairdryers; most overlook the estuary. Guests are welcomed on arrival
with home-made scones and local clotted cream in the lounge. Fresh local produce again features at
breakfast. Evening meals are available on request, or Neil and Ella can recommend local restaurants.
Recommended in the area
Polperro; Looe town and beach; St Mellion Golf Course

Tremaine Farm

★★★★ FARMHOUSE
Address: Pelynt, LOOE PL13 2LT
Tel: 01503 220417
Fax: 01503 220417
Email: rosemary@tremainefarm.co.uk
Website: www.tremainefarm.co.uk
Map ref: 1, SX25
Directions: 5m NW of Looe. B3359 N from Pelynt,
left at x-rds
Rooms: 2 (1 en suite) (1 pri facs), **S** £35–£36
D £60–£64 **Notes:** ⊗ on premises 🧒 under 4yrs **Parking:** 6

This working farm is set within an area of outstanding natural beauty. The farmhouse retains many
original features and the mature gardens provide a haven of tranquillity. Accommodation consists
of a luxury family suite with a king-sized double room, an adjoining twin room and a bathroom with
power shower; and a luxury double suite with pretty furnishings and a splendid bathroom. Each has a
hospitality tray and TV. A hearty breakfast is served in the dining room and there is a pleasant lounge.
Recommended in the area
South West Coastal Path; The Eden Project; The Monkey Sanctuary Trust

Colvennor Farmhouse

★ ★ ★ ★ B&B

Address: Cury, HELSTON TR12 7BJ
Tel: 01326 241208
Email: colvennor@aol.com
Website: www.colvennorfarmhouse.com
Map ref: 1, SW61
Directions: A3083 Helston-Lizard, over rdbt at end of airfield, next right to Cury/Poldhu Cove, farm 1.4m on right at top of hill
Rooms: 3 en suite (1 GF), **S** £36–£40 **D** £56–£66
Notes: ⊗ on premises ⁂ under 10yrs **Parking:** 4 **Closed:** Dec & Jan

A lovingly restored Grade II listed building, dating from the 17th century, set in an acre of attractive gardens surrounded by open countryside, with glimpses of the sea at Poldhu Cove. Friendly proprietors provide a range of maps and books to help guests plan their days and are happy to give advice. The beamed lounge with a granite fireplace offers the perfect setting for guests to relax at any time. The delightful cottage-style bedrooms are individually furnished with guests' comfort in mind.
Recommended in the area
Coastal Path; Helston; St Ives

Degembris

★ ★ ★ ★ FARMHOUSE

Address: St Newlyn East, NEWQUAY TR8 5HY
Tel: 01872 510555
Fax: 01872 510230
Email: kathy@degembris.co.uk
Website: www.degembris.co.uk
Map ref: 1, SW86
Directions: A30 onto A3058 towards Newquay, 3rd left to St Newlyn East & 2nd left
Rooms: 5 (3 en suite), **S** £30 **D** £60–£70
Notes: ⊗ on premises **Parking:** 8 **Closed:** Xmas

Built on the site of Degembris Manor, this delightful Grade II listed farmhouse has an unusual slate-hung exterior. Set in a south-facing valley, the house overlooks beautiful wooded countryside and seasonal fires burn in the comfortable lounge, where you will find a collection of games, books, maps and local information. The bedrooms are furnished in pine with co-ordinated soft furnishings, and are equipped with tea- and coffee-making provisions, TVs, electric blankets and hairdryers.
Recommended in the area
The Eden Project; The Lost Gardens of Heligan; Trerice Manor (NT)

Botallack Mine

The Old Mill House

★★★★ GUEST HOUSE

Address: LITTLE PETHERICK, Padstow, PL27 7QT
Tel: 01841 540388
Fax: 01841 540406
Email: enquiries@theoldmillhouse.com
Website: www.theoldmillhouse.com
Map ref: 1, SW97
Directions: 2m S of Padstow. In centre of Little Petherick on A389
Rooms: 7 en suite, **S** £80–£120 **D** £80–£120 **Notes:** ⊗ on premises ⅷ under 14yrs **Parking:** 20 **Closed:** Nov–Mar

You are assured of a warm welcome in this licensed Grade II listed mill house just two miles from the popular village of Padstow. The idyllic converted corn mill and millhouse is next to a pretty stream with ducks and a pair of swans – you may even spot a kingfisher. The seven comfortable bedrooms are individually decorated, well equipped and all have good views. An extensive breakfast menu is served in the original mill room.

Recommended in the area

The Eden Project; Lost Gardens of Heligan; Camel Trail Cycle Path

Camilla House

★★★★★ 🏠 GUEST HOUSE

Address: 12 Regent Terrace, PENZANCE TR18 4DW
Tel/Fax: 01736 363771
Email: enquiries@camillahouse.co.uk
Website: www.camillahouse.co.uk
Map ref: 1, SW53
Directions: A30 to Penzance, at railway station follow road along harbour front onto Promenade Rd. Opp Jubilee Bathing Pool, Regent Ter 2nd right
Rooms: 8 (7 en suite) (1 pri facs) (1 GF),
S £35–£39.50 D £70–£85 **Notes:** ⊗ on premises **Parking:** 6

The friendly proprietors of this attractive Grade II listed terrace house – Simon Chapman was a finalist for AA friendliest 'Landlady' of the Year award 2007 – do their utmost to ensure a comfortable stay. On arrival, guests are served with tea and coffee with 'Thunder and Lightning', a real Cornish treat. Bedrooms and bathrooms are attractively furnished, providing many added extras, such as fluffy towels and bathrobes, refreshment trays with Fairtrade products and Cornish mineral water, flat-screen Freeview TV/DVD, hairdryer, magazines and sweets. Some bedrooms and the dining room also provide delightful sea views over Mount's Bay. Wireless internet connection is available throughout, and there is also access to computers in the stylish, high-ceilinged lounge, which stocks a library of DVDs as well as Cornish Monopoly. A range of breakfast options is on offer in the dining room (home to a well-stocked residents' bar), using home-made or fresh local produce; options include Cornish cheese platters. Evening meals are available by prior arrangement. Camilla House has been registered and inspected by the Green Tourism Business Scheme award since 2006 and is committed to operating in an environmentally responsible fashion.

Recommended in the area

Land's End; Lizard Peninsula; South West Coastal Path

The Summer House

★★★★★ ⊚⊚ ⚱ GUEST ACCOMMODATION

Address: Cornwall Terrace, PENZANCE TR18 4HL
Tel: 01736 363744
Fax: 01736 360959
Email: reception@summerhouse-cornwall.com
Website: www.summerhouse-cornwall.com
Map ref: 1, SW53
Directions: A30 to Penzance, at rail station along harbour onto Promenade Rd, pass Jubilee Pool, right after Queens Hotel, 30yds on left
Rooms: 5 en suite **S** £85–£125 **D** £95–£125 **Notes:** ⊗ on premises ⍾ under 13yrs **Parking:** 6 **Closed:** Nov–Feb

The philosophy of The Summer House is to combine great food and beautiful surroundings with a happy, informal atmosphere, making it the perfect seaside retreat. Close to the seafront and harbour, this stylishly converted, stunning Grade II listed Regency house features bold decor, polished wood, bright colours, and a curving glass-walled tower that fills the building with light. Fresh flowers are among the thoughtful extras provided in the spacious twin and double en suite bedrooms, which are light, airy and individually decorated, and enhanced by interesting family pieces and collectables, as well as a range of home comforts to help you relax, such as TV, radio, DVD player, hairdryer, books and magazines. Fresh local food and regional produce is simply prepared to provide memorable dining from a weekly changing menu, with dishes distinctly Mediterranean in feel, and good wines on hand to accompany them. The rich Cornish puddings are especially hard to resist. The restaurant opens out onto a walled garden with terracotta pots, sub-tropical planting and attractive blue tables and chairs, where in warmer weather evening drinks and dinner may be enjoyed.

Recommended in the area

St Michael's Mount (NT); Land's End; The Minack Theatre

Ednovean Farm

★★★★★ FARMHOUSE
Address: PERRANUTHNOE TR20 9LZ
Tel: 01736 711883
Email: info@ednoveanfarm.co.uk
Website: www.ednoveanfarm.co.uk
Map ref: 1, SW52
Directions: Off A394 towards Perranuthnoe at Dynasty Restaurant, farm drive on left on bend by post box
Rooms: 3 en suite (3 GF), S £77.50–£105
D £77.50–£105 **Notes:** ⊗ on premises ⋈ under 16yrs **Parking:** 4 **Closed:** 24–28 Dec & New Year

Spectacular sea views over St Michael's Mount and Mount's Bay are a delightful feature of this converted 17th-century farmhouse which stands high above the village in beautiful grounds. The stylish bedrooms are furnished with comfortable beds and quality pieces, chintz fabrics, and thoughtful extras like flowers, magazines and fruit. Guests can relax in the elegant sitting room, the garden room and on several sunny patios. The coastal footpath and the beach and pub are just three minutes away.
Recommended in the area
St Michael's Mount (NT); Godolphin House; Penlee House Gallery (Newlyn School paintings)

Penryn House

★★★ GUEST ACCOMMODATION
Address: The Coombes, POLPERRO PL13 2RQ
Tel: 01503 272157
Fax: 01503 273055
Email: chrispidcock@aol.com
Website: www.penrynhouse.co.uk
Map ref: 1, SX25
Directions: A387 to Polperro, at mini-rdbt left into village (ignore restricted access). 200yds on left
Rooms: 12 (11 en suite) (1 pri facs), S £35–£40
D £70–£90 **Parking:** 13

Situated in tranquil surroundings close to the lovely fishing village of Polperro and with easy access to the coastal paths, Penryn House prides itself on having a relaxed and friendly atmosphere. Guests here will be among the few allowed to drive into the village, which has restricted access. Inside, the en suite bedrooms are neatly presented and reflect the character of the building. After a day exploring the area, residents can enjoy a drink at the bar or just relax in the comfortable lounge.
Recommended in the area
The Eden Project; Bodmin Moor; Cotehele medieval house (NT)

Trenake Manor Farm

★ ★ ★ ★ FARMHOUSE
Address: Pelynt, POLPERRO PL13 2LT
Tel: 01503 220835
Fax: 01503 220835
Email: lorraine@cornishfarmhouse.co.uk
Website: www.cornishfarmhouse.co.uk
Map ref: 1, SX25
Directions: 3.50m N of Polperro. A390 onto B3359
for Looe, 5m left at small x-rds
Rooms: 3 en suite, D £64–£70 Parking: 10

Situated midway between the historic fishing ports of Looe and Polperro, this welcoming 15th-century farmhouse is surrounded by 300 acres of its own farmland. It has been owned by the same family for five generations and makes a good base for touring Cornwall. En suite bedrooms, including one family room, are spacious and boast elegant Victorian king-sized bedsteads and a number of thoughtful finishing touches. Breakfast is made from local produce and served in the cosy dining room. Guests are welcome to relax on the sunloungers provided in the large, well-kept garden.
Recommended in the area
The Eden Project; Lost Gardens of Heligan; Polperro

The Coach House

★ ★ ★ ★ GUEST ACCOMMODATION
Address: Kuggar, RUAN MINOR, Helston, TR12 7LY
Tel: 01326 291044
Email: mjanmakin@aol.com
Website: www.the-coach-house.net
Map ref: 1, SW71
Directions: 1m N of Ruan Minor in Kuggar village
Rooms: 5 en suite (2 GF), S £35–£40 D £64–£70
Notes: ⊗ on premises Parking: 10 Closed: Xmas

This 17th-century house, close to Kennack Sands and Goonhilly Downs nature reserve, retains many interesting original features. Its location makes it an ideal base for hikers. The friendly proprietors look after their guests well, and they can relax in the spacious lounge-dining room where a fire burns in colder months and which boasts low beamed ceilings and an inglenook fireplace and old bread oven. The en suite bedrooms, two of which are in a converted stable block, are attractively decorated and offer extras such as hairdryer, tea and coffee-making facilities and Sky television.
Recommended in the area
Lizard Peninsula; The Earth Satellite Station; Flambards Theme Park

Restormel Castle

Smeaton Farm

★★★★ 🛏 🍽 FARMHOUSE
Address: PILLATON, Saltash, PL12 6RZ
Tel: 01579 351833
Fax: 01579 351833
Email: info@smeatonfarm.co.uk
Website: www.smeatonfarm.co.uk
Map: 1, SX45
Directions: 1m S of St Mellion just off A388
Rooms: 3 en suite, S £45–£55 D £60–£80
Notes: ⊗ on premises **Parking:** 8

This elegant Georgian farmhouse is surrounded by 450 acres of rolling Cornish farmland, situated within the Duchy of Cornwall. It provides a wonderfully peaceful place to stay, and the atmosphere is relaxed and hospitable, with every effort made to ensure guests have a comfortable and rewarding break. The bedrooms, including two family rooms, are spacious, light and airy and well equipped. Enjoyable dinners often feature seasonal vegetables and home-reared meats – the farm is now fully organic – and the sausages and home-cured bacon at breakfast come highly recommended.

Recommended in the area

Saltash Town Museum; Churchdown Farm Community Nature Reserve; trips on the River Tamar

Anchorage House

★★★★★ 🛏 ☕ GUEST ACCOMMODATION

Address: Nettles Corner, Tregrehan Mills
ST AUSTELL PL25 3RH
Tel: 01726 814071
Fax: 01726 813462
Email: info@anchoragehouse.co.uk
Website: www.anchoragehouse.co.uk
Map ref: 1, SX05
Directions: 2 m E of town centre off A390, opposite
St Austell Garden Centre
Rooms: 5 en suite (1 GF) S £85–£125 D £110–£150
Notes: ⊗ on premises ⋇ under 16yrs **Parking:** 6
Closed: Dec–Feb

Jane and Steve Epperson have created a very special place to stay here, with the utmost luxury and pampering in a perfect location near the Cornish coast. Little wonder that it makes it into Britain's Best Bed and Breakfast once again. This impressive Georgian-style house has a charming conservatory at the rear, overlooking the new swimming and leisure complex. The hospitality and delightful informality offered by this couple is outstanding, the rooms are impeccable, with extra-large beds, satellite TV and lots of other extras, and the ultra-modern bathrooms have everything you would expect from this award-winning lodge. But that's not all. Facilities here include a sauna, a hot tub, an indoor 15-metre lap pool and a small but well-equipped gym. When guests have finished working out or relaxing they can enjoy a bistro supper (by arrangement 24 hours in advance), served in the glass room, using the finest local fresh produce. Breakfast is also a special occasion, with an extensive cooked menu and delicious buffet to choose from.

Recommended in the area

The Eden Project; Tall Ships in Charlestown Harbour; Lost Gardens of Heligan

Highland Court Lodge

★★★★★ 🏠 GUEST ACCOMMODATION

Address: Biscovey Road, Biscovey, Par,
ST AUSTELL PL24 2HW
Tel: 01726 813320
Fax: 01726 813320
Email: enquiries@highlandcourt.co.uk
Website: www.highlandcourt.co.uk
Map ref: 1, SX05
Directions: 2m E of St Austell. A390 E to St Blazey
Gate, right onto Biscovey Rd, 300yds on right

Rooms: 5 en suite (5 GF), **S** £85–£125 **D** £90–£190 **Notes:** ⊗ on premises **Parking:** 10

There is a definite 'wow' factor to this excellent Cornish retreat, where an inspirational setting, with views over St Austell Bay and excellent walking nearby, is combined with a truly relaxing atmosphere. The bedrooms here are impressive, with quality furnishings, luxurious fabrics, fresh flowers, a beverage tray, minibar, TV, DVD and VCR players and broadband internet access. Each has a private patio and a spacious en suite bathroom, some with spa baths, where luxury toiletries, aromatherapy candles and bathrobes are all provided. For extra pampering, a range of spa treatments are available. Guests can also make use of the lounge with deep sofas, and a fire is lit to create a cosy and welcoming ambience on chillier evenings. As well as a charming dining room, Highland Court boasts a terrace with fine views, where dinner is served on summer evenings. Local Cornish fish and seafood, as well as organic produce, feature strongly in the freshly prepare dinners. Like breakfast – which might include energy shakes, full Cornish hearty breakfast and smoked salmon with free-range scrambled eggs – dining here is not to be missed. Self-catering accommodation is also available, as are photography workshops.

Recommended in the area

The Eden Project; Lost Gardens of Heligan; South West Coast Path

Dozmary Pool, Bodmin Moor

Hunter's Moon

★★★★ GUEST HOUSE

Address: Chapel Hill, Polgooth
ST AUSTELL PL26 7BU
Tel: 01726 66445
Email: enquiries@huntersmooncornwall.co.uk
Website: www.huntersmooncornwall.co.uk
Map ref: 1, SX05
Directions: 1.50m SW of town centre. Off B3273
into Polgooth, pass village shop on left, 1st right
Rooms: 4 en suite, **S** £45–£50 **D** £60–£70
Notes: ⊗ on premises ⚹ under 14yrs **Parking:** 5

A friendly welcome awaits at Hunter's Moon – the perfect location for a peaceful holiday. The en suite guest rooms are decorated and furnished to a high standard, and two rooms have super king-sized beds which can be converted into twin beds. There is plenty of space to sit and enjoy the garden and the countryside views, and with its central location this is an ideal touring base for the whole of Cornwall. The Polgooth Inn is just five minutes' walk away and there are many restaurants nearby.

Recommended in the area:

The Eden Project; Lost Gardens of Heligan; Charlestown Harbour

Lower Barn

★★★★★ GUEST ACCOMMODATION

Address: Bosue, St Ewe ST AUSTELL PL26 6ET
Tel: 01726 844881
Email: janie@bosue.co.uk
Website: www.bosue.co.uk
Map ref: 1, SX05
Directions: 3.50m SW of St Austell. Off B3273 at x-rds signed Lost Gardens of Heligan, Lower Barn signed 1m on right
Rooms: 3 en suite (1 GF), **Notes:** ⊗ on premises
Parking: 7 **Closed:** Jan

Tucked away down a meandering country lane yet with easy access to local attractions, this converted barn has huge appeal and proprietors Mike and Janie Cooksley fully deserved the award AA Guest Accommodation of the Year for England 2005/2006. The warm colours and decoration create a Mediterranean feel that is complemented by informal and genuine hospitality. It is the attention to detail that places Lower Barn a cut above the rest. The three en suite bedrooms are equipped with a host of extras from daily fresh towels and fridges to tea and coffee-making facilities. Breakfast is chosen from an extensive menu and served round a large table or on the patio deck overlooking the garden, which also has a luxurious hot tub. You can even collect your own free-range eggs for breakfast. A candlelit dinner, available most nights of the week, is served in the conservatory or on the terrace – and you can bring your own wine. After exploring the many attractions the area has to offer, including Mevagissey, where a bustling harbour shelters a fishing fleet and the narrow streets are lined with colour-washed old houses, galleries and gift shops, you can unwind with some gorgeous massage and therapy treatments to make your experience at Lower Barn even more memorable.

Recommended in the area

The Eden Project; Lost Gardens of Heligan; Mevagissey; cliff walks; Roseland Peninsula

Beach at Bude

Sunnyvale Bed & Breakfast

★★★★ B&B

Address: Hewas Water, ST AUSTELL PL26 7JF
Tel: 01726 882572
Email: jmuden@aol.com
Website: www.sunny-vale.co.uk
Map ref: 1, SX05
Directions: Off A390 in Hewas Water
Rooms: 2 en suite (2 GF), **D** £60–£65
Notes: ⊗ on premises ⛾ under 16yrs **Parking:** 4

Sunnyvale is set in pleasant gardens in a rural location in central Cornwall, within easy reach of the county's coasts, the Eden Project and the Lost Gardens of Heligan. The comfortable bedrooms are both on the ground floor, and one has been specifically designed for disabled guests and has an extensive range of facilities. There is a television and two easy chairs in each room. Tea and coffee making facilities and a fridge are available. Full English breakfast is served in the adjoining main house at separate tables, or for the less able in the bedroom, by prior arrangement. Vegetarian and special diets can be catered for. Excellent off-road parking is provided.

Recommended in the area

Wheal Martyn China Clay Centre; St Austell Brewery; Charlestown Shipwreck & Heritage Centre

Penarwyn House

★★★★★ 🏠 GUEST ACCOMMODATION

Address: ST BLAZEY, Par, PL24 2DS
Tel: 01726 814224
Fax: 01726 814224
Email: stay@penarwyn.co.uk
Website: www.penarwyn.co.uk
Map ref: 1, SX05
Directions: A390 W through St Blazey, left before
2nd speed camera into Doubletrees School,
Penarwyn straight ahead

Rooms: 4 en suite, S £68–£95 D £85–£160 **Notes:** ⊗ on premises 🚸 under 10yrs **Parking:** 6
Closed: 21 Dec–9 Jan

True Cornish hospitality and memorable breakfasts complement this spacious Victorian residence which is set in tranquil surroundings, yet close to main routes. The owners Mike and Jan Russell – who have many years' experience successfully running bed and breakfast establishments – have painstakingly restored the house to its original glory. Many of the old features have been faithfully restored alongside luxury en suites, which include a bath by candlelight for romantics. The bedrooms are most impressive – spacious, delightfully appointed and equipped with a host of extras including tea and coffee facilities, hairdryer, flat-screen TV and DVD/CD player. Treffry is a king-size double room, looking out over the front garden, with a large corner bath. Prideaux, the largest room, has large comfy chairs and an en suite with a slipper bath and a separate shower. The De Cressy suite comprises a lounge with two sofas, fridge and desk plus a large bedroom (with adaptable twin or super king-sized bed), a chaise longue and an art deco style bathroom with separate bath and shower. There is a panelled snooker room with a 3/4 size snooker table and Wi-fi access is available.

Recommended in the area

The Eden Project; Lanhydrock (NT); Lost Gardens of Heligan

Edgar's

★★★★ GUEST ACCOMMODATION

Address: Chy-an-Creet Higher Stennack,
ST IVES TR26 2HA
Tel/Fax: 01736 796559
Fax: 01736 796559
Email: stay@edgarshotel.co.uk
Website: www.edgarshotel.co.uk
Map ref: 1, SW54
Directions: 0.5m W of town centre on B3306,
opp Leach Pottery
Rooms: 8 en suite (4 GF), **S** £39–£85 **D** £58.50–£100 **Notes:** ⊗ on premises **Parking:** 8
Closed: Nov–Feb

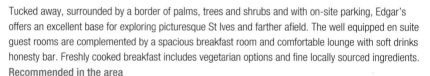

Tucked away, surrounded by a border of palms, trees and shrubs and with on-site parking, Edgar's offers an excellent base for exploring picturesque St Ives and farther afield. The well equipped en suite guest rooms are complemented by a spacious breakfast room and comfortable lounge with soft drinks honesty bar. Freshly cooked breakfast includes vegetarian options and fine locally sourced ingredients.
Recommended in the area
Leach Pottery; Penlee House Gallery; Tate St Ives

Jamies

★★★★★ GUEST ACCOMMODATION

Address: Wheal Whidden, Carbis Bay
ST IVES TR26 2QX
Tel: 01736 794718
Email: info@jamiesstives.co.uk
Website: www.jamiesstives.co.uk
Map ref: 1, SW54
Directions: A3074 to Carbis Bay, onto Pannier Ln,
2nd left
Rooms: 3 en suite (1 GF), **S** £100 **D** £110
Notes: ⊗ on premises ⊀ under 12yrs **Parking:** 4

This newly refurbished 1920s Cornish villa is just a short walk from the beaches, while the centre of St Ives can be reached by a short trip on the gaily painted Cornish Riviera train line. The en suite bedrooms are light, spacious and comfortable; all have sea views and lots of thoughtful extras, such as fresh flowers and Egyptian cotton linen. Breakfast, featuring locally sourced organic farm produce where possible, is taken in the elegant dining room at a large round table.
Recommended in the area
Tate St Ives; beaches; gardens

Nancherrow Cottage

★★★★ B&B
Address: 7 Fish Street, ST IVES, TR26 1LT
Tel: 01736 798496
Email: peterjean@nancherrowcottage.fsnet.co.uk
Website: www.nancherrow-cottage.co.uk
Map ref: 1, SW54
Directions: A30 onto A3074, along Harbour to
Sloop Inn. Left onto Fish St
Rooms: 3 (3 pri facs), **D** £75–£90 **Notes:** ⊗ on
premises 🐾 under 12yrs **Closed:** mid Nov–mid Feb

This picture-perfect 15th-century Cornish cottage is in an ideal location, on a picturesque street in old St Ives, close to the harbour and within easy reach of glorious beaches and art galleries. Originally a sail loft, the conversion features an original ship's mast that runs the full length of the cottage. The charming rooms are light and decorated in plain pastel shades, with complementing fabrics, crisp cotton bedding and non-allergenic duvets and pillows. Bathrooms are separate but private, all with Italian marble tiles and fluffy white towels. There's a good breakfast menu to suit all tastes.
Recommended in the area
Tate St Ives; Barbara Hepworth Studio and Museum; St Michael's Mount

The Old Count House

★★★★ GUEST HOUSE
Address: 1 Trenwith Square, ST IVES TR26 1DQ
Tel: 01736 795369
Fax: 01736 799109
Email: counthouse@btconnect.com
Website: www.theoldcounthouse-stives.co.uk
Map ref: 1, SW54
Directions: Follow signs to St Ives, located between
leisure centre and school
Rooms: 10 (9 en suite) (1 pri facs) (2 GF),

S £38–£42 **D** £72–£88 **Notes:** ⊗ on premises **Parking:** 8 **Closed:** 20–29 Dec

This granite stone house built in 1825 is situated in a quiet residential area with private parking, yet is just a five-minute walk from town, with its many restaurants. Bedrooms here vary in size and all are comfortably furnished and most enjoy magnificent views over the harbour and bay. One luxurious room has a four-poster bed and whirlpool-style bath. Breakfast offers extensive choices made from fresh local produce, including kippers. Guests are welcome to relax in the conservatory, garden and sauna.
Recommended in the area
Tate St Ives; Porthmeor Beach; St Ives town

The River Eye at Upper Slaughter

Primrose Valley

★★★★★ 🛏 GUEST ACCOMMODATION

Address: Porthminster Beach ST IVES TR26 2ED
Tel/Fax: 01736 794939
Email: info@primroseonline.co.uk
Website: www.primroseonline.co.uk
Map ref: 1, SW54
Directions: Contact for directions
Rooms: 9 en suite, D £100–£165 **Luxury suite**
£195–£235 **Notes:** ⊗ on premises 🌱 under 8yrs
Parking: 10 **Closed:** 23–27 Dec

An Edwardian seaside villa, Primrose Valley has been transformed to provide contemporary comfort just seconds from Porthminster Beach, and is perfect for those who enjoy art, surfing, walking or touring. There is a luxury suite, attractively finished with exposed brickwork, commissioned photographs, and Philippe Starck bathroom fittings. Bedrooms are individually designed, many with hand-made furniture, while hand-stitched mattresses, sumptuous pillows and large towels are standard issue. The business has established environmental credentials and includes a REN bio active skincare therapy room.

Recommended in the area

Tate St Ives; Barbara Hepworth Museum; St Ives Museum

The Regent

★ ★ ★ ★ 🛏 GUEST ACCOMMODATION

Address: Fernlea Terrace, ST IVES TR26 2BH
Tel: 01736 796195
Fax: 01736 794641
Email: keith@regenthotel.com
Website: www.regenthotel.com
Map ref: 1, SW54
Directions: In town centre, near bus & railway station
Rooms: 9 (7 en suite), S £33.50–£34.50
D £72–£92 **Notes:** ⊗ on premises ⭑ under 16yrs
Parking: 12

The Regent Hotel was established 78 years ago when a local architect purchased Penwyn House from a retired sea captain and converted it to provide an interest for his wife and daughter. In 1972 the late Mr and Mrs SH Varnals bought the property and in due course passed it on to Keith and Sandi Varnals the present proprietors. Sandi, a former lingerie designer, has worked her magic on the interior of the old building, while Keith, an engineer turned chef, has modernised the facilities to appeal to today's modern traveller. Bedrooms are well equipped with colour TV, radio alarm clocks and tea and coffee-making facilities. Seven rooms have facilities en suite, and most benefit from spectacular sea views. The breakfast menu offers a good choice of hot dishes, cooked to order, and an extensive buffet of cereals, yoghurts, pastries, fruit and juice. The oak-smoked fish and bacon is sourced locally. Also on offer are espresso, cappuccino, cafetière coffee, hot chocolate and a choice of teas. There is a lounge and bar for evening relaxation, and parking is provided for all rooms. If you prefer not to drive, the hotel is situated close to the local bus, coach and rail stations. The Regent is ideally located to explore the local area, being just a short stroll from the narrow cobbled streets and harbour in St Ives.

Recommended in the area

South West Coast Path; Tate St Ives; Penzance on Cornwall's south coast

The Rookery

★★★★ GUEST ACCOMMODATION
Address: 8 The Terrace, ST IVES TR26 2BL
Tel: 01736 799401
Email: therookerystives@hotmail.com
Website: www.rookerystives.com
Map ref: 1, SW54
Directions: A3074 through Carbis Bay, right fork at Porthminster Hotel, The Rookery 500yds on left
Rooms: 7 en suite (1 GF), S £42.50–£45
D £60–£90 Notes: ⊗ on premises ⊀ under 7yrs
Parking: 7

Ron and Barbara Rook's friendly establishment stands on an elevated position overlooking the harbour, sandy beaches and St Ives Bay, near the town's train and bus stations, and only a short walk to the town's shops, galleries and restaurants. The rooms are attractively decorated, and are well equipped with considerate extras such as a chiller to keep soft drinks and wines cool. A choice of full English, continental or vegetarian breakfast is served in the dining room.

Recommended in the area

Tate St Ives; Barbara Hepworth Museum; The Minack Theatre

Treliska

★★★★ ≘ GUEST ACCOMMODATION
Address: 3 Bedford Road, ST IVES TR26 1SP
Tel/Fax: 01736 797678
Email: info@treliska.com
Website: www.treliska.com
Map ref: 1, SW54
Directions: A3074 to St Ives, fork at Porthminster Hotel into town, at T-junct facing Barclays Bank left onto Bedford Rd, house on right
Rooms: 5 en suite, S £40–£60 D £70–£80
Notes: ⊗ on premises ⊀ under 10yrs

This stylish, friendly and relaxed home boasts a great location, close to the seafront, High Street, restaurants and galleries. There is a refreshing approach here and a contemporary feel throughout. Bedrooms, featuring impressive bathrooms with power showers, are designed to maximise comfort, with Egyptian cotton bedding and CD player provided as standard. Enjoyable, freshly cooked breakfasts include organic home-made breads and muesli. Additional facilities include free internet and Wi-fi.

Recommended in the area

Barbara Hepworth Museum; Bernard Leach Pottery; Paradise Park Wildlife Sanctuary, Hayle

The Woodside

★★★★ GUEST ACCOMMODATION

Address: The Belyars, ST IVES TR26 2DA
Tel: 01736 795681
Email: woodsidehotel@btconnect.com
Website: www.woodside-hotel.co.uk
Map ref: 1, SW54
Directions: A3074 to St Ives, left at Porthminster Hotel onto Talland Rd, 1st left onto Belyars Ln, Woodside 4th on right
Rooms: 10 en suite, **S** £40–£55 **D** £80–£120
Notes: ⊗ on premises 👶 under 5yrs **Parking:** 12

Suzanne and Chris Taylor are welcoming hosts who diligently attend to their beautiful property. They promise personal attention, ensuring an enjoyable holiday here. Woodside stands in peaceful grounds above St Ives Bay, with fantastic views from most bedrooms and all of the public rooms. Just a 5-minute walk away are lovely stretches of golden beaches for bathing and surfing, the picturesque harbour with its traditional fishing fleet, and the narrow cobbled streets lined with artists' studios, galleries and craft shops. The comfortable, spacious en suite bedrooms range from single, double and twin to family rooms, and all are well equipped with colour TV, a radio-alarm clock, hairdryer and a hospitality tray. Guests can relax in the comfortable lounge with a TV and games area, enjoy a drink at the bar, or relish the sea views from the attractive gardens or terrace. A heated outdoor swimming pool is open from June to August. Breakfast is another delight, you'll find a hearty choice of full English, continental or vegetarian dishes prepared from fresh local produce where possible. A short-hole golf course and a leisure centre with a superb gym and indoor pool are both within a short distance of Woodside.

Recommended in the area

Tate St Ives; Land's End; The Eden Project

Lizard Point

Oxturn House

★★★★ B&B

Address: Ladock, TRURO TR2 4NQ
Tel: 01726 884348
Email: oxturnhouse@hotmail.com
Website: www.oxturnhouse.co.uk
Map ref: 1, SW84
Directions: 6m NE of Truro. B3275 into Ladock, onto lane opp Falmouth Arms, up hill 200yds, 1st right after end 30mph sign, Oxturn on right
Rooms: 2 (1 en suite) (1 pri facs), D £58–£68

Notes: ⊗ on premises ⬥ under 12yrs **Parking:** 4 **Closed:** Dec–Jan

Bedrooms at this large family house are spacious and come with lovely southerly views of the garden and beyond to parkland. Both rooms have a super king-size double or twin beds, and have TV, hairdryer and welcome tray. The pleasant lounge has deep sofas, and in summer the French doors are opened out onto the patio. Hearty breakfasts are served in the dining room, which overlooks the large garden. The whole county is easily accessible and the owners are happy to advise on planning itineraries.

Recommended in the area

Truro; St Just in Roseland; boat trips down the River Fal to Falmouth

CUMBRIA

Wasdale from Napes Needle in the Lake District National Park

Elterwater Park

★★★★ GUEST HOUSE
Address: Skelwith Bridge, AMBLESIDE LA22 9NP
Tel: 015394 32227
Email: enquiries@elterwater.com
Website: www.elterwater.com
Map ref: 5, NY30
Directions: A593 from Ambleside to Coniston, 1m past Skelwith Bridge Hotel, layby on right fronts estate road to Elterwater Park, signed at gate
Rooms: 5 en suite (1 GF), S £40–£52 D £64–£84
Notes: ⊗ on premises ⅙ under 10yrs **Parking:** 10

Set on the hills above Langdale, this stone house is full of traditional features. All the attractive bedrooms are en suite and are furnished with TVs, radios, hairdryers, hospitality trays and fresh flowers – one room has easier access. Breakfast and dinner are served in the spacious lounge-dining room. Your hosts hold a full residential licence with a wine list chosen for quality and value to go with the freshly prepared dinners. There is a terrace for fine days – and a drying room for those other days.
Recommended in the area
Ambleside; Coniston Water; Cumbrian Way

Kent House

★★★★ GUEST HOUSE
Address: Lake Road, AMBLESIDE LA22 0AD
Tel: 015394 33279
Email: mail@kent-house.com
Website: www.kent-house.com
Map ref: 5, NY30
Directions: From town centre, by Post Office on one-way system 300yds on left on terrace above main road
Rooms: 5 (4 en suite) (1 pri facs), S £38–£45 D £60–£90
Parking: 2

Kent House, an elegant Victorian guest house, been welcoming guests from all over the world since the mid-1800s. Sandra and Simon continue this tradition, offering spacious, stylishly furnished accommodation combining many original features with the convenience of complimentary Wi-fi access and flat-screen LCD TVs in all bedrooms. Breakfast is prepared to order using fresh locally produced fare. Located in the centre of Ambleside, this establishment is ideally situated for restaurants, hostelries and the cinema.
Recommended in the area
Lake Windermere; Dove Cottage & The Wordsworth Museum; Hill Top (Beatrix Potter's home) NT

Wanslea Guest House

★★★★ GUEST HOUSE

Address: Low Fold, Lake Road AMBLESIDE
LA22 0DN
Tel/Fax: 015394 33884
Email: information@wanslea.co.uk
Website: www.wanslea.co.uk
Map ref: 5, NY30
Directions: On S side of town, opp garden centre
Rooms: 8 en suite, S £30–£45 D £50–£90 **Notes:**
⊗ on premises 🐾 under 6yrs **Closed:** 23–26 Dec

Located at the foot of Wansfell, on the quieter south side of Ambleside village, this Victorian house is an ideal base for exploring the Lake District. Guests can relax in the comfortable bedrooms, some of which are individually themed, such as the Arabian Nights Room with its canopied bed and starry ceiling or the Rock and Roll Room, with a retro feel. Rooms are well equipped with colour TV, hairdryer and tea- and coffee-making facilities; and the themed rooms have spa baths and widescreen TV. Comprehensive breakfasts are served in the spacious dining room, and there's a cosy lounge.

Recommended in the area

Hill Top (Beatrix Potter's home) (NT); Lakeside Railway; Dove Cottage & The Wordsworth Museum

Hall Croft

★★★★ B&B

Address: Dufton, APPLEBY-IN-WESTMORLAND
CA16 6DB
Tel: 017683 52902
Email: r.walker@leaseholdpartnerships.co.uk
Map ref: 6, NY62
Directions: 3m N of Appleby
Rooms: 3 (2 en suite) (1 pri facs), S £33 D £56
Parking: 3 **Closed:** 24–26 Dec

A large Victorian villa situated on the green in the tranquil village of Dufton at the foot of the Pennines with spectacular views in all directions. Owners Frei and Ray Walker extend a warm welcome and do everything to make your stay memorable. Rooms offer high quality facilities with a range of little extras for additional comfort. Substantial cooked breakfasts, including a varied range of home-made produce, are served in the period lounge/dining room; afternoon tea and cakes and packed lunches are also available. Guests can relax in the large gardens and explore the wide network of paths and walks that start from the village.

Recommended in the area

North Pennines (Area of Outstanding Natural Beauty); Northern Lake District; Appleby-in-Westmorland

Brackenthwaite, Castle Carrock

Swaledale Watch Farm

★★★★ GUEST ACCOMMODATION
Address: Whelpo, CALDBECK CA7 8HQ
Tel: 016974 78409
Fax: 016974 78409
Email: nan.savage@talk21.com
Website: www.swaledale-watch.co.uk
Map ref: 5, NY33
Directions: 1m SW of Caldbeck on B5299
Rooms: 4 en suite (4 GF), **S** £25–£31 **D** £50
Parking: 8 **Closed:** 24–26 Dec

This busy farm is set in idyllic surroundings, with views of the fells and mountains. Just a mile away is the village of Caldbeck, once renowned for its milling and mining, or take a walk through The Howk, a beautiful wooded limestone gorge with waterfalls. Nan and Arnold Savage work hard to make their hospitality seem effortless and to put you at ease. The lounges have TVs, books and games while the bedrooms have bath and shower en suite. Two bedrooms and a lounge are in the converted cowshed, ideal for a group of four. Nan's hearty Cumbrian breakfasts are delicious.

Recommended in the area

100-acre nature reserve on site; Northern Fells; Howk Walk to Caldbeck village

Rose Cottage

★★★★ GUEST HOUSE

Address: Lorton Road, COCKERMOUTH CA13 9DX
Tel: 01900 822189
Fax: 01900 822189
Email: bookings@rosecottageguest.co.uk
Website: www.rosecottageguest.co.uk
Map ref: 5, NY13
Directions: A5292 from Cockermouth to Lorton/ Buttermere, Rose Cottage on right
Rooms: 7 en suite (3 GF), S £42–£60 D £60–£85
Parking: 12 **Closed:** 13–20 Feb

This former inn is on the edge of the traditional market town of Cockermouth, famous as the birthplace of poet William Wordsworth. Refurbished to provide attractive, modern accommodation with free private parking, it offers easy access to much of the Lake District and makes a good, peaceful base especially for touring the North Lakeland. Inside, the smart, well-equipped en suite bedrooms are all comfortably furnished – with TV and tea- and coffee-making facilities. Free Wi-fi access is also available, making it a useful stop for business travellers as well as holidaymakers. Guests can opt to stay in a range of rooms, including two family rooms, three ground-floor rooms, and an attractive self-contained, self-catering studio room with its own external access and kitchen/dining area. In the main house, there is a cosy lounge for guests to relax in, as well as a smart dining room where delicious home-cooked full English breakfasts and dinners are a highlight. Most diets can be catered for, and children are also well looked after. For special group occasions, Rose Cottage can be booked exclusively for a minimum of three nights, providing accommodation and meals for up to 16 people.

Recommended in the area

Wordsworth House (NT); Theatre by the Lake; Lake Windermere

Crosthwaite House

★★★★ GUEST HOUSE
Address: CROSTHWAITE, Kendal, LA8 8BP
Tel: 015395 68264
Fax: 015395 68264
Email: bookings@crosthwaitehouse.co.uk
Website: www.crosthwaitehouse.co.uk
Map ref: 6, SD49
Directions: A590 onto A5074, 4m right to
Crosthwaite, 0.50m turn left
Rooms: 6 en suite, S £27.50–£32 D £55–£64
Parking: 8 **Closed:** mid Nov–mid Mar

A sturdy mid 18th-century house, this establishment is in the village of Crosthwaite, at the northern end of the Lyth Valley, famous for its damson orchards. You can see across the valley from the lounge, and from the dining room where guests can enjoy Aga-cooked breakfasts prepared from local ingredients. The spacious bedrooms have showers and toilets en suite, plus tea and coffee facilities. The owners create a relaxed atmosphere in which it is easy to feel at home.

Recommended in the area
Lake Windermere; Sizergh Castle and Garden (NT); three golf courses within four miles

Moss Grove Organic

★★★★★ ⌂ GUEST ACCOMMODATION
Address: GRASMERE, Ambleside, LA22 9SW
Tel: 015394 35251
Fax: 015394 35306
Email: enquiries@mossgrove.com
Website: www.mossgrove.com
Map ref: 5, NY30
Directions: From S, M6 junct 36 onto A591
signed Keswick
Rooms: 11 en suite (2 GF), S £125–£250
D £125–£250 **Notes:** ⚑ under 14yrs **Parking:** 11 **Closed:** 24–25 Dec

Located in the centre of Grasmere, this impressive Victorian house has been refurbished using as many natural products as possible, with ongoing dedication to causing minimal environmental impact. The bedrooms are decorated with beautiful wallpaper and natural clay paints, and feature hand-made beds and furnishings. Home entertainment systems, flat-screen TVs and luxury bathrooms add further comfort. Extensive continental breakfasts are taken at the large dining table in the guest lounge.

Recommended in the area
Grasmere Lake; Rydal Water; Dove Cottage & The Wordsworth Museum

Sawrey Ground

★★★★ 🛏 GUEST ACCOMMODATION

Address: Hawkshead Hill, HAWKSHEAD LA22 0PP
Tel: 015394 36683
Email: mail@sawreyground.com
Website: www.sawreyground.com
Map ref: 5, SD39
Directions: B5285 from Hawkshead, 1m to
Hawkshead Hill, sharp right after Baptist chapel,
signs to Tarn Hows for 0.25m. Sawrey Ground
on right

Rooms: 3 en suite, **D** £74–£86 **Notes:** ⊗ on premises ⛺ under 8yrs **Parking:** 6

Built by Anthony Sawrey in 1627, this picturesque oak-beamed farmhouse has a magical setting on the edge of the Tarn Hows Forest, a peaceful location in the centre of the Lake District just above Hawkshead village. Mike and Gill O'Connell offer guests a warm welcome to their home, with its friendly, relaxed atmosphere and popular home-made cakes which are served each afternoon. They have been highly rated by the AA for their care and hospitality, and will do all they can to make your stay enjoyable and memorable. The centuries of occupation have created a comfortable and lived-in feeling, from the entrance hall, lounge and dining room, to the three attractive south-facing bedrooms – all are en suite with colour TV and tea- and coffee-making facilities. Many walks are possible from the front door, leading to Coniston, Windermere and Langdale, and including the beautiful lake of Tarn Hows. The area is good for birdwatching and wildlife, and also for cycling and fishing. The central location is ideal for touring the Lakeland region, and there are some excellent places to eat within easy driving distance.

Recommended in the area

Great walks from the front door; Blackwell (The Arts & Crafts House), Bowness-on-Windermere; Brantwood (Ruskin's house), Coniston

West Vale Country House

★★★★★ ⬛ ⬱ GUEST ACCOMMODATION

Address: Far Sawrey, HAWKSHEAD, Ambleside, LA22 0LQ
Tel: 015394 42817
Fax: 015394 45302
Email: enquiries@westvalecountryhouse.co.uk
Website: www.westvalecountryhouse.co.uk
Map ref: 5, SD39
Directions: Cross Windemere by car ferry at Bowness, B5285 for 1.25m to Far Sawrey, West Vale on left leaving village
Rooms: 7 en suite, S £70–£78 D £100–£160
Notes: ⊗ on premises ⛹ under 12yrs
Parking: 8

West Vale is a lovely country house, built in the 1890s as a Victorian gentleman's residence, where you can forget all your cares. It is surrounded by the stunning countryside of the Lake District National Park on the edge of the pretty village of Far Sawrey, with views of Grizedale Forest and the Old Man of Coniston beyond the vale. Beautiful gardens have been cultivated around the property, and there is a delightful spot by the large pond to sit and soak up the sun. Your hosts Dee and Glynn Pennington have left nothing to chance in their desire to create a perfect retreat. The bedrooms are impeccably decorated, furnished and equipped to a very high standard, and the bathrooms are also stylish. After a long journey you can anticipate a welcoming decanter of sherry in the bedroom. Elegant lounges, with a roaring log fire in the winter months, help you to unwind, and afternoon tea can be taken in the lounge or, in warmer weather, on the terrace. The traditional breakfasts (there are also vegetarian and continental options) are equally delicious.

Recommended in the area

Hill Top, (Beatrix Potter's home) (NT); Brantwood; Dove Cottage & The Wandsworth Museum

Dalegarth House

★★★★ 🍽 GUEST ACCOMMODATION

Address: Portinscale, KESWICK CA12 5RQ
Tel: 017687 72817
Email: allerdalechef@aol.com
Website: www.dalegarth-house.co.uk
Map ref: 5, NY22
Directions: Off A66 to Portinscale, pass Farmers Arms,
100yds on left
Rooms: 10 en suite (2 GF), **S** £40–£45 **D** £80–£100 **Notes:** ⊗
on premises 🚸 under 12yrs **Parking:** 14 **Closed:** Dec–1 Mar

The views from this spacious Edwardian house, in the village of
Portinscale, just south of Keswick, are nothing short of stunning.
It sits on high ground, with a panoramic vista that takes in Derwent Water (just 400 metres from the door), Skiddaw, Catbells and the expanse of the fells of the northern Lakeland. It would be hard to find a better location for a walking holiday, and the full meal service here is a real bonus for hungry hikers. A full English breakfast starts the day, packed lunches are available on request and guests can return to a daily-changing four-course table d'hote dinner, prepared by the resident chef-proprietors Pauline and Bruce Jackson. Traditional and contemporary dishes feature, many of which have a regional emphasis, and there's an extensive wine list. Their appetites thus sated, guests can stroll in the gardens or relax in the comfortable lounge bar, furnished, like the rest of the house, with many antiques. The bedrooms at Dalegarth vary, with double, twin, family and single rooms all available. Each has an en suite bathroom, TV radio and tea- and coffee-making facilities. Special rates are available for guests staying on a dinner, bed and breakfast basis. The Jacksons have also embued the house with a charming family atmosphere while providing the most professional of standards.

Recommended in the area

Cars of the Stars, Keswick; Theatre by the Lake, Keswick; Mirehouse

The Grange Country Guest House

★★★★★ GUEST HOUSE

Address: Manor Brow, Ambleside Road KESWICK
CA12 4BA
Tel: 017687 72500
Fax: 0707 500 4885
Email: info@grangekeswick.com
Website: www.grangekeswick.com
Map ref: 5, NY22
Directions: M6 junct 40, A66 15m. A591 for 1m,
turn right onto Manor Brow

Rooms: 10 en suite, S £71–£83 D £98–£106 **Notes:** ⊗ on premises ⚲ under 10yrs **Parking:** 10
Closed: Jan

A stylish Victorian residence with many original features, The Grange Country Guest House stands in beautiful gardens on the outskirts of the lovely market town of Keswick, with ample off-street parking provided. It is ideally placed to explore the Lake District in a location that offers wonderful views as well as all the amenities of the town centre within strolling distance. Mark, Sally and their team offer a relaxed atmosphere with professional service and are more than happy to give advice on walks and local activities. Free Wi-fi access is available and there is a comfortable lounge and outdoor terrace for guests' use, where you can sit and enjoy a drink in the evening while watching the sun go down behind the fells. The spacious bedrooms are well equipped with quality bedding, flat-screen TVs with digital channels and additional comforts such as complimentary Fairtrade beverage trays, mineral water and toiletries. Some of the rooms have mountain views. Freshly prepared Cumbrian breakfasts include locally farmed bacon, sausage and free-range eggs. Vegetarians, coeliac and other dietary requirements can be catered for on request.

Recommended in the area

The Cumberland Pencil Museum; Castlehead Viewpoint; Keswick town

Catbells and Friar's Crag, Lake District National Park

Sunnyside Guest House

★★★★ GUEST HOUSE

Address: 25 Southey Street, KESWICK CA12 4EF
Tel: 017687 72446
Email: enquiries@sunnysideguesthouse.com
Website: www.sunnysideguesthouse.com
Map ref: 5, NY22
Directions: 200yds E of town centre. Off A5271
Penrith Rd onto Southey St, Sunnyside on left
Rooms: 7 en suite, S £40–£45 D £60–£74
Notes: ⊗ on premises ⚹ under 12yrs **Parking:** 8

Sunnyside is a stylish Victorian house set in a quiet area close to the town centre. Bedrooms, including a triple room, have all been appointed to a high standard and are equipped with refreshment-making facilities, hairdryer and flat-screen TV (digital from mid 2009). There is a spacious lounge with plenty of books, magazines and board games. A hearty breakfast is served at individual tables in the attractive dining room. Fresh Cumbrian produce provides plenty of variety, including vegetarian options. For special occasions, you can arrange to have chocolates, flowers or champagne in your room on arrival.

Recommended in the area

Derwentwater; Borrowdale; Keswick's Theatre by the Lake

New House Farm

★★★★★ ⚌ ⊜ FARMHOUSE

Address: LORTON, Cockermouth, CA13 9UU
Tel: 01900 85404
Fax: 01900 85478
Email: enquiries@newhouse-farm.co.uk
Website: www.newhouse-farm.com
Map ref: 5, NY12
Directions: 6m S of Cockermouth on B5289 between Lorton & Loweswater
Rooms: 5 en suite (2 GF), S £80–£100 D £160
Notes: ⋇ under 6yrs **Parking:** 30

Hazel Thompson bought New House Farm in 1990 and has completely renovated it to its present de luxe standard. Located in the north-west corner of the Lake District National Park, this Grade II listed house dates from 1650. The restoration discovered original oak beams and rafters, flagstone floors, and fireplaces where blazing log fires now crackle on colder days. There are lovely views from all the stylish rooms, and these can also be enjoyed by taking a relaxing Hot Spring Spa in the beautifully maintained garden. The appealing en suite bedrooms are richly furnished and equipped with many thoughtful extras including home-baked biscuits or a champagne tray and flowers for special occasions – two rooms have a magnificent oak four-poster beds. The delicious three- or five-course dinner menu uses local ingredients whenever possible and changes daily – traditional puddings are a speciality. Hearty breakfasts are another highlight. Stabling is available for guests who wish to bring their own horses. Guests are welcome to wander around the 15 acres of open fields, woods, streams and ponds.

Recommended in the area

Keswick; Cockermouth; Buttermere Lake

The Old Vicarage

★ ★ ★ ★ 🏠 ☕ GUEST HOUSE

Address: Church Lane, LORTON CA13 9UN
Tel: 01900 85656
Email: enquiries@oldvicarage.co.uk
Website: www.oldvicarage.co.uk
Map ref: 5, NY12
Directions: B5292 onto B5289 N of Lorton. 1st left signed Church, house 1st on right
Rooms: 7 en suite (1 GF), S £75–£80 D £110–£120
Notes: ⊗ on premises 🧒 under 8yrs **Parking:** 10

Set in the beautiful Lorton Vale in a quiet, unspoilt corner of the Lake District National Park, The Old Vicarage enjoys sensational views of the surrounding fells of Grasmoor, Grisedale Pike and Whinlatter. This charming country guest house is surrounded by fields and set in over an acre of lovely wooded gardens. The Old Vicarage is a wonderful Victorian property with antiques, log fires and quaint charm, an ideal place to relax and unwind. Amongst the eight tastefully-furnished guest bedrooms are a luxurious four-poster bedroom – the perfect setting for a romantic weekend – and a comfortable ground-floor room with en suite bathroom. The converted coach-house offers two welcoming rooms with exposed stone walls and en suite shower rooms and is ideal for families with older children. A hearty breakfast menu is served every morning in the elegant dining room, and a delicious home-cooked dinner is available in the evenings, if desired. The Old Vicarage, with its reputation for providing a warm, friendly and relaxed atmosphere, is perfectly situated for exploring the nearby lakes of Buttermere and Crummock Water. The nearby historical market town of Cockermouth is the site of the original Jennings brewery which offers enjoyable tours.

Recommended in the area

Buttermere Lake; Grisedale Pike; Crummock Water; Cockermouth

Winder Hall Country House

★★★★★ ♨ ☕ GUEST ACCOMMODATION

Address: LORTON CA13 9UP
Tel: 01900 85107
Fax: 01900 85479
Email: stay@winderhall.co.uk
Website: www.winderhall.co.uk
Map ref: 5, NY12
Directions: A66 W from Keswick, at Braithwaite onto B5292 to Lorton, left at T-junct signed Buttermere, Winder Hall 0.50m on right
Rooms: 7 en suite, S £52–£104 D £82–£148 **Notes:** ⊗ on premises **Parking:** 10 **Closed:** 2–31 Jan

Winder Hall, an impressive former manor house dating from the 14th century, is set in the peaceful village of Low Lorton, near Buttermere. Inside, it retains a real sense of history, yet has an informal, family-run atmosphere and provides thoughtful service. The evocatively named bedrooms, such as Greystones and Whinlatter, are smart and individually styled, some featuring luxurious furnishing such as Georgian and Tudor four-posters. All rooms are en suite and thoughtfully equipped, and all enjoy stunning fell views. The lounge is also richly furnished and the oak-panelled dining room is the perfect setting for skilfully prepared meals made using local seasonal produce – organic wines and locally produced organic ingredients all feature. The leisurely breakfast includes fresh Fairtrade coffee, croissants, fruit salad, home-cured bacon and organic Cumberland sausage. Guests are invited to wander around the garden, and they can collect their own eggs for breakfast from the free-range hens, or even help feed the pigs. For wetter days, a selection of games is on hand, and there are laundry and drying facilities available. Guests can also make sure of the hot tub and spa bath in the Summer House.

Recommended in the area

Buttermere; Keswick; beaches of west Cumbria

Hutton-in-the-Forest, near Penrith

Ees Wyke Country House

★★★★★ ◉ ≜ GUEST HOUSE

Address: NEAR SAWREY, Ambleside, LA22 0JZ
Tel: 015394 36393
Email: mail@eeswyke.co.uk
Website: www.eeswyke.co.uk
Map ref: 5, SD39
Directions: On B5285 on W side of village
Rooms: 8 en suite (1 GF), S £49–£78 D £98–£126
Notes: ⊗ on premises ⋈ under 12yrs **Parking:** 12

Visitors to this elegant Georgian country house can enjoy the same views over Esthwaite Water and the surrounding countryside that once drew Beatrix Potter to the area. The thoughtfully equipped en suite bedrooms have all been decorated and furnished with care, and there is a charming lounge with an open fire. In summer, guests can sit on the terrace and spot some of the most well-known fells in the Lake District. Above all, Ees Wyke is renowned for its splendid dining room, where a carefully prepared five-course dinner is served. Breakfasts have a fine reputation due to the skilful use of local produce.

Recommended in the area

Grizedale Forest; Coniston Old Man; Langdale Pikes

Ashness near Derwent Water, Lake District National Park

Lyndhurst Country House

★ ★ ★ ★ 🏠 🍴 GUEST HOUSE

Address: NEWBY BRIDGE, Ulverston, LA12 8ND
Tel: 015395 31245
Email: chris@lyndhurstcountryhouse.co.uk
Website: www.lyndhurstcountryhouse.co.uk
Map ref: 5, SD38
Directions: On junct of A590 and A592 at Newby
Bridge rdbt
Rooms: 3 en suite, S £45 D £65–£70
Notes: ⊗ on premises 🐾 under 8yrs **Parking:** 3
Closed: 23–28 Dec

Situated at the southern tip of beautiful Lake Windermere and set in its own lovely gardens, this 1920s house is well located within easy reach of a host of local amenities, such as hotels, restaurants and country inns. The comfortable bedrooms are well equipped and tastefully decorated. Hearty breakfasts here feature local produce as much as possible and are served in the pleasant dining room, which also has a lounge area that opens out onto the garden.

Recommended in the area

Windermere Lake Cruises; Hill Top (Beatrix Potter's home) (NT); Holker Hall Gardens and Motor Museum

Brooklands

★ ★ ★ ★ GUEST HOUSE
Address: 2 Portland Place, PENRITH CA11 7QN
Tel: 01768 863395
Fax: 01768 863395
Email: enquiries@brooklandsguesthouse.com
Website: www.brooklandsguesthouse.com
Map ref: 6, NY53
Directions: From town hall onto Portland Place, 50yds on left
Rooms: 7 en suite, S £32.50–£35 D £70–£80
Notes: ⊗ on premises **Parking:** 2

Charming and elegant, Brooklands Guest House is situated in the heart of the bustling market town of Penrith with its many attractions. This beautiful, refurbished Victorian terrace house is an excellent base for exploring the many delights of the Lake District National Park while convenient for the attractive Eden Valley. Debbie and Leon ensure you have a most enjoyable stay and that you will be keen to make a return visit. The traditional hearty breakfast, designed to satisfy the largest of appetites, offers a choice of fruit juices, fresh fruit, yoghurt, cereals, oat cakes and cheese followed by such delights as Cumberland sausage, back bacon and eggs cooked to your liking; there's also a vegetarian option. All bedrooms are furnished to the highest standard and include television and tea- and coffee-making facilties. For a romantic escape with a touch of luxury, the Brooklands' suite has a locally handcrafted four-poster bed, a sofa, television, DVD, radio-alarm clock, hairdryer, luxury branded toiletries, bath robes and a choice of light refreshments in a mini-fridge. If you intend to explore the area on two wheels then Brooklands has secure storage for your bike. Ullswater, one of the areas loveliest lakes, is nearby, and can be enjoyed at leisure aboard a 19th-century steamer.

Recommended in the area

Penrith; Coast to Coast cycle route; Ullswater lake; Rheged Discovery Centre

Lane Head Farm

★★★★ GUEST HOUSE

Address: TROUTBECK, Keswick, CA11 0SY
Tel: 017687 79220
Email: info@laneheadfarm.co.uk
Website: www.laneheadfarm.co.uk
Map ref: 5, NY32
Directions: On A66 between Penrith & Keswick
Rooms: 7 en suite (1 GF), S £45–£80 D £68–£80
Notes: ⊗ on premises ⸙ under 12yrs
Parking: 9

Visitors quickly relax in the tranquil setting of this Lakeland farmhouse, dating from 1750 and set in rolling countryside, which guests can view with pleasure from the colourful garden. Lane Head Farm is just 10 minutes' drive from Keswick and Ullswater, so makes a great base from which to explore the Lake District National Park. The park is only 40 miles long and 33 miles wide so nowhere is too far from the door. Individually designed en suite bedrooms are thoughtfully equipped with televisions, radio-alarm clocks, hairdryers and complimentary toiletries. The attention to detail extends to the provision of Fairtrade coffee, hot chocolate, sugar and ethically sourced tea. Larger, four-poster bedrooms also offer 20-inch flat-screen televisions and iPod docking radio-alarm clocks. Freshly prepared and well cooked breakfasts are served in the spacious dining room, where two- or three-course farmhouse dinners are also available in the evening, prepared from locally sourced produce. Browse the wine list in the lounge over a pre-dinner drink and chat with fellow residents. After dinner teas and coffees are also taken in the lounge, or you may prefer to sample a malt whisky, Cognac, Armagnac or one of the local beers.

Recommended in the area

Keswick Pencil Museum; Ullswater Steamers; Honister Slate Mine

Glenfield Guest House

★★★★ GUEST HOUSE

Address: Back Corkickle, WHITEHAVEN CA28 7TS
Tel: 01946 691911
Fax: 01946 694060
Email: glenfieldgh@aol.com
Website: www.glenfield-whitehaven.co.uk
Map ref: 5, NX91
Directions: 0.5m SE of town centre on A5094
Rooms: 6 en suite, **S** £35 **D** £60

Glenfield is an imposing family-run Victorian town house, with traditional large rooms and high ceilings, set in a conservation area close to the town centre and harbour. The house has been lovingly restored while retaining Victorian features such as open fires in the guest lounge and dining room. Emphasis is placed on real home cooking and baking, incorporating local and organic ingredients whenever possible, and pre-ordered evening meals are available. Guests can enjoy a drink in the residents' lounge, dining room or in the landscaped garden. Glenfield has earned a reputation for its unobtrusive, home-from-home atmosphere, with many guests making return visits. Free Wi-fi and online booking.

Recommended in the area

Cockermouth; Lake District National Park; Ennerdale Water; Crummock Water

The Coach House

★★★★ GUEST ACCOMMODATION

Address: Lake Road, WINDERMERE
LA23 2EQ
Tel: 015394 44494
Email: enquiries@lakedistrictbandb.com
Website: www.lakedistrictbandb.com
Map ref: 6, SD49
Directions: A591 to Windermere house 0.5m on right opp St Herbert's Church
Rooms: 5 en suite, **S** £45–£60 **D** £60–£80
Notes: ⊗ on premises ⁇ under 5yrs **Parking:** 5
Closed: 24–26 Dec

The property was originally a Victorian coach house, but now the interior is more chic and minimalist, achieved through the bold use of bright colours and contemporary furnishings. The modern decor continues in the bedrooms, with stylish iron beds, showers, and a host of amenities such as radios, alarm clocks and hairdryers. The breakfasts are a special feature.

Recommended in the area

Windermere lake cruises; Blackwell (The Arts & Crafts House); Holehird Gardens

Pooley Bridge Boathouse, Ullswater

The Coppice

★★★★ 🛏 🍽 GUEST HOUSE

Address: Brook Road, WINDERMERE LA23 2ED
Tel: 015394 88501
Fax: 015394 42148
Email: chris@thecoppice.co.uk
Website: www.thecoppice.co.uk
Map ref: 6, SD49
Directions: 0.25m S of village centre on A5074
Rooms: 9 en suite (1 GF), **S** £35–£45 **D** £56–£104
Parking: 10

This traditional Lakeland vicarage retains all its character and charm. Built of local stone, The Coppice sits in an elevated position between the villages of Windermere and Bowness, perfectly placed for touring or walking in the Lake District National Park. Hosts Chris and Barbara promise a memorable experience and can provide extras such as flowers, chocolates and champagne on arrival or the chance to upgrade to a four-poster bed. The en suite bedrooms, some with bath, some with shower, have been individually designed so each has its own distinctive feel. All have TV and complimentary tea and coffee trays. The renowned Lakeland breakfast and dinner are enjoyed in the light and airy dining room and a pre-dinner drink can be taken in the spacious lounge which has an open fire. Dinner is served most evenings and the restaurant has an excellent reputation in the area with locally sourced seasonal ingredients used in the dishes. This includes championship sausages and fine cured bacon, fell-bred beef, pork and lamb and fish from Fleetwood. The dinner menu also features vegetarian options, together with home-made bread and desserts. Additional facilities at The Coppice include a private car park, local leisure club membership and fishing. Dogs are welcome in some of the rooms.

Recommended in the area

Hill Top Farm (Beatrix Potter's home) (NT); Wordsworth's homes – Rydal Mount and Dove Cottage

The Cranleigh

★★★★ GUEST HOUSE

Address: Kendal Road, Bowness WINDERMERE LA23 3EW
Tel: 015394 43293
Fax: 015394 47283
Email: enquiries@thecranleigh.com
Website: www.thecranleigh.com
Map ref: 6, SD49
Directions: Lake Rd onto Kendal Rd, 150yds on right
Rooms: 17 en suite (1 GF), **S** £45–£85 **D** £60–£150
Notes: ⊗ on premises **Parking:** 13

Expect the unexpected in this new concept guest house just two minutes' walk from Lake Windermere. Owners Stephen and Louise Hargreaves have established something fresh and exciting here, maintaining a traditionally friendly and informal atmosphere while creating accommodation with all the cutting-edge style of an expensive boutique hotel. The guest lounge, with its lovely open fireplace, leather furniture and mellow decor is in classic style, and is a great place to relax with a glass of wine or one of the local ales. Hearty breakfasts are served in equally stylish surroundings. Bedrooms are simply stunning and uncompromisingly contemporary, each having received the attention of a professional interior designer and each with its own individual style. Rooms vary in size, with the largest having king-sized or super king-sized beds. All have luxurious goose-down duvets and fine cotton sheets, iPod docking stations, large-screen LCD TVs, DVD players and free Wi-fi access. The fully tiled bathrooms feature designer fittings by Villeroy & Boch, heated floors, and bathrobes. Those with air spa baths have a mirrored TV at the foot of the bath for utter indulgence. As an added bonus, guests have free use of nearby leisure facilities, including a swimming pool, sauna, gym and squash courts.

Recommended in the area

Windermere; cruises on the lake; Beatrix Potter Museum

Fairfield House and Gardens

★ ★ ★ ★ ⌂ GUEST HOUSE

Address: Brantfell Road, Bowness-on-Windermere
WINDERMERE LA23 3AE
Tel: 015394 46565
Fax: 015394 46564
Email: tonyandliz@the-fairfield.co.uk
Website: www.the-fairfield.co.uk
Map ref: 6, SD49
Directions: Into Bowness town centre, turn opp St
Martin's Church & sharp left by Spinnery restaurant,
house 200yds on right
Rooms: 10 en suite (3 GF), S £65–£110 D £70–£160 **Notes:** ✿ under 10yrs **Parking:** 10

Situated close to Bowness Bay, this establishment is the perfect place to take a tranquil break. Owners Tony and Liz Blaney offer genuine hospitality and high standards of personal service at their 200-year-old home, which is set in half an acre of its own beautifully landscaped gardens. All rooms are en suite and there are twin as well as double rooms; the deluxe rooms feature spa baths. The four-poster room has its own wet room with heated floor for that added touch of luxury – the power shower here is big enough for two, and comes with body jets and massage pebbles on the floor. A roof-space penthouse (featured on TV), has a glass shower and spa bath as well as a flat-screen TV and surround-sound. Options are available for guests to have sparkling wine or Belgian chocolates in their room on arrival and, for special occasions, to have rose petals scattered on the bed. Special facilities are available for visitors with mobility requirements. Breakfasts come in hearty or healthy versions, each made with the finest ingredients. There is free internet access via a public terminal or, for those with their own laptops, Wi-fi is available.

Recommended in the area

Blackwell (The Arts & Crafts House); Windermere lake steamers; Wordsworth House (NT)

River Irthing at Crammell Linn waterfall, near Gilsland

St John's Lodge

★ ★ ★ GUEST ACCOMMODATION

Address: Lake Road, WINDERMERE, LA23 2EQ
Tel: 015394 43078
Fax: 015394 88054
Email: mail@st-johns-lodge.co.uk
Website: www.st-johns-lodge.co.uk
Map ref: 6, SD49
Directions: On A5074 between Windermere & lake
Rooms: 12 en suite, S £40–£50 D £55–£110
Notes: ⊗ on premises ⛺ under 12yrs **Parking:** 3
Closed: Xmas

Adult-only, pet-free, eco-friendly St John's Lodge is just 10 minutes' walk from Windermere and the lake, and restaurants, pubs and shops are all nearby. A choice of bedrooms is offered to suit all pockets from budget to premium. All the rooms have en suite shower rooms, TVs, Fairtrade tea- and coffee-making facilities and hairdryers. An extensive menu offers over 30 cooked breakfasts and more than 15 vegetarian and vegan options. Gluten free options also available. Free internet access and Wi-fi.

Recommended in the area

Lake Windermere; Beatrix Potter Attraction; Blackwell

The Willowsmere

★★★★ ≙ GUEST HOUSE

Address: Ambleside Road, WINDERMERE
LA23 1ES
Tel: 015394 43575
Fax: 015394 44962
Email: info@thewillowsmere.com
Website: www.thewillowsmere.com
Map ref: 6, SD49
Directions: On A591, 500yds on left after
Windermere station, towards Ambleside
Rooms: 12 en suite, **S** £35–£50 **D** £64–£100
Notes: ⊗ on premises ⚲ under 12yrs **Parking:** 15

Wonderful views of Lake Windermere are available only a few minutes' stroll from this luxuriously renovated gentleman's residence dating from 1850. The town centre and the railway station, too, are just an eight-minute walk away, and ample off-road parking is provided on site. Willowsmere is an imposing property, built from Lakeland stone, set in large, landscaped gardens, which have won the titles 'Windermere in Bloom 2008, Winner Best Kept Garden', and 'Cumbria in Bloom 2008, Winner Best Kept Garden B&B/Guest House'. Guests can relax over a drink from the well stocked cellar, either in the secluded gardens during fine weather or in either of the two guest lounges. The large, comfortable bedrooms are all en suite and include single, twin, double and four-poster rooms. Luxury pocket sprung beds and Egyptian cotton duvets ensure a sound night's sleep. A double ground floor room has wheelchair access and a bathroom with facilities for the disabled. No family rooms are available so only children of 12 years or older can be accommodated. The English breakfast, home cooked to order, has a current AA Breakfast Award.

Recommended in the area

Brockhole Lake District Visitor Centre; Townend; The World of Beatrix Potter

DERBYSHIRE

Mam Tor, Castleton, Peak District National Park

Chatsworth

Oaktree Farm

★ ★ ★ B&B

Address: Matlock Road, Oakerthorpe, Wessington, ALFRETON DE55 7NA

Tel: 01773 832957

Email: katherine770@btinternet.com

Map ref: 8, SK45

Directions: 2m W of Alfreton. A615 W under railway bridge & past cottages, farmhouse on left

Rooms: 3 en suite, S £27–£30 D £47–£50

Notes: ⊗ on premises **Parking:** 10

Oaktree Farm is ideally situated for the glorious Peak District and convenient for Derby, Nottingham and Sheffield, with their exciting retail outlets. The working farm provides off-street parking, a coarse fishing lake free to residents and DIY livery stables, set in 22 acres of Derbyshire countryside complete with a mature flower garden and sizeable patio. The comfortable en suite bedrooms feature satellite television and tea- and coffee-making facilities. The home produce is organic and includes free-range eggs, all served in the attractive cottage-style dining room.

Recommended in the area

Crich Tramway Village; Lea Gardens; Hardwick Hall

Dannah Farm Country House

★★★★★ ⚕ ☕ GUEST ACCOMMODATION

Address: Bowmans Lane, Shottle, BELPER
DE56 2DR
Tel: 01773 550273
Fax: 01773 550590
Email: reservations@dannah.co.uk
Website: www.dannah.co.uk
Map ref: 8, SK34
Directions: A517 from Belper towards Ashbourne,
1.5m right into Shottle after Hanging Gate pub on
right, over x-rds & right
Rooms: 8 en suite (2 GF), S £75–£110 D £110–£250 **Notes:** ⊗ on premises **Parking:** 20
Closed: 24–26 Dec

Dannah, a Georgian farmhouse on a working farm on the Chatsworth Estate is home to Joan and Martin Slack and their collection of pigs, hens and cats, and Cracker the very good-natured English Setter. Each bedroom has its own individual character, beautifully furnished with antiques and old pine and filled with a wealth of thoughtful extras. Some rooms have private sitting rooms, four-poster beds and amazing bathrooms featuring a double spa bath or Japanese-style tubs – the Studio Hideaway suite even has its own private terrace with hot tub. All the bedrooms look out onto green fields and open countryside. The two delightful sitting rooms have open fires on chilly evenings and views over the gardens. The English farmhouse breakfasts are a true delight, served in relaxed and elegant surroundings. Dinner s available by arrangement, alternatively there are excellent pubs and restaurants within easy reach. Footpaths criss-cross the surrounding area in the heart of the Derbyshire Dales, making it an ideal location for walking enthusiasts.

Recommended in the area

Chatsworth; Dovedale; Alton Towers

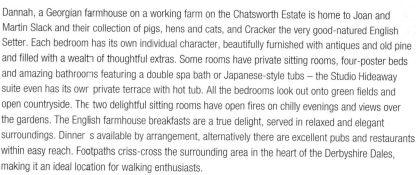

Kinder Scout, overlooking Kinder Reservoir in the Peak District National Park

Grendon Guest House

★★★★★ ♨ ☕ GUEST HOUSE

Address: Bishops Lane, BUXTON SK17 6UN
Tel: 01298 78831
Email: grendonguesthouse@hotmail.co.uk
Website: www.grendonguesthouse.co.uk
Map ref: 7, SK07
Directions: 0.75m from Buxton centre. Turn right off A53
(St Johns Rd), just past Otter Hole development
Rooms: 5 en suite, S £38–£50 D £60–£90
Notes: 👶 under 10yrs **Parking:** 8 **Closed:** 3 Jan–13 Feb

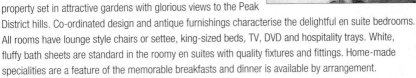

Spaciousness distinguishes this beautifully maintained Edwardian property set in attractive gardens with glorious views to the Peak District hills. Co-ordinated design and antique furnishings characterise the delightful en suite bedrooms. All rooms have lounge style chairs or settee, king-sized beds, TV, DVD and hospitality trays. White, fluffy bath sheets are standard in the roomy en suites with quality fixtures and fittings. Home-made specialities are a feature of the memorable breakfasts and dinner is available by arrangement.

Recommended in the area

Walks to the Goyt Valley from the door; Peak District National Park; Chatsworth

Roseleigh

★★★★ GUEST HOUSE

Address: 19 Broad Walk, BUXTON SK17 6JR
Tel: 01298 24904
Fax: 01298 24904
Email: enquiries@roseleighhotel.co.uk
Website: www.roseleighhotel.co.uk
Map ref: 7, SK07
Directions: A6 to Safeway rdbt, onto Dale Rd, right at lights, 100yds left by Swan pub, down hill & right onto Hartington Rd
Rooms: 14 (12 en suite) (2 pri facs) (1 GF), **Notes:** ⊗ on premises ⋈ under 6yrs **Parking:** 9 **Closed:** 16 Dec–16 Jan

Roseleigh is a comfortable and elegant Victorian property that benefits from a prime location overlooking Buxton's 23-acre Pavilion Gardens – the land on which it stands was once owned by the Duke of Devonshire. Built in 1871 and situated on the pedestrianised Broad Walk, it is just a 5-minute walk from the heart of the town and benefits from its own car park. The quality furnishings and decor throughout highlight the house's many original features. Most of the sympathetically furnished bedrooms in this family-run establishment have smart en suite shower rooms; all have colour TV and tea- and coffee-making facilities, and several have good views over the Pavilion Gardens. The comfortable guest lounge, which overlooks the lake, is the place simply to relax or you can plan the next day's itinerary by poring over the many books on the Peak District provided by the hosts, Gerard and Maggi, both of whom had interesting careers prior to opening Roseleigh; they are knowledgeable about the local area and are happy to advise on suitable pubs, restaurants and activities. The elegant dining room offers a range of breakfast choices, including vegetarian options, from a menu that makes use of local produce where possible.

Recommended in the area

Buxton Opera House; Chatsworth; Peak District National Park

Stoney Ridge

★★★★ 🏠 GUEST ACCOMMODATION

Address: Granby Road, Bradwell CASTLETON
S33 9HU
Tel: 01433 620538
Email: toneyridge@aol.com
Website: www.stoneyridge.org.uk
Map ref: 7, SK18
Directions: From N end of Bradwell, Gore Ln uphill
past Bowling Green Inn, turn left onto Granby Rd
Rooms: 4 (3 en suite) (1 pri facs), S £40–£42
D £54–£68 **Notes:** 🐾 under 10yrs **Parking:** 3

Set in the heart of the Peak District National Park, Stoney Ridge sits in an elevated position, overlooking a mature garden and large lawn. Guests can relax in the attractive heated indoor pool, or pass time in the large residents' lounge, which has a balcony. Pretty bedrooms are well equipped with TV, hairdryer, hospitality tray and toiletries, and some have fine views. Wi-fi available. Breakfast comes with a range of options, including full English, vegetarian (on request), and gluten free, all served with tea or coffee.
Recommended in the area
Chatsworth House; Derwent Valley; Castleton Caverns

Underleigh House

★★★★★ 🏠 GUEST ACCOMMODATION

Address: Off Edale Road, HOPE, Hope Valley,
S33 6RF
Tel: 01433 621372
Fax: 01433 621324
Email: info@underleighhouse.co.uk
Website: www.underleighhouse.co.uk
Map ref: 7, SK18
Directions: From village church on A6187 onto
Edale Rd, 1m left onto lane
Rooms: 5 en suite (2 GF), S £60–£65 D £80–£100 **Notes:** 🐾 under 12yrs **Parking:** 6
Closed: Xmas, New Year & 5 Jan–5 Feb

At this ideal base for walkers, Vivienne and Philip Taylor provide thoughtfully furnished bedrooms each with a hairdryer, radio-alarm, and tea and coffee facilities. Some rooms have direct access to the gardens, two have their own lounge. Enjoy an evening drink on the terrace in summer or by the log fire in the lounge in cooler weather. Breakfast is served around one large table in the dining room.
Recommended in the area
Castleton Caverns; Chatsworth; Eyam

Mount Tabor House

★★★★ B&B
Address: Bowns Hill, Crich MATLOCK DE4 5DG
Tel: 01773 857008
Fax: 01773 857008
Email: mountabor@msn.com
Map ref: 7, SK35
Directions: 6m SE of Matlock. On B5035 in Crich
Rooms: 2 en suite (1 GF), D £80 Notes: ⊗ on
premises Parking: 2 Closed: Xmas & New Year

On a steep hillside between the Peaks and the Dales, this distinctive former chapel has a lovely garden with far-reaching views. Inside, the welcoming main hall, with light streaming in through arched stained-glass windows, has a stylish, open-plan dining area. The bedrooms are equally inviting, and include high-definition TV with DVD, free Wi-fi access and garden views. All have en suite bathrooms with power showers – one also a jacuzzi and another a wet room. Breakfast, served in the dining area or on a balcony overlooking the garden and wooded countryside, is firmly based on local and organic ingredients, and special diets can be accommodated.

Recommended in the area
Chatsworth; Crich Tramway Village; Kedleston Hall

Yew Tree Cottage

★★★★ 🛏 B&B
Address: The Knoll, Tansley MATLOCK DE4 5FP
Tel: 01629 583862
Email: enquiries@yewtreecottagebb.co.uk
Website: www.yewtreecottagebb.co.uk
Map ref: 7, SK35
Directions: 1.2m E of Matlock. Off A615 into Tansley
Rooms: 3 en suite, D £75–£95
Notes: ⊗ on premises ⋈ under 14yrs Parking: 3

This 18th-century cottage, full of original character and charm and with stunning views, is set in pretty gardens in the village of Tansley. The cottage is a true home away from home, with outstanding service and hospitality, and ideally situated for all the Derbyshire Dales and Peak District attractions. The elegantly furnished and decorated bedrooms have TV/radios, DVD players, bath robes, hairdryers, toiletries and well-stocked refreshment trays. Breakfast is a memorable feast of both home-made and local produce and light refreshments are served in the sitting room where log fires cheer up the cooler days.

Recommended in the area
Chatsworth; Crich Tramway Village; Heights of Abraham cable cars

The Smithy

★★★★★ 🛏 GUEST ACCOMMODATION

Address: NEWHAVEN, Biggin, Buxton SK17 0DT
Tel: 01298 84548
Fax: 01298 84548
Email: lynnandgary@thesmithybedandbreakfast.co.uk
Website: www.thesmithybedandbreakfast.co.uk
Map ref: 7, SK16
Directions: 0.5m S of Newhaven on A515. Next to Biggin Ln, private driveway opp Ivy House
Rooms: 4 en suite (2 GF), D £80–£90 **Notes:** ⊗ on premises **Parking:** 8

Welcoming owners Lynn and Gary Jinks have restored this former drovers' inn and blacksmith's shop to a high standard with all modern comforts and a very personal service. The well-decorated good-sized bedrooms are all en suite with hospitality trays and many extras. Tasty breakfasts, including free-range eggs and home-made preserves, are served in the forge, which still has its vast open hearth, and is adjacent to a cosy lounge. The pleasant gardens are set within 4 acres of meadowland.

Recommended in the area

Chatsworth; Tissington and High Peak Trails (within walking distance); Peak District National Park

---

Braeside Guest House

★★★★ GUEST HOUSE

Address: 113 Derby Road, RISLEY DE72 3SS
Tel: 0115 939 5885
Email: bookings@braesideguesthouse.co.uk
Website: www.braesideguesthouse.co.uk
Map ref: 8, SK43
Directions: W end of village on B5010
Rooms: 6 en suite (6 GF), S £45 D £60 **Notes:** ⊗ on premises **Parking:** 10 **Closed:** 25–26 Dec

Guests here can enjoy an added element of privacy as the bedrooms – doubles and twins – are all located in converted barns close to the house, which was originally part of the Risley Hall Estate and is set in extensive grounds. Each attractively appointed room has original beams and offers many thoughtful extras, such as TV, tea- and coffee-making facilities. Two of the rooms have patio doors that open onto a sun terrace. Breakfast, made as far as possible from local ingredients, is served in the main cottage's conservatory, which has superb views over the countryside.

Recommended in the area

Donington Park Race Track; Peak District National Park; Chatsworth

Derwent Valley, Peak District National Park

The Old Manor House

★★★★★ B&B

Address: Coldwell Street, WIRKSWORTH, Matlock, DE4 4FB
Tel: 01629 822502
Email: ivan@spurrier-smith.fsnet.co.uk
Map ref: 7, SK25
Directions: On B5035 Coldwell St off village centre
Rooms: 1 (1 pri facs), S £50–£55 D £80–£85
Notes: ⊗ on premises ⚫ under 12yrs **Parking:** 1
Closed: Xmas & New Year

This impressive 17th-century house is located on the edge of the pleasant town of Wirksworth, which is well worth a visit for its period buildings, narrow streets and intricate alleyways. The house and the private bathroom and bedroom, with its four-poster bed and quality furnishings, retains many original features. A full, hearty breakfast is served in the elegant dining room and a spacious drawing room is available to relax in after a day out. There are good restaurants and pubs in the vicinity.

Recommended in the area

Peak District National Park; Chatsworth; Carsington Water

DEVON

Woolacombe beach

Gages Mill Country Guest House

★★★★ GUEST ACCOMMODATION

Address: Buckfastleigh Road, ASHBURTON
TQ13 7JW
Tel: 01364 652391
Fax: 01364 652641
Email: richards@gagesmill.co.uk
Website: www.gagesmill.co.uk
Map ref: 2, SX76
Directions: Off A38 at Peartree junct, turn right then

left at fuel station, Gages Mill 500yds on left
Rooms: 7 en suite (1 GF), **S** £45 **D** £62–£74 **Notes:** ⊗ on premises 👪 under 8yrs **Parking:** 7
Closed: 23 Oct–1 Mar

Gages Mill is a Grade II listed former wool mill on the edge of Dartmoor National Park. Bedrooms are well equipped and have views of open countryside; there is a twin room on the ground floor. The large dining room has a well-stocked corner bar, and stone archways lead through to the cosy sitting room where guests can relax.

Recommended in the area

Buckfast Abbey; Dartmoor National Park; South Devon Steam Railway; Newton Abbot Racecourse

Greencott

★★★★ GUEST HOUSE

Address: Landscove, ASHBURTON TQ13 7LZ
Tel: 01803 762649
Map ref: 2, SX76
Directions: 3m SE of Ashburton. Off A38 at Peartree
junct, Landscove signed on slip road, village green
2m on right, opp village hall
Rooms: 2 en suite, **S** £23 **D** £46 **Notes:** ⊗ on
premises **Parking:** 3 **Closed:** 25–26 Dec

Modern facilities in a traditional atmosphere are offered at this renovated house in the village of Landscove, which is just three miles from Ashburton. Greencott stands in a garden with lovely country views. The bedrooms are carefully furnished and well equipped with baths and showers en suite, and tea and coffee amenities. Television, books, maps and local information are provided in the comfortable sitting room, and traditional country cooking is served around the oak dining table. The full English breakfast includes home-made bread, and dinner is available on request. Older children are welcome, but pets cannot be accommodated, with the exception of assist dogs.

Recommended in the area

Dartington; Buckfast Abbey; riding, fishing and golf nearby

The Rising Sun

★★★★ ⇔ INN

Address: Woodland, ASHBURTON TQ13 7JT
Tel: 01364 652544
Email: admin@therisingsunwoodland.co.uk
Website: www.therisingsunwoodland.co.uk
Map ref: 2, SX76
Directions: A38, exit signed Woodland/Denbury, continue straight on for 1.5m Rising Sun on left
Rooms: 5 en suite (2 GF), **D** from £50 **Parking:** 30

Mid-way between Exeter and Plymouth, this delightful family-run country inn was taken over in 2007 by its head chef, Paul Cheakley and his wife Louise, ensuring that its reputation as a great place to eat would be maintained. Fresh fish from Brixham, local game in season and other top quality local produce features on the menu, which offers classic pub fare with gourmet touches, a choice of home-made pies and a great selection of West Country cheeses. The bedrooms, which vary in size, have a bright, unfussy decor, en suite bathrooms and television. Families are very welcome here with a play area in the large garden, where you can also eat and drink in the warmer months.

Recommended in the area

Dartmoor National Park; Torquay; Buckfast Abbey

Sladesdown Farm

★★★★ FARMHOUSE

Address: Landscove, ASHBURTON TQ13 7ND
Tel: 01364 653973
Fax: 01364 653973
Email: sue@sladesdown.co.uk
Website: www.sladesdownfarm.co.uk
Map ref: 2, SX76
Directions: 2m S of Ashburton. Off A38 at Peartree junct, Landscove signed on slip road, left at 2nd x-rds, farm 100yds right
Rooms: 4 (2 en suite) (2 pri facs) **Notes:** ⊗ on premises

Convenient for the A38, this modern farmhouse offers very spacious, attractive accommodation. There's a friendly atmosphere, with relaxation assured whether you're in the cheerful bedrooms, the lounge, with its exposed beams and open fireplace, or on the terrace in finer weather. A hearty breakfast featuring delicious local and home-made produce is the perfect start to the day, served in the breakfast room.

Recommended in the area

Buckfast Abbey; Newton Abbot Racecourse; Stover Country Park

Kerrington House

★ ★ ★ ★ ★ 🔊 GUEST ACCOMMODATION
Address: Musbury Road, AXMINSTER EX13 5JR
Tel: 01297 35333
Email: enquiries@kerringtonhouse.com
Website: www.kerringtonhouse.com
Map ref: 2, SY29
Directions: 0.5m from Axminster on A358 towards
Seaton, house on left
Rooms: 5 en suite, S £70–£77 D £95–£115
Notes: ⊗ on premises **Parking:** 6

Be prepared for a very warm welcome and genuine pampering at this lovingly-restored period house set in landscaped gardens. Bedrooms are beautifully decorated and feature quality furniture, co-ordinated fabrics and many extras while antique pieces and well-loved treasures create a personal atmosphere in the drawing room. Kerrington is renowned for its delicious food served at breakfast. Groups of families and friends are welcome to use the accommodation for small house parties.

Recommended in the area

Lyme Regis; Dorchester; East Devon Heritage Coast; West Bay; Beer, Branscombe & Sidmouth

---

The Bark House

★ ★ ★ ★ 🍵 GUEST ACCOMMODATION
Address: Oakford Bridge, BAMPTON EX16 9HZ
Tel: 01398 351236
Website: www.thebarkhouse.co.uk
Map ref: 2, SS92
Directions: A361 to rdbt at Tiverton onto A396
for Dulverton and onto Oakfordbridge, on right
Rooms: 6 (5 en suite) (1 pri facs), S £48.50–£64
D £82–£128 **Parking:** 6

A wisteria-covered, cottage-style hotel with plenty of character, Bark House is located on the edge of Exmoor in a charming garden, from where you are treated to stunning views. Strong emphasis is placed on attention to detail here: help with luggage, afternoon tea with cakes and tea/coffee tray in the room. The cosy bedrooms have many thoughtful extras, including fresh flowers from the garden and a selection of magazines. For an additional charge, beautifully cooked dinners are served in the low-beamed, candlelit dining room. Breakfast is taken very seriously, too, with produce sourced from the best of West Country suppliers.

Recommended in the area

Exmoor National Park; Knightkayes Court (NT); Dulverton

Pines at Eastleigh

★ ★ ★ ★ 🏠 GUEST ACCOMMODATION

Address: The Pines, Eastleigh BIDEFORD EX39 4PA
Tel: 01271 860561
Fax: 01271 861689
Email: pirrie@thepinesateastleigh.co.uk
Website: www.thepinesateastleigh.co.uk
Map ref: 2, SS42
Directions: A39 onto A386 signed East-the-Water. 1st left signed Eastleigh, 500yds next left, 1.5m to village, house on right

Rooms: 6 en suite (4 GF), **S** £45 **D** £65–£90 **Notes:** 🐾 under 9yrs **Parking:** 20

From its magnificent hilltop position overlooking the Torridge estuary and Lundy Island, this Georgian house, standing in 7 acres of grounds, is perfect for a relaxing break. Most of the comfortable bedrooms are in converted stables around a charming courtyard. There are two rooms in the main house. The tasty breakfasts are made from local and home-made produce.

Recommended in the area

Instow and Clovelly; cycling and walking on The Tarka Trail; Hartland Heritage Coast

Hansard House

★ ★ ★ ★ GUEST ACCOMMODATION

Address: 3 Northview Road, BUDLEIGH SALTERTON
EX9 6BY
Tel: 01395 442773
Fax: 01395 442475
Email: enquiries@hansardhotel.co.uk
Website: www.hansardhousehotel.co.uk
Map ref: 2, SY08
Directions: 500yds W of town centre
Rooms: 12 en suite (3 GF), **S** £39–£47 **D** £79–£93
Parking: 11

Set in an ideal situation a short walk from central Budleigh Salterton, Hansard House is just five minutes from the beach and the cliff path of this beautiful part of the East Devon coast. The tastefully decorated en suite bedrooms have TV, tea- and coffee-making facilities and hairdryers, and most have views across the town, to the countryside and estuary beyond. The hearty breakfast is served in the light and airy dining room. Children and pets are welcome.

Recommended in the area

Otter Estuary Bird Sanctuary; Bicton Park Botanical Gardens

St Michael's Church, Brent Tor, Dartmoor National Park

Easton Court

★ ★ ★ ★ GUEST ACCOMMODATION

Address: Easton Cross, CHAGFORD TQ13 8JL
Tel: 01647 433469
Email: stay@easton.co.uk
Website: www.easton.co.uk
Map ref: 2, SX78
Directions: 1m NE of Chagford at junct A382 & B3206
Rooms: 5 en suite (2 GF), **S** £50–£65 **D** £60–£80
Notes: ✷ under 10yrs **Parking:** 5

Debra and Paul Witting's impressive thatched Tudor farmhouse stands in acres of gardens and paddocks in the Teign Valley. Evelyn Waugh was charmed by the place and wrote *Brideshead Revisited* here, and you too should find it inspiring. An Edwardian extension houses the en suite bedrooms with fabulous views of the countryside – four rooms are superior, and there is a mixture of showers and bathrooms.

Recommended in the area

Castle Drogo (NT); Fingle Bridge; Dartmoor National Park

Tor Cottage

★ ★ ★ ★ ★ 🏠 GUEST ACCOMMODATION

Address: CHILLATON, Tavistock, PL16 0JE
Tel: 01822 860248
Fax: 01822 860126
Email: info@torcottage.co.uk
Website: www.torcottage.co.uk
Map ref: 1, SX48
Directions: A30 Lewdown exit through Chillaton towards Tavistock, 300yds after Post Office right signed 'Bridlepath No Public Vehicular Access' to end

Rooms: 4 en suite (3 GF), **S** £98 **D** £140 **Notes:** ⊗ 🐾 under 14yrs **Parking:** 8 **Closed:** 17 Dec–7 Jan

This romantic cottage offers tranquillity and seclusion in 28 acres of grounds. Nothing is too much trouble for Maureen Rowlatt, who has equipped the en suite bed-sitting rooms with everything you could desire. Each one is individually designed, from the warmth and style of the Art Deco Room to the blue and cream elegance of The Craftsman's Room – both converted from an original craftsman's workshop. One room is in the cottage wing and the others are in converted barns – each has a private terrace/garden and a log fire. Laughing Waters, the garden retreat, is nestled in its own private valley. Breakfast is an imaginative range of dishes, and can be taken in the conservatory-style dining room or on the terrace in fine weather. The gardens are a feature in their own right with many private corners, a stream and, in summer, a heated swimming pool. Woodlands cloaking the hillside behind the cottage are home to a variety of wildlife including badgers, pheasants and deer that enjoy the cover of the gorse, while buzzards and the occasional heron can be seen overhead. Children cannot be accommodated. Autumn and spring breaks are available – 3 nights for the price of 2.

Recommended in the area

Dartmoor; The Eden Project; National Trust houses and gardens

Nonsuch House

★★★★★ 🏠 ☕ GUEST ACCOMMODATION

Address: Church Hill, Kingswear DARTMOUTH
TQ6 0BX
Tel: 01803 752829
Fax: 01803 752357
Email: enquiries@nonsuch-house.co.uk
Website: www.nonsuch-house.co.uk
Map ref: 2, SX85

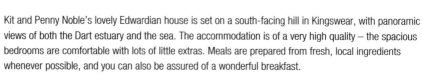

Directions: A3022 onto A379 2m before Brixham.
Fork left onto B3205. Left up Higher Contour Rd,
down Ridley Hill, house on bend on left at top of Church Hill **Rooms:** 4 en suite (2 GF),
S £65–£110 D £90–£145 **Notes:** ⊗ on premises 👶 under 10yrs **Parking:** 4

Kit and Penny Noble's lovely Edwardian house is set on a south-facing hill in Kingswear, with panoramic views of both the Dart estuary and the sea. The accommodation is of a very high quality – the spacious bedrooms are comfortable with lots of little extras. Meals are prepared from fresh, local ingredients whenever possible, and you can also be assured of a wonderful breakfast.

Recommended in the area

Dartmouth; Brixham; South West Coast Path

Mill Farm

★★★★ FARMHOUSE

Address: Kenton, EXETER EX6 8JR
Tel: 01392 832471
Email: info@millfarmstay.co.uk
Website: www.millfarmstay.co.uk
Map ref: 2, SX99

Directions: A379 from Exeter towards Dawlish, over mini-rdbt by Swans Nest, farm 1.75m on right
Rooms: 5 en suite, S £37–£40 D £55–£60
Notes: ⊗ on premises 👶 under 6yrs **Parking:** 12
Closed: Xmas

Situated on the Powderham Estate just south of the cathedral city of Exeter, this charming farmhouse is surrounded by peaceful woodland, streams and rolling hills. The spacious en suite bedrooms are sunny, well-appointed and have wide country views. An extensive breakfast menu is offered, and there are plenty of local places serving evening meals. Mill Farm is easy to find and there is ample parking space. Guests can expect a warm welcome.

Recommended in the area

Powderham Castle; Dartmoor; Exe Estuary Nature Reserve

Barn

★★★★ 🛏 GUEST ACCOMMODATION

Address: Foxholes Hill, Marine Drive EXMOUTH
EX8 2DF

Tel: 01395 224411

Fax: 01395 225445

Email: info@barnhotel.co.uk

Website: www.barnhotel.co.uk

Map ref: 2, SY08

Directions: M5 junct 30, A376 to Exmouth, then
signs to seafront. At rdbt last exit into Foxholes Hill.
Located on right

Rooms: 11 en suite, S £35–£52 D £70–£104 **Notes:** ⊗ on premises **Parking:** 30

Closed: 23 Dec–10 Jan

Close to miles of sandy beaches, this Grade II listed establishment is set in an impeccable and stunning
2-acre garden, which is sea facing and with spectacular views of the East Devon Heritage Coast.
There is a terrace and a swimming pool for summer. The building is a leading example of the Arts and
Crafts movement and was built in the early 1900s by Edward Prior, a contemporary of William Morris.
The Barn has been sympathetically modernised and furnished in keeping with its architectural design
and creates an atmosphere of country-house style. The public rooms and most of the bedrooms have
outstanding sea views. The attractively decorated, en suite bedrooms have TV, hospitality tray, hairdryer
and direct-dial telephone. Breakfast, featuring freshly squeezed juices and local produce, is served in
the bright, airy dining room. Exmouth is 15 minutes' walk away along the tree-lined and landscaped
Madeira Walk. There are also several rural and coastal walks in the area and the estuary of the River
Exe offers opportunities for birdwatching, sailing, fishing and windsurfing.

Recommended in the area

Crealy Adventure Park; Exeter; Bicton Park Botanical Gardens

The Devoncourt

★★★★ GUEST ACCOMMODATION
Address: 16 Douglas Avenue, EXMOUTH EX8 2EX
Tel: 01395 272277
Fax: 01395 269315
Email: enquiries@devoncourt.com
Website: www.devoncourthotel.com
Map ref: 2, SY08
Directions: M5/A376 to Exmouth, follow seafront to Maer Rd, right at T-junct
Rooms: 10 en suite, **S** £45–£69 **D** £70–£115
Notes: ⊗ on premises **Parking:** 50

The Devoncourt stands in 4 acres of mature, landscaped, subtropical gardens sloping down towards the sea and overlooking two miles of golden beaches. Ideally located for a seaside holiday, the house is also within easy reach of Dartmoor and the city of Exeter, which is only eight miles away. Attractions at the Devoncourt include beauty/spa facilities, a pool, sauna, steam room, snooker room and croquet lawn. Accommodation comes in a choice of single or double rooms and spacious family suites. Rooms are well furnished and generously equipped with en suite bathrooms, tea and coffee making provisions, clock radios, direct-dial telephones and digital televisions with a wide selection of channels. Porter services are available, and reception is open 24 hours. Free Wi-fi is available in the public areas, and guests can access ironing facilities and secure bicycle storage. Picture windows in the bar, lounge and restaurant afford wonderful views over the gardens and out to sea, and the restaurant serves a good range of dishes at reasonable prices. Guests can choose a continental-style or full English cooked breakfast. Cots, highchairs and games are available for children, and business people can access meeting rooms, internet connections, faxes, printers and photocopiers.

Recommended in the area

A La Ronde (NT); Powderham Castle; Exeter Cathedral

Leworthy Farm House

★ ★ ★ ★ GUEST ACCOMMODATION

Address: Lower Leworthy, Nr Pyworthy
HOLSWORTHY EX22 6SJ
Tel: 01409 259469
Fax: 01409 259469
Email: leworthyfarmhouse@yahoo.co.uk
Website: www.leworthyfarmhouse.co.uk
Map ref: 1, SS30
Directions: From Holsworthy onto Bodmin St towards
North Tamerton, 4th left signed Leworthy/Southdown
Rooms: 7 en suite, **S** £45–£65 **D** £65 **Notes:** ⊗ on premises **Parking:** 8

Pat and Phil Jennings' passions for the countryside, collecting books, curios and classical music, and meeting new people come together wonderfully at Leworthy Farm House. Spacious public rooms include a softly lit dining room with an oak parquet floor and colourful displays of old china, a peaceful drawing room with comfortable old sofas and armchairs and more displays of pictures and china, and a warmly decorated conservatory. Bedrooms, some with window seats, are beautifully furnished with pine or antique pieces and thoughtfully equipped with radio alarms, hairdryers, electric blankets, books and magazines. Hospitality trays are set with bone china, fresh milk, a selection of teas, coffees and chocolate, biscuits and fresh flowers. All the rooms are en suite and have ample supplies of soft towels and toiletries. A good choice of dishes is served at breakfast, and picnics are available by arrangement. Evening meals are not served here, but there are plenty of cafés, pubs and restaurants to choose from in the area. Leworthy is an ideal base for exploring Dartmoor and Bodmin Moor and the lovely villages of Clovelly, Tintagel, Boscastle and Padstow. Bude and its wonderful four-mile sweep of golden sand is also within easy driving distance.

Recommended in the area

Rosemoor Gardens; South West Coast Path; Dartington Glass

Courtmoor Farm

★ ★ ★ ★ FARMHOUSE
Address: Upottery, HONITON EX14 9QA
Tel: 01404 861565
Email: courtmoor.farm@btinternet.com
Website: www.courtmoor.farm.btinternet.co.uk
Map ref: 2, ST20
Directions: 4m NE of Honiton off A30
Rooms: 3 en suite, S £36–£38 D £59–£62
Notes: ⊗ on premises **Parking:** 20
Closed: 20 Dec–1 Jan

Rosalind and Bob Buxton welcome you to their spacious farmhouse with marvellous views over the Otter Valley and surrounding countryside. The extensive grounds are home to a flock of sheep and three ponies. Accommodation is provided in a family room, double room and twin, all equipped with digital televisions, hairdryers, electric blankets, clock radios as well as tea and coffee facilities. The full English breakfast should easily satisfy but special diets can be catered for. A fitness suite and a sauna are also available.

Recommended in the area

Honiton antiques shops and Lace Museum; Lyme Regis; Forde Abbey and Gardens

Norbury House

★ ★ ★ ★ GUEST HOUSE
Address: Torrs Park, ILFRACOMBE EX34 8AZ
Tel: 01271 863888
Email: info@norburyhouse.co.uk
Website: www.norburyhouse.co.uk
Map ref: 2, ST20
Directions: From A399 continue to end of High St/
Church St. At mini-rdbt after lights take 1st exit onto
Church Rd. Bear left onto Osbourne Rd. At T-junct
turn left onto Torrs Park, at top of hill on right

Rooms: 6 en suite, D £70–£100 **Notes:** ⊗ on premises **Parking:** 6

Norbury House stands in a quiet elevated position with views over the town and the sea. Adam Bess and Paula Newman have refurbished the property, bringing a stylish contemporary twist to this traditional Victorian residence. The well-equipped bedrooms come in a choice of suites, super king-size, family and superior doubles, many with sea views. Breakfast is served in the sunny dining room and local produce is used whenever possible.

Recommended in the area

Marwood Hill Gardens; Arlington Court (NT); Lundy Island; surfing beaches at Woolacombe & Croyde

Brixham Harbour

Strathmore

★ ★ ★ ★ GUEST ACCOMMODATION

Address: 57 St Brannock's Road, ILFRACOMBE
EX34 8EQ
Tel: 01271 862248
Fax: 01271 862248
Email: peter@small6374.fsnet.co.uk
Website: www.the-strathmore.co.uk
Map ref: 2, ST20
Directions: Strathmore 1.5m from Mullacot Cross
on A361
Rooms: 8 en suite, **S** £32–£35 **D** £65–£76 **Parking:** 7

There is a warm and welcoming atmosphere at this charming Victorian property close to the town centre and harbour. Cottage-style, en suite bedrooms with many thoughtful extras ensure a restful night's sleep. Relax in the cosy lounge bar with a drink or, should the weather allow, in the terraced gardens to the rear of the property. Set yourself up for the day with a choice of either continental, full English or vegetarian breakfast, all served in the relaxed setting of the elegant dining room.

Recommended in the area

Bicclescombe Park; Cairn Nature Reserve; Lundy Island; South West Coast Path

Moor View House

★★★★★ 🛏 GUEST ACCOMMODATION
Address: Vale Down, LYDFORD EX20 4BB
Tel: 01822 820220
Fax: 01822 820220
Map ref: 2, SX58
Directions: 1m NE of Lydford on A386
Rooms: 4 en suite, S £50 D £70
Notes: ⊗ on premises 🚼 under 12yrs **Parking:** 15

Built in 1869, Moor View House is a small licensed Victorian country house situated in large mature grounds on the western slopes of Dartmoor, where guests have enjoyed hospitality for more than a hundred years. The house has a very interesting history: in around 1900 it changed hands over a game of cards whilst, in Edwardian times, the writer Eden Phillpotts visited and wrote the famous play *A Farmer's Wife* and the novel *Widecombe Fair*. Today, David and Wendy Sharples offer first class accommodation and friendly hospitality. There are four en suite bedrooms, each with TV, radio, hospitality trays and bathrobes amongst other facilities. A large conservatory leads from the drawing room to the garden beyond and offers lovely views towards Cornwall in the distance. Sunsets are a delight to behold. Guests to the house are offered accommodation and a choice of English or continental breakfast. Dinner is available by prior arrangement and Wendy's award-winning cooking uses locally-produced meat, fish, game and vegetables. There are also fine, sensibly-priced wines to complement the good food. Moor View House is an ideal base from which to tour Devon and Cornwall's heritage sites, coast and, of course, Dartmoor; after which it is a delight to return and relax in the garden on warm evenings or, on cooler days, by a blazing log fire in the traditionally-furnished reception rooms.

Recommended in the area

Lydford Gorge (NT); Tavistock; The Eden Project

Bonnicott House

★★★★★ 🏠 🍴 GUEST HOUSE

Address: 10 Watersmeet Road, LYNMOUTH
EX35 6EP
Tel: 01598 753346
Email: stay@bonnicott.com
Website: www.bonnicott.com
Map ref: 2, SS74
Directions: A39 from Minehead over East Lyn River Bridge, left onto Watersmeet Rd, 50yds on right
Rooms: 8 (7 en suite) (1 pri facs), S £37–£86
D £45–£96 **Notes:** ⊗ on premises ⅱ under 14yrs

In the heart of the lovely village of Lynmouth, on a particularly scenic stretch of the north Devon coast, you will find Bonnicott House, a Grade II listed former rectory of the church opposite. It stands in an elevated location, with unparalleled panoramic views over the village, the East Lyn Valley and the sea. This is a lovely house with beautiful terraced gardens where guests can relax. But you don't have to go outside to enjoy the views – inside each of the rooms the eye is drawn to the window and the stunning vista beyond. This house also boasts a beautiful lounge where guests can congregate to chat or quietly enjoy a book, take tea or light afternoon refreshments, or have a drink from the licensed bar. In cooler months, a crackling log fire makes it even more inviting. The dining room, where award-winning breakfasts and cooked-to-order evening meals are served, has a double aspect with more of those terrific views. The bedrooms, each with its own private bathroom, are luxurious and comfortable and guests are not only provided with complimentary tea- and coffee-making supplies, but also a decanter of sherry. It is very peaceful here (children under 14 and pets are not accommodated), and the hosts ensure a charming, homely atmosphere. Wi-fi broadband internet access is available.

Recommended in the area

Cliff Railway, Lynmouth; Watersmeet Lodge and tea gardens; Valley of the Rocks, Lynton

Tarr Steps, near Dulverton, Exmoor National Park

Rock House

★★★★ GUEST ACCOMMODATION

Address: Manor Grounds, LYNMOUTH EX35 6EN
Tel: 01598 753508
Fax: 0800 7566964
Email: enquiries@rock-house.co.uk
Website: www.rock-house.co.uk
Map ref: 2, SS74
Directions: On A39
Rooms: 8 en suite (1 GF), **Parking:** 8
Closed: 24–25 Dec

Standing alone by the river at the mouth of the harbour, the 18th-century Rock House has wonderful sea views. The bedrooms, some with four-poster beds, are well appointed and furnished to a high standard with en suite facilities, central heating, televisions, hairdryers, alarm clocks and complimentary tea and coffee. Double, twin and single rooms are available. Bedrooms afford superb views of the Lyn Valley, the river or the sea. A choice of menus is offered, either in the spacious lounge/bar or in the smart dining room, and the garden is a popular venue for cream teas in the summer.
Recommended in the area
Combe Martin Wildlife & Dinosaur Park; Lyn & Exmoor Museum; Arlington Court

Sea View Villa

★ ★ ★ ★ ★ ☖ ➾ GUEST ACCOMMODATION

Address: 6 Summer House Path, LYNMOUTH EX35 6ES
Tel: 01598 753460
Fax: 01598 753496
Email: seaviewenquiries@aol.com
Website: www.seaviewvilla.co.uk
Map ref: 2, SS74
Directions: A39 from Porlock, 1st left after bridge,
Sea View Villa on right 20yds along path opp church
Rooms: 5 (3 en suite), **S** £40–£45 **D** £110–£130
Notes: ⊗ on premises ⸬ under 14yrs **Closed:** Jan

This charming Grade II listed Georgian villa, built in 1721,
has been appointed to a high standard by owners Steve Williams and Chris Bissex, who bought the
house in 2002, moving from London, where they were both involved in the arts as performers and
directors. Walking and surfing are popular local pursuits and there are wonderful walks directly from
the door, including the Two Moors Walk and Lynton's Valley of the Rocks. Tucked away from the
bustle of the main streets, the house provides elegant and peaceful accommodation. The name says
it all, and indeed all of the individually decorated bedrooms enjoy impressive views of the harbour
and sea. Many thoughtful extras are provided, including Egyptian cotton linen, luxury toiletries and
TV/VCR, with a choice of films available to borrow. The proprietors' genuine hospitality assures a
relaxed and comfortable stay. Dinner and breakfast are not to be missed, and home-made bread is a
speciality here. For guests planning a day out, picnics, hikers' feasts and ploughman's hampers can
all be provided. To top it all off, a range of beauty therapies and holistic treatments is available by
prior arrangement.

Recommended in the area

Exmoor National Park; Clovelly; Watersmeet Valley

Highcliffe House

★★★★★ 🛏 ☕ GUEST ACCOMMODATION
Address: Sinai Hill, LYNTON EX35 6AR
Tel: 01598 752235
Email: info@highcliffehouse.co.uk
Website: www.highcliffehouse.co.uk
Map ref: 2, SS74
Directions: Off A39 into Lynton, signs for Old Village, at Crown pub up steep hill, house 150yds on left
Rooms: 7 en suite, S £70–£90 D £90–£120
Notes: ⊗ on premises 👶 under 16yrs **Parking:** 7
Closed: Dec–mid Feb

Highcliffe House stands in an acre of woodland and gardens just a short walk from the Exmoor coastal town of Lynton. It has stunning sea views over the Exmoor hills, Lynton and Lynmouth and across the Bristol Channel to South Wales. Within the National Park and originally built as a Victorian summer residence, this beautifully restored house has elegant, spacious en suite bedrooms, all with sea views. Each is individually designed with matching William Morris or Laura Ashley themes, antique furniture and feature wooden beds. Four rooms have beautifully carved super king-sized beds. Each room is very well appointed, with a thoughtfully stocked hospitality tray, digital TV, DVD player and iPod docks plus Wi-fi internet access. There are two elegant guest lounges, one with exceptional views, where guests are encouraged to enjoy the peace and serenity of the surroundings. A particular feature of the house is the stunning conservatory breakfast room with unique panoramic coastal and headland views, a wonderful setting to enjoy the excellent breakfast menu offering fine West Country fare. Resident hosts Michael and Karen Orchard offer a warm welcome to guests wishing to escape to this magnificent and diverse part of Devon.

Recommended in the area

Exmoor National Park; cliff railway between Lynton and Lynmouth; South West Coast Path

Sidmouth

Pine Lodge

★★★★ GUEST HOUSE
Address: Lynway, LYNTON EX35 6AX
Tel: 01598 753230
Email: info@pinelodgelynton.co.uk
Website: www.pinelodgelynton.co.uk
Map ref: 2, SS74
Directions: 500yds S of town centre off Lynbridge
Rd opp Bridge Inn
Rooms: 4 en suite, D £60–£76
Notes: ⊗ on premises ⨷ under 12yrs **Parking:** 6

A stunning Victorian guest house located in a sunny, sheltered, traffic-free location, Pine Lodge offers panoramic views over the beautiful West Lyn Valley. A paradise for walkers; Exmoor and a variety of walks start right from the doorstep. The Victorians named Lynton as 'England's Little Switzerland' and from the village and nearby coast, attractions such as the Valley of the Rocks and Watersmeet Estate can be found. Beautiful and spacious en suite rooms have hospitality trays, TV, and sofa or chairs to make your stay relaxing. Home-made bread features at breakfast and there's a conservatory lounge.
Recommended in the area
Exmoor National Park; Cliff Railway between Lynton & Lynmouth; South West Coast Path

Victoria Lodge

★★★★★ ≙ GUEST ACCOMMODATION
Address: 30–31 Lee Road, LYNTON EX35 6BS
Tel: 01598 753203
Email: info@victorialodge.co.uk
Website: www.victorialodge.co.uk
Map ref: 2, SS74
Directions: Off A39 in village centre opp Post Office
Rooms: 8 en suite, S £59.50–£119 D £70–£140
Notes: ⊗ on premises ⚑ under 11yrs **Parking:** 6
Closed: Nov–23 Mar

Victoria Lodge is a large, elegant villa, built in the 1880s and located in the heart of Lynton. Full of character and original features, the house offers luxurious accommodation with quality furnishings including some antique pieces. The bedrooms are named after Queen Victoria's daughters and other members of the royal family and reflect the style of the period. They are decorated in rich colours and feature coronet, half-tester and four-poster beds. Guests can relax in the gardens, which include a colourful front terrace overlooking the water garden, ideal for fine weather. Otherwise there are two guest lounges with bay windows, comfortable sofas and shelves of books and magazines for guests to read. A good choice is offered at breakfast, with cooked dishes ranging from pancakes with maple syrup or porridge with (or without) Devon cream, through eggs Benedict and home-made kedgeree to the full Exmoor Works, with egg, sausage, bacon, tomato, mushrooms, hash brown and the Devon delicacy of hogs and black pudding. A meat-free full English breakfast is also offered, with vegetarian sausages, and you can finish off with toast and home-made preserves. Breakfast is served in the sumptuously decorated dining room, with its period fireplace and over mantle.

Recommended in the area

Exmoor National Park; Valley of the Rocks; The Tarks Trail

Berkeley's of St James

★★★★ GUEST ACCOMMODATION

Address: 4 St James Place East, The Hoe
PLYMOUTH PL1 3AS
Tel: 01752 221654
Fax: 01752 221654
Email: enquiry@onthehoe.co.uk
Website: www.onthehoe.co.uk
Map ref: 1, SX45
Directions: Off A38 towards city centre, left at sign
The Hoe, over 7 sets of lights, left onto Athenaeum
St, right to Crescent Av, 1st left
Rooms: 5 en suite (1 GF), **S** £40–£45 **D** £60–£65 **Notes:** ⊗ on premises **Closed:** 23 Dec–1 Jan

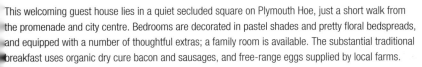

This welcoming guest house lies in a quiet secluded square on Plymouth Hoe, just a short walk from the promenade and city centre. Bedrooms are decorated in pastel shades and pretty floral bedspreads, and equipped with a number of thoughtful extras; a family room is available. The substantial traditional breakfast uses organic dry cure bacon and sausages, and free-range eggs supplied by local farms.
Recommended in the area
National Maritime Museum; Historic Barbican; Dartmoor National Park

Strete Barton House

★★★★ GUEST HOUSE

Address: Totnes Rd, STRETE, Dartmouth, TQ6 ORU
Tel: 01803 770364
Fax: 01803 771182
Email: info@stretebarton.co.uk
Website: www.stretebarton.co.uk
Map ref: 2, SX84
Directions: Off A379 into village centre
Rooms: 6 (5 en suite) (1 pri facs) (1 GF), **S** £65–£90
D £75–£100 **Notes:** ⩔ under 3yrs **Parking:** 4

This beautifully refurbished manor house is only a short distance from some of south Devon coast's finest beaches – the coastal path is 200 yards from the garden. The spacious double rooms all have king-size beds, one even has a super king-size four-poster, and all have private bathrooms, five of which are en suite. The bedrooms also have TV and DVD players, clock radios, hairdryers and hospitality trays. There is also a luxury cottage suite with a living room and dual aspect bedroom with sea views (dogs are welcome here too). Wi-fi is available throughout.
Recommended in the area
Blackpool Sands; Woodlands Adventure Park; Dartmouth

Thomas Luny House

★★★★★ ⛫ GUEST ACCOMMODATION
Address: Teign Street, TEIGNMOUTH TQ14 8EG
Tel: 01626 772976
Email: alisonandjohn@thomas-luny-house.co.uk
Website: www.thomas-luny-house.co.uk
Map ref: 2, SX94
Directions: A381 to Teignmouth, at 3rd lights turn right to quay,
50yds turn left onto Teign St, after 60yds turn right through
white archway
Rooms: 4 en suite S £65–£70 D £75–£98
Notes: ⊗ on premises ⚹ under 12yrs Parking: 8

This delightful late 18th-century house is run by John and Alison
Allan whose relaxed yet attentive approach is much appreciated by their guests. The large drawing
room and dining room are beautifully furnished and have French doors opening onto a walled garden.
The bedrooms are well equipped and very comfortable. Home-made dishes and a full cooked breakfast
are a speciality.
Recommended in the area
Tuckers Maltings; Powderham Castle; Cockington village

Headland View

★★★★ ⛫ GUEST HOUSE
Address: 37 Babbacombe Seafront, Babbacombe
TORQUAY TQ1 3LN
Tel: 01803 312612
Email: reception@headlandview.com
Website: www.headlandview.com
Map ref: 2, SX96
Directions: Off Babbacombe Rd left onto Portland Rd
& Babbacombe Downs Rd & seafront
Rooms: 6 (4 en suite) (2 pri facs), S £40–£50 D £64
Notes: ⊗ on premises ⚹ under 5yrs Parking: 4 Closed: Nov–Mar

Every comfort is thought of in this delightful guest house by the sea. There are spectacular views over
the World Heritage Coast of Lyme Bay from the sun lounge and most of the bedrooms have balconies.
Those without sea views have four poster beds. Colin and Sue Jezard and a professional team will
ensure a memorable stay. The excellent breakfast includes kedgeree, fresh fruit pancakes, home-made
yoghurt and bread. Lovely beaches, and a good choice of pubs and restaurants, are nearby.
Recommended in the area
Torquay; South-West Coastal Path; Oddicombe beach

Linden House

★ ★ ★ ★ GUEST ACCOMMODATION
Address: 31 Bampfylde Road, TORQUAY TQ2 5AY
Tel: 01803 212281
Email: lindenhouse.torquay@virgin.net
Website: www.lindenhousetorquay.co.uk
Map ref: 2, SX96
Directions: Onto A3022, 1st left opposite playing fields
Rooms: 7 en suite (1 GF), S £50–£55 D £65–£80
Notes: ⊗ on premises **Parking:** 7

Built around the 1880s, this elegant Victorian villa, ideally located for a stay in the English Riviera, has stood the test of time, and its delightful entrance and hallway give guests a taste of a bygone age. To the front of the house is a good-sized floral garden, in which guests are welcome to relax with morning coffee and home-made cheese scones or a Devonshire cream tea, weather permitting. Inside, the property has been refurbished in a classic style using soft, neutral colours and fabrics. Bedrooms are comfortably furnished, using white bed linen and cream duvets for a relaxed feel. All provide hairdryers, TV and complimentary beverages and mineral water. Some of the en suite bathrooms have a bath as well as shower, and all come supplied with good-quality toiletries. The garden room has its own private patio, and offers direct access to the garden. Delicious and home-cooked, the four-course breakfast utlilises fresh, local and organic produce, and includes delights such as fruit smoothies, organic yoghurt, flat field mushrooms with scrambled eggs or French toast with organic maple syrup; dinners are available by prior arrangement. Guests can also make use of the pretty, relaxing sitting room, which overlooks the garden.

Recommended in the area

Torre Abbey; Cockington Village; Dartmoor

Burgh Island

Millbrook House

★ ★ ★ ★ GUEST ACCOMMODATION

Address: 1 Old Mill Road, Chelston TORQUAY
TQ2 6AP
Tel: 01803 297394
Map ref: 2, SX96
Rooms: 10 en suite (2 GF), **S** £28–£30 **D** £60–£70
Notes: ⊗ on premises **Parking:** 8 **Closed:** Nov–Feb

The delightful, personally run Millbrook House is within easy walking distance of Torquay's many attractions and has a friendly and relaxed atmosphere. The well-maintained en suite bedrooms provide many useful facilities; a king-size bed and a four-poster room are available and there is a family room, thoughtfully divided by a partition wall. One room features a sunken bath. There is a cosy bar on the lower ground floor with pool and darts, and the vibrant garden has a summer house for guests to relax in on hotter days. The freshly cooked breakfasts here include local produce as much as possible.

Recommended in the area

Torquay's beaches; Paignton; Brixham

Durant Arms

★ ★ ★ ★ ⇔ INN

Address: Ashprington, TOTNES TQ9 7UP
Tel: 01803 732240
Email: info@thedurantarms.com
Website: www.thedurantarms.com
Map ref: 2, SX85
Directions: A381 from Totnes for Kingsbridge,
1m left for Ashprington
Rooms: 8 en suite (2 GF), **S** £50 **D** £80
Notes: ⊗ on premises **Parking:** 8
Closed: 25–26 Dec evenings

Immaculate whitewashed walls and masses of well-tended shrubs and plants make this traditional country inn a focal point in the picturesque village of Ashprington, deep in the heart of Devon's South Hams district. Owners Eileen and Graham Ellis proudly offer their own brand of hospitality and provide attractive accommodation in either the main building or a refurbished annexe. The bedrooms are individually designed to a very high standard, using stylish furnishings, and include a host of thoughtful touches to help ensure a memorable stay. Each room has a luxurious well-appointed en suite bathroom that adds additional comfort. The inn is renowned locally for its delicious food. A blackboard menu of home-cooked food is available in the character bar or the smart dining room, both furnished in rich red velvets. All dishes are freshly cooked to order, offering fresh vegetables and a wide variety of meat and fish; seasonal local produce is used whenever possible. To complement your meal there is a good choice of real ales, beers and wines, some from the local Sharpham Vineyard, just a 15-minute walk away and open to the public for visiting and wine tasting. There are stunning views of the River Dart from this delightful inn. Packed lunches are available.

Recommended in the area

Historic Totnes; The Eden Project; Sharpham Vineyard

Culloden House

★ ★ ★ GUEST HOUSE
Address: Fosketh Hill, WESTWARD HO! EX39 1UL
Tel: 01237 479421
Email: enquiry@culloden-house.co.uk
Website: www.culloden-house.co.uk
Map ref: 1, SS42
Directions: S of town centre. Off B3236 Stanwell Hill onto Fosketh Hill
Rooms: 7 en suite (1 GF), S £40 (only available Nov–Feb)
D £60–£70 Closed: Christmas

Set in a commanding position on a wooded hillside, overlooking Westward Ho! beach and Bideford Bay, Culloden House was built in 1865 as a Victorian gentleman's residence. It is now a family-run guest house with large, elegant rooms retaining many original features. Westward Ho! is the perfect place for a short break or family holiday, only five minutes' drive from the A39 'Atlantic Highway' with one of the safest and most beautiful Blue Flag beaches in the West Country, two miles long and perfect for surfing. It is in the middle of the North Devon Area of Outstanding Natural Beauty, the first UNESCO biosphere reserve in Europe, and a Site of Special Scientific Interest. Guests are favoured with reduced rates at the Royal North Devon Golf Club, the oldest golf course in England. All of the guest bedrooms are en suite, offering a choice of king-size, double or twin beds, with Freeview television and a hospitality tray. Children are welcome and many rooms are suitable for families. Well-behaved pets can also be accommodated with prior notice. A traditional English breakfast is served in the large dining room with its splendid views over the whole of Golden Bay.

Recommended in the area
Burton Art Gallery; RHS Garden Rosemoor; Milky Way Adventure Park

Hope Cove, near Salcombe

Harrabeer Country House

★ ★ ★ ★ GUEST ACCOMMODATION

Address: Harrowbeer Lane, YELVERTON PL20 6EA
Tel: 01822 853302
Email: reception@harrabeer.co.uk
Website: www.harrabeer.co.uk
Map ref: 3, SX56
Directions: In village. Off A386 Tavistock Rd onto Grange Rd, right onto Harrowbeer Ln
Rooms: 6 (5 en suite) (1 pri facs) (1 GF),
S £55–£80 D £65–£95 **Parking:** 10
Closed: 3rd wk Dec, 2nd wk Jan

This lovely Devon longhouse on the edge of Dartmoor has a relaxing lounge, a bar for a convivial evening drink and well-equipped comfortable bedrooms. Breakfast is a leisurely affair served in the dining room, and dinner can be served by arrangement. The Harrabeer provides an excellent base for exploring the beautiful surrounding countryside. Two self-catering units are available.

Recommended in the area

The Garden House; The Eden Project; Dartmoor National Park

DORSET

Ruins of Corfe Castle

Portman Lodge

★★★★★ B&B

Address: Whitecliff Mill Street, BLANDFORD FORUM
DT11 7BP
Tel/Fax: 01258 453727
Email: enquiries@portmanlodge.co.uk
Website: www.portmanlodge.co.uk
Map ref: 2, ST80
Directions: On NW end of one-way system, follow
signs from town centre to Shaftesbury & hospital
Rooms: 3 en suite
Notes: ⊗ on premises ✗ under 10yrs **Parking:** 6

Once used as a residence for the choristers of St Martin's Church, this fine Victorian house now
provides elegant guest accommodation. With many original features, it has been carefully decorated
with artefacts and pictures from the proprietors' extensive travels. The public rooms are spacious
and inviting, and the en suite bedrooms have been individually decorated. A delicious home-cooked
breakfast is served at a communal table. Dinner is available by prior arrangement.

Recommended in the area

Jurassic Coast; Bovington Tank Museum; Clouds Hill (NT)

The Balincourt

★★★★★ GUEST ACCOMMODATION

Address: 58 Christchurch Road, BOURNEMOUTH
BH1 3PF
Tel/Fax: 01202 552962
Email: rooms@balincourt.co.uk
Website: www.balincourt.co.uk
Map ref: 3, SZ09
Directions: On A35 between Lansdowne &
Boscombe Gardens, opp Lynton Court pub
Rooms: 12 en suite, **S** £50–£90 **D** £80–£100
Notes: ⊗ on premises ✗ under 16yrs **Parking:** 11 **Closed:** Xmas

This friendly establishment offers high standards of accommodation and is within easy reach of the
town centre and beaches. The en suite bedrooms are individually decorated and themed – examples
include the Moroccan, Victorian and Country Manor rooms. All come equipped with a host of thoughtful
extras such as hand-painted china, an iron, bottled water and luxury toiletries. There is a lounge and
bar, and freshly prepared breakfasts and evening meals are available in the attractive dining room.

Recommended in the area

Christchurch Priory; The New Forest; Brownsea Island

The Shave Cross Inn

★★★★★ ⇔ INN

Address: Marshwood Vale, BRIDPORT DT6 6HW
Tel: 01308 868358
Fax: 01308 867064
Email: roy.warburton@virgin.net
Website: www.theshavecrossinn.co.uk
Map ref: 2, SY49
Directions: From B3165 turn at Birdsmoorgate and follow brown signs
Rooms: 7 en suite (3 GF) **Parking:** 29

This is a newly built property standing in the grounds of the thatched, 700-year-old Shave Cross Inn, which was once a stopping off point for pilgrims and monks, who had their tonsures trimmed as a mark of respect. The buildings are set at the end of several narrow lanes in the centre of the lovely Marshwood Vale, three miles from the World Heritage Jurassic Coast and very much part of Thomas Hardy's Dorset. The construction of the house, from Dorset flint with beautiful stone floors and oak beams, follows in the tradition of the ancient inn, while offering luxurious accommodation in en suite bedrooms, comprising three four-poster rooms, three doubles with sleigh beds and a honeymoon suite. Individually designed by the owners, the rooms all offer flat-screen televisions, hairdryers and tea-making facilities. The original inn is renowned for its real ales and ciders and the Shavers Restaurant serves authentic Caribbean and international food. The 13th-century bar has a huge inglenook fireplace, where log fires burn from when the swallows fly and until they return the following year. The inn also boasts the oldest thatched skittle alley in Britain, with skittling most nights from September to April.

Recommended in the area

Beaminster Museum; Horn Park Gardens; Abbotsbury Swannery & Subtropical Gardens

The Lord Bute & Restaurant

★ ★ ★ ★ ★ ◉◉ GUEST ACCOMMODATION

Address: 179–185 Lymington Road, Highcliffe on Sea, CHRISTCHURCH BH23 4JS
Tel: 01425 278884
Fax: 01425 279258
Email: mail@lordbute.co.uk
Website: www.lordbute.co.uk
Map ref: 3, SZ19
Directions: A337 towards Highcliffe
Rooms: 13 en suite (6 GF), D £98–£225
Parking: 40

The elegant Lord Bute stands directly behind the original entrance lodges of Highcliffe Castle, close to the beach and the historic town of Christchurch. It was once home to Lord Bute, British Prime Minister from 1762 to 1763. Comfort and impeccable standards are key here. The luxurious and very stylish en suite bedrooms, including some family rooms and some on the ground floor, have all been finished to a very high standard, with many thoughtful extras including direct-dial telephones, trouser press, air-conditioning and well-stocked tea- and coffee-making facilities. Self-contained suites, some with their own private landscaped garden areas and including a bridal suite, are available in what were once the gatehouses to the castle. Elsewhere, guests can relax in the warm and welcoming lounge, or peruse the menu in the tranquil conservatory-styled orangery. The excellent food makes dining here memorable. Served in the smart, classically furnished restaurant with a friendly ambience, breakfast, lunch and dinner are all available, prepared by award-winning chefs. Special events include cabaret evenings and a jazz diary. Conferences and weddings are also catered for, and a conference suite is available.

Recommended in the area

New Forest; Hengistbury Head; Christchurch Priory

Baytree House Dorchester

★★★★ B&B

Address: 4 Athelstan Road, DORCHESTER DT1 1NR
Tel: 01305 263696
Email: info@baytreedorchester.com
Website: www.bandbdorchester.co.uk
Map ref: 2, SY69
Directions: 0.5m SE of town centre
Rooms: 3 en suite **Notes:** ⊗ on premises
Parking: 3

In 2006 owners Nicola and Gary Cutler completely refurbished Baytree House, creating a stylish place to stay, with spacious and light rooms, contemporary decor and luxurious fittings. Although it is set in a quiet residential area, it's just a 10-minute stroll to the historic centre of Dorchester and a short drive to many of rural Dorset's attractions. The bedrooms offer either en suite shower room or a private bathroom, which has shower and bath. The Cutlers also own the Walnut Grove Restaurant and Coffee Shop in the town centre, and employ the same high standards of cooking at Baytree House. Guests are offered a 15 percent discount on meals at the Walnut Grove.

Recommended in the area

Thomas Hardy's Cottage; Monkey World; Dorset's Jurassic coastline

Little Court

★★★★★ ≘ GUEST ACCOMMODATION

Address: 5 Westleaze Charminster, DORCHESTER
DT2 9PZ
Tel: 01305 261576
Fax: 01305 261359
Email: info@littlecourt.net
Website: www.littlecourt.net
Map ref: 2, SY69
Directions: A37 from Dorchester, 0.25m right at
Loders Garage, Little Court 0.5m on right
Rooms: 8 en suite, S £79 D £89 **Notes:** ⊗ on premises **Parking:** 10

A picture-postcard Edwardian house, Little Court nestles in 4 acres of beautiful grounds and gardens. The property has been refurbished to a very high standard and the proprietors are on hand to ensure you have an excellent stay. Bedrooms have a bath and shower en suite, and come with extras such as an umbrella. A delicious breakfast, including home-grown produce, is served in the dining room which adjoins a restful lounge with open fires. A pub nearby serves good food.

Recommended in the area

Jurassic World Heritage Coast; Dorchester; Weymouth

The Acorn Inn

★★★★ ❀ INN

Address: EVERSHOT, Dorchester, DT2 0JW
Tel: 01935 83228
Fax: 01935 83707
Email: stay@acorn-inn.co.uk
Website: www.acorn-inn.co.uk
Map ref: 2, ST50
Directions: 0.5m off A37 between Yeovil and
Dorchester, signed Evershot, Holywell
Rooms: 10 en suite
Parking: 40

This 16th-century coaching inn was immortalised as the Sow and Acorn in Thomas Hardy's *Tess of the D'Urbervilles*. It stands at the heart of the village of Evershot, in an Area of Outstanding Natural Beauty, with walking, fishing, shooting and riding all nearby. Inside are two oak-panelled bars – one flagstoned, one tiled – with logs blazing in carved hamstone fireplaces, and a cosy restaurant. There's also a skittle alley in what was once the stables, and it's rumoured that the residents' sitting room was once used by Hanging Judge Jeffreys as a court room. The en suite bedrooms are all individually styled, and each named after a character from Hardy's novel – several feature interesting four-poster beds. All of the rooms, including two family rooms, have a TV, telephone with modem and beverage tray. Hairdryers and irons are available on request. Fresh, local produce is included on the varied and interesting menu, with most of the food sourced from within a 15-mile radius, including local fish and game, and bolstered by blackboard specials. Bar snacks and lighter meals are also available, accompanied by a selection of real ales and a comprehensive wine list. Plenty of parking spaces are available.

Recommended in the area

Evershot village; Forde Abbey; Lyme Regis

Durdle Door

Farnham Farm House

★★★★★ GUEST ACCOMMODATION

Address: FARNHAM, Blandford Forum, DT11 8DG
Tel: 01725 516254
Fax: 01725 516306
Email: info@farnhamfarmhouse.co.uk
Website: www.farnhamfarmhouse.co.uk
Map ref: 2, ST91
Directions: Off A354 Thickthorn x-rds into Farnham, continue NW from village centre T-junct, 1m bear right at sign

Rooms: 3 en suite, **S** £60–£70 **D** £80 **Notes:** ⊗ on premises **Parking:** 7 **Closed:** 25–26 Dec

Farnham Farm House, with its flagstone floors, open log fires and magnificent views, dates back to the 1850s. Guests can walk around the 350-acre working farm, part of a private estate owned by the descendants of archaeologist General Pitt-Rivers. Facilities include a heated outdoor swimming pool, and the Sarpenela Natural Therapy Centre for therapeutic massage. Delicious Aga-cooked breakfasts are served in the attractive dining room. Local produce is used whenever possible.

Recommended in the area

Cranborne Chase; Kingston Lacey (NT); Larmer Tree Gardens

Longpuddle

★ ★ ★ ★ B&B

Address: 4 High Street, PIDDLEHINTON
DT2 7TD

Tel: 01300 348532

Email: ann@longpuddle.co.uk

Website: www.longpuddle.co.uk

Map ref: 2, SY79

Directions: From Dorchester (A35) take B3143, after entering village 1st thatched house on left

Rooms: 2 en suite, D £80–£100 **Parking:** 3

Set in the Piddle Valley, midway between the abbey town of Sherborne and the county town of Dorchester, Longpuddle is well placed for exploring Thomas Hardy's Dorset and the Jurassic Coast. The 400-year-old thatched cottage overlooks the embryo River Piddle, which runs between the large garden and paddocks, and off-road parking is available. Guest accommodation comprises two spacious, tastefully decorated rooms ideal for an extended stay; one double and one twin, both with en suite facilities. A third bed can be made available if required for a child. Guests have the use of a spacious, comfortable drawing room with a TV and views over the garden and paddocks. Breakfast consists of local produce personally cooked by the proprietor, including homemade marmalade. Individual tastes and vegetarians are catered for. The name Longpuddle was used by Thomas Hardy, collectively, for the villages of the Piddle Valley, where there are several pubs serving local food and the excellent Abbots Tea Room. For a special meal there are some superior restaurants within a 40-minute drive. Ann (the proprietor) and Sassy (the resident Golden Retriever) look forward to meeting you and helping you enjoy this delightful county. Well-behaved pets are welcome by prior arrangement.

Recommended in the area

Cerne Abbas Giant; Maiden Castle; Sherborne

The Piddle Inn

★★★★ INN

Address: PIDDLETRENTHIDE, Dorchester, DT2 7QF
Tel: 01300 348468
Fax: 01300 348102
Email: piddleinn@aol.com
Website: www.piddleinn.co.uk
Map ref: 2, SY79
Directions: 7m N of Dorchester on B3143 in middle of Piddletrenthide
Rooms: 3 en suite, S £45–£50 D £70–£80
Parking: 15

In the heart of Thomas Hardy walking country, nestled in the beautiful Piddle Valley and only half an hour from the Jurassic Coast, The Piddle Inn is a traditional family-owned village inn. Dating from the 1760s, it takes its name from the river that flows past the sunny beer garden, creating a picturesque foreground for a stunning view of the countryside beyond. There are three beautifully refurbished en suite rooms, two of which have views over the River Piddle and the countryside beyond. All of the comfortable rooms have tea- and coffee-making facilities, direct-dial telephones, Wi-fi, TVs, DVD players, clock radios and electric safes, and the bathrooms have high-powered electric showers. Fresh flowers are regularly placed in each room, and for special occasions you can arrange in advance to have wine or champagne in the room on arrival. The restaurant here seats 50 and offers daily specials, an à la carte menu sourced straight from local farmers, fish and produce markets, with home-made puddings and a bar and children's menu. Real ales are served straight from the barrel and there's an extensive choice of wine and other beverages. Guests can take time out to relax by the open fire while playing traditional pub games. Well-behaved dogs are welcome.

Recommended in the area

Salisbury Cathedral; Cerne Abbas Giant; Poole

Thorn Bank

★ ★ ★ ★ B&B

Address: Long Street, SHERBORNE DT9 3BS
Tel: 01935 813795
Email: savileplatt@hotmail.com
Map ref: 2, ST61
Directions: A30 onto North Rd, then St Swithin's Rd.
Right onto Long St, 75yds on right
Rooms: 2 en suite, D £70–£85
Notes: ⊗ on premises 👶 under 18yrs **Parking:** 2

A Grade II listed Georgian town house, Thorn Bank is just three minutes' walk from Sherborne's beautiful Abbey. The house is newly refurbished to a high standard and retains its period character. Offering impressive quality and comfort, attentive service is a hallmark here. The spacious double-aspect bedrooms look out on to Sherborne Long Street conservation area, while the view from the rear is over the 18th-century walled garden and listed summer house. Each en suite bathroom is decorated in black and white, with original shutters and a free-standing bath with shower attachment. Cooked or continental breakfast is served in the airy breakfast room or on the lovely patio in the summer months.

Recommended in the area

Sherborne Abbey; Sherborne Castle, Sherborne Museum

Greyhound Inn

★ ★ ★ ★ ⌐ INN

Address: 26 High Street, SYDLING ST NICHOLAS,
Dorchester, DT2 9PD
Tel: 01300 341303
Email: info@thegreyhounddorset.co.uk
Website: www.thegreyhounddorset.co.uk
Map ref: 2, SY69
Directions: Off A37 into village centre
Rooms: 6 en suite (3 GF), D £70–£90 **Parking:** 30

Situated in the traditional English village of Sydling St Nicholas, the Greyhound Inn is well located for exploring Hardy Country. The inn has a range of stylish, well-equipped en suite bedrooms, three of which are at ground-floor level. Elsewhere, flagstone floors and attractive, relaxed surroundings make this inn a popular place for dining. An interesting and wide choice of meals made from top-quality local produce, and often including fresh game, is offered in either the restaurant, which has a well as its central feature, the bar or the conservatory. Lights snacks are also available.

Recommended in the area

Keep Military Museum; Purbeck; Yeovil

George Loveless statue, Martyrs Museum, Tolpuddle

Kemps Country House

★★★★★ ❀ GUEST ACCOMMODATION

Address: East Stoke, WAREHAM BH20 6AL
Tel: 0845 8620315
Fax: 0845 8620316
Email: info@kempscountryhouse.co.uk
Website: www.kempshotel.com
Map ref: 2, SY98
Directions: Follow A352 W from Wareham,
3m on right
Rooms: 16 en suite (6 GF), **S** £95–£160
D £120–£170 **Parking:** 24

Facing south across the Frome Valley to the Purbeck Hills, this beautifully refurbished Victorian rectory offers supreme levels of relaxation and comfort, whether by the log fire in the lounge in winter or on the terrace in summer. The air-conditioned bedrooms are in contemporary style and newer rooms have super king-size beds, power showers and flat-screen TVs. Executive and family rooms also available. At dinner, locally sourced seafood and farm produce are skilfully crafted by the chef.

Recommended in the area

Monkey World; Tank Museum; Corfe Castle

The Esplanade

★★★★ GUEST ACCOMMODATION

Address: 141 The Esplanade, WEYMOUTH DT4 7NJ

Tel: 01305 783129

Fax: 01305 773896

Email: stay@theesplanadehotel.co.uk

Website: www.theesplanadehotel.co.uk

Map ref: 2, SY67

Directions: On seafront, between Jubilee Clock and Pier Bandstand

Rooms: 11 en suite (2 GF), S £40–£55 D £60–£100

Notes: ⊗ on premises **Parking:** 9

With a warm welcome assured from owners Rob and Terri Cole, The Esplanade is a Grade II listed Georgian seafront property. Built in 1835, it is located in a prime seafront location. Ideally situated for all local attractions and amenities, it is just yards from the beach and promenade. The front-facing rooms have stunning seaside views and a panorama of the beautiful golden sands of Weymouth beach. Set against the unforgettable backdrop of Weymouth Bay and the famous World Heritage Coastline, The Esplandade is a haven for those wanting peace and relaxation beside the sea, as well as those seeking a more activity-based seaside experience. The town centre, railway station, bus station and ferry terminal are all within easy walking distance. All bedrooms offer en suite facilities with baths and showers, 100% Egyptian cotton linen with a high degree of luxury and comfort. With an extensive breakfast menu supplied from the highest quality locally sourced produce wherever possible, delicious breakfasts are served overlooking the sea. With a guest lounge and bar on the first floor, the balcony is the perfect place to sip a cool drink and watch the boats sail past. Off-road parking is available.

Recommended in the area

Dorset Beaches; Portland Bill; South West Coastal Path; Monkey World; Sea Life Centre; Abbotsbury Swannery and Subtropical Gardens; Sea fishing and sailing

ESSEX

Epping Forest

Chudleigh

★★★★ GUEST ACCOMMODATION

Address: 13 Agate Road, Marine Parade West
CLACTON-ON-SEA CO15 1RA
Tel: 01255 425407
Fax: 01255 470280
Email: chudleighhotel@btconnect.com
Website: www.chudleighhotel.com
Map ref: 4, TM11
Directions: With sea on left, cross lights at pier, turn onto Agate Rd

Rooms: 10 en suite (2 GF), S £46–£48 D £75 **Notes:** ✿ under 2yrs **Parking:** 7

With its unique architecture, its front terrace with outdoor furniture and its masses of flowers spilling out of window boxes, tubs and hanging baskets, Chudleigh is a distinctive landmark near the Clacton seafront. The pier and the main shopping centre are both within a short distance, making this an ideal spot for both business and leisure visitors to the town, but it is nevertheless a peaceful place to stay. For more than three decades it has been run with dedication and enthusiasm by Carol and Peter Oleggini, who, as might be surmised from their name, can converse fluently with Italian-speaking guests. Service here is pleasantly informal, but attention to detail and high standards of housekeeping are paramount. It's a delicate balance, perfectly achieved, which brings many guests back time and time again. The bedrooms are very attractive, with coordinating decor, comfortable beds and chairs, en suite bathrooms and facilities such as TVs, direct-dial telephones and tea- and coffee-making supplies. There are also spacious family rooms. Downstairs there's a residents' lounge with a television, and an extensive breakfast menu is on offer in the dining room, where the separate tables are dressed with linen tablecloths.

Recommended in the area

Sandy beaches of the Essex coast; Colchester; Beth Chatto Gardens; Constable Country

Beth Chatto Gardens

Old Manse

★★★★ GUEST ACCOMMODATION

Address: 15 Roman Road, COLCHESTER CO1 1UR
Tel: 01206 545154
Email: wendyanderson15@hotmail.com
Website: www.theoldmanse.uk.com
Map ref: 4, TL92
Directions: In town centre, 250yds E of castle.
Off High St-East Hill onto Roman Rd
Rooms: 3 (2 en suite) (1 pri facs), S £45–£60
D £65–£75 **Notes:** ⊗ on premises 👶 under 8yrs
Parking: 1 **Closed:** 23–31 Dec

This elegant and spacious Victorian house is in a quiet location, yet is just a short walk from the castle and the town centre. The bedrooms here are carefully decorated with coordinated soft furnishings, and equipped with many thoughtful touches. Breakfast is served at a large communal table in the attractive dining room and there is a comfortable lounge. Famous for its warm welcome and friendly atmosphere, Wendy Anderson was a finalist for AA Friendliest Landlady of the Year 2007.

Recommended in the area

Colchester Castle; Colchester Zoo; Beth Chatto Gardens

GLOUCESTERSHIRE

Gloucester Cathedral, west front and tower

The Old Passage Inn

★★★★ ◎◎ ♨ RESTAURANT WITH ROOMS

Address: Passage Road, ARLINGHAM GL2 7JR
Tel: 01452 740547
Fax: 01452 741871
Email: oldpassage@ukonline.co.uk
Website: www.theoldpassage.com
Map ref: 2, SO71
Directions: A38 onto B4071 through Arlingham, located by river
Rooms: 3 en suite, S £75–£130 D £95–£130
Notes: ⊗ on premises **Parking:** 30 **Closed:** 24–27 Dec

This restaurant with rooms is delightfully located on the very edge of the River Severn. The en suite bedrooms are decorated in contemporary style and welcoming extra includes air conditioning, mini bars and tea and coffee making equipment. In the restaurant the fresh water crayfish is local, and pride is taken in using sustainably sourced fish and shellfish, with lobster fresh from the tanks, and freshly shucked oysters and fruits de mers as house specialities.

Recommended in the area

Dean Heritage Centre; Lydney Park Gardens; Edward Jenner Museum

Badger Towers

★★★★ GUEST ACCOMMODATION

Address: 133 Hales Road, CHELTENHAM GL52 6ST
Tel: 01242 522583
Fax: 01242 574800
Email: mrbadger@badgertowers.co.uk
Website: www.badgertowers.co.uk
Map ref: 2, SO92
Directions: Off A40 London Rd onto Hales Rd, 0.50m on right towards Prestbury Village and race course
Rooms: 7 en suite (2 GF), S £50–£70 D £70–£105 **Parking:** 7 **Closed:** Xmas & New Year

A comfortable, relaxed atmosphere is felt as soon as you enter this impressive Victorian property, set in a quiet residential area. Owners Claire and Peter Christensen offer elegantly decorated and furnished bedrooms, including two on the ground floor. The breakfast room, where a full English breakfast is freshly cooked from locally sourced produce, is bright and cheerful, and there is a spacious sitting room.

Recommended in the area

Sudeley Castle; Prestbury Park; Cheltenham Promenade and Montpellier

Cleeve Hill House

★★★★★ GUEST ACCOMMODATION

Address: Cleeve Hill, CHELTENHAM GL52 3PR
Tel: 01242 672052
Fax: 01242 679969
Email: info@cleevehill-hotel.co.uk
Website: www.cleevehill-hotel.co.uk
Map ref: 2, SO92
Directions: 3m N of Cheltenham on B4632
Rooms: 10 en suite (1 GF), **S** £50–£65 **D** £85–£110
Notes: ⊗ on premises ⛄ under 8yrs **Parking:** 11

Set on an elevated location north of Cheltenham with stunning views, this is an elegant and friendly boutique establishment in an ideal spot for visiting the Cotswolds. Guests will receive a warm welcome with complimentary tea and cakes on arrival and great emphasis is placed providing a relaxed atmosphere. Individually styled bedrooms, including one with a four-poster, have flat-screen TV and free Wi-fi. The deep sofas, superb decor and soft furnishings in the spacious lounges provide a relaxed atmosphere. The quality breakfasts are served in a conservatory that looks out to the Malvern Hills.

Recommended in the area

National Hunt Racecourse; Stratford-upon-Avon; Bath

The Malt House

★★★★★ GUEST HOUSE

Address: Broad Campden, CHIPPING CAMPDEN
GL55 6UU
Tel: 01386 840295
Fax: 01386 841334
Email: info@malt-house.co.uk
Website: www.malt-house.co.uk
Map ref: 3, SP13
Directions: By church in village
Rooms: 7 en suite (1 GF), **S** £85 **D** £143
Notes: ⊗ on premises **Parking:** 10 **Closed:** 22–28 Dec

The Malt House nestles in the English countryside. There are fresh flowers everywhere, preserves made from fruit grown in the garden are served at breakfast, and the large bedrooms have been elegantly decorated and fitted with quality fabrics by helpful owner Judy Wilkes. She has thought of everything for guests' comfort, including hot water bottles, irons and boards, umbrellas, torches and more, hidden away in every room. Good local restaurants are recommended to ensure a wide choice for dinner.

Recommended in the area

Chipping Campden; Kiftsgate Court Gardens; Snowshill Manor

The Moda House

★★★★ GUEST ACCOMMODATION
Address: 1 High Street, CHIPPING SODBURY
BS37 6BA
Tel: 01454 312135
Fax: 01454 850090
Email: enquiries@modahouse.co.uk
Website: www.modahouse.co.uk
Map ref: 2, ST78
Directions: In town centre
Rooms: 10 en suite (3 GF), S £65 D £82–£95

Over 300 years old, The Moda House is an exquisite and impressive three storey Grade II listed building, with wonderful views of the town and countryside beyond. The modern bedrooms of various shapes and sizes have their own distinctive character with well-appointed bathrooms and satellite television. The superb breakfasts are sourced from local suppliers and cooked on the Aga. Chipping Sodbury is an excellent base from which to explore the area.

Recommended in the area

Bath; Westonbirt Arboretum; Dyrham Park (NT)

Hare & Hounds

★★★★  INN
Address: Fosse-Cross, Chedworth CHELTENHAM
GL54 4NN
Tel: 01285 720288
Email: stay@hareandhoundsinn.com
Website: www.hareandhoundsinn.com
Map ref: 3, SP00
Directions: 4.50m NE of Cirencester. On A429 by speed camera
Rooms: 10 en suite (8 GF), S £60–£70 D £90–£125
Notes: ⊗ on premises Parking: 40

This country inn is close to the historic Fosse Way and perfectly situated for visiting nearby Cirencester and the Cotswolds. The smart bedrooms surround a peaceful courtyard and have full disabled access. Guests can dine outside on warm summer days, in the orangerie, or in one of the three elegant dining areas in the main pub. The delicious home-cooked food is highly regarded, chef Gerry Ragosa, an advocate of Cotswold produce, creates superb results using local ingredients where possible.

Recommended in the area

Chedworth Roman Villa (NT); Cheltenham; Cotswold Wildlife Park

The Plough Inn

★★★★ ⊜ INN

Address: FORD, Temple Guiting, GL54 5RU
Tel: 01386 584215
Fax: 01386 584042
Email: info@theploughinnatford.co.uk
Website: www.theploughinnatford.co.uk
Map ref: 3, SP02
Directions: On B4077 in village
Rooms: 3 en suite **Notes:** ⊗ on premises
Parking: 50

The Plough Inn, popular with locals and the racing fraternity, is a charming 16th-century inn, well located for visiting the Cotswolds. Inside it retains many original features including Cotswold stone walls, open fires and beamed ceilings, while the en suite bedrooms are located across a courtyard in a quaint cobble-stoned building – once a hayloft with stabling, it has now been restored to provide comfortable, modern accommodation. Home-cooked food featuring local produce is a highlight here, as are the well-kept Donnington ales, which can be enjoyed in the delightful beer garden.
Recommended in the area
Cheltenham Racecourse; Bourton-on-the-Water; Chipping Campden

Guiting Guest House

★★★★ GUEST HOUSE

Address: Post Office Lane, GUITING POWER,
Cheltenham, GL54 5TZ
Tel: 01451 850470
Email: info@guitingguesthouse.com
Website: www.guitingguesthouse.com
Map ref: 3, SP02
Directions: In village centre
Rooms: 6 (4 en suite, 2 pri facs) (2 GF)
S £45 **D** £85 **Parking:** 2

Guiting Guest House is an engaging family home at one with its surroundings in a beautiful Cotswold village. Bedrooms are individually decorated and full of charm. Most have en suite facilities, some have four-poster beds, and all of them are equipped with hairdryers, bathrobes, quality toiletries, and hospitality trays, fresh fruit and flowers. Exposed beams, inglenook fireplaces and solid elm floorboards provide character in the inviting public rooms. Breakfast and evening meals, based on fresh local produce, are served in the dining room. Please give at least 48 hours' notice for a dinner booking.
Recommended in the area
Cotswold Farm Park; Sudeley Castle; Blenheim Palace

Cambrai Lodge

★★★★ GUEST ACCOMMODATION

Address: Oak Street, LECHLADE-ON-THAMES
GL7 3AY
Tel: 01367 253173
Email: cambrailodge@btconnect.com
Website: www.cambrailodgeguesthouse.co.uk
Map ref: 3, SU29
Directions: In town centre, off High St onto A361
Oak St
Rooms: 5 en suite (2 GF), **S** £45–£65 **D** £55–£75
Parking: 12

This attractive house, on the edge of the market town of Lechlade, is only a stroll from a number of recommended pubs serving food. The bedrooms are all carefully decorated and furnished. Some rooms are in a pretty cottage across the garden and include a king-sized bed and corner bath, and there are two ground-floor bedrooms. All the rooms are en suite, have tea and coffee facilities and central heating. Hearty breakfasts are served in the conservatory overlooking the large gardens.

Recommended in the area

Cirencester; Oxford; the Cotswolds

Hyde Wood House

★★★★ B&B

Address: Cirencester Road, MINCHINHAMPTON
GL6 8PE
Tel: 01453 885504
Email: info@hydewoodhouse.co.uk
Website: www.hydewoodhouse.co.uk
Map ref: 2, SO80
Directions: From Stroud A419 to Cirencester, after village of Chalford, turn right at top of hill signed Minchinhampton & Aston Down. House 1m on right

Rooms: 3 en suite, **D** £65 **Notes:** ⊗ on premises 🚼 under 14yrs **Parking:** 6

Located within extensive mature grounds, this well-proportioned mellow-stone house was originally built as a farmhouse. Guests are greeted with tea and delicious home-made cake on arrival. Bedrooms come filled with a range of homely extras. Comprehensive breakfasts are taken in an elegant dining room, served straight from the Aga, though lighter options are also available. A spacious, comfortable lounge awaits you after a day out, and the log fire is lit on cold nights.

Recommended in the area

Westonbirt Arboretum; WWT Slimbridge; Cirencester

Hailes Abbey, near Winchcombe

Heavens Above

★★★★ ◉◉ RESTAURANT WITH ROOMS

Address: 3 Cossack Square, NAILSWORTH
GL6 0DB
Tel: 01453 832615
Email: info@wild-garlic.co.uk
Map ref: 2, ST89
Directions: In town centre. Off A46 onto Spring Hill,
left onto Old Market Street, left onto Chestnut Hill
Rooms: 3 (1 en suite), S £75–£85 D £75–£85
Notes: ⊗ on premises

Heavens Above is situated over the Wild Garlic Restaurant in the picture postcard Cossack Square of a town renowned for its wonderful craft shops and award-winning farmers market. It provides a tranquil base from which to explore the Cotswolds, with its wealth of cultural attractions, and just a short walk from the bustling town centre. Meals can be taken in the restaurant below, where everything is hand made on the premises, from the fresh pasta, ice creams and sorbets to the daily baked bread, but bookings are essential so don't forget to reserve your table when booking your room.

Recommended in the area

Chavenage; Owlpen Manor; Woodchester Mansion

143

Northfield Guest House

★★★★ GUEST ACCOMMODATION

Address: Cirencester Road, NORTHLEACH
GL54 3JL
Tel: 01451 860427
Fax: 01451 860427
Email: p.loving@sky.com
Website: www.northfieldbandb.co.uk
Map ref: 3, SP11
Directions: Signed off A429 Northleach-Cirencester road, 1m from Northleach lights
Rooms: 3 en suite (3 GF), **D** £65–£75 **Notes:** ⊗ on premises **Parking:** 10 **Closed:** Dec–Feb

Animals graze in the fields around this Cotswold stone house set in immaculate gardens. Indoors there is a clear commitment to presentation and the bedrooms are a pleasure to stay in – two rooms have direct access to the gardens. The relaxing atmosphere extends to the lounge. The friendly dining room is the scene of delicious country breakfasts including eggs from the resident hens. Northleach is convenient for Cirencester and Gloucester.

Recommended in the area

Chedworth Roman Villa (NT); Keith Harding's Musical Museum; Cheltenham; Stow-on-the-Wold

Aston House

★★★★ B&B

Address: Broadwell, MORETON-IN-MARSH
GL56 0TJ
Tel: 01451 830475
Email: fja@astonhouse.net
Website: www.astonhouse.net
Map ref: 3, SP12
Directions: A429 towards Moreton-in-Marsh, 1m right at x-rds to Broadwell, 0.5m on left
Rooms: 3 (2 en suite) (1 pri facs) (1 GF), **D** £62–£68
Notes: ⊗ on premises 🧒 under 10yrs **Parking:** 3 **Closed:** Nov–Feb

The enthusiastic owner ensures that the accommodation has every comfort, with armchairs in all the rooms, electric blankets and fans. Other amenities include quality toiletries in the en suite bathrooms, televisions, radios and hairdryers, tea-making facilities and bedtime drinks and biscuits. Although rooms are not suitable for wheelchair-bound visitors, the stair lift is a boon for those with limited mobility. A full English breakfast is served and there is a good pub within walking distance.

Recommended in the area

Cotswolds villages; Blenheim Palace; Hidcote Manor Gardens

Kings Head Inn & Restaurant

★★★★ ◉ INN

Address: The Green, Bledington CHIPPING NORTON
OX7 6XQ
Tel: 01608 658365
Fax: 01608 658902
Email: kingshead@orr-ewing.com
Website: www.kingsheadinn.net
Map ref: 3, SP12
Directions: 4m SE off B4450
Rooms: 12 en suite (3 GF) **Notes:** ⊗ on premises
Parking: 24 **Closed:** 25–26 Dec

Located next to the picturesque village green with a brook running past, this classic English country pub is well worth seeking out. In the 16th century it was used as a cider house, and its timeless interior, full of charm and character, has low ceilings, beams, exposed stone walls and open fires. Nicola Orr-Ewing was once a milliner in London, and she has used her creative talents to transform the accommodation. Husband Archie, born in the next village, helps to maintain a relaxed but efficient atmosphere. The stylish bedrooms are individually decorated and each has a modern bathroom. Some rooms are above the inn (these are full of character and have standard double beds), while others are in a quiet courtyard annexe set well back from the pub. These annexe rooms have king-size beds and are more spacious than those in the main building. All rooms have wireless internet access and televisions. Excellent meals, using locally sourced and organic produce where possible, are served in the smart restaurant. The Aberdeen Angus beef comes from the family's own farm in a neighbouring village and the vegetables from the Vale of Evesham. The interesting breakfast menu offers a choice of delicious and sustaining dishes.

Recommended in the area

Blenheim Palace; Cotswold Farm Park; Cheltenham Races

1 Woodchester Lodge

★ ★ ★ ★ 🛏 B&B

Address: Southfield Road, North Woodchester
STROUD GL5 5PA
Tel: 01453 872586
Email: anne@woodchesterlodge.co.uk
Website: www.woodchesterlodge.co.uk
Map ref: 2, SO80
Directions: A46 onto Selsley Rd, take 2nd left,
200yds on the left
Rooms: 2 (1 en suite) (1 pri facs), S £40–£45
D £60–£65 **Notes:** ⊗ on premises **Parking:** 4 **Closed:** Xmas & Etr

This large, late Victorian house, which was once the home of a timber merchant, is set in the peaceful village of North Woodchester, just a short drive from Stroud. Surrounded by attractive gardens, it has been sympathetically restored to make the most of its unusual features. The central hallway has a barrel vaulted ceiling, a grand stairway, oak-turned banisters and etched glass doors. Spacious bedrooms offer king-size beds, television and hospitality tray, and comfortable chairs have been provided from which to enjoy the peaceful countryside views. Bathrooms come with large baths, heated towel rails and quality toiletries. The colourful gardens here have been well tended, and guests can sit in the sun on the patio or find a spot in the shade from which to enjoy the tranquil setting; otherwise, the comfortable lounge/dining room offers an open fire, satellite television and books, magazines and games. Guests are greeted on arrival with home-made cakes and tea. Meals, prepared by a fully qualified chef, often using fruit and vegetables from the garden, are not to be missed. The delicious dinners are served by candlelight, while the freshly prepared breakfasts might include smoked salmon and scrambled egg made from newly laid eggs.

Recommended in the area

Woodchester Mansion and grounds; WWT Slimbridge; Westonbirt Arboretum

Cheltenham

Beaufort House

★ ★ ★ ★ ★ B&B

Address: Willesley, TETBURY
GL8 8QU
Tel: 01666 880444
Map ref: 2, ST89
Directions: 4m SW of Tetbury. A433 to Willesley,
House set back from road
Rooms: 4 en suite, S £75 D £90
Notes: ⊗ on premises ⛹ under 10yrs **Parking:** 8

Located near the market town of Tetbury, within easy reach of Bath and Bristol, this former staging post and inn built from beautiful local stone, dates back to the 17th century. The bedrooms, all with spacious en suite bathrooms, are elegantly furnished and thoughtfully equipped with colour TV, beverage-making facilities and radio alarm. There is also a deeply comfortable guest lounge. Breakfast, featuring organic items (when available), is served in the dining room around one grand table. A delightful walled garden may be enjoyed in warmer weather.

Recommended in the area

Worcester Cathedral; Blenheim Palace; Berkeley Castle; Westonbirt Arboretum (opposite)

Arlington Row, Bibury

Exbury Gardens, New Forest National Park

Beech Barns Guest House

★ ★ ★ ★ GUEST ACCOMMODATION

Address: 61 Wellhouse Road, Beech, ALTON
GU34 4AQ
Tel: 01420 85575
Fax: 01420 85575
Email: timsiggs@yahoo.com
Website: www.beechbarns.co.uk
Map ref: 3, SU73
Directions: 1.50m W of Alton. Off A339 towards
Beech, 2nd right onto Wellhouse Rd, 0.50m on left
Rooms: 9 en suite (6 GF), S £55–£80 D £80–£110 **Parking:** 12

This rambling house and barn conversion, believed to date from the early 18th century, is set in its own grounds on the outskirts of Alton, where there are plenty of opportunities for walking and cycling in glorious countryside. The en suite bedrooms are attractively decorated with a blend of contemporary and traditional styles. There is a games and TV room and a separate lounge. Outside a large patio area is perfect for relaxing when enjoying tea and home-made cakes. Dinner is available on request.
Recommended in the area
Jane Austen's House; Gilbert White's House and The Oates Museum; Winchester

The Cottage Lodge

★ ★ ★ ★ ★ GUEST ACCOMMODATION

Address: Sway Road, BROCKENHURST SO42 7SH
Tel: 01590 622296
Fax: 01590 623014
Email: enquiries@cottagelodge.co.uk
Website: www.cottagelodge.co.uk
Map ref: 3, SU30
Directions: Off A337 opp Careys Manor Hotel
onto Grigg Ln, 0.25m over x-rds, cottage next
to war memorial
Rooms: 12 en suite (6 GF), S £50–£120 D £50–£170 **Notes:** ⚹ under 10yrs **Parking:** 12
Closed: Xmas & New Year

Owners David and Christina welcome guests to their cosy award-winning 17th-century B&B with tea or coffee, served in front of the roaring fire. Brockenhurst is one of the few New Forest settlements where grazing ponies and cattle still have right of way. Conveniently close to the high street and the open forest. The individually furnished bedrooms are en suite and a local New Forest breakfast is served.
Recommended in the area
National Motor Museum, Beaulieu; Exbury Gardens; walking, cycling and horse riding

36 on the Quay

★★★★ ◉◉◉ RESTAURANT WITH ROOMS
Address: 47 South Street, EMSWORTH PO10 7EG
Tel: 01243 375592
Website: www.36onthequay.co.uk
Map ref: 3, SU70
Rooms: 5 en suite, S £70–£100 D £95–£200
Parking: 6
Closed: 3wks Jan, 1wk late May & 1 wk late Oct

Located in a picturesque fishing village, this 16th-century house occupies a prime position with far-reaching views over the bay. It is the ideal setting to experience some accomplished and exciting cuisine. The stylish en suite rooms are a joy to relax in with their muted colours and sense of space. Charmingly named Nutmeg, Vanilla, Clove and Cinnamon, they have great views and come equipped with colour TV, bathrobes, hospitality tray and toiletries. The lounge and summer terrace are perfect for breakfast or a drink. Centre stage goes to the elegant restaurant with its peaceful pastel shades where you can enjoy expertly cooked dishes, using fresh produce to create flavoursome, quality cuisine.

Recommended in the area

Chichester; Weald and Downland Open Air Museum; Portsmouth Historic Dockyard

---

Wisteria House

★★★★ B&B
Address: 14 Mays House, Stubbington FAREHAM
PO14 2EP
Tel: 01329 511940
Email: info@wisteria-house.co.uk
Website: www.wisteria-house.co.uk
Map ref: 3, SU50
Directions: Exit M27 junct 9, take A27 to Fareham.
Turn right onto B3334, at rdbt turn left onto Mays Ln
Rooms: 2 en suite (2 GF), S £47 D £62
Notes: ⊗ on premises ✸ under 8yrs **Parking:** 2

Wisteria House, a comfortable and tastefully decorated guest house, is just a short walk from local amenities and a mile from the beach at Lee-on-the-Solent, with its stunning panoramic views of the Isle of Wight. The charming and comfortable bedrooms, both on the ground floor, are packed with homely touches such as king-size bed, Freeview colour TV with video recorder, radio alarm, hairdryer and well-stocked hospitality tray. A full English breakfast is served in the pretty dining room.

Recommended in the area

Portsmouth Historic Dockyard; The New Forest; Winchester

Tudorwood Guest House

★★★★ GUEST HOUSE

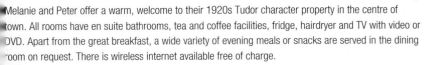

Address: 164 Farnborough Road, FARNBOROUGH
GU14 7JJ
Tel: 01252 541123
Email: pshutak@btinternet.com
Website: www.tudorwood.net
Map ref: 3, SU85
Directions: Off A325 (Farnborough Rd) left onto
Sycamore Rd, next 2 left turns onto Cedar Rd, right
onto Old Farnborough Rd
Rooms: 6 en suite (4 GF), **S** £45–£60 **D** £60–£75 **Notes:** ⊗ on premises **Parking:** 7
Closed: 24–29 Dec

Melanie and Peter offer a warm, welcome to their 1920s Tudor character property in the centre of town. All rooms have en suite bathrooms, tea and coffee facilities, fridge, hairdryer and TV with video or DVD. Apart from the great breakfast, a wide variety of evening meals or snacks are served in the dining room on request. There is wireless internet available free of charge.

Recommended in the area

London; Farnborough Air Show; RHS Garden Wisley; Thorpe Park

Alderholt Mill

★★★★ GUEST ACCOMMODATION

Address: Sandleheath Road, FORDINGBRIDGE
SP6 1PU
Tel: 01425 653130
Fax: 01425 652868
Email: alderholt-mill@zetnet.co.uk
Website: www.alderholtmill.co.uk
Map ref: 3, SU11
Directions: 1m W from Fordingbridge, left at x-rds
in Sandleheath, 0.50m over bridge on right
Rooms: 5 (4 en suite), **S** £28–£32 **D** £35–£75 **Notes:** ⋈ under 8yrs **Parking:** 10 **Closed:** 24–26 Dec

This picturesque group of brick buildings beside a working watermill, is perfectly placed for exploring the New Forest. The rooms all have en suite bathrooms, television, tea and coffee-making facilities and there's a residents' lounge. Breakfast features freshly baked bread made with milled flour from locally grown wheat. Three self-catering apartments are also available.

Recommended in the area

Rockbourne Roman Villa; Breamore House; Salisbury Cathedral

Bremore Wood

Ravensdale

★★★★ B&B

Address: 19 St Catherines Road, HAYLING ISLAND
PO11 0HF
Tel/Fax 023 9246 3203
Email: phil.taylor@tayloredprint.co.uk
Website: www.ravensdale-hayling.co.uk
Map ref: 3, SU70
Directions: A3023 at Langstone, cross Hayling
Bridge & continue 3m to mini rdbt, right onto Manor
Rd 1m. Right by Barley Mow onto Station Rd, 3rd left
onto St Catherines Rd
Rooms: 3 (2 en suite), **S** £40 **D** £66
Notes: ⊗ on premises 🚼 under 8yrs **Parking:** 4 **Closed:** last 2 wks Dec

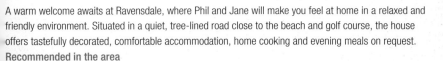

A warm welcome awaits at Ravensdale, where Phil and Jane will make you feel at home in a relaxed and friendly environment. Situated in a quiet, tree-lined road close to the beach and golf course, the house offers tastefully decorated, comfortable accommodation, home cooking and evening meals on request.
Recommended in the area
Chichester Cathedral; Portsmouth Historic Dockyard; walking on the South Downs

West Wind Guest House

★★★★ GUEST ACCOMMODATION

Address: 197 Portsmouth Road, LEE-ON-THE-
SOLENT,Gosport, PO13 9AA
Tel: 023 9255 2550
Email: maggie@west-wind.co.uk
Website: www.west-wind.co.uk
Map ref: 3, SU50
Directions: M27 junct 11, A32, then B3385 for
Lee-on-the-Solent, left at beach, 800mtrs on left
Rooms: 6 en suite (1 GF), **S** £45–£55 **D** £60
Notes: ⊗ on premises 🚼 under 10yrs **Parking:** 6 **Closed:** Xmas & New Year

A long established, family-run guest house, West Wind is just 50 metres from the beach. The white-painted, double-fronted house makes an ideal base for visiting the cities of Portsmouth, Southampton and Winchester as well as the beautiful New Forest. Bedrooms are individually decorated to a high standard and equipped to offer en suite facilities, televisions, hairdryers and well-stocked hospitality trays. Wi-fi internet access is also available in all rooms. The freshly cooked breakfasts include locally made sausages.
Recommended in the area
Portsmouth Historic Dockyard; Winchester Cathedral; Southampton Maritime Museum

The ruins of Odiham Castle

The Rufus House

★★★★ GUEST ACCOMMODATION

Address: Southampton Road, LYNDHURST SO43 7BQ
Tel: 023 8028 2930
Email: stay@rufushouse.co.uk
Website: www.rufushouse.co.uk
Map ref: 3, SU30
Directions: From Lyndhurst centre onto A35
Southampton Rd, 300yds on left
Rooms: 10 en suite (2 GF), S £30–£50 D £50–£130
Notes: ⊗ on premises ⋈ under 5yrs **Parking:** 12

A welcoming, peaceful haven in the heart of the New Forest National Park, Rufus House overlooks the forest. Within ten minutes' walk of this grand Victorian house, you will be spoilt with the choice of restaurants, tea houses and pubs. Golf courses, equestrian centres, cycle hire and swimming are all a short distance from Rufus House. A 'stress relief short break' with yoga, meditation and a healthy natural food experience is on offer, as is the equally popular 'spa short break' in collaboration with a New Forest spa. Newly developed self-catering holiday cottages with Wi-fi are available.

Recommended in the area

National Motor Museum and Palace House, Beaulieu; Exbury Gardens; New Forest Otter & Wildlife Park

Temple Lodge

★ ★ ★ ★ GUEST ACCOMMODATION

Address: 2 Queens Road, LYNDHURST SO43 7BR
Tel: 023 8028 2392
Fax: 023 8028 4910
Email: templelodge@btinternet.com
Website: www.templelodge-guesthouse.com
Map ref: 3, SU30
Directions: M27 junct 2/3 onto A35 to Ashurst/
Lyndhurst, Temple Lodge on 2nd corner on right,
opposite forest

Rooms: 6 en suite, D £60–£120 **Notes:** ⊗ on premises ⋈ under 12yrs **Parking:** 6

Temple Lodge is a beautiful Victorian residence, lovingly restored by its present owners and retaining many original features, such as the large entrance hall with its grand wooden staircase and beautiful stained-glass windows. The six spacious bedrooms, including a family suite and a family room, all have en suite facilities, generous hospitality trays, TVs/DVDs and mini fridges. The attractive guest lounge has a good selection of books and magazines and comfortable leather sofas. There is a wide choice of breakfasts, ranging from continental to full English breakfasts which are freshly prepared, using local ingredients, and served in the elegant dining room, which overlooks the well-stocked gardens. This is an ideal place for a relaxing stay, just a few minutes' level walk from the village of Lyndhurst with its numerous pubs and restaurants, and directly opposite the New Forest National Park. It makes a superb base for walking, cycling and exploring the surrounding countryside and nearby coastal areas. The owners, Mike and Teresa, are always pleased to be of service and make every effort to ensure their guests have a truly memorable stay. Free Wi-fi and good off-road parking is available.

Recommended in the area

National Motor Museum Beaulieu; Exbury Gardens; Buckler's Hard; Lymington; Bournemouth; Christchurch

New Forest National Park

Alma Mater

★★★★ B&B

Address: 4 Knowland Drive, MILFORD ON SEA,
Lymington, SO41 0RH
Tel: 01590 642811
Email: bandbalmamater@aol.com
Website: www.newforestalmamater.co.uk
Map ref: 3, SZ29
Directions: A337 at Everton onto B3058 to Milford
on Sea. Pass South Lawn Hotel, right onto Manor Rd,
1st left onto Knowland Dr, 3rd bungalow on right

Rooms: 3 en suite (1 GF), **S** £50 **D** £64–£70 **Notes:** ⊗ on premises ⚲ under 15yrs **Parking:** 4

Eileen and John Haywood enjoy welcoming guests to their beautifully kept home overlooking
landscaped gardens in a quiet residential area. It is a good base for exploring the New Forest and coast,
the yachting centre of Lymington is close by and the village and the beach are just a walk away. A full
four-course or continental breakfast is served in the dining room. The bedrooms are centrally heated
and have extras such as radios, tea and coffee provisions, toiletries and bathrobes.

Recommended in the area

Hurst Castle; Exbury Gardens; National Motor Museum, Beaulieu

Pilgrims Rest

★★★★ GUEST ACCOMMODATION

Address: Westover Road, MILFORD ON SEA
SO41 0PW
Tel: 01590 641167
Email: pilgrimsrestbandb@yahoo.co.uk
Website: www.milfordonseabandb.co.uk
Map ref: 3, SZ29
Directions: From Lymington follow signs New Milton, continue 2m left onto B3058 through village, 2nd left
Rooms: 4 en suite, S £40–£50 D £60–£70
Notes: ⊗ on premises 🐾 under 10yrs **Parking:** 6

Between the south coast and the woods and heathland of the New Forest National Park, Pilgrims Rest has an elegance and spaciousness that belies its modern exterior. Set back from the road, it has off-street parking and is conveniently located for exploring the historic village of Milford-on-Sea on foot. The coast is just two minutes' walk away, with a shingle bank leading out to Hurst Castle. The bedrooms are roomy and decorated with considerable flair, each with its own colour scheme, interesting pieces of furniture, Egyptian cotton sheets, sumptuous soft furnishings and fresh flowers. Each has a flat-screen television with Freeview channels, tea- and coffee-making facilities and an en suite bathroom with Molton Brown toiletries, but the place still maintains a nice home-from-home atmosphere. Breakfast is a real treat – served in the bright, sunny breakfast room, with its beautiful pine grandfather clock. The dishes feature ingredients that come from local producers who employ high standards of animal welfare and good husbandry. It's certainly reflected in the taste, and provides a great energy boost for a day's sightseeing. Dinner is not served here, but there are restaurants and pubs in the village or in nearby Lymington.

Recommended in the area

Sammy Miller Motorcycle Museum; Buckler's Hard; Beaulieu National Motor Museum

View across River Hamble

Sunrise on Boscombe beach

Quinhay Farmhouse

★ ★ ★ ★ ☗ B&B

Address: Alton Road, Froxfield PETERSFIELD
GU32 1BZ
Tel: 01730 827183
Fax: 01730 827184
Email: janerothery@hotmail.com
Website: www.quinhaybandb.co.uk
Map ref: 3, SU72
Directions: 4m NW of Petersfield. Off A3 at A272
junct towards Petersfield, at rdbt exit signed Froxfield/
Steep, 3.50m on right

Rooms: 3 (1 en suite) (2 pri facs), **S** £35 **D** £70–£80 **Notes:** ⊗ on premises ⚲ under 12yrs
Parking: 10 **Closed:** 15 Dec–15 Jan

Jane Rothery takes great delight in welcoming you to her delightful farmhouse, set in rolling countryside outside Petersfield. The spacious bedrooms have a wealth of thoughtful extras, and the large lounge has comfy sofas and access to a terrace. Quinhay is popular with walkers and cyclists.
Recommended in the area
Winchester; Portsmouth Historic Dockyard; Jane Austen's House, Chawton

Moortown Lodge

★ ★ ★ ★ GUEST ACCOMMODATION

Address: 244 Christchurch Road, RINGWOOD
BH24 3AS

Tel: 01425 471404

Fax: 01425 476527

Email: enquiries@moortownlodge.co.uk

Website: www.moortownlodge.co.uk

Map ref: 3, SU10

Directions: 1m S of Ringwood. Off A31 at Ringwood
onto B3347, signs to Sopley, Lodge next to David
Lloyds Leisure Club

Rooms: 7 en suite (2 GF), **S** £67.50 **D** £84–£94 **Parking:** 9

Moortown Lodge is a charming, family-run Georgian property in the attractive market town of Ringwood, the western gateway to the New Forest, where there is a wide range of unusual shops, traditional pubs and lovely restaurants. It offers guests a warm welcome and luxury grade B&B accommodation with many of the features found in a good class hotel. The seven elegantly furnished en suite rooms, include one with a romantic four-poster bed and two easy access ground-floor rooms. All suites have digital TV and DVD, free broadband connection and free national direct-dial phones. Generous traditional breakfasts are cooked to order with lighter and vegetarian breakfast options available. Wherever possible fresh New Forest produce is used in the cooking. The peace and tranquillity of the open forest as well as the unspoilt water meadows of the River Avon are only minutes away. Moortown Lodge is the ideal stopover for business people as well as an excellent base for touring and leisure visitors. There are special arrangements for guests wishing to use the bar, restaurant and outstanding recreational facilities at the adjacent private David Lloyd Leisure Club.

Recommended in the area

Bournemouth; New Forest National Park; Stonehenge

Bolderwood Deer Sanctury, New Forest National Park

Greenvale Farm

★ ★ ★ ★ B&B

Address: Melchet Park, Sherfield English, ROMSEY
SO51 6FS
Tel: 01794 884858
Email: suebrown@greenvalefarm.com
Website: www.greenvalefarm.com
Map ref: 3, SU32
Directions: 5m W of Romsey. On S side of A27
through archway for Melchet Court, farm 150yds
on left, left at slatted barn

Rooms: 1 en suite (1 GF), D £60–£65 **Notes:** ⊗ on premises ⚹ under 14yrs **Parking:** 10

Greenvale Farm in Melchet Park is located on the Hampshire/Wiltshire border, just four miles from the New Forest, near the historic market town of Romsey. The cathedral cities of Salisbury and Winchester are also within easy reach for days out. The working farm offers spacious, self-contained, ground floor accommodation with twin or double rooms, en suite facilities, television and Wi-fi access. A hearty breakfast is served to set you up for the day and, if you're lucky, you can have freshly-laid eggs.

Recommended in the area

The Hillier Arboretum; Mottisfont Abbey and Gardens; Florence Nightingale's Grave

White Star Tavern, Dining and Rooms

★★★★ ❀ INN

Address: 28 Oxford Street, SOUTHAMPTON, SO14 3DJ
Tel: 023 8082 1990
Fax: 023 8090 4982
Email: reservations@whitestartavern.co.uk
Website: www.whitestartavern.co.uk
Map ref: 3, SU41
Directions: M3 junct 14 onto A33, towards Ocean Village
Rooms: 13 (13 en suite), D £79–£179

This award-winning bar, restaurant and boutique establishment is set in the historic maritime district of Southampton in cosmopolitan Oxford Street. Named after the prominent British shipping company, the White Star Line, each of the luxury en suite bedrooms bears the name of one of its vessels. Seriously comfortable beds are made up with soft Egyptian linen, and the bathrooms feature roll top baths and oversized showers. Thoughtful extras include mini bars stocked with your favourite products and personal safes big enough to accommodate your laptop. Rooms are also equipped with the latest technology and entertainment facilities, such as broadband Wi-fi and 20-inch Freeview flat-screen televisions. The elegant building has now been completely restored to include a gastro-pub, serviced apartments, a conference room, lounge, reception and sun deck, while retaining its unique period charm. The ground floor restaurant and bar attract a lively mix of drinkers and diners and offer an imaginative menu of modern British dishes in a relaxed and informal atmosphere. The breakfast menu provides healthy eating and traditional options: porridge and poached eggs from the former and pastries or full English from the latter, including a vegetarian alternative.

Recommended in the area

Hall of Aviation; Maritime Museum; Southampton Art Gallery

Old Drapery Guesthouse

★ ★ ★ ★ B&B

Address: Middle Wallop, STOCKBRIDGE SO20 8HN
Tel: 01264 781301
Fax: 01264 781301
Email: amanda@olddraperyguesthouse.co.uk
Website: www.olddraperyguesthouse.co.uk
Map ref: 3, SU33
Directions: A303 onto A343, turn right at x-rds by George Inn, 2nd on left
Rooms: 4 en suite, S £45 D £80–£95
Notes: ⊗ on premises ⚲ under 12yrs **Parking:** 5 **Closed:** 24–26 & 31 Dec–1 Jan

Mike and Amanda Daly welcome you to their home at the Old Drapery, where guests return time and again to enjoy a level of hospitality which is second to none. The Georgian family home is located in the heart of the Test Valley, close to Stockbridge, among beautiful thatched cottages with Wallop Brook meandering through the mature garden. Good off-street parking is provided and there are many places of interest within easy reach, such as the beautiful cities of Winchester and Salisbury with their magnificent cathedrals, and the megalithic structure of Stonehenge on Salisbury Plain. London is only 55 minutes by train with a direct link to London's Waterloo Station. The pretty bedrooms provide all the modern comforts a guest could need, including free Wi-fi connection, and there is a spacious guests' lounge with an array of books to read. The en suite bedrooms include one with a four-poster bed and a large spa bath, and all are furnished for maximum comfort, with bathrobes and complimentary toiletries. Breakfasts are freshly prepared using local ingredients, with dishes ranging from smoked trout and scrambled eggs to pancakes and maple syrup.

Recommended in the area

The Museum of Army Flying; Sir Harold Hillier Gardens; Mottisfont Abbey Garden, House & Estate

Nurse's Cottage Restaurant with Rooms

★★★★ 🏠 🍽 GUEST ACCOMMODATION

Address: Station Road, SWAY, Lymington,
S041 6BA
Tel: 01590 683402
Email: nurses.cottage@lineone.net
Website: www.nursescottage.co.uk
Map ref: 3, SZ29
Directions: Off B3055 in village centre
Rooms: 5 en suite, **S** 90 **D** £180–£190
Notes: 🚫 under 10yrs **Parking:** 5
Closed: Feb–Mar & Nov (3 wks)

The Nurse's Cottage is located in the centre of Sway on the edge of the New Forest National Park. For 70 years it was home to a succession of the village's District Nurses, who now lend the bedrooms their names. Each of the ground-floor rooms is individually designed and offers many home comforts, such as digital flat-screen TVs with video/DVD, CD/radios, central heating or air conditioning, direct-dial telephones, free Wi-fi access and fridges (containing fresh organic milk, fruit juices, New Forest spring water and snacks). Well equipped bathrooms feature White Company toiletries. Accessibility is also high on the agenda, with facilities for those with mobility, hearing or visual difficulties. Chef/proprietor Tony Barnfield has been welcoming guests here since 1992 and has attracted many awards over the years, including the AA Best Breakfast in Britain. Where possible, fresh produce is sourced locally and/ or organically, but quality is deemed to be paramount. The wine list has over 80 bins from some 18 countries and at dinner there is a seasonally changing menu of British classics and house specialities. All rates include dinner, bed and breakfast.

Recommended in the area

ArtSway Gallery (opposite); walking and cycling in the New Forest; shopping in Lymington

The Needles

13th-century Stokesay Castle

Linton Brook Farm

★★★★ FARMHOUSE

Address: Malvern Road, Bringsty, BROMYARD
WR6 5TR
Tel: 01885 488875
Fax: 01885 488875
Map ref: 2, SO65
Directions: Off A44 1.5m E of Bromyard onto B4220
signed Malvern. Farm 0.5m on left
Rooms: 3 (2 en suite) (1 pri facs) **S** £30–£40
D £60–£70 **Notes:** ⊗ on premises **Parking:** 12
Closed: Xmas & New Year

Sheila and Roger Steeds's 400-year old farmhouse stands on an ancient site. With such a history behind it, this charming house is filled with atmosphere, fostered by the inglenook fireplace and enormous beam in the dining room, and the wood-burning stove in the sitting room. Bedrooms are spacious and homely. At breakfast, enjoy Sheila's tasty home-smoked food, and afterwards wander through the 68-acre grassland farm with access to wonderful scenic walks.

Recommended in the area

Brockhampton Estate (NT); Elgar Birthplace Museum; Berrington Hall (NT)

Little Hegdon Farm House

★★★★ B&B

Address: Hegdon Hill, Pencombe, BROMYARD
HR7 4SL
Tel: 01885 400263
Email: howardcolegrave@hotmail.com
Website: www.littlehegdonfarmhouse.co.uk
Map ref: 2, SO65
Directions: 4m SW of Bromyard. From Bromyard to
Pencombe, 1.5m towards Risbury, at top of Hegdon
Hill down farm lane for 500yds
Rooms: 2 en suite, **S** £35 **D** £60 **Parking:** 4

A 17th-century former farmhouse, Little Hegdon lies in the heart of Herefordshire with clear views over farmland, cider orchards and hop yards to the Malvern and Cotswold hills. Restored to provide high standards of comfort, the period character of the house survives in the open fires and plenty of exposed oak beams. Facilities include a drawing room and attractive garden. There is one double and one twin room with hairdryers and tea and coffee facilities. Children and pets are welcome.

Recommended in the area

Lower Brockhampton Estate (NT); historic towns of Hereford and Ledbury; Worcester

Somerville House

★★★★★ GUEST ACCOMMODATION

Address: 12 Bodenham Road, HEREFORD HR1 2TS
Tel: 01432 273991
Fax: 01432 268719
Email: enquiries@somervillehouse.net
Website: www.somervillehouse.net
Map ref: 2, SO53
Directions: A465, at Aylestone Hill rdbt continue towards city centre, left at Southbank Rd, leading to Bodenham Rd
Rooms: 12 en suite (1 GF), S £50 D £65–£99
Notes: ⊗ no dogs **Parking:** 10

An imposing Victorian villa set in a quiet tree-lined road, Somerville House is run by Bill and Rosie, who provide modern boutique-style accommodation. The house is just a short walk from the railway station, bus station and Hereford city centre shops, restaurants and main attractions, and off-street parking is available within the grounds. To relax after a busy day, guests can sit with a drink on the terrace or in the lovely lounge with its open fire and later, perhaps, take a stroll around the garden. A mixture of large, luxury and smaller character bedrooms all have high quality en suite bathrooms, Wi-fi access, flat-screen Freeview televisions, ironing equipment, hairdryers, hospitality trays and mini bars. Luxury rooms are more spacious and have large beds, CD and DVD players. Flavours of Herefordshire are supported in-house, so enjoy locally produced drinks and snacks, such as Lulham Court wine and Tyrrell's crisps. The dining room has contemporary appeal and here the full English breakfast is a speciality, using quality, locally sourced, organic produce with vegetarian options. There are also delicious local organic yoghurts, fruit juices, cereals, muesli and fresh fruit. Continental breakfast and healthy options are also offered. Fun breaks available.

Recommended in the Area

Hereford Cathedral, Mappa Mundi & Chained Library; Hereford Museum; beautiful country walks

Hills Farm

★★★★★ FARMHOUSE
Address: Leysters, LEOMINSTER, HR6 0HP
Tel: 01568 750205
Email: j.conolly@btconnect.com
Website: www.thehillsfarm.co.uk
Map ref: 2, SO45
Directions: Off A4112 Leominster to Tenbury Wells, on outskirts of Leysters
Rooms: 3 en suite (1 GF), S £35–£39 D £70–£78
Notes: ⊗ on premises ❦ under 12yrs **Parking:** 8
Closed: Dec & Jan

On high ground, with panoramic views over the Teme Valley, this 15th-century farmhouse is a splendid base for exploring the Welsh Marches. The accommodation is located in beautifully converted barns; each room has its own front door, en suite bathroom, TV, radio and hospitality tray. Guests head to the main farmhouse for breakfast, which is served at separate tables. There's also a pleasant sitting room with lots of reading matter, including maps and guidebooks for planning the next day out.

Recommended in the area
Berrington Hall (NT); Hereford Cathedral and city; Burton Court

Cwm Craig

★★★★ FARMHOUSE
Address: LITTLE DEWCHURCH HR2 6PS
Tel: 01432 840250
Fax: 01432 840250
Map ref: 2, SO53
Directions: Off A49 into Little Dewchurch, turn right in village, Cwm Craig 1st farm on left
Rooms: 3 en suite, S £28–£34 D £52–£64
Notes: ⊗ on premises **Parking:** 6

Cwm Craig Farm is midway between Hereford and Ross-on-Wye and stands on the edge of a village surrounded by superb countryside. The Georgian property retains many original features and offers spacious accommodation furnished with fine period pieces. The bedrooms are all en suite and include two doubles and a family room. Guests have access to their rooms all day, and hospitality trays are provided. Home-cooked breakfasts are served in the dining room and morning room around large tables, and you can relax in the sitting room or the games room with its three-quarter-size snooker/pool table and dartboard. Pets cannot be accommodated.

Recommended in the area
Hereford Cathedral and city; Forest of Dean; Wye Valley

Lumleys

★★★★ B&B

Address: Kern Bridge, Bishopswood ROSS-ON-WYE
HR9 5QT
Tel: 01600 890040
Fax: 0870 706 2378
Email: helenmattis@tiscali.co.uk
Website: www.thelumleys.co.uk
Map ref: 2, SO52
Directions: Off A40 onto B4229 at Goodrich, over
Kern Bridge, right at Inn On The Wye, 400yds opp
picnic ground
Rooms: 3 en suite, D £70 **Parking:** 15

Its setting, on the banks of the River Wye, makes Lumleys a favourite with those who appreciate the unspoilt countryside of this corner of Herefordshire. The mellow stone Victorian house retains much of its original character, aided by the period pieces and ornaments that adorn the public areas. These include two sitting rooms and a dining room where breakfasts and early evening meals are served.
Recommended in the area
Symonds Yat; Forest of Dean; Goodrich Castle

Norton House

★★★★ 🛏 🍽 GUEST ACCOMMODATION

Address: Whitchurch, ROSS-ON-WYE HR9 6DJ
Tel: 01600 890046
Fax: 01600 890045
Email: su@norton.wyenet.co.uk
Website: www.norton-house.com
Map ref: 2, SO51
Directions: 0.5m N of Symonds Yat West.
Off A40 into Whitchurch village and left onto
Old Monmouth Rd
Rooms: 3 en suite, S £40–£45 D £60–£80 **Notes:** 🐾 under 12yrs **Parking:** 5 **Closed:** 25–26 Dec

Norton House is just a short walk from the River Wye and close to all the opportunities for outdoor pursuits that the area has to offer. The 16th-century house retains some exposed beams and has a generous range of extra facilities to enhance a stay. The cooking at both dinner and breakfast is a particular strength here, with accomplished skills making the best of fresh local produce.
Recommended in the area
Symonds Yat; Goodrich Castle; Forest of Dean

Ross-on-Wye, beside the River Wye

Portland House Guest House

★★★ GUEST ACCOMMODATION

Address: WHITCHURCH, Ross-on-Wye, HR9 6DB
Tel: 01600 890757
Email: info@portlandguesthouse.co.uk
Website: www.portlandguesthouse.co.uk
Map ref: 2, SO51
Directions: Off A40 between Monmouth and Ross-on-Wye. Take turn for Whitchurch/Symonds Yat West
Rooms: 6 en suite (1 GF), S £40–£50 D £60–£86
Notes: ⊗ on premises **Parking:** 6
Closed: 25–26 Dec & Jan

This impressive dwelling dates in part from the 17th century. The comfortable bedrooms, including a large family suite and a four-poster suite, all have many thoughtful extras. Guests can make use of the Boot Room, the laundry, the terrace garden area and the attractive lounge. Breakfasts, cooked on the Aga, include local ingredients, home-made bread and preserves, and are served in the elegant dining room. With prior arrangement, evening meals can be provided.

Recommended in the area

Forest of Dean; Ross-on-Wye; Tintern Abbey

Knebworth House

Brick Kiln Wood in North Mymms Country Park

Rushen

★★★★★ B&B

Address: Mount Pleasant, HERTFORD HEATH
SG13 7QY

Tel: 01992 581254

Fax: 01992 534737

Email: wilsonamwell@btinternet.com

Map ref: 3, TL31

Directions: From A10 exit at Hertford slip road, 1st left onto B1502. 1st right at top of lane, bear left at village green. Rushen on left at end of green

Rooms: 2 (1 en suite), **S** £35–£40 **D** £60–£70 **Notes:** ⊗ on premises **Parking:** 3
Closed: 22 Dec–3 Jan

Rushen is a well-presented detached house with one twin and one double room – both comfortable and well appointed, with a range of thoughtful extras such as TV/DVD, hairdryer, Wi-fi, dressing gowns and slippers and well-stocked tea and coffee-making facilities, including mineral water and chocolates. Breakfast offers a good range of choices, based on local and organic produce when possible.

Recommended in the area

Hertford Castle; Henry Moore Foundation; Forge Museum and Victorian Cottage Garden

KENT

Dover Castle

Bay Tree Broadstairs

★★★★ GUEST ACCOMMODATION

Address: 12 Eastern Esplanade, BROADSTAIRS CT10 1DR
Tel: 01843 862502
Fax: 01843 860589
Map ref: 4, TR36
Directions: A255 onto Rectory Rd & Eastern Esplanade
Rooms: 10 en suite (1 GF), S £41–£71 D £82–£92
Notes: ⊗ on premises 🐾 under 10yrs **Parking:** 11
Closed: Xmas & New Year

This family-run establishment is situated on an elevated position overlooking East Cliff, with panoramic views over the English Channel, yet is close to the town centre with all its amenities. Inside, the attractive en suite bedrooms, one of which is on the ground floor, are well equipped with colour TV, hairdryer and tea and coffee-making facilities, and some have their own balcony with a sea view. There is a comfortable lounge bar, and a good breakfast and dinner menu is offered in the dining room. Car parking is available.

Recommended in the area

Dickens House Museum; Viking Bay; Deal

Chislet Court Farm

★★★★ FARMHOUSE

Address: Chislet, CANTERBURY CT3 4DU
Tel: 01227 860309
Fax: 01227 860444
Email: kathy@chisletcourtfarm.com
Website: www.chisletcourtfarm.com
Map ref: 4, TR15
Directions: Off A28 in Upstreet, farm on right 100yds past church
Rooms: 2 en suite, S £45–£50 D £75–£80
Notes: ⊗ on premises 🐾 under 12yrs **Parking:** 4 **Closed:** Xmas

Chislet Court is an 800-acre arable farm, with an 18th-century farmhouse, set in mature gardens overlooking the village church and surrounding countryside. There are two spacious double bedrooms, each with modern bath and shower rooms, and tea and coffee facilities. You are welcome to relax in the garden and in the conservatory dining room where breakfast is served. There is a good choice of pubs and restaurants in the area for lunch and dinner.

Recommended in the area

Canterbury Cathedral; Sandwich; Howletts Zoo Park

Blériot's

★ ★ ★ GUEST ACCOMMODATION

Address: Belper House, 47 Park Avenue DOVER
CT16 1HE
Tel: 01304 211394
Email: info@bleriots.net
Website: www.bleriots.net
Map ref: 4, TR34
Directions: A20 to Dover, left onto York St, right at
lights to Ladywell. Bear left at next lights onto Park Av
Rooms: 8 en suite, **S** £25–£40 **D** £54–£62
Notes: ⊗ on premises **Parking:** 8

Named after the intrepid French aviator, Louis Blériot, who made his pioneering cross-Channel flight to Dover in 1909, this is a charming Victorian house in a leafy avenue between Dover Castle and the ferry terminals. The off-road parking is a real boon in this busy town. You can expect an outstanding welcome from the owner, a Friendliest Landlady finalist in the AA Centenary Awards, and high level of comfort in the spacious bedrooms. These vary in size and each has an en suite bathroom.

Recommended in the area

Dover Castle and Secret Wartime Tunnels; Roman Painted House; Walmer Castle and Gardens

Court Lodge B&B

★ ★ ★ ★ GUEST ACCOMMODATION

Address: Court Lodge, Church Road, Oare,
FAVERSHAM ME13 0QB
Tel: 01795 591543
Fax: 01795 591543
Email: d.wheeldon@btconnect.com
Website: www.faversham.org/courtlodge
Map ref: 4, TR06
Directions: A2 onto B2045, left onto The Street,
right onto Church Road, 0.25m on left
Rooms: 2 (1 en suite) (1 pri facs), **S** £40 **D** £60 **Notes:** ⊗ on premises **Parking:** 10 **Closed:** Dec–Jan

This sympathetically restored 16th-century listed farmhouse stands in 1.5 acres of gardens amid arable farmland – the perfect place to relax. The spacious rooms have private bathrooms, TV, and tea- and coffee-making facilities. Breakfast is served in the farmhouse kitchen, using the best of local produce including fish and home-made preserves. Court Lodge is ideal for those visiting Oare Creek or walking the Saxon Shore Way. Several pubs and restaurants are only a short distance away.

Recommended in the area

Faversham; Canterbury; Whitstable

The Relish

★★★★★ GUEST ACCOMMODATION

Address: 4 Augusta Gardens, FOLKESTONE
CT20 2RR
Tel: 01303 850952
Fax: 01303 850958
Email: reservations@hotelrelish.co.uk
Website: www.hotelrelish.co.uk
Map ref: 4, TR23
Directions: Off A2033 Sandgate Rd
Rooms: 10 en suite, **S** £65 **D** £90–£140
Notes: ⊗ on premises **Closed:** 22 Dec–2 Jan

You will get a warm welcome at this stylish Victorian property overlooking Augusta Gardens in the fashionable West End of town. On arrival you will be greeted with a complimentary glass of wine or beer and fresh coffee, tea and home-made cakes are available throughout your stay. The bedrooms feature lovely coordinated fabrics, great showers and all have DVD players. Public rooms include a modern lounge-dining room and a terrace where breakfast is served during summer.

Recommended in the area

Dover Castle; Romney, Hythe and Dymchurch Railway; Canterbury

Seabrook House

★★★★ GUEST ACCOMMODATION

Address: 81 Seabrook Road, HYTHE CT21 5QW
Tel: 01303 269282
Fax: 01303 237822
Email: seabrookhouse@hotmail.co.uk
Website: www.seabrook-house.co.uk
Map ref: 4, TR13
Directions: 0.9m E of Hythe on A259
Rooms: 13 en suite (4 GF), **S** £35–£45 **D** £65–£75
Notes: ⊗ on premises **Parking:** 13

This striking Victorian property, easily recognised by the heavily timber-framed frontage and pretty gardens, is conveniently located for the M20 and Eurotunnel. Many of the art-deco style bedrooms have lovely sea views. These spacious en suite rooms, with their attractive decor and furnishings, also have hospitality trays, TV and hairdryers. A memorable full English breakfast sets you up for the ferries from Folkestone or Dover or for sightseeing in the local area, and there are plenty of comfortable places for relaxation, including a sunny conservatory and an elegant lounge.

Recommended in the area

Romney, Hythe and Dymchurch Railway; Dover Castle; Port Lympne Animal Park; Royal Military Canal

Langley Oast

★ ★ ★ ★ GUEST ACCOMMODATION

Address: Langley Park, Langley MAIDSTONE
ME17 3NQ

Tel: 01622 863523

Fax: 01622 863523

Email: margaret@langleyoast.freeserve.co.uk

Map ref: 4, TQ75

Directions: 2.5m SE of Maidstone off A274. After
Parkwood Business Estate lane signed Maidstone
Golf Centre

Rooms: 3 (2 en suite), **S** £40–£60 **D** £55–£95 **Notes:** ⊗ on premises **Parking:** 5 **Closed:** Xmas

This is an authentic Kentish oasthouse, built in 1873 and originally used for drying hops used in the making of local beer. The interior has been the subject of a tasteful conversion, with exposed brick, clean white walls and period furniture, and the distinctive shape of the oast towers adds extra interest to the two 24-ft diameter "roundel" bedrooms, which include sofas and en suite bathrooms, one of which has a jacuzzi bath. Breakfasts are served in an elegant dining room around a single table.

Recommended in the area

Leeds Castle; Sissinghurst Castle Gardens; Canterbury

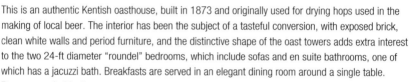

Merzie Meadows

★ ★ ★ ★ ★ B&B

Address: Hunton Road, MARDEN TN12 9SL

Tel: 01622 820500

Fax: 01622 820500

Email: pamela@merziemeadows.co.uk

Website: www.merziemeadows.co.uk

Map ref: 4, TQ74

Directions: A229 onto B2079 for Marden, 1st right
onto Underlyn Ln, 2.5m large Chainhurst sign, right
onto drive

Rooms: 2 en suite (2 GF), **D** £85–£95 **Notes:** ⊗ on premises ⚹ under 15yrs **Parking:** 4 **Closed:** mid Dec–mid Feb

Uniquely designed Merzie Meadows is set in peaceful, idyllic, mature grounds that have been designed with conservation in mind – a haven for birds and wildlife. It is situated near many historic houses and glorious gardens, including Sissinghurst and Leeds Castle. The superb bedrooms are housed in two wings providing space, comfort and privacy. The breakfast room has superb garden views.

Recommended in the area

Sissinghurst Castle Garden (NT); Leeds Castle; The Hop Farm Country Park, Yalding Organic Gardens

Danehurst House

★★★★★ B&B

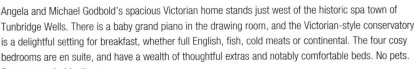

Address:	41 Lower Green Road, Rusthall
	TUNBRIDGE WELLS TN4 8TW
Tel:	01892 527739
Fax:	01892 514804
Email:	info@danehurst.net

Website: www.danehurst.net

Map ref: 4, TQ53

Directions: 1.5m W of Tunbridge Wells in Rusthall. Off A264 onto Coach Rd & Lower Green Rd

Rooms: 4 en suite, **S** £59.50–£69.50 **D** £69.50–£99.50 **Notes:** ⊗ on premises ⚲ under 8yrs

Parking: 6 **Closed:** Xmas & 1st 2wks Feb

Angela and Michael Godbold's spacious Victorian home stands just west of the historic spa town of Tunbridge Wells. There is a baby grand piano in the drawing room, and the Victorian-style conservatory is a delightful setting for breakfast, whether full English, fish, cold meats or continental. The four cosy bedrooms are en suite, and have a wealth of thoughtful extras and notably comfortable beds. No pets.

Recommended in the area

Groombridge Place; Hever Castle; Chartwell (NT)

Pretty Maid House B&B

★★★★ GUEST ACCOMMODATION

Address:	London Road, WROTHAM HEATH,
	Sevenoaks, TN15 7RU
Tel:	01732 886445
Fax:	01732 886439
Email:	stay@prettymaid.co.uk

Website: www.prettymaidhouse.com

Map ref: 4, TQ65

Directions: M26 junct 2A Maidstone on A20, over lights, 300mtrs on L. Adjacent Vineyard Restaurant

Rooms: 7 (6 en suite) (1 pri facs) (2 GF), **S** £55 **D** £65–£75 **Parking:** 7

Sue and Andy drew on over 30 years' experience in the hotel and catering industry to open Pretty Maid House in 2004. They offer the highest of standards, comfort and style in a home-from-home atmosphere. The house is set in the heart of Kent, convenient for Dover port, airports and Bluewater shopping complex, plus numerous golf courses including the London Golf Club. Each of the bedrooms has en suite facilities and super king-size double or large single beds, free Wi-fi, TVs and Freeview.

Recommended in the area

Leeds Castle; Lullingstone Castle and World Garden of Plants; Brands Hatch Race Circuit

LANCASHIRE

The Victoria Monument in Williamson Park, Lancaster

Hartshead

★ ★ ★ GUEST ACCOMMODATION

Address: 17 King Edward Avenue, North Shore,
BLACKPOOL FY2 9TA
Tel: 01253 353133
Email: info@hartshead-hotel.co.uk
Website: www.hartshead-hotel.co.uk
Map ref: 5, SD33
Directions: M55 junct 4, A583 & A584 to North
Shore, off Queens Promenade onto King Edward Av
Rooms: 10 en suite, **S** £20–£33 **D** £40–£60
Notes: ⊗ on premises **Parking:** 6

Set about 100 metres back from Queen's Promenade on Blackpool's North Shore, this is a peaceful place, handy for the bright lights and entertainments of the central area. Guests can congregate over cups of tea in the lounge, or relax in the sun lounge or cosy bar. The comfortable bedrooms are tastefully decorated and well equipped. All have an en suite bathroom and TV with Freeview channels. A three-course dinner menu offers a small choice of traditional British home cooking.

Recommended in the area
Blackpool Grand Theatre; Blackpool Tower; Stanley Park

Whitestake Farm

★ ★ ★ ★ ★ B&B

Address: Pope Lane, Whitestake PRESTON PR4 4JR
Tel: 01772 619392
Fax: 01772 611146
Email: enquiries@gardenofedenspa.co.uk
Website: www.gardenofedenspa.co.uk
Map ref: 6, SD52
Directions: M6 junct 29, A582 Lytham St Annes
Penwortham Way, left onto Chain House Ln, right
onto Pope Ln, on right
Rooms: 2 en suite, **S** £60 **D** £120 **Notes:** ⊗ on premises **Parking:** 6

This attractive white farmhouse is peacefully located just minutes from Preston and is within easy reach of Southport and Lytham. Inside, the beautifully appointed bedrooms and en suite bathrooms are spacious and thoughtfully equipped, and there is a guest lounge for relaxing. Carefully prepared, substantial breakfasts are taken around a huge table in the elegant dining room. Guests can also make use of the indoor swimming pool and two treatment rooms for added luxury.

Recommended in the area
The National Football Museum; Beacon Fell Country Park; The Ribble Steam Museum

LEICESTERSHIRE

Battlefield Steam Railway

Castle ruins, Ashby-de-la-Zouch

The Swan Inn

★★★★ INN

Address: 10 Loughborough Road, MOUNTSORREL
LE12 7AT
Tel: 0116 230 2340
Fax: 0116 237 6115
Email: office@swaninn.eu
Website: www.the-swan-inn.eu
Map ref: 3, SK51
Directions: In village centre
Rooms: 1 en suite, S £70–£98 D £70–£98
Parking: 12

This is a traditional 17th-century inn, a Grade II listed building located on the banks of the River Soar. The accommodation consists of one luxury suite with everything you could want – a large en suite bedroom, a fully equipped office with PC and Wi-fi, an en suite bathroom with shower and antique roll-top cast-iron bath, a fitted kitchen and a private lounge. Meals are served inside or, weather permitting, in the secluded riverside garden. A continental breakfast is served in the suite.

Recommended in the area

Beacon Hill Country Park; Charnwood Museum; Great Central Railway

Battlements of Lincoln Castle

Tulip fields

Wesley Guest House

★★★★ GUEST ACCOMMODATION
Address: 16 Queen Street, EPWORTH DN9 1HG
Tel: 01427 874512
Fax: 01427 874592
Email: enquiries@wesleyguesthouse.com
Website: www.wesleyguesthouse.com
Map ref: 8, SE70
Directions: In town centre, 200yds off Market Place
Rooms: 6 en suite (1 GF), **S** £50–£60 **D** £80–£150
Notes: ⊗ on premises **Parking:** 6

A pleasurable stay is a certainty at this friendly and well-maintained detached house (open all year) in the market town of Epworth. Epworth is the birthplace of John Wesley, founder of Methodism, and places associated with Wesley are all within walking distance. The good-size bedrooms, decorated in soft pastels, have mini-fridges, fresh flowers and complimentary toiletries. Cheerful tablecloths and lovely views over the large garden enhance the pristine breakfast room. Unwind with a game on the full-size snooker table or try one of the leisure options nearby, such as golf and fishing.
Recommended in the area
Normanby Hall and Park; Sandtoft Museum; John Wesley Museum; St Andrew's Church, Epworth

Church Farm B & B

★★★★ B&B

Address: High Street, FILLINGHAM, Gainsborough
DN21 5BS
Tel: 01427 668279
Email: enquiries@churchfarm-fillingham.co.uk
Website: www.churchfarm-fillingham.co.uk
Map ref: 8, SK98
Directions: Off B1398 into village, 1st house on right
Rooms: 3 (1 en suite), S £38 D £55
Notes: ⊗ on premises ⚲ under 5yrs
Parking: 6 **Closed:** 24 Dec–1 Jan

Church Farm lies on the edge of the small, peaceful stone village of Fillingham, which nestles at the base of the Lincolnshire Scarp, the limestone edge that slices through the country and extends down to the Cotswolds. Relax and unwind in this large 19th-century stone farmhouse set in secluded mature gardens overlooking farmland. The traditional bedrooms decorated in various styles offer one en suite twin, and a double and a single that share a bathroom. Plush sofas and chairs and an open fire in the lounge make for a relaxed atmosphere. The English breakfast includes cereals, porridge, yoghurts and fresh fruit to start, followed by local bacon and sausages, free-range eggs cooked to your liking and fresh mushrooms and tomatoes, plus a choice of breads and a selection of preserves. Special dietary needs can be catered for and packed lunches can be provided if advance notice is given. Host Kathleen Needham is very proud (and rightly so) of her housekeeping and warm hospitality – if you arrive before 6pm you are greeted with complimentary tea and home-made cake. For the keen angler, there is a large, privately owned lake in the village offering fishing with a daily permit (£10) open to Church Farm's guests.

Recommended in the area

Lincoln's cathedral, castle and museums; RAF Scampton; antiques at Newark, Swinderby and Hemswell

The Brownlow Arms

★★★★★ ❀ INN

Address: High Road, HOUGH-ON-THE-HILL,
Grantham NG32 2AZ
Tel: 01400 250234
Fax: 01400 271193
Email: paulandlorraine@thebrownlowarms.com
Website: www.thebrownlowarms.com
Map ref: 8, SK94
Rooms: 4 en suite, S £65–£70 D £96–£110
Notes: ⊗ on premises ⛥ under 14yrs
Parking: 20 **Closed:** 25–27 Dec & 31 Dec–20 Jan

The Brownlow Arms is a 17th-century country inn that enjoys a peaceful location in the heart of this picturesque stone village, located between Newark and Grantham. Once owned by Lord Brownlow, today it offers peace and relaxation alongside the twin delights of exceptional modern comforts and good old-fashioned country hospitality. The establishment is tastefully decorated throughout, and all of its comfortable double bedrooms are en suite; extras such as LCD flat-screen TVs, DVD players and DVDs, power/drench showers, and hairdryers make them particularly well equipped. The friendly bar here serves prize-winning ales from a hand pump, while the elegant restaurant offers a setting and atmosphere reminiscent of an intimate country house. Chef Paul Vidic works with premium produce to produce imaginative dishes from a menu that has both traditional and modern influences – examples include house potted brown shrimps with avruga caviar, tiger prawns in tempura batter, braised blade of beef with horseradish mash, and caramelised passionfruit crême brulée – all supported by an interesting wine list. Guests may also make use of the luxurious lounge, a landscaped terrace in summer, or they can sit back and relax by an open log fire in winter.

Recommended in the area

Belton House; Lincoln Castle; Lincoln Cathedral

The Old Bakery

★★★★ ⍟⍟ RESTAURANT WITH ROOMS
Address: 26/28 Burton Road, LINCOLN LN1 3LB
Tel: 01522 576057
Email: enquiries@theold-bakery.co.uk
Website: www.theold-bakery.co.uk
Map ref: 8, SK94
Directions: Exit A46 at Lincoln North follow signs for cathedral.
3rd exit at 1st rdbt, 1st exit at next rdbt
Rooms: 4 (2 en suite) (2 pri facs), S £50–£53 D £53–£63
Notes: ⊗ on premises

Situated close to the castle in the Uphill area at the top of the town, this converted bakery is close to Lincoln Cathedral and the castle. It was originally built in 1837 and operated as a bakery until 1954. In 1994 the property was restored and many of the original bakery features remain. Today it offers well-equipped bedrooms and a delightful and informal dining operation. The pretty bedrooms come with en suite or private facilities, and all benefit from digital colour TV with Freeview, broadband wireless internet access, radio alarm clock, hairdryer and tea- and coffee-making facilities. Ironing facilities are available on request. The restaurant here is popular, and the characterful dining room at the Old Bakery has been created in the location of the original ovens. A superb room has recently been created and described as a 'Garden under Glass' which extends the restaurant from 45 to 85 covers and is fully climate controlled for all year use. The cooking is Modern British with an Italian accent and has a dedication toward the use of local produce – the Old Bakery even has its own garden allotment that provides many of the vegetables served in the restaurant. Expect good friendly service from a dedicated staff at all times.

Recommended in the area

Lincoln Cathedral; Viking Way walking route; The Museum of Lincolnshire Life

Black Swan Guest House

★★★★ GUEST ACCOMMODATION

Address: 21 High Street, MARTON, Gainsborough
DN21 5AH
Tel: 01427 718878
Email: info@blackswanguesthouse.co.uk
Website: www.blackswanguesthouse.co.uk
Map ref: 8, SK88
Directions: On A156 in village centre at junct A1500
Rooms: 10 en suite (4 GF), S £45–£55 D £68–£75
Parking: 10

Located in the village centre, the 18th-century Black Swan offers good hospitality and comfortable bedrooms with modern facilities. A four-poster bedroom is also available. The guest house caters to business travellers, tourists and local families, who return frequently for the home-from-home comforts. Generous, tasty breakfasts are served in the dining room and a comfortable lounge is available. An added bonus is transport to and from nearby pubs and restaurants.

Recommended in the area

Lincoln Cathedral; Lincoln Castle; Lincoln Showground; Museum of Lincolnshire Life

---

La Casita

★★★★★ 🛏 B&B

Address: Frith House, Main Street NORMANTON,
Grantham NG32 3BH
Tel: 01400 250302
Fax: 01400 250302
Email: jackiegonzalez@btinternet.com
Website: www.lacasitabandb.co.uk
Map ref: 8, SK94
Directions: In village centre on A607
Rooms: 1 en suite (1 GF), S £95 D £125
Notes: ⊗ on premises **Parking:** 2

Set independently in the grounds of the owner's house, this converted stable offers considerable luxury. The suite provides complete privacy in sumptuous, spacious open-plan accommodation with its own entrance and terrace. There is a living room with kitchen area and log fire, and the slate-tiled bathroom is pure 'state of the art' complete with luxury toiletries and bathrobes. Extras include two flat-screen TVs, DVD, CD and broadband.

Recommended in the area

Lincoln; Nottingham; Grantham

Scott's Government Offices, St James' Park

MIC Conferences and Accommodation

★★★★ 🛏 GUEST ACCOMMODATION

Address: 81–103 Euston Street, LONDON NW1 2EZ
Tel: 020 7380 0001
Fax: 020 7387 5300
Email: sales@micentre.com
Website: www.micentre.com
Map ref: 3, TQ38

Directions: Euston Rd left at lights onto Melton St, 1st left onto Euston St, MIC 100yds on left

Rooms: 28 en suite **Notes:** ⊗ on premises

The top floor of the MIC building was completely overhauled in 2004 and has been designed to offer the highest standards and value for money. Staffed around the clock, a safe environment is assured. The stylish, air-conditioned bedrooms are en suite and come with LCD TVs and radios, room safes, a desk space with internet access, complimentary hospitality trays and mineral water. The spacious and airy Atrium Bar and Restaurant is perfect for an informal meeting, drink or meal. For breakfast, a traditional English buffet features eight hot items with eggs cooked to order, pancakes and waffles served with maple syrup or sauces, fruit juices, a good selection of cereals, a fruit and yoghurt bar, plus assorted teas and fresh coffee. The centre also offers a range of meeting rooms and private dining rooms for special events, which can be catered for. There are special weekend discount rates. The building is located in a quiet street close to Euston, which has a mainline station, an underground and local bus connections.

Recommended in the area

West End theatres; The BA London Eye; Madame Tussauds; British Museum; near St Pancras Eurostar Terminal

The New Inn

★ ★ ★ INN
Address: 2 Allitsen Road, St Johns Wood, LONDON
NW8 6LA
Tel: 020 7722 0726
Fax: 020 7722 0653
Email: thenewinn@gmail.com
Website: www.newinnlondon.co.uk
Map ref: 3, TQ38
Directions: Off A41 by St Johns Wood tube station
onto Acacia Rd, last right, to end on corner
Rooms: 5 en suite, **S** £75 **D** £75 **Notes:** ⊗ on premises

Built in 1810, this traditional inn is located in a leafy suburb just a stroll from Regents Park, and close
to many central London places of interest. The en suite bedrooms are appointed to a high standard and
are popular with business and leisure guests alike. Rooms are equipped with TVs, free Wi-fi, hairdryers
and tea- and coffee-making facilities. A good choice of English ales, continental beers, wines and
spirits is served alongside Thai and English cuisine in the bar lounge. Live music is played at weekends
Recommended in the area
Madame Tussaud's; London Zoo; Lord's Cricket Ground

The Gallery

★ ★ ★ ★ GUEST ACCOMMODATION
Address: 8–10 Queensberry Place, South
Kensington, LONDON SW7 2EA
Tel: 020 7915 0000
Fax: 020 7970 1805
Email: reservations@eeh.co.uk
Website: www.eeh.co.uk
Map ref: 3, TQ38
Directions: Off A4 Cromwell Rd opp Natural History
Museum, near South Kensington tube station
Rooms: 36 en suite **Notes:** ⊗ on premises

This boutique establishment is a tribute to the art of the Victorian era. Everything from the Oriental
porcelain in the lobby to the furniture and decor of the aptly named Morris Room has been selected
with care. William Morris, Lord Leighton and Dante Gabriel Rossetti would surely feel at home here.
The Gallery offers attentive service and sumptuously furnished en suite bedrooms, some with a private
terrace. Public areas include a choice of lounges and an elegant bar. 24-hour room service is available
Recommended in the area
Kensington Gardens; Hyde Park; Science & Natural History Museums

View of London from the London Eye, South Bank

The Cottage

★★★ GUEST ACCOMMODATION

Address: 150–152 High Street, CRANFORD,
Hounslow, TW5 9WB

Tel: 020 8897 1815

Email: info@the-cottage.eu

Website: www.the-cottage.eu

Map ref: 3, TQ17

Directions: M4 junct 3, A312 towards Feltham,
left at lights, left after 1st pub on left

Rooms: 20 en suite (12 GF), **S** £55–£65
£74.50–£84.50 **Notes:** ⊗ on premises **Parking:** 20 **Closed:** 24–26 Dec & 31 Dec–1 Jan

A family-run guest house, The Cottage provides accommodation in a warm, friendly atmosphere just 10 minutes from Heathrow Airport. The beautiful, 19th-century property attracts many returning guests who appreciate its unique charm and comfortable bedrooms. The ground-floor rooms are spacious and well equipped with TVs, hairdryers and hospitality trays. Newer rooms are located in the garden, connected to the house by a covered walkway overlooking the courtyard. There is secure parking.

Recommended in the area

Kew Gardens; Windsor Castle; Hampton Court Palace

NORFOLK

Horsey Mere at sunset

Bon Vista

★★★★ GUEST HOUSE

Address: 12 Alfred Road, CROMER NR27 9AN
Tel: 01263 511818
Email: jim@bonvista-cromer.co.uk
Website: www.bonvista-cromer.co.uk
Map ref: 4, TG24
Directions: From pier onto A148 Coast road, 100yds left onto Alfred Rd
Rooms: 5 en suite
Notes: ⊗ no dogs
Parking: 2

One might consider this the epitome of the traditional seaside guest house, a sturdy, three-storey Victorian home, peacefully set in a residential area near the town and beach, which, along with its neighbours, sums up much of the character of this charming east-coast resort. Jim and Margaret have renovated the house to a very high standard, while retaining many of its 100-year-old features and have dedicated more than a decade to endowing it with a warm and friendly atmosphere. The first-floor lounge, with its original fireplace and big bay window, makes the most of the sea views and is a cosy place to relax in the evening. The dining room is on the ground floor and it's here that the traditional English breakfasts can be enjoyed, bathed in the light of the morning sun. The five bedrooms, each with an en suite bathroom, are very prettily decorated with cottagey wallpapers and colour-coordinated fabrics. Some still have their original fireplaces, and the climb up to the front room on the first floor is rewarded with a sea view. The other first-floor bedroom can accommodate a family, with bunk beds for the children. Each room has a TV, and Sky channels are available in the lounge. Another plus point here is the off-street parking, but it is limited so early arrival is recommended.

Recommended in the area

Cromer Pier Pavilion Theatre; North Norfolk Railway; Sheringham Park (NT)

Incleborough House

★★★★★ B&B

Address: Lower Common, East Runton CROMER
NR27 9PG
Tel: 01263 515939
Email: enquiries@incleboroughhouse.co.uk
Website: www.incleboroughhouse.co.uk
Map ref: 4, TG24
Directions: On A149 turn left onto Felbrigg road,
150mtrs on left
Rooms: 3 en suite (1 GF), **S** £112.50–£123.75
D £150–£165 **Notes:** ✖ under 14yrs **Parking:** 7

Guests at this award-winning B&B can look forward to tea and home-made cake on arrival, and indeed every afternoon, at this large 17th-century property, situated on the heritage North Norfolk Coast and close to the beach. A Grade II listed building built in 1687, it has been lovingly restored by the current owners. The attractively decorated bedrooms, one of which is on the ground floor and has a National Accessible Scheme rating, are carefully furnished throughout with lovely coordinated fabrics, huge beds and fine garden or common views. All have a wealth of useful extras, such as a comfortable sitting area, small fridge, LCD TV with Freeview, DVD, CD and radio, as well as broadband internet access. The spacious public areas include a luxurious drawing room with plush leather sofas and an open fireplace. Breakfast made from local produce is freshly cooked on the Aga and served at individual tables in the large open-plan conservatory, which has a lush indoor tropical garden. For special occasions, a champagne breakfast can be served in guests' own rooms. Evening meals can be prepared with prior notice from October to June, and the owners are happy to advise on nearby eating places.

Recommended in the area

Cromer and Sheringham beaches; Blakeney Point; North Norfolk Steam Railway

Shrublands Farm

★ ★ ★ ★ FARMHOUSE

Address: Church Street, Northrepps CROMER
NR27 0AA
Tel/Fax: 01263 579297
Email: youngman@farming.co.uk
Website: www.shrublandsfarm.com
Map ref: 4, TG24
Directions: Off A149 to Northrepps, through village,
past Foundry Arms, cream house 50yds on left
Rooms: 3 (1 en suite) (2 pri facs), **S** £42–£45
D £64–£70 **Notes:** ⊗ on premises 👶 under 12yrs **Parking:** 5

Shrublands is a working farm set in mature gardens amid 300 acres of arable farmland, an ideal base for exploring the coast and countryside of rural north Norfolk. Traditional hospitality is a distinguishing feature at the 18th-century farmhouse, with good cooking using home-grown and fresh local produce. Breakfast is served at a large table in the dining room, and there is also a cosy lounge, with a log fire, books and a television. The bedrooms have TVs, radio alarms and tea and coffee facilities. No pets.
Recommended in the area
Blickling Hall and Felbrigg Hall (NT); Sandy beaches at Cromer and Overstrand; Blakeney Point

Knights Court

★ ★ ★ ★ GUEST ACCOMMODATION

Address: 22 North Drive, GREAT YARMOUTH
NR30 4EW
Tel: 01493 843089
Fax: 01493 850780
Email: enquiries@knights-court.co.uk
Website: www.knights-court.co.uk
Map ref: 4, TG50
Directions: 600yds N of Britannia Pier
Rooms: 20 en suite (6 GF), **S** £30–£42 **D** £56–£70
Notes: ⊗ on premises **Parking:** 21 **Closed:** 28 Oct–16 Mar

Overlooking the sea and the Venetian Gardens, on a quieter stretch of the seafront, Knights Court is just a few minutes' walk from the town's main attractions. Behind the fine looking 1920s architecture you will find a stylish interior, with an elegant lounge and cosy bar and a bright dining room. With free Wi-fi, the bedrooms are well planned, some with sea views, and include some ground-floor motel-style rooms with individual patios.
Recommended in the area
Norfolk Broads; Somerleyton Hall and Gardens; Caister Roman Site

Sandpipers Bed & Breakfast

★★★★ B&B

Address: The Street, KELLING NR25 7EL
Tel: 01263 588604
Email: ina@sandpipersbandb.co.uk
Website: www.sandpipersbandb.co.uk
Map ref: 4, TG04
Directions: From A149 into Kelling, 200mtrs on right
Rooms: 1 en suite (1 GF), **D** £70
Notes: ⊗ on premises **Parking:** 1

Located in Kelling, a small village on the North Norfolk Coast, Sandpipers offers bed and breakfast accommodation in a completely self-contained unit. Close by are Kelling Quags, the beach, Kelling and Salthouse Heaths and Cley Marshes, perfect for birdwatching, walking or relaxing in beautiful surroundings. Completely refurbished to a high standard with an emphasis on space and comfort, Sandpipers comprises a large en suite bedroom with a king-sized bed; a separate lounge complete with a settee, armchair, dining table and chairs, and a kitchenette with a small fridge, microwave and toaster. The comprehensive breakfast menu specialises in locally sourced food and Fairtrade products.

Recommended in the area

Blakeney Point; NWT Cley Reserve; Sheringham Park

White House Farm

★★★★★ GUEST ACCOMMODATION

Address: Knapton, NORTH WALSHAM NR28 0RX
Tel: 01263 721344
Email: info@whitehousefarmnorfolk.co.uk
Website: www.whitehousefarmnorfolk.co.uk
Map ref: 4, TG23
Rooms: 3 en suite, **S** £50 **D** £55–£65
Notes: ⊗ on premises ⋈ under 12yrs **Parking:** 6

A delightful Grade II listed, 18th-century flint cottage that is close to sandy beaches of Norfolk's Heritage Coastline. Surrounded by open farmland it has been carefully restored to ensure the modern decor blends beautifully with historic features. The three large bedrooms have luxury en suite bathrooms and are equipped with many thoughtful touches. The Pulford Room has a four-poster bed and far-reaching views, while the Orton Room, also with a four-poster, has an additional single bedroom that can be used to provide twin accommodation if preferred. The traditional full English breakfast features home-made and local produce. Two self-catering cottages available.

Recommended in the area

Sandringham; Blickling Hall and Felbrigg Hall (NT); Norfolk Broads

Gothic House Bed & Breakfast

★ ★ ★ ★ GUEST ACCOMMODATION

Address: King's Head Yard, Magdalen Street NORWICH
NR3 1JE
Tel: 01603 631879
Email: charvey649@aol.com
Website: www.gothic-house-norwich.com
Map ref: 4, TG20
Directions: Follow signs for A147, turn off at rdbt past flyover
into Whitefriars. Right again onto Fishergate, at end, turn right
Rooms: 2 pri facs, **S** £65 **D** £95 **Notes:** ⊗ on premises
👶 under 18yrs **Parking:** 2 **Closed:** Feb

Set in a quiet courtyard in the heart of the most historic part
of Norwich, Gothic House is a Grade II listed building barely five minutes' walk from the cathedral.
The area has a wealth of gracious Georgian and earlier architecture. Gothic House has been lovingly
restored and retains much of its original character. With Wi-fi access available, the bedrooms are
spacious, individually decorated and stylishly presented. Breakfast is served in the elegant dining room.
Recommended in the area
Norwich Castle; Norwich Aviation Museum; Norwich Gallery

Old Thorn Barn

★ ★ ★ ★ GUEST ACCOMMODATION

Address: Corporation Farm, Wymondham Road,
Hethel, NORWICH NR14 8EU
Tel: 01953 607785
Fax: 01953 601909
Email: enquires@oldthornbarn.co.uk
Website: www.oldthornbarn.co.uk
Map ref: 4, TG20
Directions: 6m SW of Norwich. Follow signs for
Lotus Cars from A11 or B1113, on Wymondham Rd

Rooms: 7 en suite (7 GF), **S** £34–£38 **D** £58–£60 **Notes:** ⊗ on premises **Parking:** 12

Reconstruction of a group of derelict buildings has resulted in this delightful conversion. The substantial
17th-century barns and stables feature a stylish open-plan dining room, where you can linger over
breakfast around individual oak tables. At the other end of the room there is a cosy lounge area with a
wood-burning stove. Antique pine furniture and smart en suites are a feature of the spacious bedrooms
which have tea and coffee trays, trouser presses and hairdryers.
Recommended in the area
Fairhaven Woodland and Water Garden; Pettitts Animal Adventure Park; Wolterton Park

At Knollside

★ ★ ★ ★ B&B
Address: 43 Cliff Road, SHERINGHAM NR26 8BJ
Tel: 01263 823320
Fax: 01263 823320
Email: avril@at-knollside.co.uk
Website: www.at-knollside.co.uk
Map ref: 4, TG14
Directions: 250yds E of town centre. A1082 to
High St, onto Wyndham St & Cliff Rd
Rooms: 3 en suite **Notes:** ⊗ on premises
Parking: 3

You're welcomed with a glass of sherry and fresh fruit in your room at this guest house a short walk along the promenade from the centre of Sheringham. The beds are either king size or sleigh, and one room has a carved cedar four-poster – all are enhanced with crisp white linen. Some bedrooms have sea views. Easy chairs and tea and coffee facilities, trouser press, hair dryer, thoughtful toiletries and TV are provided for extra comfort. Start the day with an impressive full English breakfast.

Recommended in the area

Felbrigg Hall (NT); North Norfolk Heritage Coast – Blakeney; Holkam Hall

Holly Lodge

★ ★ ★ ★ ★ ⊜ B&B
Address: The Street, THURSFORD NR21 0AS
Tel/Fax: 01328 878465
Email: info@hollylodgeguesthouse.co.uk
Website: www.hollylodgeguesthouse.co.uk
Map ref: 4, TF93
Directions: Off A148 into Thursford village
Rooms: 3 en suite (3 GF), **S** £70–£100 **D** £90–£120
Notes: ⊗ on premises ⚘ under 14yrs **Parking:** 5
Closed: Jan

This 18th-century property is situated in a picturesque location surrounded by open farmland. The lovely landscaped gardens include a large sundeck, which overlooks the lake and water gardens, providing a great place to relax. The lodge and its guest cottages have been transformed into a splendid guest house, with stylish ground-floor bedrooms that are individually decorated and beautifully furnished. En suite bathrooms, TVs and lots of thoughtful extras make for a pleasant stay. The attractive public areas are full of character, with flagstone floors, oak beams and open fireplaces.

Recommended in the area

North Norfolk Coast; Thursford Museum; Walsingham

Stracey Arms Mill, near Acle, Norfolk Broads National Park

NORTHAMPTONSHIRE

St Mary and All Saints Collegiate Church, Fotheringhay

Braunston Manor

★ ★ ★ ★ GUEST ACCOMMODATION

Address: BRAUNSTON, Daventry NN11 7HS
Tel: 01788 890267
Fax: 01788 891515
Email: info@braunstonmanor.com
Website: www.braunstonmanor.co.uk
Map ref: 3, SP56
Directions: From A45 join High St at T-junct, right
into parking area
Rooms: 10 (9 en suite) (1 pri facs) (2 GF),
S £60–£85 D £85–£140 **Notes:** ⊗ on premises **Parking:** 50

Braunston Manor is a real find in a delightful corner of the heart of England. While relaxing in the 10-acre hillside grounds, you can enjoy the peaceful sight of a narrow boat or cruiser gliding through on the canal, perhaps as a brief interruption from a game of croquet, boules or giant chess. The manor, built of mellow, golden-hued Northamptonshire stone, dates back some 400 years and has been in the same family for more than a century. Presiding over the south western edge of the village, it has been lovingly restored to provide a high standard of accommodation, with rooms ranging from plush and elegant to a more rustic-style luxury with exposed stone walls and sturdy wooden beams. Four rooms are in a cottage wing. All are stylishly enhanced by individual features and antiques, but the four-poster room is, perhaps, the most reminiscent of the origins of the building. Not all of the bedrooms overlook the canal or marina, so if you want the view it's worth mentioning it when you book. With its romantic ambience and setting, it's hardly surprising that this is a popular place (and is licensed) for civil weddings. There are also conference rooms. Two village pubs, under the same ownership, are both just three minutes' walk away.

Recommended in the area

Stanford Hall; Althorp; Garden Organic Ryton

Hunt House Quarters

★★★★ GUEST ACCOMMODATION
Address: Main Road, KILSBY, Rugby CV23 8XR
Tel: 01788 823282
Email: luluharris@hunthouse.fsbusiness.co.uk
Website: www.hunthousekilsby.com
Map ref: 3, SP57
Directions: On B3048 in village
Rooms: 4 en suite (4 GF), **S** £59.95–£75
D £75–£85 **Notes:** ⊗ on premises **Parking:** 8

Hunt House Quarters in Kilsby is set in a beautiful peaceful courtyard and forms one part of a magnificently restored 1656 thatched hunting lodge and covered stables. Steeped in history, the lodge was originally used for deer hunting. The property is ideally placed as a touring base for visiting Stratford-upon-Avon, the Cotswolds and Warwick. Nearby there are stately homes, castles and gardens to visit as well as opportunities for some excellent walking. The spacious en suite bedrooms have their own character and are named the Manger, the Smithy, the Saddlery and the Tack Room. Set around a large courtyard, they retain features such as oak beams and old glass but are furnished in a modern, contemporary style. All rooms are equipped to a high standard and have internet broadband connection, colour TV, tea- and coffee-making facilities and hairdryer. Breakfast is served in the restaurant where guests are offered the choice of full English, continental or vegetarian breakfast. All breakfasts are freshly cooked and prepared to order at times convenient to the guests. For other meals, there are two village pubs serving food seven days per week, and a selection of Indian, Chinese, Italian, Mexican, English, and Thai restaurants only 5–10 minutes away. The gardens surrounding Hunt House Quarters are a peaceful haven in which to relax and take a stroll.

Recommended in the area

Rugby School; Crick Boat Show; National Exhibition Centre

Sir Thomas Tresham's triangular lodge representing the Holy Trinity, Rushton

Bridge Cottage Bed & Breakfast

★★★★ B&B

Address: Oundle Road, Woodnewton
PETERBOROUGH PE8 5EG
Tel: 01780 470779
Fax: 01780 470860
Email: judycolebrook@btinternet.com
Website: www.bridgecottage.net
Map ref: 3, TL08
Directions: A1 onto A605, right at 1st rdbt, through
Fortheringham to Woodnewtown. 1st house on left
Rooms: 3 (2 en suite) (1 pri facs), **S** £37.50–£50 **D** £70–£85 **Parking:** 3

Bridge Cottage enjoys a delightful and peaceful location on the periphery of the village of Woodnewton and bordered by open countryside. This friendly and relaxing B&B offers real home-from-home comforts and tastefully appointed accommodation, with Wi-fi available in every room. Freshly cooked Northamptonshire breakfasts, made from local ingredients, are taken in the open-plan kitchen, which overlooks the lovely gardens. Easy access to Stamford, Peterborough and Oundle.

Recommended in the area

Burghley House; Peterborough Cathedral; Fotheringhay village

Dove Crag in the Simonside Hills in Northumberland National Park

Bondgate House

★★★★ ⌂ GUEST HOUSE

Address: 20 Bondgate Without, ALNWICK
NE66 1PN
Tel: 01665 602025
Email: enquiries@bondgatehouse.co.uk
Website: www.bondgatehouse.co.uk
Map ref: 10, NU11
Directions: A1 onto B6346 into town centre,
200yds past war memorial on right
Rooms: 6 en suite (1 GF), **D** £75–£85
Notes: ⊗ on premises **Parking:** 8 **Closed:** Xmas

Experience relaxed hospitality of the highest standards in an elegant Grade II listed Georgian town house; with comfortable, restful en suite bedrooms, private car park and a delightful herb garden and patio. The lounge has a splendid selection of local literature. It is an easy stroll to Alnwick Garden, the castle and town. Alnwick is an ideal centre for visiting both inland and coastal Northumberland. Anne also offers local herb walks in spring and summer, as well as tours of her herb garden.

Recommended in the area

Alnwick Castle & Gardens; Lindisfarne; Northumberland National Park

Market Cross

★★★★★ ⌂ GUEST ACCOMMODATION

Address: 1 Church Street, BELFORD NE70 7LS
Tel: 01668 213013
Email: info@marketcross.net
Website: www.marketcross.net
Map ref: 10, NU13
Directions: Off A1 into village, opp church
Rooms: 3 en suite, **S** £40–£70 **D** £75–£110
Parking: 3

Set in the heart of the charming village of Belford, just off the Great North Road, this Grade II listed building is well placed for visiting the Northumbrian coast. The northern hospitality here is matched by the high quality of the accommodation, with bedrooms large enough for easy chairs and sofas. Each has a flat-screen TV, a fridge with fresh milk for the complimentary beverages, fruit and fresh flowers. The breakfasts, which may include kedgeree, smoked salmon, scrambled eggs, pancakes and griddle scones, have an AA Breakfast Award. Many ingredients are sourced locally and there are vegetarian options. Runner-up in the AA's Friendliest Landlady of the Year Award 2008–9.

Recommended in the area

Lindisfarne (Holy Island); Alnwick Castle and gardens; the Farne Islands; Northumberland National Park

Lindisfarne Inn

★★★ INN

Address: Beal, BERWICK UPON TWEED TD15 2PD
Tel: 01289 381223
Fax: 01289 381223
Email: enquiries@lindisfarneinn.co.uk
Website: www.lindisfarneinn.co.uk
Map ref: 10, NT95
Directions: On A1, turn off for Holy Island
Rooms: 21 en suite (10 GF), S £55 D £75
Parking: 25

There could hardly be a more convenient location for anyone wanting to visit Lindisfarne, but this inn has much more to offer than simply being in the right place. Its modernised rustic style presents an appealing setting, and the high standard of the food and accommodation make this a destination in itself. It's also a very convenient stop-over for travellers pounding the A1. The bedrooms, each with an en suite bathroom, occupy the ground and first floors of the adjacent lodge-style wing, and are comfortable, unfussy and well equipped, with digital television and refreshment trays. The bar is warm and welcoming, with its deep red ceiling, wooden floor and exposed stone wall, and a full range of cask ales, fine wines, liqueurs and spirits. Food is available all day, cooked to order by the head chef and his team, and ranges from snacks and sandwiches to full meals. The choice is exceptional, with as many as 10 daily specials and a long menu of British and international dishes, featuring ingredients from Northumberland producers and locally caught fish. There are vegetarian choices and a children's menu alongside classics such as steak and ale pie and 21-day hung Aberdeen Angus steaks.

Recommended in the area

Holy Island and Lindisfarne Castle (NT); Bamburgh Castle; Farne Islands (NT)

Ivy Cottage

★ ★ ★ ★ ★ ⌂ GUEST ACCOMMODATION

Address: 1 Croft Gardens, Crookham
CORNHILL-ON-TWEED TD12 4ST
Tel: 01890 820667
Fax: 01890 820667
Email: stay@ivycottagecrookham.co.uk
Website: www.ivycottagecrookham.co.uk
Map ref: 10, NT83
Directions: 4m E of Cornhill. Off A697 onto B6353
into Crookham village
Rooms: 3 (2 pri facs) (1 GF), **S** £45 **D** £68–£78 **Notes:** ⚬ under 5yrs **Parking:** 2

This pristine stone-built modern cottage is testament to the many years spent in the hospitality industry by owner Doreen Johnson, and guests soon feel the benefit of her experience and dedication. Set in delightful gardens, the summerhouse provides a welcome spot in which to take tea on fine afternoons. Inside, everything is bright and spotless, and the two spacious bedrooms offer a choice of furnishings – the downstairs room is smart and modern while the room upstairs is beautifully done out in antique pine. With fresh flowers, crisp embroidered bedding, home-baked biscuits and tea-making facilities, they are immediately welcoming and relaxing. Each room has its own private bathroom with a deep tub, Crabtree & Evelyn toiletries, huge terry towels and bathrobes. Breakfasts, served in the formal dining room or in the farmhouse-style kitchen, with its Aga cooking range, are sumptuous. Whichever room is used, the feast always includes local free-range eggs, organic produce where possible, home-made preserves, freshly squeezed orange juice and home-baked bread made from stone-ground flour from nearby Heatherslaw Mill. Ivy Cottage is perfectly located for exploring the Northumberland coast and the Cheviot Hills.

Recommended in the area
Holy Island; Alnwick Castle and Gardens; Flodden Battlefield

Pheasant Inn

★★★★ INN

Address: Stannersburn, HEXHAM NE48 1DD
Tel: 01434 240382
Fax: 01434 240382
Email: enquiries@thepheasantinn.com
Website: www.thepheasantinn.com
Map ref: 6, NY78
Directions: 1m S of Falstone. Off B6320 to Kielder Water, via Bellingham or via Hexham A69 onto B6320 via Wall-Wark-Bellingham
Rooms: 8 en suite (5 GF), **S** £50–£55 **D** £90–£95 **Parking:** 40 **Closed:** Xmas

Set close to the magnificent Kielder Water, this classic country inn, built in 1624, has exposed stone walls, original beams, low ceilings, open fires and a display of old farm implements in the bar. Run by the welcoming Kershaw family since 1985, the inn was originally a farmhouse and has been refurbished to a very high standard. The bright, modern en suite bedrooms, some with their own entrances, are all contained in stone buildings adjoining the inn and are set round a pretty courtyard. All the rooms, including one family room, are spotless, well equipped, and have tea and coffee facilities, hairdryer, colour TV and radio-alarm clock; all enjoy delightful country views. Delicious home-cooked breakfasts and evening meals are served in the bar or in the attractive dining room, or may be taken in the pretty garden courtyard if the weather permits. Irene and her son Robin are responsible for the traditional home cooking using local produce and featuring delights such as game pie and roast Northumbrian lamb, as well as imaginative vegetarian choices. Drying and laundry facilities are available and, for energetic guests, cycle hire can be arranged.

Recommended in the area

Hadrian's Wall; Scottish Borders region; Northumberland's castles and stately homes

Bush Nook

★ ★ ★ ★ GUEST HOUSE

Address: Upper Denton, GILSLAND, Nr Haltwhistle
CA8 7AF
Tel/Fax: 016977 47194
Email: info@bushnook.co.uk
Website: www.bushnook.co.uk
Map ref: 6, NY66
Directions: Halfway between Brampton and
Haltwhistle, off A69 signed Birdoswald, Bush Nook
Rooms: 7 en suite, **S** £35–£40 **D** £70–£100
Notes: ⊗ on premises **Parking:** 6 **Closed:** Xmas & New Year

Set in wonderful open countryside, Bush Nook overlooks Birdoswald Roman Fort on Hadrian's Wall. It was built using stones 'borrowed' from the nearby Roman fortifications. Today this converted farmhouse offers comfortable bedrooms, split between the main house and the barn; each has many thoughtful extras and a lovely countryside view. Dinners are made using fresh local produce, and there are good breakfast choices. As well as dining room, there is a cosy lounge and impressive conservatory.

Recommended in the area

Lanercost Priory; Birdoswald Roman Fort; Hadrian's Wall

Vallum Lodge

★ ★ ★ ★ GUEST HOUSE

Address: Military Road, Twice Brewed,
HALTWHISTLE NE47 7AN
Tel: 01434 344248
Fax: 01434 344488
Email: stay@vallum-lodge.co.uk
Website: www.vallum-lodge.co.uk
Map ref: 6, NY76
Directions: On B6318, 400yds W of Once Brewed
National Park visitors centre

Rooms: 6 en suite (6 GF), **S** £50–£60 **D** £70 **Notes:** ⊗ on premises **Parking:** 15 **Closed:** Nov–Feb

This licensed roadside guest house provides a home from home in the heart of the Northumberland National Park. It is perfectly placed for walking and cycling in this unspoiled part of England. The refurbished bedrooms are all on the ground floor and feature hospitality trays and complimentary toiletries. Laundry and drying facilities are also available. Breakfast is served in the smart dining room and there is a cosy lounge with a television and a selection of books and games.

Recommended in the area

Hadrian's Wall; Vindolanda; Housesteads; Roman Army Museum; the Pennine Way

Peth Head Cottage

★ ★ ★ ★ B&B

Address: Juniper, HEXHAM NE47 0LA
Tel: 01434 673286
Fax: 01434 673038
Email: peth_head@btopenworld.com
Website: www.peth-head-cottage.co.uk
Map ref: 7, NY96
Directions: B6306 S from Hexham, 200yds fork right, next left. Continue 3.5m, house 400yds on right after Juniper sign
Rooms: 2 en suite, **S** £29 **D** £58 **Notes:** ⊗ on premises
Parking: 2

This lovingly maintained rose-covered cottage dates back to 1825 and is popular for its warm welcome, idyllic setting, and home comforts. Tea and hand-made biscuits are offered on arrival, and the delicious home cooking is enjoyed at breakfast too, along with freshly baked bread and delicious homemade preserves. The inviting sandstone cottage is set in peaceful, well-kept gardens. There are two bright, south-facing bedrooms, both overlooking the garden, with shower rooms en suite, a hairdryer, TV, radio alarm and hospitality trays. The relaxing lounge is heavily beamed and furnished with comfortable chairs. Peth Head Cottage is ideallly situated for visiting Durham and Newcastle as well as nearby Roman sites, and there are plenty of opportunites for walking and cycling in the area. A wide range of tourist information and maps are on hand for visitors to browse through and plan the day. The owner, Joan Liddle, is an excellent host who knows how to ensure her guests have an enjoyable stay. There is private off-road parking. Sorry, no pets can be accommodated.

Recommended in the area

Beamish Open Air Museum; Hadrian's Wall; the Northumberland coast; Durham Cathedral; Finchale Priory; Lanercost Priory

View across Bolam Lake, Bolam Lake Country Park

The Old Manse

★ ★ ★ ★ ★ 🛏 GUEST ACCOMMODATION

Address: New Road, Chatton, ALNWICK NE66 5PU
Tel: 01668 215343
Email: chattonbb@aol.com
Website: www.oldmansechatton.co.uk
Map ref: 10, NT92
Directions: 4m E of Wooler. On B6348 in Chatton
Rooms: 3 en suite (1 GF), S £40–£60 D £80–£95
Notes: ⊗ on premises 👣 under 13yrs **Parking:** 4
Closed: Nov–Feb

Built in 1875 and commanding excellent views over the open countryside, this imposing former manse stands on the edge of the pretty village of Chatton between the Cheviot Hills and the scenic North Northumberland Heritage Coast. Approached by a sweeping gravel drive, you can explore the extensive gardens, which include a wildlife pond. The Rosedale Suite is an elegant four-poster room with a Victorian-style bathroom en suite; Buccleuch has a sitting room and private patio. All rooms are well appointed, spacious and luxurious. Enjoy hearty breakfasts in the elegant conservatory dining room.

Recommended in the area

Alnwick Garden; Chillingham Castle and wild cattle; Bamburgh Castle

Blenheim Palace, Woodstock

The ruined hall at Minster Lovell

The Mill House

★ ★ ★ ★ GUEST ACCOMMODATION

Address:	North Newington Rd, BANBURY OX15 6AA
Tel:	01295 730212
Fax:	01295 730363
Email:	lamadonett@aol.com
Website:	www.themillhousebanbury.com
Map ref:	3, SP44

Directions: M40 junct 11, signs to Banbury Cross, B4035 (Shipston-on-Stour), 2m right for Newington

Rooms: 7 en suite, S £69–£85 D £85–£125

Notes: ⊗ on premises **Parking:** 20 **Closed:** 2wks Xmas

The former miller's house, surrounded by countryside, offers luxurious accommodation in three rooms in the house and four refurbished self-contained cottages in the courtyard. Most of the en suite rooms have DVD players and/or digital TV; all have telephones and tea- and coffee-making facilities. The cottages are available on a self-catering or bed and breakfast basis, and have a separate lounge. Free Wi-fi available.

Recommended in the area

Blenheim Palace; Stratford-upon-Avon; The Cotswolds

The Angel at Burford

★ ★ ★ ★ ◎◎ RESTAURANT WITH ROOMS

Address: 14 Witney Street, BURFORD OX18 4SN
Tel: 01993 822714
Fax: 01993 822069
Email: paul@theangelatburford.co.uk
Website: www.theangelatburford.co.uk
Map ref: 3, SP21
Directions: Off A40 at Burford rdbt, down hill, 1st right onto Swan Ln, 1st left to Pytts Ln, left at end onto Witney St
Rooms: 3 en suite, **S** £70–£85 **D** £93–£110 **Notes:** ⅷ under 9yrs

Just 100 yards from Burford's bustling high street, The Angel is a haven of tranquillity and comfort. Built in 1652, this cosy restaurant with rooms is packed with original features. Old oak beams adorn the ceilings, and in the winter months flickering log fires reflect on the gleaming copper and brass, while in the summer you can relax in the peaceful courtyard or in the walled garden. The bedrooms are en suite, individually decorated for comfort and style, and have everything that you need to make you feel comfortable and at home. In the residents' lounge you will find information on local attractions, and literature to help you plan long or short walks. In the candlelit restaurant the menus reflect all that is good about the local Cotswold produce, with an imaginative range of seasonal dishes, incorporating game from local estates, great fish dishes, and stunning desserts, all created using the freshest and best ingredients available. In the bar you'll find well-kept Hook Norton Ales, and arguably the finest bar counter in Burford, made from the increasingly rare Burr Elm. You may also find some locals, enjoying a pint or two of Cotswold hospitality!

Recommended in the area

Stratford-upon-Avon; The Cotswolds; Bicester Shopping Village

The Cherry Tree Inn

★ ★ ★ ★ ❀ INN

ddress: Stoke Row, HENLEY-ON-THAMES
RG9 5QA
el: 01491 680430
mail: info@thecherrytreeinn.com
ebsite: www.thecherrytreeinn.com
ap ref: 3, SU78
rections: W of Henley. Off B841 into Stoke Row
ooms: 4 en suite (4 GF), **D** £95 **Parking:** 30
osed: 25–26 Dec

his stylish inn, which has housed a pub for over 200 years, is situated in a peaceful rural setting at ne of the highest points in the Chilterns Area of Outstanding Natural Beauty, yet it is just 20 minutes vay from Reading and motorway connections. Originally three flint cottages, today the 400-year-old ted building successfully combines classic features, such as original flagstone floors and beamed eilings, with contemporary features and strong colours, and the result is a comfortable and informal stablishment. The bedrooms, located in a converted barn to the side of the inn, are of a modern esign and have spacious en suite bathrooms with power showers and luxury toiletries, as well as ng-sized beds, flat-screen TVs and tea- and fresh coffee-making facilities; two can be converted into mily rooms. The cosy, contemporary dining room is the setting for imaginative and hearty dishes from menu that describes itself as classic European with a twist. Daily specials appear on the chalkboard id there's a hearty Sunday roast featuring Scottish prime roast beef and home-made horseradish. ood is prepared using fresh local ingredients and seasonal produce; there's an eat-anywhere policy side and, weather permitting, diners may also eat outside in the large garden.

ecommended in the area

ne Maharajah's Wall; Windsor Castle; Basildon Park

Chowle Farmhouse

★★★★ FARMHOUSE

Address: Great Coxwell, FARINGDON SN7 7SR
Tel: 01367 241688
Fax: 07775 669102
Email: info@chowlefarmhouse.co.uk
Website: www.chowlefarmhouse.co.uk
Map ref: 3, SU29
Directions: From Faringdon rdbt on A420, 2m W
on right. From Watchfield rdbt 1.5m E on left
Rooms: 4 en suite (1 GF), **S** £55 **D** £75 **Parking:** 10

This delightful, friendly establishment makes an ideal base for visiting the Thames Valley and surrounding area. The bedrooms and large en suite bathrooms in this modern farmhouse are all very well equipped, with flat-screen TV, hairdryer, fresh flowers, complimentary soft drinks, bath and/ or power shower and good toiletries. One room has its own balcony, overlooking the outdoor pool. Downstairs is the charming and airy breakfast room, where breakfasts are prepared to order from fresh local ingredients, including home-produced eggs, family-reared bacon and local honey.

Recommended in the area

Market town of Faringdon; Blenheim Palace

Crowsley House

★★★★★ B&B

Address: Crowsley Road, Lower Shiplake
HENLEY-ON-THAMES RG9 3JT
Tel: 0118 940 6708
Email: info@crowsleyhouse.co.uk
Website: www.crowsleyhouse.co.uk
Map ref: 3, SU78
Directions: A4155 onto Station Rd in Shiplake.
Right onto Crowsley Rd, 2nd house on right
Rooms: 3 (2 en suite) (1 pri facs), **S** £75–£95
D £95–£125 **Notes:** ⊗ on premises ⚫ under 14yrs **Parking:** 6

Set in beautifully landscaped grounds in a pretty village by the River Thames, Crowsley House is renowned for its hospitality and the wonderful breakfasts cooked by French chef, Philippe, who has cooked at some of the world's finest establishments. Dinner is also available on request, served in the delightful dining room overlooking the garden. Bedrooms are sunny and bright, with good en suite or private bathrooms. Guests can relax in the lovely gardens and a short stroll leads to the river.

Recommended in the area

Thames Path; Greys Court (NT); River and Rowing Museum

The Tollgate Inn & Restaurant

★★★★ ⊜ INN

Address: Church Street, KINGHAM
OX7 6YA
Tel: 01608 658389
Email: info@thetollgate.com
Website: www.thetollgate.com
Map ref: 3, SP22
Rooms: 9 en suite (4 GF), S £65 D £95
Parking: 12

Situated in the idyllic Cotswold village of Kingham, this Grade II listed Georgian farmhouse blends in perfectly with its surroundings. It has been lovingly restored to provide a complete home-from-home among some of the most beautiful and historic countryside in Britain, and makes a good base for exploring the local area. Inside, there is an informal yet stylish atmosphere, with flagstone floors, beamed ceilings and huge inglenook fireplaces adding to the charm. The Tollgate provides a range of comfortable, well-equipped en suite bedrooms, three of which are on the ground floor and have adjacent parking. Each room has its own individual identity – one features a four-poster, while another, the spacious Hayloft, is designed as a family suite. The inn serves some of the best food in the area – including a hearty breakfast – from a constantly changing menu based on fresh and local produce. Meals are served in the modern, well-equipped dining room or in the less formal bar and lounge areas, as guests prefer, and to wash it all down there's a range of well-kept beers and good wines. When the weather allows, food is also served outside, on the front terraced garden and in the rear courtyard.

Recommended in the area

Blenheim Palace; Batsford Park Arboretum; Oxford

Byways

★★★★ 🛏 B&B

Address: Old London Road, MILTON COMMON,
Thame, OX9 2JR
Tel & Fax: 01844 279386
Email: byways.molt@tiscali.co.uk
Website: www.bywaysbedandbreakfast.co.uk
Map ref: 3, SP60
Directions: Between M40 junct 7 & 8A
Rooms: 3 (2 en suite) (1 pri facs) (3 GF), **S** £35–£40
D £60–£70 **Notes:** ⊗ on premises ✝ under 7yrs
Parking: 3

Situated in 3 acres of English country garden, yet just a few minutes from the M40, Byways is a TV-free establishment with the emphasis on providing a peaceful and relaxing stay away from it all. The bedrooms are comfortable and tastefully decorated, with extras such as robes and radios. Breakfast makes use of organic and local produce where possible, and includes home-made bread, home-grown fruit preserves and eggs from Byway's own free roaming chicken Special diets can be catered for.

Recommended in the area

Waterperry Gardens; Le Manoir aux Quat'Saisons; The Swan Antique Centre

---

Duke of Marlborough Country Inn

★★★★ INN

Address: A44, Woodleys, WOODSTOCK OX20 1HT
Tel: 01993 811460
Fax: 01993 810165
Email: sales@dukeofmarlborough.co.uk
Website: www.dukeofmarlborough.co.uk
Map ref: 3, SP41
Directions: 1m N of Woodstock on A44 x-rds
Rooms: 13 en suite (7 GF), **S** £65–£95 **D** £80–£120
Notes: ⊗ on premises **Parking:** 42

This inn is located in a stunning rural location, just outside the popular town of Woodstock. It features a large garden area, making it popular with families, but it is also fully equipped to cater for business travellers. The bedrooms and en suite bathrooms are housed in an adjacent lodge-style building and offer high standards of quality and comfort. Dinner is served in either the bar restaurant, with its log fires, or in the modern function-room restaurant, and includes many tempting home-cooked dishes featuring seasonal ingredients and complemented by a good selection of ales and wines.

Recommended in the area

Blenheim Palace; Broughton Castle; Ashmolean Museum

SHROPSHIRE

Wenlock Priory

Field House

★★★★★ GUEST HOUSE
Address: Cardington Moor, Cardington CHURCH
STRETTON SY6 7LL
Tel: 01694 771485
Email: pjsecrett@talktalk.net
Website: www.fieldhouse.info
Map ref: 2, SO49
Rooms: 3 en suite (1 GF), **D** £57–£63 **Notes:** ⊗
Seasonal offers **Parking:** 3 **Closed:** Nov–Feb

Field House is a delightful old cottage in a picturesque valley surrounded by 20 acres of grounds and gardens leading to a wildlife pool. A perfectly relaxing spot, it affords stunning views of fields, trees, hills, craggy outcrops and open skies. Offering a friendly welcome, owners Phil and Jane provide cosy twin, double and ground floor rooms with en suite baths and showers, easy chairs, televisions and beverages. A varied breakfast menu is offered, and home-cooked evening meals using local and home-grown produce are served at individual tables, with coffee to follow in the conservatory. If you're looking for diversion, there's the games room or a visit to Phil's wood workshop. Courtyard parking available.
Recommended in the area
Acton Scott Historic Working Farm; Shipton Hall; Stokesay Castle; Attingham Park; Ironbridge

The Orchards

★★★★★ B&B
Address: Eaton Road, Ticklerton CHURCH
STRETTON SY6 7DQ
Tel: 01694 722268
Email: lnutting@btinternet.com
Website: www.theorchardsticklerton.com
Map ref: 2, SO49
Directions: Off B4371 to Ticklerton village
Rooms: 3 (2 en suite) (1 pri facs), **S** £28–£35
D £56–£70 **Notes:** ⊗ on premises ⚹ under 3yrs
Parking: 6

This modern house, set in more than 4 acres of grounds, gardens and, of course, an orchard, offers high standards of comfort throughout. The bedrooms are thoughtfully equipped with hairdryers, tea- and coffee-making facilities, TV, armchairs and radio alarms, (an iron and ironing board are available on request) and each has a private bathroom, all but one of them en suite. Ann and Lloyd Nutting, the owners, not only maintain the quality but also provide the exceptionally warm, welcoming atmosphere.
Recommended in the area
Long Mynd and the Carding Mill Valley; Shropshire Hills Discovery Centre; Ironbridge Gorge museums

Saracens at Hadnall

★★★★ ◉ RESTAURANT WITH ROOMS

Address: Shrewsbury Road, HADNALL SY4 4AG
Tel: 01939 210877
Fax: 01939 210877
Email: reception@saracensathadnall.co.uk
Website: www.saracensathadnall.co.uk
Map ref: 6, SJ52
Directions: M54 onto A5, at junct of A5/A49 take A49 towards Whitchurch. Follow A49 until Hadnall, diagonal from church
Rooms: 5 en suite, **S** £45 **D** £60–£75 **Notes:** ⊗ on premises **Parking:** 20

This 18th-century Grade II listed coaching inn offers a warm welcome, excellent food and wine and comfortable accommodation. Each room offers Egyptian cotton bed linen, goose-down duvets and pillows, and all have been designed to be comfortable and cosy. There are many original features, including a 35-foot glass-topped well and beautiful parquet flooring. Wake up to a full English breakfast with Gloucester Old Spot sausages and free-range eggs from the owners' family farm.

Recommended in the area

Shrewsbury; Ironbridge; Wroxeter, Hawkstone Follies

The Library House

★★★★ ☖ GUEST ACCOMMODATION

Address: 11 Severn Bank, IRONBRIDGE, Telford,
TF8 7AN
Tel: 01952 432299
Email: info@libraryhouse.com
Website: www.libraryhouse.com
Map ref: 2, SJ60
Directions: 50yds from Iron Bridge
Rooms: 4 en suite, **S** £60–£75 **D** £70–£90
Notes: ⊗ on premises

Located just 60 yards from the famous Iron Bridge, this Grade II listed Georgian building is tucked away in a peaceful thoroughfare yet is close to good pubs and restaurants. Hanging baskets and window boxes enhance the creeper-covered walls of the former library, and in the spring and summer the gardens are immaculate. All of the bedrooms have a television with DVD, a small DVD library, and a hospitality tray. Excellent breakfasts are served in the pine-furnished dining room.

Recommended in the area

Ironbridge World Heritage Site; Telford International Exhibition Centre; Blists Hill Victorian Town

Woodlands Farm Guest House

★★★★ B&B

Address: Beech Road, IRONBRIDGE TF8 7PA
Tel: 01952 432741
Fax: 01952 432741
Email: woodlandsfarm@ironbridge68.fsnet.co.uk
Website: www.woodlandsfarmguesthouse.co.uk
Map ref: 2, SJ60
Directions: Off B4373 rdbt in Ironbridge onto Church
Hill & Beech Rd, house on private lane 0.5m on right
Rooms: 5 en suite (3 GF), **S** £30–£60 **D** £50–£80
Notes: 🐾 under 5yrs **Parking:** 8 **Closed:** 24 Dec–1 Jan

This green oasis, set in 2 acres of garden, features a host of comforts and well-equipped suites.
The three ground floor rooms have garden facing lounges and upstairs studio bedrooms also provide
comfortable seating arrangements. All suites have fridges and a generous selection of toiletries and
refreshments are supplied. The grounds are open to guests and include pleasant seating areas and a
car park. A comprehensive breakfast is served in the cheerful, welcoming dining room.

Recommended in the area

Ironbridge Gorge Museums; Telford International Exhibition Centre; Blists Hill Victorian Town

Top Farm House

★★★★ 🛏 GUEST HOUSE
Address: KNOCKIN SY10 8HN
Tel: 01691 682582
Fax: 01691 682070
Email: p.a.m@knockin.freeserve.co.uk
Website: www.topfarmknockin.co.uk
Map ref: 5, SJ32
Directions: Off B4396 in village centre
Rooms: 3 en suite, **S** £35–£45 **D** £65–£75
Parking: 6

Set in pretty gardens and retaining many original features, including exposed beams and open log
fires, Top Farm House combines traditional hospitality with elegant surroundings. The bedrooms are
equipped with many thoughtful extras. There is a relaxing beamed drawing room with a grand piano,
and imaginative and comprehensive breakfasts are served in the spacious period dining room which
overlooks the garden. The village of Knockin is one of the prettiest in this part of Shropshire.

Recommended in the area

Shrewsbury; Powis Castle (NT); Llanthaedr Waterfall

The Iron Bridge

The Clive Bar & Restaurant with Rooms

★★★★★ ◉◉ RESTAURANT WITH ROOMS

Address: Bromfield, LUDLOW SY8 2JR
Tel: 01584 856565
Fax: 01584 856661
Email: info@theclive.co.uk
Website: www.theclive.co.uk
Map ref: 2, SO57
Directions: 2m N of Ludlow on A49 in village of Bromfield
Rooms: 15 en suite (11 GF), S £60–£85 D £85–£110 **Notes:** ⊗ **Parking:** 100 **Closed:** 25–26 Dec

A stylish makeover of a former farmhouse has given The Clive a smart contemporary look. The well-known restaurant has an emphasis on fresh produce ranging from local meats to Cornish fish. The spacious en suite bedrooms have been refurbished to provide well-equipped modern accommodation. Family suite and room with disability facilities are available.

Recommended in the area

Stokesay Castle, Craven Arms; Ludlow Food Hall; Ludlow Race Course and Golf Club; Offa's Dyke

De Greys of Ludlow

★★★★★ GUEST HOUSE

Address: 5–6 Broad Street, LUDLOW SY8 1NG
Tel: 01584 872764
Fax: 01584 879764
Email: degreys@btopenworld.com
Website: www.degreys.co.uk
Map ref: 2, SO57
Directions: Off A49, in town centre, 50yds beyond the clock tower
Rooms: 9 en suite (1 GF), S £60–£120 D £80–£180
Notes: ⊗ on premises **Closed:** 26 Dec & 1 Jan

This 16th-century timber-framed property houses De Grey's Tea Rooms, a well-known establishment in Ludlow town centre. It now also provides high-quality accommodation with luxurious modern facilities. All of the individually decorated and spacious bedrooms – including two suites and one room on the ground floor – have been carefully renovated, the design of each governed by the labyrinth of historic timbers that comprise this Tudor building. Sporting evocative names such as The Buttercross, Valentines View, Castle View and Market View, all the rooms have en suite facilities, and some feature stunning bathrooms with roll-top baths and large, powerful showers; one even has his and hers bathrooms separated by a 4-foot beam. Furnishings are tasteful, with lots of lush fabrics used throughout and four-poster beds in some rooms. Combined with the latest in entertainment technology, this creates a successful fusion of past and present, and guests are encouraged to return to their rooms, unwind and relax with a bottle of wine. Breakfast, taken in the adjacent tearoom/restaurant and bakery shop, includes award-winning breads and pastries freshly made on the premises, and is served by smartly dressed waitresses, helping make a stay at De Grey's even more memorable.

Recommended in the area

Ludlow Castle; Long Mynd; Cardin Mill Valley

Number Twenty Eight

★ ★ ★ ★ ⌂ B&B

Address: 28 Lower Broad Street, LUDLOW SY8 1PQ
Tel/Fax: 01584 875466
Email: enquiries@no28ludlow.co.uk
Website: www.no28ludlow.co.uk
Map ref: 2, SO57
Directions: In town centre. Over Ludford Bridge onto Lower Broad St, 3rd house on right
Rooms: 2 en suite, S £65–£75 D £80–£90
Notes: ⊗ on premises ⚹ under 16yrs **Closed:** Jan–May

A property with a wealth of period character, this half-timbered, 16th-century town house is just a stroll from the centre of historic Ludlow with its attractions. Guests have the use of a cosy sitting room and in fine weather you can relax in the pretty courtyard or on the roof terrace. The en suite bedrooms are well equipped and offer many thoughtful extras, such as welcoming home-made biscuits. Breakfast options include fresh orange juice, fruit salad, local bacon, sausages, eggs and breads, plus a fish and vegetarian option.
Recommended in the area
Berrington Hall; Stokesay Castle; Ironbridge World Heritage Site

Crown Country Inn

★ ★ ★ ★ ⊛⊛ ⌂ INN

Address: MUNSLOW, Craven Arms SY7 9ET
Tel: 01584 841205
Email: info@crowncountryinn.co.uk
Website: www.crowncountryinn.co.uk
Map ref: 2, SO58
Directions: Off B4368 into village
Rooms: 3 en suite (1 GF), S £55 D from £85
Notes: ⊗ on premises **Parking:** 20 **Closed:** 25 Dec

The historic character of this impressive Tudor inn is retained in the massive oak beams, flagstone floors and a large inglenook fireplace in the main bar area. The bedrooms, in a converted stable block at the rear, have sitting areas, mini bars stocked with locally produced items, hospitality trays, fresh fruit and mineral water, plus Wi-fi. Traditional ales and food prepared from local produce are served in the bar and restaurant, and the day begins with a substantial English breakfast.
Recommended in the area
Ironbridge Gorge Museums; Seven Valley Railway; Long Mynd

Ruins of 13th-century Clun Castle

Fieldside

★★★★ GUEST HOUSE

Address: 38 London Road, SHREWSBURY SY2 6NX
Tel: 01743 353143
Fax: 01743 354687
Email: robrookes@btinternet.com
Website: www.fieldsideguesthouse.co.uk
Map ref: 2, SJ41
Directions: A5 onto A5064, premises 1m on left
Rooms: 4 en suite, S £40 D £60–£65
Notes: ⊗ on premises ⚶ under 10yrs **Parking:** 8

Fieldside, which dates back to 1835, is just one mile from the centre of Shewsbury and a 5-minute walk from Shrewsbury Abbey. This delightful house is attractively furnished and decorated and offers both single and double/twin rooms, all en suite. The bedrooms feature period-style furniture and are equipped with tea and coffee facilities. Breakfast is served at individual tables in the spacious dining room. Traditional English or vegetarian or lighter options are available. There is ample private parking.

Recommended in the area

Shrewsbury Castle and Abbey; Attingham Park (NT); Ironbridge Gorge and museums

Tudor House

★ ★ ★ ★ 🏠 GUEST HOUSE

Address: 2 Fish Street, SHREWSBURY SY1 1UR
Tel: 01743 351735
Email: enquiry@tudorhouseshrewsbury.co.uk
Website: www.tudorhouseshrewsbury.co.uk
Map ref: 2, SJ41
Directions: Enter town over English Bridge, ascend Wyle Cop, in 50yds take 1st right
Rooms: 3 (2 en suite) (1 pri facs)
Notes: ⊗ on premises 👶 under 11yrs

Located in the beautiful medieval town centre of Shrewsbury, on a quiet street, this fine Grade II listed 15th-century house makes an ideal base for visiting the town with its many attractions and excellent shopping. This is a family-run establishment with the emphasis on a relaxed atmosphere, and guests are well looked after, whether staying for business or pleasure; much attention is paid to detail throughout. Inside, the house retains a wealth of historical features, such as the original oak beams and fireplaces, enhanced by the tasteful decor and furnishings. The attractively decorated and cosy bedrooms – all with en suite or private facilities – are filled with thoughtful extras such as wall-mounted LCD TV and crisp white sheets, so that guests can retire to their rooms and relax after exploring all that Shrewsbury has to offer. Broadband wireless internet connection is available for an additional charge. The hearty full English breakfast served in the dining room features local organic produce where possible, and special dietary needs will be catered for where possible. Parking is available at a secure car park nearby, for a small charge.

Recommended in the area

Attingham Park; Wroxeter Roman Vineyard; Ironbridge

Soulton Hall

★★★★ ⬡ GUEST ACCOMMODATION

Address: Soulton, WEM SY4 5RS
Tel: 01939 232786
Fax: 01939 234097
Email: enquiries@soultonhall.co.uk
Website: www.soultonhall.co.uk
Map ref: 6, SJ52
Directions: A49 between Shrewsbury & Whitchurch turn onto B5065 towards Wem. Soulton Hall 2m NE of Wem on B5065
Rooms: 7 en suite (3 GF), **S** £56.50–£74.75 **D** £83–£119.50 **Parking:** 50

The Ashton family can trace their tenure of this impressive hall back to the 16th century, and much evidence of the building's age remains. The family and their staff offer excellent levels of personal service where the care of guests is of the utmost importance. The welcoming entrance lounge leads into the well-stocked bar on one side and an elegant dining room on the other. Here a good range of freshly prepared dishes, using fresh local produce wherever possible, are served in a friendly and relaxed formal setting. After the meal, coffee and liqueurs are served in the lounge hall in front of a blazing log fire in season. The house has central heating as well as log fires. The bedrooms in the hall reflect the character of the house with mullioned windows and exposed timbers; one room also has wood panelling. The converted carriage house across the garden offers ground-floor accommodation in two spacious double rooms each with spa baths. Standing in its own grounds beyond the walled garden, Cedar Lodge provides a choice of a peaceful four-poster suite or more modest family accommodation. Soulton Hall stands in 500 acres of open farmland, parkland and ancient oak woodland and you are welcome to explore the grounds.

Recommended in the area

Chester; Ironbridge; Shrewsbury

...iperstones, Shropshire Hills

SOMERSET

A Rhodesian Railways locomotive, East Somerset Railway, Cranmore

Apsley House

★★★★ ≙ B&B

ddress: Newbridge Hill, BATH BA1 3PT
el: 01225 336966
ax: 01225 425462
mail: info@apsley-house.co.uk
ebsite: www.apsley-house.co.uk
ap ref: 2, ST76
irections: 1.2m W of city centre on A431
ooms: 11 en suite (2 GF), S £55–£120
£70–£165 **Notes:** ⊗ on premises **Parking:** 12
osed: 1wk Xmas

uilt by the Duke of Wellington in 1830, this country house in the city, owned by Nick and Claire Potts, fers a gracious taste of Georgian Bath at its finest. Here guests can really soak up the atmosphere Britain's only World Heritage City. The location of Apsley House, in a peaceful residential area about mile from the city centre, ensures a truly relaxing stay, and this is enhanced by the presence of a arming and secluded rear garden, to which two of the bedrooms have direct access. The on-site rking and walking distance into the heart of the Bath are also great benefits in a city that can at nes seem besieged by traffic. Public rooms include a large drawing room with bar and a light and egant dining room, where the outstanding, freshly cooked breakfasts are served. All of the bedrooms ve en suite bathrooms, complete with Molton Brown toiletries, and each is individually decorated d furnished. The beds are either super king-size or four-posters, and other in-room facilities include at-screen TVs, Freeview, hospitality trays, direct-dial telephones and wireless internet access. osley House is an aristocrat among bed and breakfast establishments and, maintained to the highest andards, is, in fact, fit for a duke.

ecommended in the area

oman Baths and Pump Room and the many museums in Bath; Longleat; Cheddar Gorge

Ayrlington

★ ★ ★ ★ ★ GUEST ACCOMMODATION

Address: 24/25 Pulteney Road, BATH BA2 4EZ
Tel: 01225 425495
Fax: 01225 469029
Email: mail@ayrlington.com
Website: www.ayrlington.com
Map ref: 2, ST76
Directions: A4 onto A36, pass Holburne Museum, premises 200yds on right
Rooms: 16 en suite (3 GF), S £80–£195

D £80–£195 **Notes:** ⊗ on premises ⚲ under 14yrs **Parking:** 16 **Closed:** 22 Dec–5 Jan

Built of golden Bath stone, this impressive Grade II listed Victorian house is full of splendour and set right in the heart of Bath. Owners Simon and Mee-Ling Roper fuse western and eastern themes to stunning effect throughout. Asian antiques, artworks and fine fabrics sit comfortably alongside classical fireplaces, drapes and seating. All of the spacious bedrooms are furnished and decorated to individual themes, including a Chinese room, an Empire room, and the Pulteney room which has a four-poster bed. Other facilities include hospitality trays, direct-dial telephones, in-room safes, ironing facilities, TV and radio, and free wireless broadband access (a laptop is available for guests' use). Bathrooms are equipped with quality fixtures and fittings, and luxurious towels and toiletries, and some have a spa bath. While you enjoy your freshly cooked breakfast you can also enjoy superb views over the Oriental-style walled gardens to Bath and the medieval abbey. There is also a bar and a welcoming lounge. This hotel offers a tranquil atmosphere and has ample secure parking. Simon and Mee-Ling also own the Lopburi Art & Antiques gallery, which is within walking distance. Bath's magnificent historic sites and many excellent restaurants are also close by.

Recommended in the area

Bath Abbey; Thermal Bath Spa; Museum of East Asian Art

The Bailbrook Lodge

★ ★ ★ ★ GUEST HOUSE

Address: 35/37 London Road West, BATH BA1 7HZ
Tel: 01225 859090
Fax: 01225 852299
Email: hotel@bailbrooklodge.co.uk
Website: www.bailbrooklodge.co.uk
Map ref: 2, ST76
Directions: M4 junct 18, A46 S to A4 junct, left signed
Batheaston, Lodge on left
Rooms: 15 (14 en suite) (1 pri facs) (1 GF), **S** £59–£70
D £75–£160 **Notes:** ⊗ on premises **Parking:** 15

Bailbrook Lodge is a Grade II listed country house in a delightful
location just one and a half miles from the city centre and only 10 minutes' drive from the M4, with
free parking provided. The setting is peaceful and relaxed amid lovely lawns and gardens. The house,
built in 1850, has been totally redecorated and refurbished. It offers all en suite bedrooms, five with
four-poster beds and eight rooms with views of the gardens, lawns and the Avon Valley. The remaining
rooms overlook the grounds of Bailbrook House, a splendid Georgian mansion designed by the famous
architect John Everleigh. All rooms are equipped with Freeview television, clock radios, hairdryers,
trouser presses and complimentary tea and coffee, biscuits, mineral water and cotton slippers. The
four-poster rooms have additional facilities, such as dressing gowns, DVD players and a private safe.
Children are welcome, and cots, highchairs and children's portions are available on request. Bedroom
rates include a full English breakfast together with a glass of champagne. Breakfast is served in
the elegant dining room, and there is an inviting lounge with a small bar overlooking the patio. The
proprietors are happy to recommend nearby restaurants for dinner.

Recommended in the area

Roman Baths; Bath Abbey; Thermal Spa

Glastonbury Tor

Brocks Guest House

★ ★ ★ ★ GUEST ACCOMMODATION

Address: 32 Brock Street, BATH BA1 2LN
Tel: 01225 338374
Fax: 01225 338425
Email: brocks@brocksguesthouse.co.uk
Website: www.brocksguesthouse.co.uk
Map ref: 2, ST76
Directions: Just off A4 between Circus & Royal Crescent
Rooms: 6 en suite, S £65–£70 D £79–£99
Notes: ⊗ on premises **Closed:** 24 Dec–1 Jan

For an authentic taste of Georgian Bath, there are few places
to surpass Brocks, which enjoys a superb location, between
the Royal Crescent and The Circus. The accommodation, in rooms that retain all the elegance of that
bygone age, is supremely comfortable and all the expected conveniences are there. The service and
atmosphere is pleasantly informal and the hosts will help guests plan their sightseeing trips to make the
most of their time here.

Recommended in the area

Royal Crescent; Prior Park; Thermae Bath Spa

Cheriton House

★★★★★ GUEST ACCOMMODATION

Address: 9 Upper Oldfield Park, BATH BA2 3JX
Tel: 01225 429862
Fax: 01225 428403
Email: info@cheritonhouse.co.uk
Website: www.cheritonhouse.co.uk
Map ref: 2, ST76
Directions: A36 onto A367 Wells Rd, 1st right
Rooms: 11 en suite (2 GF) **Notes:** ⊗ on premises
⚬ under 12yrs **Parking:** 11

This grand Victorian house has panoramic views over Bath and is only a short walk from the city centre. Expect a friendly welcome from proprietors Iris and John who work hard to achieve a relaxed atmosphere at Cheriton House. The carefully restored en suite bedrooms are all charmingly individual and are furnished with a mix of antiques and modern furniture, and include a two-bedroom suite in a converted coach house. All rooms have colour TV and a well-stocked hospitality tray. Wireless internet access is also available for guests' use. A substantial breakfast is served in the large conservatory-breakfast room overlooking beautifully manicured and secluded gardens which are ablaze with colour during the summer months. The morning gets off to a good start with an excellent buffet of cereals, fruits and juices with a traditional full English breakfast to follow. Special dietary requirements can be catered for. Plan your day in the comfortable lounge, where you can browse the ample supply of brochures and guide books and discover all that the city and the surrounding area has to offer. Dinner is not available but Bath has many excellent restaurants and Iris and John are happy to make recommendations to help you with your choice. Cheriton House is a non-smoking establishment.

Recommended in the area

The Abbey and the many museums in Bath; Cheddar Gorge; Wells; Longleat

Chestnuts House

★★★★★ 🏛 GUEST ACCOMMODATION
Address: 16 Henrietta Road, BATH BA2 6LY
Tel: 01225 334279
Fax: 01225 312236
Email: reservations@chestnutshouse.co.uk
Website: www.chestnutshouse.co.uk
Map ref: 2, ST76
Rooms: 5 en suite (2 GF), S £65–£85 D £75–£110
Notes: ⊗ on premises
Parking: 5

Chestnuts House, a fine Edwardian house with an enclosed garden, is ideally situated off the main road and adjacent to Henrietta Park, but is within a few minutes' level stroll of the city centre with its many attractions. Built from natural Bath stone, it offers fresh, airy accommodation. The bedrooms feature stylish contemporary furnishings and decor, and some have king-size and wrought-iron beds. All offer colour TV, broadband wireless internet connection, hairdryer and refreshment tray; one has its own private patio area. Breakfast features an extensive buffet and daily specials, and there is a cosy lounge
Recommended in the area
Bath's Roman Baths; Royal Crescent; Thermae Bath Spa

Devonshire House

★★★ GUEST ACCOMMODATION
Address: 143 Wellsway, BATH BA2 4RZ
Tel: 01225 312495
Email: enquiries@devonshire-house.uk.com
Website: www.devonshire-house.uk.com
Map ref: 2, ST76
Directions: 1m S of city centre. A36 onto A367 Wells Rd & Wellsway
Rooms: 4 en suite (1 GF), S £42–£63 D £68–£78
Notes: ⊗ on premises **Parking:** 6

Located within walking distance of the city centre, this charming house, built in 1880, maintains its Victorian style. The attractive en suite bedrooms, some appointed to a high standard, have TVs and tea- and coffee-making facilities. There is a small lounge area, and the freshly cooked breakfasts, with a range of choices, are served in the pleasant dining room, which was originally a Victorian grocer's shop. Secure parking is in the walled courtyard, and the proprietors make every effort to ensure your stay is pleasant and memorable.
Recommended in the area
Roman Baths; Longleat House and Safari Park; Wells Cathedral

Dorian House

★ ★ ★ ★ ★ GUEST ACCOMMODATION

Address: 1 Upper Oldfield Park, BATH BA2 3JX
Tel: 01225 426336
Fax: 01225 444699
Email: info@dorianhouse.co.uk
Website: www.dorianhouse.co.uk
Map ref: 2, ST76
Directions: A36 onto A367 Wells Rd, right onto Upper Oldfield Park, 3rd building on left
Rooms: 11 en suite (2 GF), **S** £65–£95 **D** £89–£165
Notes: ⊗ on premises **Parking:** 9

Extensively refurbished in 2007, Dorian House is a fully restored Victorian town house with stunning views over the city. The period charm of the en suite bedrooms is enhanced by luxurious fabrics and furnishings, including Egyptian cotton sheets, large flat-screen TVs, and the award-winning breakfasts and lovely gardens. Several bedrooms have fine oak four-poster beds and all the rooms are named after famous musical figures, including Jacqueline du Pre, the owner's cello teacher.
Recommended in the area
Roman Baths and Abbey; Royal Crescent and The Circus; Stourhead (NT)

Grove Lodge

★ ★ ★ ★ GUEST ACCOMMODATION

Address: 11 Lambridge, BATH BA1 6BJ
Tel: 01225 310860
Fax: 01225 429630
Email: stay@grovelodgebath.co.uk
Website: www.grovelodgebath.co.uk
Map ref: 2, ST76
Directions: 0.6m NE of city centre. Off A4, 400yds W from junct A46
Rooms: 5 (4 en suite) (1 pri facs) (1 GF), **S** £50–£60
D £70–£90 **Notes:** ⊗ on premises ♨ under 6yrs **Closed:** Xmas & New Year

Owners Isobel Miles and her husband Peter Richards have refurbished their Grade II listed Georgian home to highlight the period features. Bedrooms are spacious with original marble or stone fireplaces. Furnishings blend modern and antique styles, and all rooms have large bathrooms. Each room has a radio-alarm clock, hairdryer, king-size bed and a courtesy tray. Healthy breakfasts are served in the sunny dining room; vegetarian and gluten-free diets are catered for with prior notice. Free on-street parking.
Recommended in the area
Georgian Bath; Roman Baths; Bath Abbey

The Kennard

★★★★ GUEST ACCOMMODATION

Address: 11 Henrietta Street, BATH BA2 6LL
Tel: 01225 310472
Fax: 01225 460054
Email: reception@kennard.co.uk
Website: www.kennard.co.uk
Map ref: 2, ST76
Directions: A4 onto A36 Bathwick St, 2nd right onto Henrietta Rd & Henrietta St
Rooms: 12 (10 en suite) (2 GF), **S** £58–£89 **D** £98–£140 **Notes:** ⊗ on premises 👶 under 8yrs **Closed:** 2 wks Xmas

This Georgian town house, now restored as a charming small hotel with its own special character, was built as a lodging house in 1794. Situated just off the famous Great Pulteney Street, it is only five minutes from the Abbey, the Roman Baths, the new spa complex and the railway station. All of the bedrooms are thoughtfully and individually furnished, most are en suite, and some are located at ground-floor level. Breakfast includes a cold buffet as well as a selection of hot items.

Recommended in the area

Stonehenge; Castle Combe; Wells

Marlborough House

★★★★ GUEST ACCOMMODATION

Address: 1 Marlborough Lane, BATH BA1 2NQ
Tel: 01225 318175
Fax: 01225 466127
Email: mars@manque.dircon.co.uk
Website: www.marlborough-house.net
Map ref: 2, ST76
Directions: 450yds W of city centre, at A4 junct
Rooms: 6 en suite (1 GF), **S** £75–£95 **D** £85–£130
Parking: 3 **Closed:** 24–26 Dec

This enchanting Victorian town house is owned and run in a friendly and informal style by Peter Moore. The location is walking distance from Bath's major attractions. This large and impressive house has spacious, well proportioned bedrooms, all fully en suite and presented with complimentary organic shampoo, conditioners and soap. The rooms are elegantly furnished with antiques, including some antique four-poster or king-size beds, and feature free Wi-fi and flat-screen TVs with Freeview. A hospitality tray is provided including organic teas and coffees and a decanter of sherry.

Recommended in the area

Roman Baths; Abbey Tower Tour; Thermal Spa

Clanville Manor

★ ★ ★ ★ 🏛 FARMHOUSE

Address: CASTLE CARY BA7 7PJ
Tel: 01963 350124
Fax: 01963 350719
Email: info@clanvillemanor.co.uk
Website: www.clanvillemanor.co.uk
Map ref: 2, ST63
Directions: A371 onto B3153, 0.75m entrance to Clanville Manor via white gate & cattle grid under bridge

Rooms: 4 en suite, **S** £35–£45 **D** £70–£90 **Facilities:** ⚐ **Notes:** ⊗ on premises ⚑ under 12yrs **Parking:** 6 **Closed:** 21 Dec–2 Jan

Built in 1743 from local honey-coloured Cary stone, Clanville Manor has been owned by the Snook family since 1898 and still functions as a beef-rearing farm. On hot summer days guests can enjoy the heated outdoor swimming pool, relax in the walled garden or take a walk along the banks of the River Brue. There are often newborn calves in the fields near the house. Guests enter the farmhouse by the flagstone entrance hall and climb a polished oak staircase up to the individually decorated bedrooms, which retain much original character and offer fine views. The rooms, including one with a four-poster, each have flat-screen TV, hairdryer and complimentary tea and coffee. Hearty breakfasts made mainly from local produce are served in the elegant dining room overlooking the pond and driveway. Fresh, golden-yolked eggs come from the farm's own hens, honey comes from Chris Wright's bees, and the Aga is called into play to cook the full English breakfast – lighter alternatives are also on the menu. In the evenings, you can dine at one of several excellent local restaurants and pubs, or unwind in the spacious drawing room. Assistance dogs only are allowed. Free Wi-fi available.

Recommended in the area

Glastonbury; Stourhead (NT); Wells Cathedral; Cheddar Gorge and Wookey Hole Caves; Glastonbury Tor

Bellplot House & Thomas's Restaurant

★★★★★ ◉ 🏠 GUEST ACCOMMODATION

Address: High Street, CHARD TA20 1QB
Tel/Fax: 01460 62600
Email: info@bellplothouse.co.uk
Website: www.bellplothouse.co.uk
Map ref: 2, ST30
Directions: In town centre, 500yds from Guildhall
Rooms: 7 en suite (2 GF), **S** £79.50 **D** £89.50 **Notes:** ⊗ on premises **Parking:** 12

This Grade II listed town house is a delightful Georgian bolthole, with its own private car park, Chard is surrounded by beautiful countryside in an area with many historical houses and gardens to explore. You arrive to a warm welcome from Betty and Dennis, who ensure that their guests have all they need. The bedrooms are named after the women who once owned Bellplot, and offer en suite facilities, free Wi-fi and complimentary tea and coffee. Breakfast is a feast of excellent local ingredients.

Recommended in the area

Forde Abbey and Gardens; Barrington Court; East Lambrook Manor Gardens; River Cottage

Tarr Farm Inn

★★★★★ ◉ 🏠 INN

Address: Tarr Steps, Exmoor National Park
DULVERTON TA22 9PY
Tel: 01643 851507
Fax: 01643 851111
Email: enquiries@tarrfarm.co.uk
Website: www.tarrfarm.co.uk
Map ref: 2, SS92
Directions: 4m NW of Dulverton. Off B3223 signed
Tarr Steps, signs to Tarr Farm Inn
Rooms: 9 en suite (4 GF), **D** £150 **Notes:** 🐾 under 14yrs **Parking:** 10

Tarr Farm dates from the 16th century and nestles just above Tarr Steps and the River Barle. The new bedrooms with en suite bathrooms display careful attention to detail with thick fluffy bathrobes, fridge organic toiletries and much more. When it comes to food you will not be disappointed with wonderful cream teas, scrumptious breakfasts and delicious dinners with ingredients sourced from Devon and Somerset farms and suppliers. The farm is set in beautiful countryside ideal for walkers.

Recommended in the area

Exmoor National Park; South West Coast Path; Dunster Castle (NT)

Harptree Court

★★★★★ 🏠 🍽 GUEST ACCOMMODATION

Address: EAST HARPTREE BS40 6AA
Tel: 01761 221729
Email: location.harptree@tiscali.co.uk
Website: www.harptreecourt.co.uk
Map ref: 2, ST55
Directions: From A368 take B3114 for Chewton
Mendip. After 0.5m turn right into drive entrance
Rooms: 3 (2 en suite) (1 pri facs), **S £**75
D £95–£110 **Notes:** ⊗ on premises 👶 under 12yrs
Parking: 10 **Closed:** 23 Dec–Jan

This elegant Georgian country house is at the end of a long tree-lined driveway, surrounded by 17
acres of parkland and gardens amid a designated Area of Outstanding National Beauty. With just three
guest rooms, there's something of a house-party feel, enhanced by the cream tea on arrival and the
flowers, fruit, mineral water and magazines in the bedrooms. These are spacious and sumptuously
furnished. Breakfast is served in the elegant dining room or sitting room. All have glorious views.
Recommended in the area
Wookey Hole Caves and Papermill; Wells Cathedral and Bishop's Palace; Cheddar Gorge and Caves

Cannards Grave Farmhouse

★★★★ GUEST ACCOMMODATION

Address: Cannards Grave, SHEPTON MALLET
BA4 4LY
Tel: 01749 347091
Fax: 01749 347091
Email: sue@cannardsgravefarmhouse.co.uk
Website: www.cannardsgravefarmhouse.co.uk
Map ref: 2, ST64
Directions: On A37 between Shepton Mallet & The
Bath & West Showground, 100yds from Highwayman
Pub towards showground on left
Rooms: 5 en suite (1 GF), **S £**40–£50 **D £**60–£70 **Notes:** ⊗ on premises **Parking:** 6

Charming host Sue Crockett offers quality accommodation at this welcoming 17th-century farmhouse.
The bedrooms are delightful and have thoughtful touches such as hospitality trays, mineral water,
biscuits and mints. One room has a four-poster bed and a fridge with fresh milk. Delicious breakfasts
are served in the garden conservatory and there is a comfortable lounge to relax in.
Recommended in the area
Bath and West Showground; Historic Wells; Glastonbury Tor; City of Bath

Greyhound

★ ★ ★ ★ 🛏 INN

Address: STAPLE FITZPAINE,Taunton, TA3 5SP
Tel: 01823 480227
Fax: 01823 481117
Email: thegreyhound-inn@btconnect.com
Website: www.greyhoundinn.biz
Map ref: 2, ST21
Directions: M5 junct 25, A358 signed Yeovil.
In 3m turn right, signed Staple Fitzpaine.
Rooms: 4 en suite, **S** £60 **D** £90
Notes: 🐾 under 10yrs **Parking:** 40

The creeper-clad Greyhound Inn is set in an Area of Outstanding Natural Beauty; it is a picturesque village inn tucked away in the village of Staple Fitzpaine. It makes an ideal base for touring the local countryside, yet being close to the M5 it is also a good choice for business travellers. Inside it has great atmosphere and character, and has been extended over the years to provide a series of rambling, connecting rooms with a rustic mix of flagstone floors, old timbers, natural stone walls and open fires. The delightful en suite bedrooms are spacious, comfortable and well equipped, with many extras such as colour TV, direct-dial telephone, trouser press, hairdryer and hospitality tray, as well as a good supply of toiletries, coming as standard. Wireless internet connection is also available. In the candlelit restaurant, an imaginative choice of freshly prepared seasonal dishes using locally sourced ingredients is featured on the ever-changing blackboard menu, complemented by a good choice of wines, and the hearty full English breakfasts are definitely worth getting up for. Award-winning, properly kept ales can be enjoyed in the locals' bar, with its barrel stools and wood-burning stove. Parking is available for guests.

Recommended in the area

Taunton; Blackdown Hills; Longleat

Cutsey House

★ ★ ★ ★ GUEST ACCOMMODATION

Address: Cutsey, Trull TAUNTON TA3 7NY
Tel: 01823 421705
Fax: 01823 421294
Email: cutseyhouse@btconnect.com
Website: www.cutseyhouse.co.uk
Map ref: 2, ST22
Directions: M5 junct 26, into West Buckland,
right at T-junct, 2nd left, next right
Rooms: 3 en suite, **S** £35–£45 **D** £60–£70
Notes: ⊗ on premises **Parking:** 10 **Closed:** Xmas–Etr

This Victorian house is set in over 20 acres of gardens and grounds, with parts of the building dating back to the 15th and 16th century, including a Tudor staircase. Inside, careful renovation has resulted in an elegant and traditional establishment. The comfortable, spacious bedrooms have glorious views of the countryside. Public rooms are well proportioned and comfortable and include the library, main dining room, billiards room and parlour dining room. Dinner is available by arrangement.

Recommended in the area

Blackdown Hills (Area of Outstanding Natural Beauty); Barrow Mump (NT); Somerset County Museum

Lower Farm

★ ★ ★ ★ FARMHOUSE

Address: Thornfalcon, TAUNTON TA3 5NR
Tel: 01823 443549
Email: doreen@titman.eclipse.co.uk
Website: www.thornfalcon.co.uk
Map ref: 2, ST22
Directions: M5 junct 25, 2m SE on A358, left opp
Nags Head pub, farm signed 1m on left
Rooms: 11 (8 en suite) (3 pri facs) (7 GF),
S £45–£50 **D** £70–£75 **Notes:** ⊗ on premises
⊶ under 5yrs **Parking:** 10

This charming thatched 15th-century longhouse is full of character. Lovely gardens and open farmland surround this pretty property, where beamed ceilings and inglenook fireplaces testify to its age. The bedrooms include some in a converted granary and byre, and all are en suite or have private facilities. All rooms have high standards of furnishings. A hearty breakfast is cooked on the Aga and served in the farmhouse kitchen, using local bacon and sausages, and eggs from the proprietor's own hens.

Recommended in the area

Hestercombe Gardens; Willow and Wetlands Visitors Centre; Quantock Hills

Crown & Victoria

★★★★ ⊛ INN

Address: Farm Street, TINTINHULL,Yeovil
BA22 8PZ
Tel: 01935 823341
Fax: 01935 825786
Email: info@thecrownandvictoria.co.uk
Website: www.thecrownandvictoria.co.uk
Map ref: 2, ST41
Directions: Off A303, signs for Tintinhull Gardens
Rooms: 5 en suite, **S** £65 **D** £85 **Parking:** 60

The Crown and Victoria country inn stands in the heart of the pretty village of Tintinhull. In days gone by, as well as being the village pub, the inn was also a private school – lessons took place where the existing bar is situated. Today, above the new restaurant, the unfussy bedrooms are light and airy and very well equipped with hairdryers, TVs with DVD players, tea and coffee facilities, and wireless broadband internet access. The staff ensure you are well cared for. The contemporary bar and restaurant offers a successful combination of traditional pub atmosphere and quality dining. Carefully presented dishes are available for lunch and dinner under the direction of head chef, London-trained Stephen Yates. The menu ranges from traditional English dishes such as steak and ale pie to the more elaborate pan-roasted breast of duck on a bed of spinach with a potato rösti, plum and port jus. The extensive wine list includes ten fine house wines and there is a choice of local real ales. When the weather is kind, guests can relax in the garden with a drink or a light meal or enjoy a candlelit dinner in the conservatory with lovely garden views.

Recommended in the area

Tintinhull House Garden (NT); Montacute House (NT); Barrington Court (NT); Yeovil; Fleet Air Arm Museum, Yeovilton

Double-Gate Farm

★★★★ FARMHOUSE

Address: Godney, WELLS BA5 1RX
Tel: 01458 832217
Fax: 01458 835612
Email: doublegatefarm@aol.com
Website: www.doublegatefarm.com
Map ref: 2, ST54
Directions: A39 from Wells towards Glastonbury, at Polsham right signed Godney/Polsham, 2m to x-rds, continue to farmhouse on left after inn
Rooms: 6 en suite (1 GF), **S** £55–£60 **D** £70–£80 **Notes:** ⊗ on premises **Parking:** 10
Closed: 21 Dec–4 Jan

A special welcome awaits you not just from the owners but from Jasper and Paddy, the very friendly retrievers, at this fine stone farmhouse situated on the banks of the River Sheppey on the Somerset Levels, which has good views of Glastonbury Tor. There's fishing from the bottom of the garden and cycle rides on the quiet roads of the Levels which abound with birds and wildlife. Guests can play table-tennis or snooker (on a full-size table), or watch their own DVDs in the well equipped bedrooms, all of which are en suite and offer hairdryers, complimentary beverages and Freeview TV. Summer 2009 sees the addition of four ground-floor, triple bedrooms and a lovely garden dining room. There is free internet access in the guest lounge. Double-Gate Farm is well known for its beautiful summer flower garden, home-grown tomatoes and fruit. Delicious breakfasts are served at two refectory tables in the farmhouse. Choose from a selection of fruit, cereals, juice, yoghurt, compote and local cheeses, as well as full English breakfasts with home-made bread, kippers and American pancakes. Evening meals are available on certain days, or alternative dining can be found at the inn next door.

Recommended in the area

Wells (England's smallest city); Glastonbury; Cheddar Gorge

Collett Park, Shepton Mallet

Camellia Lodge

★★★★ B&B

Address: 76 Walliscote Road,
WESTON-SUPER-MARE BS23 1ED
Tel: 01934 613534
Fax: 01934 613534
Email: dachefscamellia@aol.com
Website: www.camellialodge.net
Map ref: 2, ST36
Directions: 200yds from seafront
Rooms: 5 (4 en suite) (1 pri facs), S £27.50–£35
D £55–£65

With the mile-long promenade and pier right on the doorstep, Camellia Lodge is a great choice for a seaside break. The proprietors create a warm atmosphere – they will even collect you from the train or bus stations. Inside their three-storey Victorian home you will find immaculate, mainly good size, well equipped bedrooms. Breakfast is a wide choice using local produce and excellent home-cooked evening meals are available by prior arrangement. Both are served the dining room.

Recommended in the area

Weston Golf Club; Sea Life Centre; Cheddar Gorge

North Wheddon Farm

★★★★ 🛏 🍴 FARMHOUSE

Address: WHEDDON CROSS TA24 7EX
Tel: 01643 841791
Email: rachael@go-exmoor.co.uk
Website: www.go-exmoor.co.uk
Map ref: 2, SS93
Directions: 500yds S of village x-rds on A396.
Pass Moorland Hall on left, driveway next right
Rooms: 3 (2 en suite) (1 pri facs), **S** £35–£37.50
D £70–£75 **Parking:** 5

Country hospitality at its best is provided at North Wheddon Farm, which is delightfully friendly and comfortable, whether you are looking for a quiet, relaxing stay or a family holiday. Built in 1840, it is a listed farmhouse with a Georgian country house feel, featuring high ceilings and large open fires. The property is set in the vibrant green patchwork of Exmoor, a private estate of 20 acres with a very pleasant garden. Within the grounds there are streams, a waterfall and a bottom paddock crossed with natural springs – very picturesque – and of course there's the classic Somerset farmyard with all the animals you would expect. The bedrooms have great views; they are individually decorated, bright, airy and calming, and thoughtfully equipped with extras such as televisions and DVD players, a film library, books galore and classic games to play. Tea and coffee making facilities are provided and the comfortable beds are finished with hot water bottles. Food is particularly memorable. If it can't be grown or raised on the farm, then you can be sure that it will be locally sourced and of the very best quality. From the home-smoked bacon to the Aga-baked breads, you won't go hungry.

Recommended in the area

Minehead; Exmoor; Dunster

Bishop's Palace, Wells

Karslake House

★★★★ @ GUEST HOUSE

Address: Halse Lane, WINSFORD, Exmoor National
Park, TA24 7JE
Tel/Fax: 01643 851242
Email: enquiries@karslakehouse.co.uk
Website: www.karslakehouse.co.uk
Map ref: 2, SS93
Directions: In village centre, past the pub and up
the hill
Rooms: 6 (5 en suite) (1 pri facs) (1 GF), **S** £60–£80
D £85–£120 **Notes:** ✷ under 12yrs **Parking:** 15 **Closed:** Feb & Mar

This small country house is very much a family home where guests are made to feel like old friends.
Original beams and fireplaces feature and quality is evident in the furnishings throughout the house.
The bedrooms are attractively decorated and thoughtfully equipped – one has a four-poster bed. Food
is a highlight, and interesting menus, home-baked bread, and home-made preserves are offered in the
spacious restaurant. Riding, fishing and shooting can be arranged. Dogs are welcome.
Recommended in the area
Tarr Steps (medieval clapper bridge); Holnicote Estate (NT); Minehead

Roaches, Peak District National Park

Oakwood Barn B&B

★ ★ ★ B&B

Address: Oakwood Barn, Lullington Road,
EDINGALE B79 9JA
Tel: 01827 383916
Email: judith@oakwoodbarn.com
Map ref: 3, SK21
Directions: Fom Lichfield take A38, right onto A513.
left towards Croxall, then right towards Edingdale,
900mtrs on Lullington road, B&B on right
Rooms: 2 en suite (1 GF), **D** £65–£75
Notes: ⊗ on premises **Parking:** 4 **Closed:** Xmas & New Year

The name of this rural retreat could not be more appropriate. Dating back to the 15th century, it is a fine old timbered barn that has been converted to provide luxurious accommodation with wonderful views over the rolling landscape. The two bedrooms are self-contained, with their own access, and have exposed beams, gleaming wood floors and fine old pieces of furniture. Each has a king-size bed, flat-screen TV and a modern bathroom. Breakfast includes eggs from the hens that roam the gardens.
Recommended in the area
Lichfield Cathedral; The Belfry; Tamworth and Tutbury castles; National Memorial Arboretum

The Black Grouse

★ ★ ★ ★ ⊛ RESTAURANT WITH ROOMS
Address: LONGNOR, Buxton SK17 0NS
Tel: 01298 83205
Fax: 01298 83689
Email: food@theblackgrouse.co.uk
Website: www.theblackgrouse.co.uk
Map ref: 7, SK06
Directions: In village centre on B5053
Rooms: 11 (8 en suite) (1 GF), **S** £60–£100
D £100–£160 **Parking:** 100

Situated in the heart of the Peak District, high on the Staffordshire moors, this Georgian pub has been stylishly renovated, maintaining original features and ambience. The en suite bedrooms have luxury Italian-style bathrooms with under-floor heating and heated towel rails. All rooms have flat-screen TVs with digital Sky, and tea and coffee facilities. Real ales are served in the oak-panelled bar and meals can be taken in the separate dining room. There are three self-catering cottages in the courtyard.
Recommended in the area
Buxton; Haddon Hall; Peak Rail

Thor's Cave, Manifold Valley

The Beehive Guest House

★★★★ GUEST HOUSE

Address: Churnet View Road, OAKAMOOR
ST10 3AE
Tel: 01538 702420
Fax: 01538 703735
Email: thebeehiveoakamoor@btinternet.com
Website: www.thebeehiveguesthouse.co.uk
Map ref: 7, SK04
Directions: Off B5417 in village N onto Eaves Ln,
sharp left onto Churnet View Rd

Rooms: 5 en suite (1 GF), **S** £35–£54 **D** £54–£58 **Notes:** ⊗ on premises 🚼 under 5yrs **Parking:** 6

This spacious detached house offers a choice of thoughtfully equipped and comfortable bedrooms, one of which is a triple. All of the rooms, which benefit from central heating, TV, hairdryer and tea- and coffee-making facilities, are en suite and come with four-poster beds, making this an ideal place for a romantic break or just a stress-free trip away from it all. The family-run Beehive has a comfortable lounge/dining room, where individually prepared breakfasts are served. Dinner by prior arrangement.

Recommended in the area

Peak District National Park; Stoke-on-Trent potteries; Chatsworth House

Mow Cop

Haywood Park Farm

★★★★ FARMHOUSE

Address: Shugborough, STAFFORD ST17 0XA
Tel: 01889 882736
Fax: 01889 882736
Email: haywood.parkfarm@btopenworld.com
Website: www.haywoodparkfarm.co.uk
Map ref: 7, SJ92
Directions: 4m SE of Stafford off A513. Brown signs to Shugborough, on right 400yds past estate exit
Rooms: 2 en suite, D £70–£80
Notes: ⊗ on premises ⚲ under 14 yrs **Parking:** 4

The attractive farmhouse stands on a 120-acre arable and sheep farm on Cannock Chase, part of the Shugborough Estate. The large, attractively furnished bedrooms have a host of extras such as fresh flowers, fruit, tea facilities and shortbread. Large fluffy towels are provided in the luxury bathrooms. Breakfast, using local produce, is served in the lounge-dining room. The area is a paradise for walkers and cyclists. Fishing is offered in the lake, which is well stocked with carp and other coarse fish.

Recommended in the area

Shugborough Estate (NT); Wedgewood Museum; Alton Towers; Trentham Gardens

atford Mill in East Bergholt

The Chantry

★★★★ 🛏 GUEST ACCOMMODATION

Address: 8 Sparhawk Street, BURY ST EDMUNDS IP33 1RY
Tel: 01284 767427
Fax: 01284 760946
Email: chantryhotel1@aol.com
Website: www.chantryhotel.com
Map ref: 4, TL86
Directions: From cathedral S onto Crown St, left onto Sparhawk St
Rooms: 15 en suite (1 GF), **S** £69–£84 **D** £89–£99
Parking: 16

A delightful Grade II listed building where parking for each room is provided via a 19th-century carriage access. Bedrooms are decorated in period style, and the spacious superior double rooms have antique beds. There is a cosy lounge bar, and breakfast and dinner are served in the restaurant. Dishes are home cooked and prepared from the freshest of ingredients.

Recommended in the area

Abbey Gardens and ruins; Theatre Royal (NT); Ickworth House, Park & Gardens (NT)

Clarice House

★★★★★ 🏵 GUEST ACCOMMODATION

Address: Horringer Court, Horringer Road, BURY ST EDMUNDS IP29 5PH
Tel: 01284 705550
Fax: 01284 716120
Email: bury@claricehouse.co.uk
Website: www.claricehouse.co.uk
Map ref: 4, TL86
Directions: 1m SW from town on A143 towards Horringer
Rooms: 13 en suite, **S** £55–£75 **D** £85–£100
Notes: ⊗ on premises 🚸 under 5yrs **Parking:** 85
Closed: 24–26 Dec & 31 Dec–1 Jan

This large mansion is set in 20 acres of landscaped grounds just a short drive from Bury St Edmunds. The family-run residential spa, with superb leisure facilities, has spacious, well-equipped bedrooms. Public rooms include a smart lounge bar, an intimate restaurant offering quality food and a changing menu, a further lounge and a conservatory.

Recommended in the area

Bury St Edmunds; Abbey Gardens; Ickworth House, Park and Gardens (NT)

Framlingham Castle

Racehorses, near Newmarket

Valley Farm

★★★★★ B&B

Address: Bungay Road, HOLTON IP19 8LY
Tel: 01986 874521
Email: mail@valleyfarmholton.co.uk
Website: www.valleyfarmholton.co.uk
Map ref: 4, TM47
Directions: A144 onto B1123 to Holton, left at fork
in village, left at school, 500yds on left
Rooms: 2 en suite, **S** £60–£70 **D** £60–£80
Notes: ⊗ on premises **Parking:** 15

The owners of Valley Farm are keen advocates of green tourism, and this is reflected in many aspects of the charming red brick farmhouse situated in a peaceful rural location, a short drive or walk from the small market town of Halesworth. The individually decorated en suite bedrooms are tastefully appointed with many thoughtful touches. Breakfast, featuring locally sourced and home-grown produce, is served at a large communal table in the smartly appointed dining room. The property also boasts two and a half acres of lovely landscaped grounds and an indoor heated swimming pool.

Recommended in the area

Southwold; Minsmere RSPB sanctuary; The Cut arts centre

Lavenham Priory

★ ★ ★ ★ ★ 🛏 B&B

Address: Water Street, LAVENHAM, Sudbury
CO10 9RW
Tel: 01787 247404
Fax: 01787 248472
Email: mail@lavenhampriory.co.uk
Website: www.lavenhampriory.co.uk
Map ref: 4, TL94
Directions: A1141, turn by side of Swan onto
Water St, right after 50yds onto private drive
Rooms: 6 en suite, **S** £75–£85 **D** £100–£165 **Notes:** 🐾 under 10yrs **Parking:** 8
Closed: 21 Dec–2 Jan

Gilli and Tim Pitt have created a sumptuous haven in the midst of historic Lavenham, one of England's prettiest medieval villages. The building dates back to the 15th century and retains many fine early features, including an oak Jacobean staircase, leading to beautiful bedrooms with crown posts, Elizabethan wall paintings and oak floors. Each room has a spectacular bed – a four poster, lit bateau (sleigh) bed, or domed canopy polonaise bed – and some were made for the rooms by a Lavenham cabinetmaker. All are en suite, some with a slipper bath, and all have TV and tea and coffee facilities. The house stands in 3 acres of private grounds, all attractively landscaped and stocked with period herbs, plants and shrubs. Breakfast, taken in the Merchant's Room at an imposing polished table, is a choice of fruit compotes, yoghurts, orange juice, cereals, a traditional English breakfast, kippers, haddock, smoked salmon and scrambled eggs, and various breads, croissants, jams and preserves. The great hall with its Tudor inglenook fireplace and an adjoining lounge are lovely places to relax, and are well stocked with books and board games.

Recommended in the area

Lavenham Guildhall (NT); Sutton Hoo (NT); Kentwell Hall

Sandpit Farm

★★★★ B&B

Address: Bruisyard, SAXMUNDHAM IP17 2EB
Tel: 01728 663445
Email: smarshall@aldevalleybreaks.co.uk
Website: www.aldevalleybreaks.co.uk
Map ref: 4, TM36
Directions: 4m W of Saxmundham. A1120 onto
B1120, 1st left for Bruisyard, house 1.5m on left
Rooms: 2 en suite, S £35 D £70 **Parking:** 4
Closed: 24–26 Dec

This delightful Grade II listed farmhouse set in 20 acres of grounds, with the River Alde meandering along the boundary of the gardens, is well located for visiting the many places of interest in Suffolk. The en suite bedrooms have lots of thoughtful touches and enjoy lovely country views; one is located in its own wing of the house. There is also a cosy sitting room for relaxing, as well as a secret garden, a wild-flower orchard and a hard tennis court. Breakfast features quality local and home-made produce as well as freshly laid free-range eggs.

Recommended in the area

Framlingham; Minsmere RSPB reserve; Sutton Hoo (NT)

Bays Farm

★★★★★ ☖ GUEST ACCOMMODATION

Address: Forward Green, STOWMARKET IP14 5HU
Tel: 01449 711286
Email: information@baysfarmsuffolk.co.uk
Website: www.baysfarmsuffolk.co.uk
Map ref: 4, TM05
Directions: A14 junct 50, onto A1120. 1m after
Stowupland, turn right at sharp left hand bend signed
Broad Green. Bays Farm 1st house on right
Rooms: 3 en suite, S £60–£100 D £70–£110
Notes: ✿ under 12yrs **Parking:** 3

Lavish restoration has turned this charming 17th-century farmhouse into a quality destination. A moat and 4 acres of mature gardens surround the property, while the interior has a wealth of oak beams and a roaring open fire. The individually designed bedrooms are luxuriously furnished with antiques, colour co-ordinated fabrics and en suite facilities. Extras include goose-down duvets, Egyptian cotton bed linen, bathrobes and hand-made toiletries. Breakfasts are served in the oak-beamed dining room.

Recommended in the area

Museum of East Anglian Life; Mechanical Music Museum and Bygones; Otley Hall

Blythburgh, Suffolk

Marden Park Farm, Woldingham

Pembroke House

★★★★ GUEST ACCOMMODATION

Address: Valley End Road, CHOBHAM GU24 8TB
Tel: 01276 857654
Fax: 01276 858445
Email: pembroke_house@btinternet.com
Map ref: 3, SU96
Directions: A30 onto B383 signed Chobham,
3m right onto Valley End Rd, 1m on left
Rooms: 4 (2 en suite) (2 pri facs), **S** £40–£70
D £100–£140 **Notes:** 🐾 under 6yrs **Parking:** 10

Julia Holland takes great pleasure in treating guests as friends at this spacious neo-Georgian home set amid rolling fields. The elegant public areas include an imposing entrance hall and a dining room with views over the surrounding countryside. The bedrooms are filled with thoughtful extras. Two single rooms share a bathroom, while the other rooms are en suite. There are many top-class golf clubs in the vicinity, as well as polo, horseracing and shooting. There is a tennis court in the attractive grounds.

Recommended in the area

Windsor Castle; Wisley RHS Gardens; shooting at Bisley

Bentley Mill

★★★★★ B&B

Address: Gravel Hill Road, Bentley, FARNHAM
GU10 5JD
Tel: 01420 23301
Fax: 01420 22538
Email: ann.bentleymill@supanet.com
Website: www.bentleymill.com
Map ref: 3, SU84
Directions: Off A31 Farnham-Alton road,
opp Bull Inn, turn left onto Gravel Hill Rd
Rooms: 4 (2 en suite) (2 pri facs) (1 GF), **S** £80–£100 **D** £105–£150
Notes: ⊗ on premises 🐾 under 8yrs **Parking:** 6

Ann and David welcome you to their lovely home, a former corn mill beside the River Wey and set in acres of beautiful grounds. Guests are greeted with fresh flowers in their room and chocolates on the pillow. The two spacious main suites are former mill rooms with original beams. They have countryside views and feature antiques, luxurious beds and deep sofas. A full breakfast is cooked on the Aga.

Recommended in the area

Jane Austen's House, Chawton; The Watercress Line, Alresford; Portsmouth Historic Dockyard

Sunken Gardens, Hampton Court

Asperion Hillside

★★★★ 🛏 GUEST ACCOMMODATION

Address: Perry Hill, Worplesdon, GUILDFORD
GU3 3RF
Tel: 01483 232051
Fax: 01483 237015
Email: info@thehillsidehotel.com
Website: www.asperionhillside.com
Map ref: 3, SU94
Rooms: 15 en suite (6 GF), S £65 D £80–£120
Notes: ⊗ on premises **Parking:** 15
Closed: 21 Dec–5 Jan

Located just a short drive from central Guildford, this high-quality accommodation, which uses organic and Fairtrade produce, is popular with both business and leisure travellers. The en suite bedrooms are comfortable and well equipped with good facilities, including free Wi-fi; one suite features a king-size four-poster bed. There is a lounge bar and a bistro-style restaurant. The gardens, including a Koi carp pond, include a guest terrace. Conferences and events can be catered for.

Recommended in the area

St Mary's Church, Worplesdon; RHS Garden, Wisley; Clandon Park (NT)

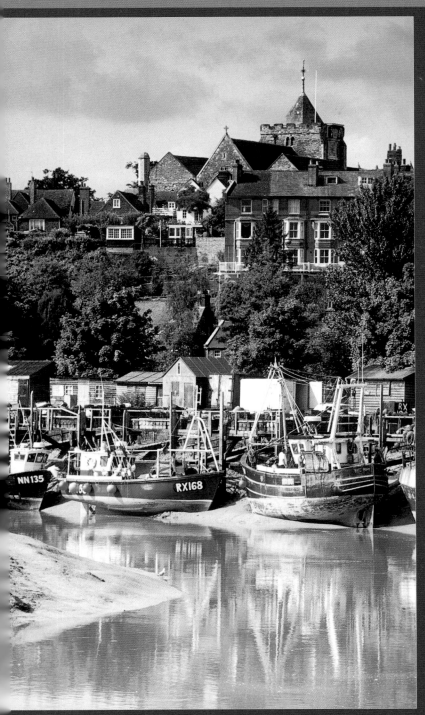

e Harbour

Brighton House

★★★★ ☖ GUEST ACCOMMODATION

Address: 52 Regency Square, BRIGHTON BN1 2FF
Tel: 01273 323282
Email: info@brighton-house.co.uk
Website: www.brighton-house.co.uk
Map ref: 3, TQ30
Directions: Opp West Pier
Rooms: 16 en suite, S £40–£60 D £65–£125
Notes: ⊗ on premises 🧒 under 12yrs

This charming Regency town house is perfectly placed for all
Brighton's attractions, including the beach, the Brighton Centre,
and shopping in The Lanes, and parking arrangements have
been made with nearby car parks for guests' benefit. Owners Christine and Lucho try to minimise
the impact that Brighton House has on the environment without compromising guests' comfort. Their
electricity supplies are from renewable sources, such as wind, and a new extension to the kitchen has
sedum roof. Recycling is taken seriously, with packaging kept to a minimum and through arrangement
with a local recycling co-operative. Bio-degradable waste is processed through a wormery. The smart
furnished bedrooms all have high quality beds and linens, TVs, Wi-fi access, hairdryers, tea- and
coffee-making facilities and fans for summer use. Double rooms come in a choice of small, standard
and superior, and single, twin and triple rooms are also available. The continental-style buffet breakfas
provides a broad choice of primarily organic and locally sourced produce, including locally smoked wil
salmon, large local organic eggs, free-range ham, organic cheeses, a good choice of cereals, fresh or
soya milk, and organic fruits and fruit juices. Children under the age of 12 cannot be accommodated.

Recommended in the area

Brighton Pavilion; Brighton seafront; South Downs

Five

★ ★ ★ ★ GUEST ACCOMMODATION

Address: 5 New Steine, BRIGHTON BN2 1PB
Tel: 01273 686547
Fax: 01273 625613
Email: info@fivehotel.com
Website: www.fivehotel.com
Map ref: 3, TQ30
Directions: Along A259 heading E, 8th turning on left into the square
Rooms: 10 (8 en suite), S £35–£75 D £70–£160
Notes: ⊗ on premises

Five, a period town house overlooking a classic Regency square, has far-reaching views and is only a few steps to the beach, bars and restaurants of the famous Lanes. The contemporary rooms are comfortable and well equipped, and benefit from crisp white linen, luxurious duvet, TV (some have DVD), Wi-fi and tea and coffee facilities. Some triple and family rooms are available. Breakfast, which includes organic bacon, eggs, mushrooms and fresh berries, is served in the bay-fronted dining room.
Recommended in the area
Brighton Pier; Brighton Pavilion; shopping in The Lanes

Lansdowne Guest House

★ ★ ★ ★ 🏠 GUEST ACCOMMODATION

Address: 3 The Red House, 21 Lansdowne Rd
HOVE BN3 1FE
Tel: 07803 484775
Fax: 01273 773718
Email: lansdowneguesthouse@hotmail.co.uk
Map ref: 3, TQ30
Rooms: 2 (1 en suite) (1 pri facs), S £65–£75
D £75–£85 **Notes:** ⊗ on premises
Closed: 24–27 Dec

Lansdowne Guest House is set in the middle of Pimlico-by-the-Sea, with its grand white Regency terraces close to the beach and promenade. The building is a 1920s mansion, built for a lord's mistress, with its own grounds just a few minutes' walk from the main shopping centre and the cobbled Lanes. Attentive, interesting, well-travelled hosts welcome guests into a big, friendly sitting room with a fire and candles for winter nights. The under-the-eaves bedrooms are stylish and modern with sitting areas, TVs, internet, fridges and kettles, and the compact bathrooms are stocked with toiletries.
Recommended in the area
Brighton Pavilion; The Lanes, Brighton Beach & Pier

New Steine

★ ★ ★ ★ GUEST ACCOMMODATION

Address: 10 New Steine, BRIGHTON & HOVE
BN2 1PB
Tel: 01273 695415 & 681546
Fax: 01273 622663
Email: reservation@newsteinehotel.com
Website: www.newsteinehotel.com
Map ref: 3, TQ30
Directions: A23 to Brighton Pier, left onto Marine
Parade, New Steine on left after Wentworth St
Rooms: 20 (16 en suite) (2 GF), **S** £32–£49 **D** £49–£125 **Notes:** ⛔ under 5yrs

Elegant and fashionable, this five-storey Georgian town house is located in central Brighton and is favoured by both business travellers and leisure guests. Decorated in chocolate and cream contemporary design, chic bedrooms are equipped with free Wi-fi, desk space, hairdryers, flat-screen LCD TVs, tea and coffee facilities and luxury toiletries. French food is served in the New Steine Bistro, prepared from local produce. A concierge service is 24 hours, and conference rooms are available.

Recommended in the area

The Royal Pavilion; Devil's Dyke; Brighton Museum & Art Gallery

Twenty One Guest House

★ ★ ★ ★ GUEST ACCOMMODATION

Address: 21 Charlotte Street, Marine Parade
BRIGHTON & HOVE BN2 1AG
Tel: 01273 686450
Email: enquiries@thetwentyone.co.uk
Website: www.thetwentyone.co.uk
Map ref: 3, TQ30
Directions: From Brighton Pier turn left on to
Marine Parade, 16th turning on left
Rooms: 8 en suite, **S** £45–£58 **D** £85–£139
Notes: ⊗ on premises

Just a few steps from the sea, at the heart of the lively and cosmopolitan Kemp Town area, this recently refurbished property is nonetheless quietly situated in a residential side street. All the bedrooms have new en suite shower rooms, flat-screen TVs with Freeview and a DVD player, DAB digital radio/alarms, iPod docks, hairdryers, toiletries, bathrobes, slippers, complimentary tea, coffee and mineral water and a mini fridge. Principal rooms have oblique sea views. Full English breakfast is available until 10.30am.

Recommended in the area

Royal Pavilion; The Lanes; Brighton Pier

Netherwood Lodge

★★★★ B&B

Address: Muddles Green, CHIDDINGLY, Nr Lewes
BN8 6HS
Tel: 01825 872512
Email: netherwoodlodge@hotmail.com
Website: www.netherwoodlodge.co.uk
Map ref: 4, TQ51
Directions: A22 at Golden Cross pub turn left. 0.5m
to T-junct then sharp right at white house & round
house. Down private road, Lodge 2nd on left
Rooms: 2 (1 en suite) (1 pri facs) (2 GF), **S** £45–£65 **D** £80–£90
Notes: ⊗ on premises ⛱ under 16yrs **Parking:** 5

In a village that was mentioned in the Domesday Book, surrounded by glorious countryside, this former coach house is now a mellow brick rural retreat with a pretty and secluded garden. The two bedrooms are both on the ground floor, and one has lovely views across farmland and woods. They are decorated with elegant simplicity and have oak furniture, Egyptian cotton bed linen and towels, silk and linen curtains and wool carpets. Extras include robes and slippers, TV with DVD player, a refrigerator and exclusive, eco-friendly toiletries imported from France. The private bathrooms are modern, with effective use made of pine and checkerboard floors. The traditional breakfast, featuring local organic produce and home-made bread, preserves and yoghurt, is just the start of the satisfying home cooking experience offered here. A three-course evening meal, by prior arrangement, might feature home-made soup, main courses such as steak and mushroom pie, and classic British desserts like fruit crumble. A vegetarian menu is also available. The dining room and drawing room are furnished with antiques and the latter has a log fire in winter, both looking out on to the beautifully seasonally changing gardens.

Recommended in the area

Glyndebourne; Herstmonceux Castle and Science Centre; Eastbourne

The Gables

★★★★★ B&B

Address: 21 Southfields Road, EASTBOURNE BN21 1BU
Tel: 01323 644600
Email: info@gablesbandb.co.uk
Website: www.gablesbandb.co.uk
Map ref: 4, TV69
Directions: A2270 into town centre, 2nd exit at rdbt by station, bear right into Southfields Rd
Rooms: 3 (2 en suite) (1 pri facs), D £68–£76
Notes: ⊗ on premises **Parking:** 2

Occupying a fine Edwardian detached house on a tree-lined street, this lovely guest house is personally run with great enthusiasm by owners Chrissy and Andy Mills, who are always on hand to offer knowledgeable suggestions to help visitors get the best from this corner of Sussex. The location offers the best of both worlds, being in a peaceful residential area yet only 15 minutes' walk from the seafront and five minutes from town-centre restaurants, pubs, theatre, cinema and station. The lounge is very relaxing, complete with a good range of books, board games and DVDs. Bedrooms are spacious, with light pouring in through the big windows, and there's a choice of king-size, double or twin beds. Two of the rooms have a fireplace, and all have en suite or private bathrooms. In-room facilities include a CD radio, Wi-fi access, a refreshment tray, mineral water and bathrobes. Breakfast is served at individual tables in the elegant dining room, and includes continental and freshly cooked choices, home-grown fruit in season, local free-range eggs and vegetarian sausages. There's a pretty garden to enjoy when the weather is fine.

Recommended in the area

South Downs Way; Long Man at Wilmington; Eastbourne Marina

The Manse B & B

★★★★★ B&B

Address: 7 Dittons Road, EASTBOURNE BN21 1DW
Tel: 01323 737851
Email: anne@themansebb.com
Website: www.themansebb.com
Map ref: 4, TV69
Directions: A22 to town centre railway station, onto Old Orchard Rd, right onto Arlington Rd
Rooms: 3 en suite, **S** £45–£55 **D** £74–£84
Notes: ⊗ on premises **Parking:** 2

This character home is in a quiet residential area only a 5-minute walk from the town centre. It was built as a Presbyterian manse in 1906 in the Arts and Crafts style and retains many original features such as oak panelling and stained-glass windows. The beautifully decorated en suite bedrooms are spacious and comfortable, and come with armchairs, digital TV/radio/DVD/CD, Wi-fi, tea and coffee trays and hairdryers. There is a wide variety of delicious breakfast options, using top quality, locally sourced produce. There's also continental or vegetarian options. Off-street parking for two vehicles.

Recommended in the area

South Downs and Beachy Head; Charleston Farmhouse (Bloomsbury group); Michelham Priory

The Mowbray

★★★★ GUEST ACCOMMODATION

Address: 2 Lascelles Terrace, EASTBOURNE
BN21 4BJ
Tel: 01323 720012
Email: info@themowbray.com
Website: www.themowbray.com
Map ref: 4, TV69
Directions: Opp Devonshire Park Theatre
Rooms: 13 en suite (1 GF), **S** £34–£45 **D** £68–£90

Just yards from the seafront and convenient for theatres and conference centres, this stylish place is on the corner of an elegant Edwardian terrace. The lounge bar on the ground floor is popular for afternoon tea or pre-theatre drinks, and the spacious dining room transforms from bright and sunny at breakfast time to a more sophisticated ambience for dinner. Home-cooked three-course meals are served early to suit theatre-goers, and lighter meals and snacks are available. The bedrooms, featuring particularly comfortable beds and a pillow menu, DVD players and welcome trays, are all front facing, some with views of the South Downs, and free Wi-fi is available throughout the building.

Recommended in the area

The South Downs Way; Pevensey Castle; Drusillas Park

Ocklynge Manor

★ ★ ★ ★ ★ B&B

Address: Mill Road, EASTBOURNE BN21 2PG
Tel: 01323 734121
Email: ocklyngemanor@hotmail.com
Website: www.ocklyngemanor.co.uk
Map ref: 4, TV69
Directions: From Eastbourne Hospital follow town centre/seafront sign, 1st right onto Kings Av, Ocklynge Manor at top of road
Rooms: 3 (2 en suite) (1 pri facs), S £45–£60 D £70–£80 **Notes:** ⊗ on premises ✦ under 16yrs **Parking:** 3

Instantly inviting, this 300-year-old house is set in extensive grounds and it's hard to imagine that you are just 10 minutes' walk from the centre of Eastbourne. The manor is on land that was previously occupied by a monastery, and this was also the site of a 12th-century Commandery of the Knights of St John of Jerusalem. More recently, according to a blue plaque, the house was once the home of the renowned children's book illustrator Mabel Lucie Atwell. Today, David and Wendy Dugdill welcome guests to the manor, providing a charming personal touch to every aspect of the place. The bedrooms, all accessed via the main staircase, are spacious and sunny, with views across the garden from the large windows. The decor and furnishings are comfortable and elegant, and top quality Egyptian cotton bed linen and towels are provided. Fresh flowers, a TV, DVD, radio, hairdryer and plenty of lamps are among the extra touches that so enhance a stay here. The bathrooms are modern and luxurious, and two adjoining rooms can be used as a suite which sleeps three. The public rooms include a gracious drawing room with grand piano and the beautiful garden is a lovely place to stroll on a summer evening. A full English breakfast is served in the dining room.

Recommended in the area

South Downs Way; Beachy Head; Great Dixter; Bodiam Castle; Bateman's

Tamberry Hall

★★★★★ GUEST ACCOMMODATION

Address: Eastbourne Road, HALLAND, Lewes
BN8 6PS

Tel: 01825 880090

Fax: 01825 880090

Email: rosi@tamberryhall.co.uk

Website: www.tamberryhall.co.uk

Map ref: 4, TQ41

Directions: In Halland on A22, 200yds N of junct
with B2192 at Black Lion Inn

Rooms: 3 en suite, **S** £65–£80 **D** £73–£85 **Notes:** ⊗ on premises **Parking:** 3

Tamberry Hall stands in 3.5 acres of grounds just six miles from Lewes. The house is beautiful, with exposed beams and a large inglenook fireplace. Furnished to a high standard, there is a drawing room and elegant dining room. The bedrooms vary in size and style, but all are en suite and equipped with beverage-making facilities, TV, fridge and hairdryer. An extensive breakfast is offered.

Recommended in the area

Lewes Castle; Barbican Museum; Anne of Cleves House

Parkside House

★★★★ GUEST ACCOMMODATION

Address: 59 Lower Park Road, HASTINGS
TN34 2LD

Tel: 01424 433096

Fax: 01424 421431

Email: bkentparksidehse@aol.com

Map ref: 4, TQ80

Directions: A2101 to town centre, right at rdbt,
1st right

Rooms: 5 (4 en suite), **D** £65–£75

Notes: ⊗ on premises

Parkside House is in a quiet conservation area opposite Alexandra Park, with its lakes, tennis courts and bowling green, yet is only a 15-minute walk from the seafront. The rooms are stylishly furnished, with many antique pieces, and generously equipped with video recorders, hairdryers, tongs, toiletries, bathrobes, and beverage trays. A good choice of breakfast – English or continental – is served at individual tables in the elegant dining room, and there is also an inviting lounge.

Recommended in the area

Battle Abbey; Bodiam Castle (NT); Michelham Priory

The Blacksmiths Arms

★★★★ ⬭ INN

Address: London Road, Offham, LEWES BN7 3QD
Tel: 01273 472971
Email: blacksmithsarms@tiscali.co.uk
Website: www.theblacksmithsarms-offham.co.uk
Map ref: 3, TQ41
Directions: 2m N of Lewes. On A275 in Offham
Rooms: 4 en suite, S £45–£55 D £60–£80
Notes: ⊗ on premises 🦺 under 5yrs **Parking:** 22

Situated just outside Lewes, this charming 18th-century inn is set amid beautiful surroundings in an Area of Outstanding Natural Beauty. Nestled beneath the Sussex Downs, this is a great location for touring the south coast. Each of the high-quality, comfortable double bedrooms at the Blacksmiths Arms features en suite bathroom, flat-screen TV and tea- and coffee-making facilities. All have been refurbished and are delightfully decorated. Downstairs, open log fires and a warm, relaxed atmosphere welcome you to the cosy bar, where excellent dinners and hearty breakfasts are freshly cooked to order. Evening diners can choose from the inventive brasserie-style menu, which draws from only the best local produce wherever possible, including fresh fish and seafood landed at local ports. Dishes here are much more than pub food, and might include roast local estate free-range venison, wild sea bass fillets on a seafood risotto with a lobster velouté drizzle, or Auntie Kate's fresh crispy roast duckling. Bernard Booker, the owner and chef of the Blacksmiths, has won awards for his seafood dishes, and award-winning, locally brewed Harveys Sussex Bitter is properly served in superb condition, another indication that the owners here like to do things properly.

Recommended in the area

Brighton; South Downs Way; Sheffield Park Gardens; Bluebell Railway; Glyndebourne Opera House

Nightingales

★ ★ ★ ★ GUEST ACCOMMODATION

Address: The Avenue, Kingston, LEWES BN7 3LL
Tel: 01273 475673
Fax: 01273 475673
Email: nightingalesbandb@googlemail.com
Website: www.users.totalise.co.uk/~nightingales
Map ref: 3, TQ41
Directions: please phone for directions
Rooms: 2 en suite (2 GF), **S** (occupancy) £45–£65
D £65–£75 **Notes:** ⊗ on premises **Parking:** 2

A spacious bungalow with a light and airy feel, Nightingales is set in a tree-lined avenue in the village of Kingston, with off-street parking provided. A footpath from the gardens leads directly to the South Downs Way, so it is a perfect base from which to explore this lovely area. Bedrooms are en suite and furnished with comfortable beds and equipped with flat-screen TVs and tea- and coffee-making facilities. Aga-cooked breakfasts are prepared from locally sourced produce, including eggs from the household hens. Afternoon tea is served beneath the tree in the front garden or by the log fire indoors.

Recommended in the area

Lewes Castle; Anne of Cleves House; Charleston; Glyndebourne Opera

Manor Farm Oast

★ ★ ★ ★ ★ 🛏 🍵 GUEST ACCOMMODATION

Address: Windmill Lane, ICKLESHAM TN36 4WL
Tel: 01424 813787
Fax: 01424 813787
Email: manor.farm.oast@lineone.net
Website: www.manorfarmoast.co.uk
Map ref: 4, TQ92
Directions: A259 W past church, left at x-rds onto Windmill Ln, after sharp left bend left into orchards
Rooms: 3 (2 en suite) (1 pri facs), **S** £69 **D** £99
Notes: ⊗ on premises 🧒 under 11yrs **Parking:** 7 **Closed:** 23 Dec–15 Jan

Built in 1860 and surrounded by a working orchard on the edge of the Icklesham, Manor Farm Oast is ideal for a quiet break. The oast house has been converted to keep the unusual original features both inside and out – the double bedroom in one tower is completely round. Your host Kate Mylrea provides a very friendly welcome. Kate is passionate about food: as well as a traditional English breakfast or a healthier alternative, she can prepare a top quality five-course dinner by arrangement.

Recommended in the area

Battle Abbey; historic Rye; Ellen Terry's House (NT)

Herstmonceux Castle

Strand House

★★★★ 🛏️ 🍴 GUEST ACCOMMODATION

Address: Tanyards Lane, Winchelsea RYE TN36 4JT
Tel: 01797 226276
Fax: 01797 224806
Email: info@thestrandhouse.co.uk
Website: www.thestrandhouse.co.uk
Map ref: 4, TQ92
Directions: A2070 to Lydd. A259 to Winchelsea
Rooms: 10 (9 en suite) (1 pri facs) (1 GF),
S £50–£75 D £70–£125 **Notes:** 🧒 under 12yrs
Parking: 12

Strand House provides a calm retreat from the stresses of modern living, with elegant rooms set in a historic Tudor house full of period detail, such as low, oak-beamed ceilings, winding stairs and inglenook fireplaces in the large lounge. Bedrooms are full of quality furniture and include thoughtful extras such as hand-made biscuits. Sussex breakfasts are provided. Afternoon tea, packed lunches and evening meals are all available – using organic local meat, fish from the boats at Rye Bay, plus home-made cakes.

Recommended in the area

Great Dixter; Sissinghurst; Romney Hythe and Dymchurch Railway

The Avondale

★ ★ ★ GUEST ACCOMMODATION
Address: Avondale Road, SEAFORD BN25 1RJ
Tel: 01323 890008
Fax: 01323 490598
Email: avondalehotel@btconnect.com
Website: www.theavondale.co.uk
Map ref: 3, TV49
Directions: In town centre, off A259 behind war memorial
Rooms: 14 (8 en suite), S £30–£42 D £55–£75
Notes: ⊗ on premises

The Avondale is conveniently positioned for both the town centre and the seafront, with Seaford Leisure Centre close by. Brighton, Eastbourne, the South Downs and many other places of interest are within easy reach. Guests frequently comment on how well they sleep in the spotlessly clean bedrooms. The beds are certainly comfortable, but the friendly service, relaxed atmosphere and fresh flowers also play their part in the home-from-home experience. Jane and Martin Home and their experienced staff spare no effort to make your stay relaxing and enjoyable, offering a perfect blend of modern comforts and traditional courtesy and service. First-floor bedrooms are accessible by stair lift and eight rooms have en suite facilities. All are equipped with free Wi-fi access, a hospitality tray, complimentary toiletries, radio and television, with a DVD player on request. An inviting lounge is available during the day for guests' use, and breakfast is served at individual tables in the spacious dining room. Guests appreciate the quality and choice of the breakfasts, and dinners and hot/cold buffets featuring home-cooked local produce can be catered for by arrangement. There are also plenty of good pubs and restaurants serving food in the area.

Recommended in the area

Beachy Head Countryside Centre; Firle Place; Clergy House Alfriston (NT)

11th-century Arundel Castle

The Townhouse

★ ★ ★ ★ ◉ RESTAURANT WITH ROOMS
Address: 65 High Street, ARUNDEL BN18 9AJ
Tel: 01903 883847
Website: www.thetownhouse.co.uk
Map ref: 4, TQ00
Directions: Follow A27 to Arundel, onto High Street,
establishment on left at top of hill
Rooms: 4 en suite, D £85–£120 **Notes:** ⊗ on
premises **Closed:** 2wks Feb & 2wks Oct

The Townhouse, an elegant Grade II listed building dating from around the 1800s, occupies a prime position opposite Arundel Castle. The spectacular carved ceiling in its dining room, however, is much older than the rest of the house; it originated in Florence and is a beautiful example of late Renaissance architecture. All of the en suite bedrooms here are sympathetically and tastefully decorated, and all benefit from TV, hairdryer and tea- and coffee-making facilities. The restaurant, too, is stylish, though informal, with owner/chef Lee Williams offering a diverse menu based on local produce and featuring fresh bread made on the premises, earning The Townhouse an AA Rosette.

Recommended in the area
Glorious Goodwood; Arundel Castle; Chichester Theatre

White Barn

★ ★ ★ ★ B&B
Address: Crede Lane, BOSHAM,Chichester,
PO18 8NX
Tel: 01243 573113
Fax: 01243 573113
Email: chrissie@whitebarn.biz
Website: www.whitebarn.biz
Map ref: 3, SU80
Directions: Please phone for directions
Rooms: 3 en suite (3 GF), S £60–£65 D £70–£95
Notes: ⊗ on premises ⋈ under 12yrs **Parking:** 3

The comfortable bedrooms at this guest house all have colour co-ordinated soft furnishings and many thoughtful extras. The Goodwood Room is a mini-suite with its own access and is themed round the nearby Goodwood Estate, while the twin Honeysuckle Room has a small patio for rest and relaxation. The open-plan and glass-walled dining room overlooks an attractive garden, where breakfasts, made from fresh, locally sourced ingredients, are served if weather permits.

Recommended in the area
Chichester; Goodwood Race Circuit; Portsmouth; South Downs

West Stoke House

★★★★★ ◉◉◉ RESTAURANT WITH ROOMS
Address: Downs Road, West Stoke, CHICHESTER
PO18 9BN
Tel: 01243 575226
Fax: 01243 574655
Email: info@weststokehouse.co.uk
Website: www.weststokehouse.co.uk
Map ref: 3, SU80
Directions: 3m NW of Chichester. Off B286 to West
Stoke, next to St Andrew's Church
Rooms: 8 (7 en suite) (1 pri facs), **S** £95–£115 **D** £130–£215 **Parking:** 20 **Closed:** 24–28 Dec

This fine country house, part Georgian and part medieval, with over 5 acres of manicured lawns and gardens, lies on the edge of the South Downs. Guests can enjoy a game of croquet on the lawns, or view the artworks exhibited in the semi-permanent West Stoke House Art Space. The large, uncluttered bedrooms at this exclusive restaurant with rooms have smart modern bathrooms and great country views, and parts of the original timber beams can still be seen in the attic bedrooms. Thoughtful touches include white linen bedding and fresh flowers in every room, as well as flat-screen televisions and DVD players. For those looking for something different, one room has a round double bed, providing Hollywood glamour. The restaurant has a relaxed atmosphere and produces very good food from a modern British menu with French influences; wines can be chosen from an interesting and varied list. Hearty breakfasts are made from local produce where possible, with eggs coming from West Stoke free-range hens. Public rooms, including the spacious Grand Ballroom, have a light-filled elegance and are adorned with an eclectic mix of period furniture and contemporary art.

Recommended in the area

The Witterings; Chichester Cathedral; Goodwood

The Lawn Guest House

★★★★ GUEST HOUSE

Address: 30 Massetts Road, HORLEY RH6 7DF
Tel: 01293 775751
Fax: 01293 821803
Email: info@lawnguesthouse.co.uk
Website: www.lawnguesthouse.co.uk
Map ref: 3, TQ24
Directions: In Massetts Rd, 200yds on left
Rooms: 12 en suite, S £45–£50 D £60 **Parking:** 15

This imposing Victorian house is set in pretty gardens just five minutes' drive from Gatwick Airport and two minutes' walk from Horley's centre with its shops, restaurants, pubs and banks. The main line railway station is 300 yards away. All en suite bedrooms, some with both bath and shower, include colour/text televisions, hairdryers, hospitality trays, direct-dial telephones, modem sockets and adjustable central heating. There's online computer access in the lounge. Full English breakfast and healthy alternatives are served, and an extensive continental breakfast for early departures. Overnight parking is available on site and long-term parking/airport transfers are available by arrangement.

Recommended in the area

The Old Mill; Saint Hill Manor; High Beeches Gardens

Amberfold

★★★★ GUEST ACCOMMODATION

Address: Amberfold, Heyshott, MIDHURST
GU29 0DA
Tel: 01730 812385
Fax: 01730 813559
Email: erlingamberfold@aol.com
Website: www.amberfold.co.uk
Map ref: 3, SU82
Directions: Off A286 signed Graffham/Heyshott, after 1.5m pass pond, Amberfold on left
Rooms: 2 en suite (2 GF), S £55–£75 D £75–£95 **Notes:** ⊗ on premises ❧ under 14yrs **Parking:** 2
Closed: 16 Dec–8 Feb

This delightful 17th-century, Grade II listed cottage is set in mature and attractive gardens in quiet, idyllic countryside on the outskirts of Heyshott – only a five-minute drive from historic Midhurst. Each of the charming bedrooms (one twin, two doubles and one suite) has its own private entrance, a shower room, TV, hospitality trolley, fridge and hairdryer. Breakfast is served in the Amberfold main house.

Recommended in the area

Singleton Open-Air Museum; Goodwood Estate; Cowdrey Park ruins and polo grounds

Rivermead House

★★★★★ B&B

Address: Hollist Lane, MIDHURST GU29 9RS
Tel: 01730 810907
Email: mail@bridgetadler.com
Website: www.bridgetadler.com
Map ref: 3, SU82
Directions: 1m NW of Midhurst. Off A286
towards Woolbeding
Rooms: 1 en suite Notes: ⊗ on premises
Parking: 2 Closed: 24–26 Dec

This gracious Sussex home is set in a semi-rural location on the edge of Midhurst, and the bedroom has glorious country views, with the South Downs in the distance. It is light and spacious, with room for a pur-up bed or cot for children, and is equipped with TV, tea- and coffee-making facilities, hairdryer and radio alarm. A full English breakfast is served informally in the farmhouse-style kitchen, and evening meals are available if booked in advance. Pets are welcome, though not in the bedroom.
Recommended in the area
Weald and Downland Open-Air Museum; Goodwood; Chichester

Orchard Mead

★★★★ B&B

Address: Toat Lane, PULBOROUGH RH20 1BZ
Tel: 01798 872640
Email: siggy.rutherford@ukonline.co.uk
Map ref: 3, TQ01
Directions: Off A29 1m N of Pulborough onto
Blackgate Ln, left onto Pickhurst Ln & right onto
Toat Ln, Orchard Mead at end
Rooms: 2 en suite (2 GF), D £75–£80
Notes: ⊗ on premises ✹ under 12yrs
Parking: 2 Closed: Xmas & Etr

A long, winding road leads you to this delightful detached home. It is set in a peaceful rural location, yet is only a short drive from the local train station. The en suite bedrooms are comfortably furnished and provide thoughtful touches, such as pure cotton sheets and fluffy towels. As well as breakfast, a delicious light supper or full dinner can be provided on request, and there are also many good eateries nearby. Guests at Orchard Mead are welcome to make use of the drawing room and the garden.
Recommended in the area
Arundel Castle; Pulborough Brooks RSPB Nature Reserve; Horsham Museum

Landseer House

★★★★ B&B

Address: Cow Lane, SIDLESHAM, Chichester,
PO20 7LN
Tel/Fax: 01243 641525
Email: enq@landseerhouse.co.uk
Website: www.landseerhouse.co.uk
Map ref: 3, SZ89
Directions: Please phone for directions
Rooms: 4 (3 en suite) (1 pri facs), **S** £75–£120
D £80–£150 **Notes:** ✿ under 12yrs **Parking:** 12

This elegant country house is set in 4.5 acres of landscaped gardens and meadowland with meandering footpaths. With far-reaching views across the Solent and to the Isle of Wight, it is well located for the beautiful West Sussex coast. Close to Pagham harbour and nature reserve, there's a lovely relaxed atmosphere here, amid a decor of pale walls, antiques and fine paintings. The comfortable bedrooms are spacious, furnished to an excellent standard and full of sunlight from windows that offer lovely views. Full English and continental breakfasts are served in a lovely conservatory-style breakfast room.
Recommended in the area
Chichester Festival Theatre; Goodwood; Fishbourne Roman Palace

The Beacons

★★★★ GUEST ACCOMMODATION

Address: 18 Shelley Road, WORTHING BN11 1TU
Tel: 01903 230948
Email: thebeacons@btconnect.com
Map ref: 3, TQ10
Directions: 0.5m W of town centre. Off A259
Richmond Rd onto Crescent Rd & 3rd left
Rooms: 8 en suite (3 GF), **S** £40–£45 **D** £70–£80
Parking: 8

The Beacons is conveniently situated for all local amenities, including the shopping centre, marine garden, theatres, nightclubs, pier and promenade. The bowling greens at Beach House Park and Marine Gardens are only a short walk from the house. It is also well placed for touring the south coast and the towns of Brighton, Chichester and Arundel are within easy reach. The bedrooms all have TV, tea- and coffee-making facilities, hairdryer and clock. Breakfast, served at individual tables, is taken in the dining room and there is a comfortable lounge to relax in after a busy day sightseeing. There is ample parking on the premises. Dogs are allowed in rooms with prior arrangement.
Recommended in the area
Brighton Pavilion; The Lanes, Brighton; South Downs

Fulking Escarpment

The Conifers

★★★★ GUEST ACCOMMODATION

Address: 43 Parkfield Road, WORTHING BN13 1EP
Tel: 01903 265066
Email: conifers@hews.org.uk
Website: www.theconifers.org.uk
Map ref: 3, TQ10
Directions: A24 or A27 onto A2031 at Offington rdbt, over lights, Parkfield Rd 5th right
Rooms: 2 (1 pri facs), S £40–£50 D £70–£100
Family suite £140 **Notes:** ⊗ on premises
👪 under 12yrs **Parking:** 2 **Closed:** Xmas

The Conifers is an immaculately kept art deco building quietly located in West Worthing, with on-street parking. Complimentary tea and home-made cakes are served in the award-winning garden on arrival. South-facing bedrooms comprise a twin and a large double room with a king-size bed; both have TVs, courtesy trays, hairdryers, fluffy robes and complimentary chocolates. A varied menu is offered at breakfast, including the full English or a lighter meal with rolls, croissants, yoghurts and fresh fruit.
Recommended in the area
Tarring village; Highdown Gardens; Arundel

Moorings

★★★★ GUEST ACCOMMODATION

Address: 4 Selden Road, WORTHING BN11 2LL
Tel: 01903 208882
Email: themooringsworthing@hotmail.co.uk
Website: www.mooringsworthing.co.uk
Map ref: 3, TQ10
Directions: 0.5m E of pier off A259 towards Brighton
Rooms: 6 en suite **Notes:** ⊗ on premises

Colourful container plants and window boxes greet guests to this fine Victorian house, in a quiet residential area yet handy for the seafront and town centre. Inside, the spacious rooms are beautifully decorated, in keeping with the age of the house, and the good-sized bedrooms have co-ordinated colour schemes, original fireplaces, teddy bears on the beds and light flooding in from the big windows. Each has a TV and tea- and coffee-making facilities, and two are large enough to accommodate a family. In addition to the stylish dining room, there's a cosy lounge, with books, magazines and games.
Recommended in the area
Pier and seafront; Aquarena; Bowling Greens

Henley Street in Stratford-upon-Avon

Chapel House

★★★★★ ◎ RESTAURANT WITH ROOMS

Address:	Friar's Gate, ATHERSTONE, CV9 1EY
Tel:	01827 718949
Fax:	01827 717702
Email:	info@chapelhouse.eu
Website:	www.chapelhouse.eu
Map ref:	3, SP39

Directions: A5 to town centre, right onto Church St.
Right onto Sheepy Rd & left onto Friar's Gate
Rooms: 12 en suite **Notes:** ⊗ on premises
Closed: Etr wk, Aug BH wk & Xmas wk

Peacefully set in the heart of a charming market town, this fine Georgian town house glows with a mellow ambience that befits its age. Built in 1728, it retains many original features and is set in a pretty walled garden. Each of the spacious bedrooms has an individual decor, luxurious linens and the en suite bathrooms have power showers. Wi-fi internet access is available. Dinner is a highlight, offering a menu of impressive dishes. Crisp white linen, fine silverware and candlelight add to the atmosphere.
Recommended in the area
Warwick Castle; National Exhibition Centre; National Memorial Arboretum

Fulready Manor

★★★★★ ⌂ B&B

Address:	Fulready, ETTINGTON,
	Stratford-upon-Avon, CV37 7PE
Tel:	01789 740152
Fax:	01789 740247
Email:	stay@fulreadymanor.co.uk
Website:	www.fulreadymanor.co.uk
Map ref:	3, SP24

Directions: 2.50m SE of Ettington. 0.5m S off A422
at Pillerton Priors
Rooms: 3 en suite, **D** £120–£140 **Notes:** ⊗ on premises ⚊ under 15yrs **Parking:** 6

Set in 125 acres, this luxury new home appears from afar to be a 16th-century castle. Full of character, the entrance hall has a stone fireplace and a floor-to-ceiling front window while one of the en suite bedrooms has a four-poster bed with gold-embroidered muslin. The Manor offers old-fashioned comfort and the breakfasts are a feast.
Recommended in the area
Warwick Castle; Warwick; Royal Shakespeare Theatre, Stratford-upon-Avon; The Cotswolds

Victoria Lodge

★★★★ GUEST ACCOMMODATION

Address: 180 Warwick Road, KENILWORTH
CV8 1HU
Tel: 01926 512020
Fax: 01926 858703
Email: info@victorialodgehotel.co.uk
Website: www.victorialodgehotel.co.uk
Map ref: 3, SP27
Directions: 250yds SE of town centre on A452 opp
St John's Church
Rooms: 10 en suite (2 GF), **S** £49–£62 **D** £72–£80 **Notes:** ⊗ on premises **Parking:** 9
Closed: 24 Dec–1 Jan

Victoria Lodge is a family-run establishment which has been extended to provide a range of well-equipped, individually styled bedrooms. The smart contemporary breakfast room serves up full English or vegetarian options, and there is a licensed bar and comfortable guest lounge. In addition, guests have access to private, off-road parking and Wi-fi broadband internet connection.

Recommended in the area

Warwick Castle; NEC, Birmingham; NAC Royal Show Ground, Stoneleigh

---

The Adams

★★★★ GUEST ACCOMMODATION

Address: 22 Avenue Road, LEAMINGTON SPA
CV31 3PQ
Tel: 01926 450742
Fax: 01926 313110
Email: bookings@adams-hotel.co.uk
Website: www.adams-hotel.co.uk
Map ref: 3, SP36
Directions: Off A452 Adelaide Rd onto Avenue Rd
Rooms: 10 en suite (2 GF), **S** £68.50 **D** £85–£90

Notes: ⊗ on premises ✦ under 12yrs **Parking:** 14 **Closed:** 23 Dec–2 Jan

Built in 1827, The Adams is an elegant Regency townhouse, where the emphasis is on peace and quiet, a comfortable night's sleep and freshly cooked breakfasts from the Aga. Guests can relax in the bar/lounge or sit outside in the charming walled garden. The Adams is situated just a few minutes' level walk from the town centre, the Pump Rooms, Jephson Gardens, Royal Spa Centre Theatre and several highly recommended restaurants. Off road parking is available. The house is totally non-smoking.

Recommended in the area

Warwick Castle; Stratford-upon-Avon; The Cotswolds

Holly End Bed & Breakfast

★★★★ 🛏 B&B

Address: London Road, SHIPSTON ON STOUR
CV36 4EP
Tel: 01608 664064
Email: hollyend.hunt@btinternet.com
Website: www.holly-end.co.uk
Map ref: 3, SP24
Directions: 0.5m S of Shipston on Stour on A3400
Rooms: 3 (2 en suite) (1 pri facs), **S** £50–£60
D £75–£100 **Notes:** ⊗ on premises 🚼 under 9yrs
Parking: 6

Holly End provides top-drawer accommodation on the edge of the Cotswolds, midway between Moreton-in-Marsh and Stratford-upon-Avon. Whether your preferences lie with long country hikes and exploring quaint Cotswold villages or discovering the history and culture of Shakespeare country, this bed and breakfast is suitably placed for both. The modern detached family house, immaculately maintained and spotlessly clean, is just a short walk from the centre of Shipston on Stour. Shipston, once an important sheep market town, was also an important stop for coaches, and many of the inns in the High Street date from that era. The spacious, comfortable bedrooms – king-size, twin and double – with subtle soft furnishings and decor have shower-baths, while dormer windows add to the character. You can pamper yourself with the Sanctuary spa products provided in each room. Colour televisions and tea- and coffee-making facilities are also provided. A comprehensive freshly cooked English breakfast uses the best of local produce (organic wherever possible). Afternoon tea or sherry and snacks are offered on arrival. There is a beautiful sunny garden with a lawn and patio dotted with many container plants.

Recommended in the area

Stratford-upon-Avon; Hidcote Manor (NT); Warwick Castle; Cotswold Falconry Centre

Beauchamp Chapel in St Mary's church

Ambleside

★ ★ ★ ★ GUEST HOUSE

Address: 41 Grove Road, STRATFORD-UPON-AVON
CV37 6PB
Tel: 01789 297239
Fax: 01789 295670
Email: ruth@amblesideguesthouse.com
Website: www.amblesideguesthouse.com
Map ref: 3, SP25
Directions: On A4390 opp Firs Park
Rooms: 6 (5 en suite) (1 GF), **S** £28–£32
D £60–£80 **Notes:** ⊗ on premises ⬥ under 5yrs **Parking:** 7

Ambleside is a comfortable guest house in the heart of Stratford-upon-Avon, where owners Ruth and Peter provide a warm welcome. A refurbishment has left the house in sparkling condition, and the accommodation can suit every need. Choose from the family rooms, one of which is situated on the ground floor, a double, twin or singles. Many rooms have shower rooms en suite, and each room is equipped with a TV, hairdryer and a hospitality tray. Ironing facilities are also available. The choice at breakfast ensures that everyone is satisfied and both the traditional full English breakfast and vegetarian options are freshly cooked. Breakfast is served in the bright and spacious dining room, which looks over the charming front patio garden. Ambleside stands opposite the attractive gardens of Firs Park and is just a short stroll into the town centre where there is a good choice of restaurants, cafés and inns. As well as the Shakespeare attractions, Stratford-upon-Avon offers a wide range of shops and ancient buildings and the benefit of town trails to guide the visitor around this interesting town. Free on-site parking and Wi-fi.

Recommended in the area

Shakespeare's birthplace; The Courtyard Theatre; Anne Hathaway's Cottage; Warwick Castle; Warwick

Arden Way Guest House

★★★ GUEST HOUSE
Address: 22 Shipston Road,
STRATFORD-UPON-AVON, CV37 7LP
Tel/Fax: 01789 205646
Email: info@ardenwayguesthouse.co.uk
Website: www.ardenwayguesthouse.co.uk
Map ref: 3, SP25
Directions: On A3400 S of River Avon, 100mtrs
Rooms: 6 (5 en suite) (1 pri facs) (2 GF), **S** £28–£55
D £56–£68 **Parking:** 6

A friendly, family-run guest house close to all the amenities of the town centre and just a few minutes from the theatres. To the back of the house there is a large garden with a summer house, while at the front there is ample space for guests' cars. The bedrooms are attractively decorated and all have en suite facilities except for one single room, which has a private bathroom. All the rooms have Freeview flat-screen TVs, Wi-fi access and tea- and coffee-making equipment. A hearty breakfast is served in the dining room which overlooks the garden. Special diets are catered for on request.
Recommended in the area
Shakespeare properties; The Cotswolds; Warwick Castle

Victoria Spa Lodge

★★★★ GUEST HOUSE
Address: Bishopton Lane, Bishopton
STRATFORD-UPON-AVON CV37 9QY
Tel: 01789 267985
Fax: 01789 204728
Email: ptozer@victoriaspalodge.demon.co.uk
Website: www.stratford-upon-avon.co.uk/
victoriaspa.htm
Map ref: 3, SP25
Directions: A3400 1.5m N to junct A46, 1st left
onto Bishopton Ln, 1st house on right
Rooms: 7 en suite, **S** £50–£55 **D** £65–£70 **Notes:** ⊗ **Parking:** 12 **Closed:** Xmas & New Year

An elegant Victorian Grade II listed building originally opened by Queen Victoria in 1837. It was also the home of cartoonist Bruce Bairnsfather. Overlooking the canal it is only a 20-minute walk from the town. The beautifully appointed bedrooms offer spacious comfort with quality furniture, stylish fabrics and thoughtful touches as well as Wi-fi. Expect a warm welcome and high standards of service.
Recommended in the area
Warwick Castle; Shakespeare theatres & properties; The Cotswolds

ISLE OF WIGHT

The Needles on the Isle of Wight

The ruins of Carisbrooke Castle

Blandings

★★★★ B&B

Address: Horringford, ARRETON, Nr Newport,
PO30 3AP
Tel: 01983 865720
Fax: 01983 862099
Email: robin.oulton@horringford.com
Website: www.horringford.com/bedandbreakfast.htm
Map ref: 3, SZ58
Directions: S through Arreton (B3056), pass
Stickworth Hall on right, 300yds on left farm entrance
signed Horringford Gdns. U-turn to left, at end of poplar trees turn right. Blandings on left
Rooms: 1 en suite (1 GF), **D** £60 **Parking:** 3

Set within a small group of farm buildings, Blandings has a delightful rural setting with pleasant views
of the Downs. On warm sunny days its wooden sun deck is a good place to enjoy breakfast or relax
with an evening sundowner. The cycle route from Cowes to Sandown (A23) runs past the front gate and
cycles and equipment are available for hire in the village and can be delivered ready for use.
Recommended in the area
Osborne House; beaches at Sandown, Shanklin and Ryde; Bembridge; Newport

The Lawns

★★★★ GUEST ACCOMMODATION

Address: 72 Broadway, SANDOWN PO36 9AA
Tel: 01983 402549
Email: lawnshotel@aol.com
Website: www.lawnshotelisleofwight.co.uk
Map ref: 3, SZ58
Directions: On A3055 N of town centre
Rooms: 13 en suite (2 GF),
S £29–£36 D £58–£88
Notes: ⊗ on premises
Parking: 15

A warm welcome always awaits you at the Lawns, which has been lovingly upgraded by owners Nick and Stella to provide every home comfort. The Lawns was built in 1865 and stands in its own southwest-facing gardens offering ample parking. Situated in the pleasing area of Sandown, it is just a short walk away from a blue-flag beach, public transport and the town centre, with its restaurants and shops, and is an ideal base from which to explore the rest of the island. Other local attractions on offer include the pier, go-karting, crazy golf and the Tiger and Big Cat Sanctuary, as well as many opportunities to take part in water sports. The Lawns has a comfortable lounge, with Freeview TV and a selection of games available, as well as a bar. Evening meals are available by arrangement. Service is friendly and attentive, and the bedrooms, two of which are on the ground floor, include a four-poster room and two superior rooms. All are comfortably equipped with flat-screen TVs and hospitality trays. All bathrooms are of a very high standard and include wall-mounted hairdryers.

Recommended in the area

Isle of Wight Zoo; Dinosaur Isle; Sandown Pier

Foxhills

★★★★★ 🛏 GUEST ACCOMMODATION

Address: 30 Victoria Avenue, SHANKLIN PO37 6LS
Tel: 01983 862329
Fax: 01983 866666
Email: info@foxhillsofshanklin.co.uk
Website: www.foxhillsofshanklin.co.uk
Map ref: 3, SZ58
Directions: A3020 from Shanklin centre towards Newport, Foxhills 450yds on left
Rooms: 8 en suite (1 GF) **S** £44–£108 **D** £88–£118
Notes: ⊗ on premises 👪 under 14yrs **Parking:** 13 **Closed:** 3–31 Jan

Every effort is made to pamper guests at this superbly maintained establishment. It is set in beautiful gardens just a short walk from Shanklin town and Old Village with its multitude of restaurants and pubs, the Chine and the downs. Hospitality is exemplary, and you are welcomed with tea and chocolates on arrival. There are high levels of comfort in the en suite bedrooms, with DVD/CD players (plus comprehensive library of DVDs), direct-dial telephones, hairdryers and refreshment trays all provided. Wi-fi is also available. For that special occasion the four-poster Osborne suite has a touch of modernised Victorian luxury. Bathrooms are beautifully fitted with quality units, and furnished with luxury towels, dressing gowns and toiletries. The large whirlpool spa is free and available for private sessions. Health and beauty treatments are relaxing options, or else take a drink or afternoon tea in front of the log fire. Comprehensive room packs are supplied with routes for local walks, bike rides and car tours.

Recommended in the area

Shanklin Chine; Carisbrooke Castle; Osborne House; Bembridge Down

The Grange

★★★★ GUEST ACCOMMODATION

Address: 9 Eastcliff Road, SHANKLIN PO37 6AA
Tel: 01983 867644
Fax: 01983 865537
Email: jenni@thegrangebythesea.com
Website: www.thegrangebythesea.com
Map ref: 3, SZ58
Directions: Off A3055, High St
Rooms: 16 en suite (6 GF), **S** £73–£81 **D** £96–£112
Notes: ⊗ on premises **Parking:** 8

Situated in the heart of Shanklin's Old Village, and only moments from its long, sandy beach, The Grange is the perfect retreat from the hectic pace of modern life. It enjoys a tranquil yet convenient setting and its atmosphere is friendly and relaxed. Built in the 1820s, it has original features such as the ornate, carved fireplace in the lounge which is now complemented by a collection of paintings and sculptures ranging in style from bold and striking to classic and elegant. The beautifully presented bedrooms, some on the ground floor, are decorated in natural tones that mirror the surrounding environment, and power showers and complimentary luxury toiletries ensure a great start to each day. In addition, there are a wide range of inspirational courses and activities available including yoga, massage and beauty treatments, coastline walks, creative writing and art. The cuisine uses the freshest ingredients, local and organic where possible, and breakfast and morning coffee can be enjoyed in the garden in fine weather. There is a sauna, and Wi-fi is available.

Recommended in the area

Shanklin Chine; Tiger Sanctuary in Sandown; Brading Roman Villa

The Leconfield

★★★★★ ✪ ♨ GUEST ACCOMMODATION

Address: 85 Leeson Road, Upper Bonchurch
VENTNOR PO38 1PU
Tel: 01983 852196
Fax: 01983 856525
Email: enquiries@leconfieldhotel.com
Website: www.leconfieldhotel.com
Map ref: 3, SZ57
Directions: On A3055, 3m from Old Shanklin village
Rooms: 12 en suite (3 GF), **S** £48–£57 **D** £92–£194
Notes: ⊗ on premises ☆ under 16yrs **Parking:** 14

Paul, Cheryl and their small team welcome you to their home on the Isle of Wight. The delightful Victorian house is elevated 400-feet above sea level and nestles into St Boniface Down in an Area of Outstanding Natural Beauty. There are views of the sea from nearly all the bedrooms, the sitting rooms, dining room, conservatory and garden. The Leconfield is on the island's south side and its unique micro climate is perfect for a break in the quieter winter months, while in the summer months guests can enjoy the heated outdoor swimming pool in the delightful gardens; a strictly adults-only oasis. Luxurious, individually designed bedrooms, some at ground-floor level, are equipped with en suite facilities, TVs with DVD players, hairdryers, hospitality trays, bathrobes and quality complimentary toiletries. A hearty breakfast prepared from local produce and free-range eggs is served in the Seascape Dining Room with its panoramic sea views. After a day of exploring the island's many treasures you'll be welcomed back to an AA rosette standard evening meal with your choice from a wide selection of wines and other drinks. Your only distraction from this relaxing ambience will be tranquil shipping activity on the open seas.

Recommended in the area

Ventnor Gardens; Carisbrooke Castle; Osborne House

St Maur

★★★★ GUEST ACCOMMODATION

Address: Castle Road, VENTNOR PO38 1LG
Tel: 01983 852570
Fax: 01983 852306
Email: sales@stmaur.co.uk
Website: www.stmaur.co.uk
Map ref: 3, SZ57
Directions: Exit A3055 at end of Park Ave onto Castle Rd, premises 150yds on left
Rooms: 9 en suite, D £76–£110
Notes: ⊗ on premises ⚲ under 5yrs
Parking: 9 **Closed:** Dec

Built in 1876, this Victorian villa has been run by the same family since 1966. St Maur is set in an elevated position overlooking Ventnor Park in one of the prettiest areas of the island, with sandy beaches, idyllic countryside, quaint villages and a variety of entertainment to suit every mood. The large sub-tropical gardens are a delight; there is a profusion of colour the whole year round and wonderful fragrances to waft about your pathway to the front door. In summer the lawn provides the perfect place for soaking up the sun. Most of the ample bedrooms, with double, twin or queen-size beds, have been refurbished. All have good size bathrooms and are equipped with TVs, tea- and coffee-making facilities, clock radios, complimentary toiletries and hairdryers. Some rooms have sea views, and balconies or decking. A spacious lounge on the grand Victorian scale overlooks the garden and provides a quiet place to sit, read and enjoy your coffee and mints after dinner. Alternatively there is a cosy licensed bar where you can relax over a drink. A comprehensive full English breakfast gets the day off to a satisfying start and a six-course dinner is on offer.

Recommended in the area

Appuldurcombe House; Blackgang Chine Fantasy Park; Ventnor Botanic Gardens

Stourhead

Sunset over Stonehenge

Home Farm

★ ★ ★ ★ B&B

Address: Farleigh Road, Wingfield TROWBRIDGE
BA14 9LG
Tel/Fax: 01225 764492
Email: info@homefarm-guesthouse.co.uk
Website: www.homefarm-guesthouse.co.uk
Map ref: 2, ST86
Directions: 2m S in Wingfield village on A366
Rooms: 3 en suite (1 GF) **Notes:** ⊗ on premises
Parking: 30

Home Farm is an imaginative conversion of what were originally cattle stalls, feeding rooms and a hay loft belonging to Wingfield House. It fronts onto the original farmyard, which provides ample private parking. There is a 2-acre garden and a large, comfortably furnished lounge to relax in. Breakfasts, cooked on an Aga, offer a wide selection including fish dishes, and home-made bread is a feature. Spacious bedrooms comprise a family room, a double, and a ground-floor twin. All en suite rooms have dual-aspect windows, television, radio, hairdryer, trouser press, bathrobes and hospitality tray.
Recommended in the area
Roman Baths, Bath; Longleat; Stonehenge

The George & Dragon

★★★★ ◉◉ RESTAURANT WITH ROOMS
Address: High Street, ROWDE, Devizes, SN10 2PN
Tel: 01380 723053
Email: thegandd@tiscali.co.uk
Website: www.thegeorgeanddragonrowde.co.uk
Map ref: 2, ST96
Directions: 1.5m from Devizes on A350 towards Chippenham
Rooms: 3 (2 en suite) (1 pri facs), D £75
Notes: ⊗ on premises **Parking:** 15

A 16th-century coaching inn, the George & Dragon retains many original features, including exposed beams with the carved Tudor rose and large open fireplaces. Wooden floors, antique rugs and candlelit tables create a warm atmosphere in the bar and restaurant. The inn is located on the village high street in Rowde which is only a couple of miles from Devizes and not far from the Caen Hill lock flight on the Kennet & Avon Canal. Accommodation is provided in individually designed bedrooms, furnished with large double beds made up with luxurious bed linens. Two of the bedrooms are en suite while the third has its own private bathroom. All are equipped with flat-screen televisions with DVD players, iPod stations and tea- and coffee-making facilities. The inn has AA rosettes for its food, so dining in the bar or restaurant should not be missed. The house speciality is fresh fish delivered daily from Cornwall, but a full carte menu is offered featuring local produce, meats and game and is available in both the restaurant and bar. Events are held throughout the year, including the likes of summer barbeques, wine and cheese tastings, games nights and charity quizzes.

Recommended in the area

Bowood House & Gardens; Roman Baths & Pump Room; Stonehenge

The Old House

★★★★ GUEST ACCOMMODATION

Address: 161 Wilton Road, SALISBURY SP2 7JQ
Tel: 01722 333433
Fax: 01722 335551
Map ref: 3, SU12
Directions: 1m W of city centre on A36
Rooms: 7 en suite, **S** £38–£60 **D** £60–£65
Notes: ⊗ on premises ⋠ under 7yrs **Parking:** 10

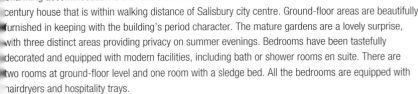

Charming accommodation is offered at this 17th-century house that is within walking distance of Salisbury city centre. Ground-floor areas are beautifully furnished in keeping with the building's period character. The mature gardens are a lovely surprise, with three distinct areas providing privacy on summer evenings. Bedrooms have been tastefully decorated and equipped with modern facilities, including bath or shower rooms en suite. There are two rooms at ground-floor level and one room with a sledge bed. All the bedrooms are equipped with hairdryers and hospitality trays.

Recommended in the area

Stourhead (NT); Heale Garden; Wilton House

Salisbury Old Mill House

★★★★ B&B

Address: Warminster Road, South Newton,
SALISBURY SP2 0QD
Tel: 01722 742458
Email: salisburymill@yahoo.com
Map ref: 3, SU12
Directions: 4m NW of Salisbury on A36
Rooms: 4 en suite, **S** £30–£45 **D** £55–£85 **Notes:**
⊗ on premises **Parking:** 10 **Closed:** 25 Dec & 1 Jan

This establishment offers the opportunity to stay in a beautifully converted mill mentioned in the Domesday Book. Only four miles from Salisbury, the Old Mill is set in the rolling hills of the Wylie Valley, within easy reach of Bath and the New Forest. It is also within striking distance of the South Coast, including Poole Harbour and the Portsmouth Historical Dockyard. The area is excellent for outdoor activities and you could learn fly fishing or shooting with the Old Mill's fully qualified APSI instructor. The premises are licensed and delicious meals are prepared from local produce. Broadband is provided for guests, and a luxury private apartment is available.

Recommended in the area

Stonehenge; Longleat House; Salisbury Cathedral

Ardecca

★★★★ GUEST ACCOMMODATION

Address: Fieldrise Farm, Kingsdown Lane,
Blunsdon, SWINDON SN25 5DL
Tel: 01793 721238
Email: chris-graham.ardecca@fsmail.net
Website: www.ardecca-bedandbreakfast.co.uk
Map ref: 3, SU18
Directions: Off A419 for Blunsdon & Swindon, onto
B4019. Right at Cold Harbour pub, 1st on left
Rooms: 4 pri facs (4 GF), S £40–£60 D £60
Notes: ⊗ on premises ⋇ under 6yrs **Parking:** 5

Ardecca (the name is an amalgamation of the names Rebecca and Richard, the owners' children) has been the family home of Chris and Graham Horne for over 25 years. The large modern bungalow is immaculate inside and out and sits in 16 acres of pastureland on the edge of Blunsdon village, in a quiet rural setting in north Wiltshire within easy reach of Swindon and Cirencester, the Cotswolds and the Marlborough downs. A great find and an asset to the area, the bungalow offers spacious first-class accommodation in a friendly and relaxed atmosphere created by Chris and Graham. All the rooms are on the ground floor, larger than average and are equipped with modern amenities including Wi-fi access, TV, video, radio alarm and tea- and coffee-making facilities. A full English breakfast is provided and freshly cooked evening meals are available by arrangement, alternatively there are many good pubs and restaurants in the area. There is an outdoor patio area with seating and you can explore the immediate area on public footpaths leading through meadows. Ample parking is available. Please note that credit cards are not accepted. Arts and Crafts workshops are available on site.

Recommended in the area

Cotswold Water Park; Avebury stone circle; Marlborough, the Savernake Forest; Lydiard Park; Thames Path; Buscot Park (NT); Stonehenge

The Old Post Office Guest House

★★★★ GUEST HOUSE

Address: Thornhill Road, South Marston SWINDON
SN3 4RY
Tel: 01793 823114
Fax: 01793 823441
Email: theoldpostofficeguesthouse@yahoo.co.uk
Website: www.theoldpostofficeguesthouse.co.uk
Map ref: 3, SU18
Directions: A420 onto Thornhill Rd at Gablecross
rdbt 0.75m on left before Old Vicarage Lane
Rooms: 5 en suite, **S** £45–£55 **D** £55–£75
Notes: ⊗ on premises **Parking:** 5

Sympathetically extended, this attractive property is about two miles from Swindon and makes an excellent base for touring the West Country, with places of interest at every point of the compass. Guests are welcomed by the enthusiastic owner, a professional opera singer with a wonderful sense of humour. It has been owned by the Sansum family for four generations and was originally a smallholding farm. A post office was added in the 1850s, and it became a focal point in the village. The comfortable and prettily decorated en suite bedrooms – including one family room – vary in size, and all come with numerous facilities, including Freeview widescreen TV, free Wi-fi internet connection and tea- and coffee-making facilities. An extensive choice is offered at breakfast, from a sumptuous full English to a delicious continental. All dishes are freshly cooked using the best of local produce to make sure that no one leaves the table hungry. It is served in the breakfast room, which still contains the original well from the days when the Old Post Office was home to a bake house. Free off-street parking is available.
Recommended in the area
Cotswold Water Park; Lacock Abbey; Avebury Stone Circle

The Bell Tower in Evesham

Boot Inn

★★★★ 🛌 INN

Address: Radford Road, FLYFORD FLAVELL,
Worcester WR7 4BS
Tel: 01386 462658
Fax: 01386 462547
Email: enquiries@thebootinn.com
Website: www.thebootinn.com
Map ref: 2, SO95
Directions: In village centre, signed from A422
Rooms: 5 en suite (2 GF), **S** £50–£60 **D** £60–£90
Parking: 30

An inn has occupied this site since the 13th century, though 'The Boot' itself, as it is called locally, dates from the Georgian period. It provides an ideal base for anyone wishing to explore Stratford-upon-Avon, the Cotswolds or the Malvern Hills. The inn has undergone modernisation, yet it has managed to retain much of its historic charm. The comfortable bedrooms in the converted coach house, furnished in antique pine, are equipped with practical extras such as tea- and coffee-making facilities, trouser press and radio-alarm clock, and all have modern bathrooms. Two rooms have disabled access. Guests can relax and indulge in the range of options available at this family-run pub, which prides itself on its friendly staff and lively atmosphere. Traditional ales and an extensive wine list complement the varied and imaginative menus, which are adapted according to availability of ingredients, with everything from sandwiches to bar meals to full carte on offer. The award-winning food here, made from fine local produce, can be enjoyed in the cosy public areas, which include an attractive restaurant, a light and airy conservatory and a shaded patio area especially suited to summer dining.

Recommended in the area

Worcester Cathedral; Stratford-upon-Avon; Evesham

View over the River Severn

The Dell House

★★★★ B&B

Address: Green Lane, Malvern Wells MALVERN
WR14 4HU
Tel: 01684 564448
Fax: 01684 893974
Email: burrage@dellhouse.co.uk
Website: www.dellhouse.co.uk
Map ref: 2, SO74
Directions: 2m S of Great Malvern on A449. Turn
left off A449 onto Green Ln. House at top of road
on right

Rooms: 3 en suite, S £35–£45 D £62–£75 **Notes:** ⊗ on premises ✗ under 10yrs **Parking:** 4

The Dell House was built around 1820 when one of Malvern's famous healing springs was diverted to its grounds. Ian and Helen Burrage offer spacious, individually styled bedrooms where period elegance is combined with homely comforts and Wi-fi access; two rooms have wonderful views to the Cotswolds. Breakfast is served in the impressive Morning Room with superb views over the Severn Valley.

Recommended in the area

Malvern Hills; Malvern Theatre; Three Counties Showground; Malvern Springs & Wells

Thornton Force, Yorkshire Dales National Park

Burton Mount Country House

★★★★★ GUEST ACCOMMODATION

Address: Malton Road, Cherry Burton, BEVERLEY
HU17 7RA
Tel: 01964 550541
Fax: 01964 551955
Email: pg@burtonmount.co.uk
Website: www.burtonmount.co.uk
Map ref: 8, TA03
Directions: 3m NW of Beverley. B1248 for Malton, 2m right at x-rds, house on left
Rooms: 3 en suite **Notes:** ⊗ on premises 🐾 under 12yrs **Parking:** 20

Burton Mount is a charming country house three miles from Beverley, set in delightful gardens and offering luxurious accommodation. Nestling in a corner of the Yorkshire Wolds, it sits in its own secluded grounds and small woodland and makes a relaxing retreat for anyone travelling on business or for pleasure. Inside, a spacious hall leads up to the en suite bedrooms, all of which are located on the first floor and are well equipped with thoughtful extra touches, such as TV, hairdryer, tea- and coffee-making facilities, bathrobes and toiletries. Downstairs, the dining room has French windows that open onto a terrace, and this in turn leads through to the spacious and elegant drawing room, which has a blazing fire in the cooler months. A second large and comfortable sitting room has a TV and another log fire. An excellent, Aga-cooked Yorkshire breakfast is served in the morning room and includes smoked bacon, free-range eggs, home-made preserves and delicious bread, or a continental breakfast is available if preferred. The house is home to the Greenwood family, and Pauline Greenwood is renowned locally for her customer care, culinary skills and warm hospitality.

Recommended in the area

Beverley Minster; Bishop Burton Horse Trials; Wilberforce House, Kingston upon Hull

Brighouse Bay

The Royal Bridlington

★★★★ GUEST ACCOMMODATION

Address: 1 Shaftesbury Road, BRIDLINGTON
YO15 3NP
Tel: 01262 672433
Fax: 01262 672118
Email: info@royalhotelbrid.co.uk
Website: www.royalhotelbrid.co.uk
Map ref: 8, TA16
Directions: A615 N to Bridlington (Kingsgate),
right onto Shaftesbury Rd

Rooms: 18 (17 en suite) (1 pri facs) (3 GF), **S** £36–£42 **D** £62–£74 **Notes:** ⊗ on premises **Parking:** 7

In an ideal location, just 100 yards from beautiful South Beach, this immaculate property also has a lovely, enclosed garden. The thoughtfully furnished bedrooms all have bathrooms and are very well equipped. Some rooms are ground floor with level access to the bar and restaurant. Many rooms have fine sea views, and Wi-fi is available throughout. Spacious public areas include a dining room serving breakfasts and dinners, a cosy lounge with plasma TV and a well-stocked bar with open fire.

Recommended in the area

Yorkshire Belle; Burton Agnes; Bridlington South Beach

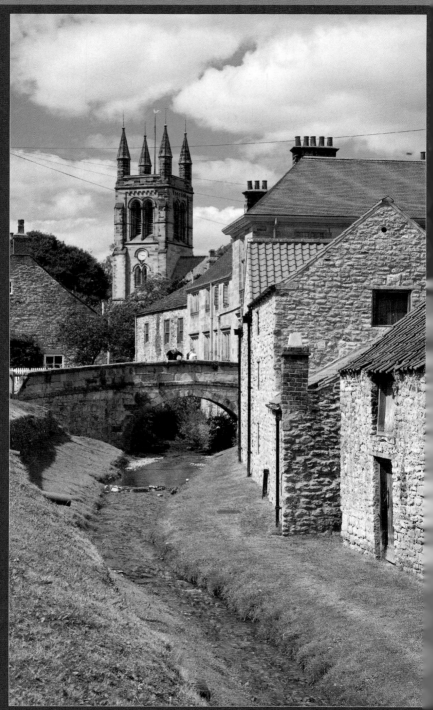

Castle gate and All Saints Church in Helmsley

Lucy Cross Farm

★ ★ ★ GUEST ACCOMMODATION

Address: ALDBROUGH ST JOHN, Richmond,
DL11 7AD
Tel: 01325 374319
Email: sally@lucycross.co.uk
Website: www.lucycross.co.uk
Map ref: 7, NZ21
Directions: A1 junct 56 onto B6275 at Barton, white house 3m from Barton rdbt on left towards Piercebridge
Rooms: 5 (3 en suite) (2 pri facs) (1 GF), **S** £30–£40 **D** £56–£65 **Parking:** 10

This working farm is located near the picturesque village of Aldbrough St John, yet is close to major road links and makes a good base for visiting North Yorkshire and the Dales. There is a relaxed atmosphere here, and the traditionally furnished bedrooms are very comfortably equipped; all have free Wi-fi. A lounge is available for guests, and hearty breakfasts are served in the pleasant dining room. Home-cooked evening meals, based on local produce, can be arranged – Aga roasts are a speciality.
Recommended in the area
Yorkshire Dales; Barnard Castle; Croft Racing Circuit

Shallowdale House

★ ★ ★ ★ ★ ▤ ➾ GUEST ACCOMMODATION

Address: West End, AMPLEFORTH YO62 4DY
Tel: 01439 788325
Fax: 01439 788885
Email: stay@shallowdalehouse.co.uk
Website: www.shallowdalehouse.co.uk
Map ref: 8, SE57
Directions: Off A170 at W end of village, on turning to Hambleton
Rooms: 3 (2 en suite) (1 pri facs), **S** £75–£85
D £95–£115 **Notes:** ⊗ on premises ⋫ under 12yrs **Parking:** 3 **Closed:** Xmas & New Year

Owned by Anton van der Horst and Phillip Gill, Shallowdale House is in a stunning location overlooking an Area of Outstanding Natural Beauty. The spacious south-facing bedrooms have huge picture windows and lovely views, and the atmosphere is relaxed and friendly. The four-course dinners are a highlight, featuring local and seasonal produce, and equal care is taken with breakfast, which can feature Whitby kippers and local sausages, as well as home-made preserves.
Recommended in the area
Castle Howard; Rievaulx Abbey; Nunnington Hall (NT)

Standing Stone above Fryupdale, North York Moors National Park

Elmfield House

★ ★ ★ ★ GUEST HOUSE

Address: Arrathorne, BEDALE DL8 1NE
Tel: 01677 450558
Fax: 01677 450557
Email: stay@elmfieldhouse.co.uk
Website: www.elmfieldhouse.co.uk
Map ref: 7, SE28
Directions: 4m NW of Bedale. A684 from Bedale for Leyburn, right after Patrick Brompton towards Richmond, B&B 1.5m on right

Rooms: 7 en suite (2 GF), **S** £55–£70 **D** £75–£88 **Notes:** ⊗ on premises **Parking:** 7

Enjoy a warm welcome at this friendly and relaxing country guest house. Set in peaceful countryside with 24 tranquil acres of garden, paddocks, woodland and fishing lake – this is a great base for exploring North Yorkshire. There are comfortable en suite bedrooms for a good night's sleep, followed by a hearty Yorkshire breakfast, using local produce and the guest house's own free-range eggs. There is an honesty bar, and home-cooked evening meals are available by arrangement.
Recommended in the area:
Bedale; Richmond; Yorkshire Dales and moors

Goldsborough Hall

★ ★ ★ ★ ★ GUEST ACCOMMODATION

Address: Church Street, GOLDSBOROUGH HG5 8NR
Tel: 01423 867321
Fax: 0870 285 1327
Email: accommodation@goldsboroughhall.com
Website: www.goldsboroughhall.com
Map ref: 8, SE35
Directions: A1(M) junct 47, take A59 to
Knaresborough. Take 2nd left onto Station Rd,
at T-junct left onto Church St
Rooms: 6 en suite, **D** £150–£395 **Parking:** 50

A luxurious experience is assured in the former home of Princess Mary, who was daughter of George V and aunt to the current queen. Built in 1625, the Hall is stately in every respect – size, architecture, glorious landscaped grounds and sumptuous furnishings. After periods used as a school and later a nursing home, it is back in private ownership, and six magnificent guest suites have been created. Rooms are vast, with sitting areas and writing desks, and all but one has a large hand-made mahogany four-poster bed, complete with curtains (the other has a beautiful king-size mahogany sleigh bed), plus hypo-allergenic bedding, a 125cm (50-inch) high-definition digital plasma television and many other luxuries. The ultra-modern bathrooms are spacious too, and all have whirlpool baths – one sunken and set into a bay window, another big enough for four – and monsoon showers. The opulent dining room offers an excellent range of breakfast choices, or you can have a continental breakfast in bed, and leisure options include the use of one of the chauffeur-driven Bentleys. In the grounds you can see the avenue of lime trees planted by royal visitors, cherry trees that were a gift from the Emperor of Japan, or simply relax in the outdoor hot tub.

Recommended in the area

City of York; Fountains Abbey; RHS Gardens Harlow Carr

The Kings Head at Newton

★★★★ GUEST ACCOMMODATION
Address: The Green, NEWTON-UNDER-ROSEBERRY,
          Nr Great Ayton TS9 6QR
Tel: 01642 722318
Fax: 01642 724750
Email: info@kingsheadhotel.co.uk
Website: www.kingsheadhotel.co.uk
Map ref: 8, NZ61
Directions: A171 towards Guisborough, at rdbt onto
A173 to Newton-under-Roseberry, under Roseberry
Topping landmark
Rooms: 8 en suite (2 GF), S £59.50–£85 D £75–£110 Notes: ⊗ on premises Parking: 100
Closed: 25–26 Dec & 1 Jan

This family-owned establishment offers stylish, thoughtfully equipped bedrooms. The restaurant, next door, offers quality food with produce sourced from the local area. A full English or continental breakfast is served in the glass-roofed breakfast area with unspoiled views of Roseberry Topping.
Recommended in the area
Cleveland Way; North York Moors National Park; Whitby

Laskill Grange

★★★★ GUEST ACCOMMODATION
Address: HELMSLEY YO62 5NB
Tel: 01439 798268
Email: laskillgrange@tiscali.co.uk
Website: www.laskillgrange.co.uk
Map ref: 8, SE58
Directions: 6m N of Helmsley on B1257
Rooms: 3 (2 en suite) (1 pri facs) (3 GF), S £35–£40
D £70–£80 Parking: 20 Closed: 25 Dec

Laskill is a charming 19th-century house in the North York Moors National Park. There are splendid walks in the surrounding countryside and fishing on the River Seph, which runs through the grounds. The elegant house has exposed beams and open fireplaces, and the immaculate bedrooms are decorated to a very high standard and come with hot-drink trays and flowers. Generous breakfasts are prepared using home-grown produce wherever possible. Across the courtyard from the farmhouse are converted barns for self catering. There is an activity centre for children too.
Recommended in the area
Rievaulx Abbey; Castle Howard; Nunnington Hall (NT)

The Druids Temple at Ilton

Gallon House

★★★★★ 🛏 ☕ GUEST HOUSE

Address: 47 Kirkgate, KNARESBOROUGH HG5 8BZ
Tel: 01423 862102
Email: gallon-house@ntlworld.com
Website: www.gallon-house.co.uk
Map ref: 8, SE35
Directions: Adjacent to railway station
Rooms: 3 en suite, S £60–£85 D £90–£120

Situated overlooking Knaresborough's beautiful Nidd Gorge, Gallon House is an award-winning bed and breakfast. The combination of breathtaking views, home-from-home comfort and Rick's delicious menus makes this establishment a real treat at any time of year. Careful attention to detail ensures guests enjoy their stay. The stylish bedrooms are individually furnished with many extras, including CD players, bathrobes and superb refreshment trays. Rick delights in serving locally sourced, seasonal dishes including venison casserole with dumplings during the winter months and Nidderdale trout in summer.

Recommended in the area

Leeds; York; Fountains Abbey (NT)

Newton House

★ ★ ★ ★ ⌂ GUEST ACCOMMODATION

Address: 5–7 York Place, KNARESBOROUGH
HG5 0AD
Tel: 01423 863539
Fax: 01423 869748
Email: newtonhouse@btinternet.com
Website: www.newtonhouseyorkshire.com
Map ref: 8, SE35
Directions: On A59 in Knaresborough, 500yds from
town centre
Rooms: 11 (10 en suite) (1 pri facs) (3 GF), **S** £50–£85 **D** £75–£100 **Parking:** 10 **Closed:** 1wk Xmas

This delightfully elegant, Grade II listed former coaching inn, entered by an archway into a courtyard, is only a short walk from the river, castle and market square in the picturesque town of Knaresborough. Owners Mark and Lisa Wilson place the emphasis on relaxation, informality and comfort, and the generously proportioned and refurbished bedrooms, most of them en suite, include some four-posters and king-size doubles, as well as family rooms and a pair of interconnecting rooms. All are very well equipped with Egyptian cotton bedding, Molton Brown toiletries, flat-screen TV with Freeview and DVD player, mini bar, a well-stocked refreshment tray, DAB radio with MP3 player input and free Wi-fi coming as standard. There is a comfortable lounge offering guests newspapers, books, magazines, games, sweets and fresh fruit, while memorable breakfasts are served in the attractive dining room. Meals are freshly cooked and the sophisticated menu includes eggs Benedict, poached smoked haddock, and porridge with sultanas in malt whisky, as well as the traditional full English. Free-range eggs, sausages and bacon are sourced locally and complemented by seasonal fruit and home-made preserves.

Recommended in the area

Fountains Abbey; Yorkshire Dales; Newby Hall; RHS Harlow Carr Gardens

River House

★★★★ 🏨 ☕ GUEST HOUSE

Address: MALHAM, Skipton BD23 4DA
Tel: 01729 830315
Email: info@riverhousehotel.co.uk
Website: www.riverhousehotel.co.uk
Map ref: 7, SD96
Directions: Off A65, N to Malham
Rooms: 8 en suite (1 GF), S £45–£60 D £60–£100
Parking: 5 **Notes:** 🐾 under 9yrs

This attractive, family-run Victorian guest house, parts of which date back to 1664, is set in the beautiful village of Malham, in the heart of the Yorkshire Dales. The surrounding countryside is excellent for walking, mountain-biking and horse-riding. Inside, the Victorian hallway has the original cornicing and archway moulding, while the newly decorated en suite bedrooms are all bright and comfortable, with a good selection of homely extras such as colour TV, large luxury towels, well-stocked hospitality tray, good-quality toiletries and hairdryer. Some rooms have the original fireplace, and one large twin room on the ground floor is equipped with grab rails in the shower room. Public areas include a cosy, licensed lounge, with an extensive list of New World wines and a large, well-appointed dining room, where locally sourced produce, including the local butcher's scrumptious sausages and black pudding, is incorporated into the excellent breakfasts and imaginative evening meals that offer choice and quality above expectation, and make River House well worthy of its Breakfast and Dinner Awards. Packed lunches can be made up on request, as can meals for vegetarians and those on special diets, and catering for walking parties, groups and family get-togethers is a speciality here.

Recommended in the area

Malham Cove and Gordale Scar; Yorkshire Dales; Pennine Way; Skipton; Settle to Carlisle Railway

From Cliff Ridge to Cleveland Hills, North York Moors National Park

Bank Villa

★★★★ ⬚ ⬚ GUEST HOUSE

Address: MASHAM, Ripon HG4 4DB
Tel: 01765 689605
Email: bankvilla@btopenworld.com
Website: www.bankvilla.com
Map ref: 7, SE28
Directions: Enter on A6108 from Ripon, property on right
Rooms: 6 (4 en suite) (2 pri facs), **S** £50–£65
D £55–£95 **Notes:** ⊗ on premises ⋈ under 5yrs
Parking: 6

Graham and Liz Howard-Barker have created a welcoming atmosphere in their charming Georgian home, a great base for exploring the Dales. Relax in the lovely terraced gardens, in one of two comfortable lounges, or the conservatory, all of which have plenty of character. Individually decorated bedrooms feature beams, stripped pine period furniture and crisp white linens. Liz's cooking uses home-grown and local produce whenever possible, served in the relaxed licensed restaurant.

Recommended in the area

Black Sheep and Theakstons breweries; Rievaulx Abbey; Fountains Abbey; Yorkshire Dales

Three Tuns

★★★★ ⇔ RESTAURANT WITH ROOMS

Address: 9 South End, Osmotherley
NORTHALLERTON DL6 3BN
Tel: 01609 883301
Fax: 01609 883988
Email: enquiries@threetunsrestaurant.co.uk
Website: www.threetunsrestaurant.co.uk
Map ref: 8, SE39
Directions: NE of Northallerton. Off A19 into
Osmotherley village
Rooms: 7 en suite (1 GF), S £55 D £85

This family-run establishment, situated in the picturesque village of Osmotherley in the North Yorkshire Moors, is full of character. With its friendly, informal atmosphere and great food, it is a popular destination for business travellers, tourists and locals alike – 'Delicious food in a beautiful restaurant' was how Paddy Burt described it in The Telegraph. The Charles Rennie Mackintosh-inspired decor sets it apart, and the bedrooms – some situated above the bar, some located in an adjoining annexe – vary in size but are stylishly furnished in pine throughout. All rooms are en suite, including one family room and one on the ground floor, and have colour TV, large beds, fluffy pillows and tea and coffee-making facilities; some rooms enjoy stunning views of the Cleveland Hills. The homely lounge contains a video and CD player, and there's a film and music collection available for guests to browse through and enjoy. The restaurant is a real draw, offering an imaginative range of wholesome, modern British dishes with the emphasis on fine local produce and with fine wines and traditional cask conditioned ales to wash it all down. A hearty breakfast, lunch, afternoon tea and dinner are all on offer. There is also a beautiful, peaceful, secret garden to enjoy.

Recommended in the area

The Forbidden Corner; Wensleydale Railway; Mount Grace Priory

17 Burgate

★ ★ ★ ★ ★ ⌂ GUEST ACCOMMODATION

Address: 17 Burgate, PICKERING YO18 7AU
Tel: 01751 473463
Email: info@17burgate.co.uk
Website: www.17burgate.co.uk
Map ref: 8, SE78
Directions: From A170 follow sign to Castle passing 17 Burgate on right
Rooms: 5 en suite, S £70–£75 D £85–£115
Notes: ⊗ on premises ⊀ under 10yrs **Parking:** 7

This elegant market town house, close to the town centre and the castle, has been expertly renovated, and the owners have gone the extra mile to make sure you enjoy your stay here. The comfortable, individually designed bedrooms all have modern facilities including free broadband, flat-screen TV, DVD player and a range of spa cosmetics and aromatic candles. Public areas include a comfortable lounge bar with a log-burning stove and well-stocked bar, and breakfast includes a wide choice of local, healthy foods. The peaceful garden includes a terrace on which to relax and enjoy a bottle of wine.

Recommended in the area

Flamingo Land; Castle Howard; North Yorkshire Moors Railway

Mallard Grange

★ ★ ★ ★ ★ ⌂ FARMHOUSE

Address: Aldfield, RIPON HG4 3BE
Tel: 01765 620242
Fax: 01765 620242
Email: maggie@mallardgrange.co.uk
Website: www.mallardgrange.co.uk
Map ref: 7, SE37
Directions: B6265 W from Ripon, Mallard Grange 2.5m on right
Rooms: 4 en suite (2 GF), D £75–£105
Notes: ⊗ on premises ⊀ under 12yrs **Parking:** 6 **Closed:** Xmas & New Year

Set in glorious countryside and ideally placed for touring the Yorkshire Dales and Moors, this fine 16th-century Yorkshire farmhouse retains many original features. Each room is en suite and has a distinct character with quality furnishings and extra touches to ensure complete comfort and convenience. There are two ground floor bedrooms in the converted smithy. As an AA Breakfast Award winner, breakfast is high standard and a real farmhouse treat using locally sourced produce such as Whitby kippers.

Recommended in the area

Fountains Abbey (NT); Harrogate; Newby Hall; Harlow Carr; Ripley Castle

St George's Court

★ ★ ★ ★ FARMHOUSE

Address: Old Home Farm, Grantley RIPON HG4 3PJ
Tel: 01765 620618
Email: stgeorgescourt@bronco.co.uk
Website: www.stgeorges-court.co.uk
Map ref: 7, SE37
Directions: B6265 W from Ripon, right signed
Grantley & Winksley, up hill 1m past Risplith sign
& next right
Rooms: 5 en suite (5 GF), S £45–£55 D £65–£75
Parking: 12

Warm hospitality is the hallmark of this renovated farmhouse complex on the edge of Wensleydale and close to Fountains Abbey World Heritage Site. The elegant house is set in 20 acres and includes a small lake. The ground floor rooms, each with their own front door, are located around a pretty courtyard, and have quality beds, refreshment trays and spacious bathrooms. One unit with two bedrooms is ideal for families. Imaginative breakfasts, using fine local ingredients, are served in the conservatory.

Recommended in the area

Fountains Abbey (NT); Brimham Rocks; Newby Hall

The Flask Inn

★ ★ ★ INN

Address: Fylingdales, WHITBY YO22 4QH
Tel: 01947 880305
Email: admin@theflaskinn.com
Website: www.theflaskinn.com
Map ref: 8, NZ90
Directions: On A171, 7m S from Whitby
Rooms: 6 en suite **Parking:** 20

Set amid the unspoilt landscape of the North York Moors National Park and a short drive from the coast, this is an appealing 17th-century inn offering a range of cosy, traditional-style rooms, each with en suite bathroom. It's a friendly, family-run place, with a regular clientele of locals enjoying the hand-pulled ales and adding to the ambience in the bar in the evenings. The chef offers a comprehensive menu of dishes based on high quality, locally sourced ingredients. The Sunday lunch carvery is particularly popular, and breakfasts will certainly set you up for a day of busy sightseeing. Children are well catered for, with family rooms, cots and highchairs, a children's menu and play area.

Recommended in the area

Whitby; Robin Hood's Bay; North Yorkshire Heritage Coast

The Blackwell Ox Inn

★★★★ ◉ INN

Address: Huby Road, SUTTON-ON-THE-FOREST
YO61 1DT
Tel: 01347 810328
Fax: 01347 812738
Email: enquiries@blackwelloxinn.co.uk
Website: www.blackwelloxinn.co.uk
Map ref: 8, SE56
Directions: Off A1237, onto B1363 to Sutton-on-
the-Forest. Left at T-junct, 50yds on right

Rooms: 7 en suite, **S** £65–£110 **D** £95–£110 **Notes:** ⊗ on premises **Parking:** 18

A picturesque village just seven miles from the centre of York is the location of this friendly, renovated inn, which dates back to around 1823 and is named after a memorable 2,278lb, 6ft-tall (at the shoulders) animal that was bred locally. The finest local meat and produce still figures prominently in the inn's renowned restaurant, where Head Chef Tom Kingston and his team create serious gastro-pub food. There's a separate area where you can relax with an aperitif and browse the menu before being served in the traditional-style dining room. For less formal eating, a selection from the restaurant menu is also available in the bar, where logs blaze in an open fireplace in winter and fine, hand-pulled ales are kept in top condition (children are allowed in the bar until 8pm). There's also a pleasant terrace for alfresco dining on warm summer days. Accommodation at the inn offers stylish en suite bedrooms which have been individually designed – you could even opt for a four-poster room with a big, claw-foot bathtub right in the bedroom, and perhaps upgrade to the Champagne Break for a really romantic stay. All of the rooms include a television with DVD player and the bathrooms have Molton Brown toiletries.

Recommended in the area

Sutton Park and Gardens; the City of York; Beningbrough Hall (NT)

Spital Hill

★★★★★ ⌂ 🍴 GUEST ACCOMMODATION

Address: York Road, THIRSK YO7 3AE
Tel: 01845 522273
Fax: 01845 524970
Email: spitalhill@spitalhill.entadsl.com
Website: www.spitalhill.co.uk
Map ref: 8, SE48
Directions: 1.5m SE of town, set back 200yds from A19, driveway marked by 2 white posts
Rooms: 5 (4 en suite) (1 pri facs) (1 GF), **S** £60–£66 **D** £90–£103 **Notes:** ⊗ on premises 🚸 under 12yrs **Parking:** 6

Robin and Ann Clough warmly welcome guests to their beautiful home, a fine country house set in its gardens and parkland surrounded by open countryside. Ann produces an excellent set dinner each evening as an optional extra, using good fresh produce, much of which comes from the garden. Breakfast is also a highlight. Bedrooms are furnished with quality and style, and thoughtfully equipped with many extras; there is no tea-making equipment as Ann prefers to offer tea as a service.

Recommended in the area

Herriott Centre, Thirsk; Byland Abbey; York Minster

Woodhouse Farm

★★★★ FARMHOUSE

Address: WESTOW,York, YO60 7LL
Tel: 01653 618378
Fax: 01653 618378
Email: stay@wood-house-farm.co.uk
Website: www.wood-house-farm.co.uk
Map ref: 8, SE76
Directions: Off A64 to Kirkham Priory & Westow. Right at T-junct, farm drive 0.5m out of village on R
Rooms: 2 en suite, **S** £40–£45 **D** £60–£70

Notes: ⊗ on premises **Parking:** 6 **Closed:** Xmas, New Year & mid Mar–mid Apr

This 500-acre family-run working farm is set in rolling countryside nestled between the Vale of York, the Yorkshire Wolds and the Howardian Hills. The 18th-century farmhouse has been sympathetically restored retaining original beams and open log fires to provide a homely feel. All rooms are well equipped and consist of king-size and family rooms. Start the day with a delicious country breakfast sourced from locally produced sausages and bacon, plus home-made preserves, cakes and scones.

Recommended in the area

Castle Howard; York Minster; North Yorkshire Moors

Staithes village from Cowbar

Corra Lynn

★★★★ GUEST ACCOMMODATION

Address: 28 Crescent Avenue, WHITBY YO21 3EW
Tel: 01947 602214
Fax: 01947 602214
Map ref: 8, NZ81
Directions: Corner A174 & Crescent Av
Rooms: 5 en suite, **S** £28–£30 **D** £56–£60
Notes: ⊗ on premises **Parking:** 5
Closed: 21 Dec–5 Jan

Bruce and Christine Marot have a passion for what they do, mixing traditional values of cleanliness, comfort and friendly service with a modern trendy style. The house is set in a prominent corner position on the West Cliff within easy walking distance of the town of Whitby and its picturesque harbour. The bedrooms are thoughtfully equipped with colour TV, radio alarm and hospitality tray, and are individually furnished and colourfully decorated. The delightful dining room, with a corner bar and a wall adorned with clocks, really catches the eye. Breakfasts at Corra Lynn are hearty, with a vegetarian option, and the menu changes with the seasons. There is off-street parking.

Recommended in the area

Whitby Abbey; Captain Cook Memorial Museum; Robin Hood's Bay

Estbek House

★ ★ ★ ★ ⓐ ⌂ RESTAURANT WITH ROOMS
Address: East Row, Sandsend WHITBY YO21 3SU
Tel: 01947 893424
Fax: 01947 893625
Email: info@estbekhouse.co.uk
Website: www.estbekhouse.co.uk
Map ref: 8, NZ81
Directions: On Cleveland Way, within Sandsend, next to East Beck
Rooms: 4 (3 en suite) (1 pri facs), **S** £60–£90
D £90–£130 **Notes:** ⊗ on premises ⨁ under 14yrs **Parking:** 6

Estbek House, a beautiful Georgian establishment located in a small coastal village north-west of Whitby, is a restaurant with rooms that specialises in seafood. Here, diners can indulge themselves in the first-floor restaurant while listening to the relaxing break of the waves from the nearby Yorkshire Moors coastline. Chef/co-proprietor Tim Lawrence has nearly 30 years' experience of seafood cookery and he and his team present a range of mouth-watering dishes, including non-fish alternatives, on daily-changing menus. An innovative wine chalk board shows a large selection of bottles and wines by the glass, especially notable for the large Australian contingent, with over 100 wines listed. Surroundings in the restaurant are modern and stylishly simple – airy and bright by day, thoughtfully lit in the evenings; when the weather allows, diners may eat outside in the flower-bordered courtyard. On the ground floor is a small bar and breakfast room, while above are the individually decorated and luxurious bedrooms. Each has its own name – such as Florence or Eva – and character, and comes with a wealth of thoughtful extras such as flat-screen TV, CD/radio alarm clock, hairdryer, tea and coffee-making facilities and complimentary guest pack.

Recommended in the area

Mulgrave castles; Mulgrave woods; Cleveland Way

Kilburn White Horse, Coxwold

The ruins of Rievaulx Abbey

Netherby House

★★★★ ⌂ ⬚ GUEST ACCOMMODATION

Address: 90 Coach Road, Sleights, WHITBY
YO22 5EQ

Tel/Fax: 01947 810211

Email: info@netherby-house.co.uk

Website: www.netherby-house.co.uk

Map ref: 8, NZ81

Directions: In village of Sleights, off A169
Whitby-Pickering road

Rooms: 11 en suite (5 GF), **S** £37–£46.50
D £74–£93 **Notes:** ⊗ on premises ⚼ under 2yrs **Parking:** 17 **Closed:** 25–26 Dec

For owners Lyn and Barry Truman their bed and breakfast business is a labour of love; the beautifully kept gardens and the delightful day rooms and bedrooms, all contribute to a restful stay. Hospitality is another strength of Netherby House, and imaginative evening meals using fresh garden produce are served in the candlelit dining room. There are twin, double and family rooms, and a four-poster room adds that extra touch of luxury. There is a lounge-bar and a conservatory for relaxing in.

Recommended in the area

Historic Whitby; North Yorkshire Moors National Park; North Yorkshire Moors Railway

Ascot House

★★★★ GUEST ACCOMMODATION

Address: 80 East Parade, YORK YO31 7YH
Tel: 01904 426826
Fax: 01904 431077
Email: admin@ascothouseyork.com
Website: www.ascothouseyork.com
Map ref: 8, SE65
Directions: 0.5m NE of city centre. Off A1036 Heworth Green onto Mill Ln, 2nd left
Rooms: 13 (12 en suite) (1 pri facs) (2 GF),
S £55–£70 D £70–£80 **Parking:** 14 **Closed:** 21–28 Dec

This Victorian villa was built for a prominent family in 1869 close to the city centre. The owners have retained many original features, yet they have improved the building to provide modern standards of comfort. Bedrooms are equipped with period furniture, and most of the spacious rooms on the first floor have four-poster or canopy beds. Two rooms are on the ground floor, and most have en suites along with hospitality trays and colour TV. The curved stained-glass window on the landing is a particularly attractive feature. There is a spacious and comfortable lounge where you can relax, watch television or enjoy a drink from the Butlers Pantry. Tea and coffee are also served in the lounge throughout the day. Delicious traditional, vegetarian and continental breakfasts are served in the dining room; the generous portions are sure to set you up for the day. Ascot House is a welcoming property that can be reached from the city by bus in just a few minutes, or by a short brisk walk. It has an enclosed car park, and the public park next door has two tennis courts and two bowling greens. A nearby pub serves good food, and there are also many restaurants, wine bars and theatres within walking distance.

Recommended in the area

Jorvik Viking Centre; National Railway Museum; York Minster

Burswood Guest House

★ ★ ★ ★ 🛏 GUEST HOUSE

Address: 68 Tadcaster Road, Dringhouses, YORK
YO24 1LR
Tel: 01904 702582
Fax: 01904 708377
Email: burswood.guesthouse@virgin.net
Website: www.burswoodguesthouse.co.uk
Map ref: 8, SE65
Directions: Tadcaster Rd A1036 opposite
racecourse, from the A64 on S side of the city

Rooms: 5 en suite (3 GF), **D** £70–£85 **Notes:** ⊗ on premises **Parking:** 6

Guests can be sure of a warm welcome indeed at this modern dormer bungalow, with attractive window-boxes, whose owner strives to offer a level of excellence that he believes is not usually found outside of a five-star hotel. Bedrooms are richly furnished and very well equipped – providing guests with numerous home comforts such as fridges supplied with milk and bottled water, air-conditioning, ceiling fans, feather pillows, comfortable armchairs, ironing board stations, bathmats, velour bathrobes and slippers and digital television. Chocolate biscuits, sweets and good-quality toiletries add to the feeling that you are being well looked after. Good, freshly cooked breakfasts are on offer, and are served in the conservatory/breakfast room, which overlooks the guest house's well-tended garden. Ample car parking is available at the front of the house and Burswood is easily accessible for visiting the walled city of York, with its host of world-class attractions, such as York Minster, the York Dungeon, the Shambles shopping centre, York Castle Museum, and the racecourse, as well as the countless restaurants, pubs, tea rooms and coffee shops the city has to offer.

Recommended in the area

Medieval York; National Railway Museum; York Races

Robin Hood's Bay

The Heathers

★★★★ GUEST ACCOMMODATION

Address: 54 Shipton Rd, Clifton-Without, YORK
YO30 5RQ
Tel/Fax: 01904 640989
Email: thghyork@globalnet.co.uk
Website: www.heathers-guest-house.co.uk
Map ref: 8, SE65
Directions: N of York on A19, halfway between
A1237 ring road & York city centre
Rooms: 6 (4 en suite) (2 pri facs), D £56–£120
Notes: ⊗ on premises ⛌ under 10yrs **Facilities:** Wi-fi **Parking:** 9 **Closed:** Xmas

Recent remodelling and refurbishment at this large 1930s house has resulted in a most comfortable and welcoming establishment. Heather and Graham Fisher have designed each room individually using quality fabrics and decor and there is a feeling of luxury in the bedrooms, all of which have en suite or private facilities and benefit from TV, Wi-fi and well-stocked tea and coffee making facilities. The light and airy breakfast room looks out onto a well-tended garden area, and off-street parking is available.

Recommended in the area

North York Moors; Castle Howard; Ryedale Folk Museum

etit Pot Bay

The Panorama

★ ★ ★ ★ ★ GUEST ACCOMMODATION

Address: La Rue du Crocquet, ST AUBIN, JERSEY
JE3 8BZ
Tel: 01534 742429
Fax: 01534 745940
Email: info@panoramajersey.com
Website: www.panoramajersey.com
Map ref: 13
Directions: In village centre
Rooms: 14 en suite (3 GF), S £40–£65 D £80–£130
Notes: ⊗ on premises 🧒 under 18yrs
Closed: mid Oct–mid Apr

The Panorama is aptly named indeed, with its spectacular views across St Aubin's Bay. A long established favourite with visitors, not least because of the genuinely warm welcome, it is situated on a pretty seafront street. Inside are antiques aplenty, including a number of elegant fireplaces, and it is well known for its collection of over 500 teapots. Wireless internet access is now also available. A feature of the recently upgraded bedrooms is the luxurious pocket-sprung beds, most well over six feet long. The breakfasts, each individually cooked to order, are another draw, with dishes such as Grand Slam and Elegant Rarebit among the inventive choices on the lengthy menu. For lunch or dinner there are many restaurants in close proximity, providing ample opportunity to sample the best produce that Jersey has to offer. Many are within walking distance, and the owners will happily make recommendations. A good base for walking, cycling (a cycle track along the promenade leads to St Helier) or travelling around the island by bus. Day trips by boat are available to the neighbouring islands of Guernsey, Herm and Sark, and also to St Malo in Brittany. The accommodation is unsuitable for children.

Recommended in the area

Picturesque village of St Aubin; Railway Walk to Corbière; Beauport and Les Creux Country Park

Sandy beach in Alderney

ISLE OF MAN

The world's largest working water wheel, 'Lady Isabella', Laxey

Dreem Ard

★ ★ ★ ★ B&B
Address: Ballanard Road, DOUGLAS IM2 5PR
Tel: 01624 621491
Fax: 01624 621491
Map ref: 5, SC37
Directions: From St Ninian's Church along Ballanard
Rd for 1m, over Johnny Watterson Ln x-rds, past
farm on left, Dreem Ard on left
Rooms: 3 en suite (2 GF), **S** £40–£60 **D** £59–£79
Notes: ⊗ on premises 👶 under 8yrs **Parking:** 6

Dreem Ard is a relaxing sanctuary, with superb views over the glens just to the north of the Isle of
Man's capital, Douglas. The en suite bedrooms here are spacious and well equipped, with one family
room available and two on the ground floor, and the caring hosts are genuinely hospitable and attentive.
Home-cooked breakfasts are served around a large table, where good food and good company go
hand-in-hand. Special diets and vegetarian meals can also be catered for. There is a fine garden for
guests to relax in, and ample off-road parking.

Recommended in the area

Manx Electric Railway; Laxey Wheel; TT Grandstand; Gaiety Theatre; Villa Marina

Aaron House

★ ★ ★ ★ ★ 🛏 GUEST HOUSE
Address: The Promenade, PORT ST MARY IM9 5DE
Tel: 01624 835702
Website: www.aaronhouse.co.uk
Map ref: 5, SC26
Directions: Signs for South & Port St Mary, left
at Post Office, house in centre of Promenade
overlooking harbour
Rooms: 4 en suite (2 pri facs), **S** £59–£98
D £70–£98 **Notes:** ⊗ on premises 👶 under 14yrs
Closed: 21 Dec–3 Jan

Overlooking Chapel Bay's stunning harbour, this family-run establishment lovingly recreates the
property's original Victorian style, with exquisite interior design, cast-iron fireplaces in the public
rooms and sparklingly polished period furniture. Delicious home-made cakes served on arrival and the
luxurious bedrooms have a hot water bottle placed in your bed at night. Breakfast is a treat and evening
meals are offered in the winter only (Monday–Friday). There is free parking 70 yards away.

Recommended in the area

Cregneash Folk Village; Victorian Steam Railway; Sound and Calf of Man (bird sanctuary)

SCOTLAND

Glamis Castle

Callater Lodge Guest House

★★★★ GUEST HOUSE

Address: 9 Glenshee Road, BRAEMAR AB35 5YQ
Tel: 013397 41275
Email: info@hotel-braemar.co.uk
Website: www.callaterlodge.co.uk
Map ref: 12, NO19
Directions: Next to A93, 300yds S of Braemar centre
Rooms: 6 en suite, S £35–£40 D £66–£72
Notes: ⊗ on premises **Parking:** 6 **Closed:** Xmas

A warm welcome is assured at Callater Lodge which stands in spacious, attractive grounds. Sink into deep leather chairs after a day spent walking, climbing, golfing, cycling, fishing or skiing. The individually-styled, en suite bedrooms have lovely soft furnishings, TV, and tea- and coffee-making facilities. A wide choice is offered at breakfast, and later, soup of the day, snacks and sandwiches are served. Surrounded by fine hills, Braemar Castle can be reached via a pretty walk, and a number of local trails includes the Whisky Trail. For guests returning from a day out on the hills or ski slopes, there is a drying room, plus storage for bicycles, golf clubs and skis.

Recommended in the area

Balmoral Castle; Cairngorm National Park; Glenshee Ski Centre, Cairnwell

Kirkton House

★★★★★ GUEST ACCOMMODATION

Address: Darleith Road, CARDROSS G82 5EZ
Tel: 01389 841951
Fax: 01389 841868
Email: aa@kirktonhouse.co.uk
Website: www.kirktonhouse.co.uk
Map ref: 9, NS37
Directions: 0.5m N of village. Turn N off A814 onto Darleith Rd at W end of village. Kirkton House 0.5m on right
Rooms: 6 en suite (2 GF), S £40–£45 D £50–£70 **Parking:** 12 **Closed:** Dec–Jan

Guests feel at ease here thanks to Gillian and Stewart Macdonald's warm hospitality and their comfortable home. The converted 18th-century farmhouse stands in peaceful countryside with panoramic views of the River Clyde. Stone walls and large fireplaces give a cosy, rustic atmosphere, while the mainly spacious bedrooms are individually styled. The full Scottish breakfast is a high point.

Recommended in the area

Loch Lomond; The Hill House, Helensburgh (NTS); Burrell Collection, Glasgow

Crathes Castle Gardens

Dunvalanree

★ ★ ★ ★ ⚜ GUEST ACCOMMODATION

Address: Port Righ Bay, CARRADALE, Campbeltown
PA28 6SE
Tel: 01583 431226
Fax: 01583 431339
Email: stay@dunvalanree.com
Website: www.dunvalanree.com
Map ref: 9, NR83
Directions: From centre of Carradale, turn right at
x-rds and continue to end of road
Rooms: 5 en suite (1 GF), **S** £75–£90 **D** £130–£150 **Notes:** ⊗ on premises **Parking:** 8

Dunvalanree is a family-run establishment, stunningly situated on the Mull of Kintyre, where a warm welcome is guaranteed. It offers high quality, individually decorated, en suite bedrooms; one room is suitable for wheelchair users and has its own patio area. Chef-proprietor, Alyson Milstead, creates award-winning menus based on the locally sourced seafood and farm produce, which is complemented by a carefully chosen wine list; there is also a wide selection of malt whiskies.

Recommended in the area

Campbeltown; Springbank Distillery; Carradale Nature Reserve

Lethamhill

★ ★ ★ ★ ★ GUEST ACCOMMODATION

Address: West Dhuhill Drive, HELENSBURGH
G84 9AW
Tel: 01436 676016
Fax: 01436 676016
Email: lethamhill@talk21.com
Website: www.lethamhill.co.uk
Map ref: 9, NS28
Directions: 1m N of town. Off A818 onto West
Dhuhill Dr. Cross Upper Colcough St, 3rd on right
Rooms: 3 en suite, **S** from £65 **D** from £85 **Notes:** ⊗ on premises **Parking:** 6

This large spacious property with lovely well-tended gardens offers superb hospitality and impressive bedrooms. Jane's delicious breakfasts made from fresh Scottish produce are a highlight. The rooms come with superb bathrooms, great beds and flat-screen TVs, along with many thoughtful extras. Public areas are equally comfortable, with a spacious lounge and a dining room that looks out to the garden. The minimum stay is two nights. Smoking is not permitted on the premises or in the grounds.

Recommended in the area

The Hill House, Helensburgh (NTS); Loch Lomond; Glasgow Airport

Alltavona House

★★★★ GUEST HOUSE
Address: Corran Esplanade, OBAN PA34 5AQ
Tel/Fax: 01631 565067
Email: carol@alltavona.co.uk
Website: www.alltavona.co.uk
Map ref: 9, NM82
Directions: From seafront past cathedral, 5th house from end of Esplanade
Rooms: 10 en suite, S £35–£80 D £60–£90
Notes: ⊗ ♨ under 12yrs **Parking:** 6 **Closed:** 12–30 Dec

An elegant Victorian villa close to central Oban, Alltavona House has stunning views over Oban Bay. It offers a warm and friendly, family atmosphere. The attractive en suite bedrooms feature quality furnishings, and have TVs and tea- and coffee-making facilities. There is an elegant dining room and a small, cosy reading room. For breakfast choose from porridge, cereals or fruit, then enjoy a full Scottish breakfast, or a lighter option of free-range eggs, Mull smoked salmon or local smoked haddock.

Recommended in the area

Oban Rare Breeds Farm Park; Scottish Sea Life Sanctuary; Dunstaffnage Castle; Barcaldine Castle

---

Craigadam

★★★★ ☲ ⇔ GUEST HOUSE
Address: Craigadam, CASTLE DOUGLAS DG7 3HU
Tel: 01556 650233
Fax: 01556 650233
Email: inquiry@craigadam.com
Website: www.craigadam.com
Map ref: 5, NX76
Directions: From Castle Douglas E on A75 to Crocketford. In Crocketford turn left on A712 for 2m. House on hill
Rooms: 10 en suite (7 GF), S £42–£84 D £84 **Parking:** 12 **Closed:** Xmas & New Year

Set on a working farm, this elegant country house offers gracious living in a relaxed environment. The strikingly individual and large en suite bedrooms are housed in a converted 18th-century farmstead, with antique furnishings and French windows opening out onto a courtyard. Public areas include a well-furnished lounge with a log fire and a snooker room with comprehensive honesty bar. The dining room features a magnificent 15-seater table, the setting for Celia Pickup's delightful meals.

Recommended in the area

Dalton Pottery; Cream o' Galloway; Mill on the Fleet

Southpark House

★★★★ GUEST ACCOMMODATION

Address: Quarry Road Locharbriggs, DUMFRIES
DG1 1QR
Tel: 01387 711188
Fax: 01387 711155
Email: info@southparkhouse.co.uk
Website: www.southparkhouse.co.uk
Map ref: 5, NX97
Directions: 3.5m NE of Dumfries. Off A701 in
Locharbriggs onto Quarry Rd, last house on left
Rooms: 4 en suite, **S** £30–£50 **D** £50–£75 **Notes:** ⊗ on premises **Parking:** 10

Southpark House, a substantial and well-maintained property in a peaceful location on the edge of town, is renowned for its comfortable accommodation, good food and hospitality. It offers stunning views across five valleys, yet is only a short drive from the centre of the bustling market town of Dumfries with all its amenities. All of the en suite bedrooms here, including one family room as well as doubles and twins, are comfortable, attractively decorated and well equipped. There is a relaxing lounge for the use of guests with the added comfort of a roaring log fire when the weather is cold outside. Email and fax facilities are also available, as well as a laundry room – making this an ideal choice for business travellers as well as those simply visiting for pleasure. The friendly proprietor, Ewan Maxwell, personally oversees the hearty Scottish breakfast, which offers a wide range of cereals, traditionally made porridge, a choice of breads and fruit juice as well as a full cooked breakfast menu to choose from. Breakfast is served in the light and airy conservatory breakfast room, a recently built addition to the house that offers beautiful views over the surrounding countryside. There is ample secure parking for guests. Free Wi-fi in all rooms.

Recommended in the area

Mabie Park Farm; Farmers Den; Kippford beach; Drumlanrig Castle; Caerlaverock Castle

Wallamhill House

★ ★ ★ ★ B&B

Address: Kirkton, DUMFRIES
DG1 1SL
Tel: 01387 248249
Email: wallamhill@aol.com
Website: www.wallamhill.co.uk
Map ref: 5, NX97
Directions: 3m N of Dumfries. Off A701 signed
Kirkton, 1.5m on right
Rooms: 3 en suite, **S** £35–£40 **D** £60
Notes: ⊗ on premises **Parking:** 6

Hospitality is a real strength at Wallamhill House, an attractive house set in well-tended gardens and peaceful countryside three miles from Dumfries. The large bedrooms are extremely well equipped and there is a drawing room and a mini health club, with sauna, steam shower and gym equipment. Evening meals (by arrangement) are served in the dining room around one large table, and you can bring your own wine. The area offers great walking, cycling, or mountain biking in the Ae and Mabie forests.
Recommended in the area
Nithdale; Sweetheart Abbey, New Abbey; Caerlaverock Castle

Hartfell House & The Limetree Restaurant

★ ★ ★ ★ ⊛ GUEST HOUSE
Address: Hartfell Crescent, MOFFAT DG10 9AL
Tel: 01683 220153
Email: enquiries@hartfellhouse.co.uk
Website: www.hartfellhouse.co.uk
Map ref: 10, NT00
Directions: Off High St at war memorial onto Well St
& Old Well Rd. Hartfell Crescent on right
Rooms: 7 en suite (1 GF), **S** £40 **D** £70 **Notes:** ⊗ on premises **Parking:** 6 **Closed:** Xmas

A stunning Victorian manor house standing in gardens with commanding countryside views. Offering spacious and tastefully furnished bedrooms, and a large, first-floor guest lounge. The choice of a continental breakfast or a full Scottish breakfast is served in the magnificent dining room. A memorable meal can be enjoyed in the restaurant where the Scottish and international menus use local produce.
Recommended in the area
Galloway Forest Park; Dumfries; Carlisle

Gillbank House

★★★★★ GUEST ACCOMMODATION

Address: 8 East Morton Street, THORNHILL
DG3 5LZ
Tel: 01848 330597
Fax: 01848 331713
Email: hanne@gillbank.co.uk
Website: www.gillbank.co.uk
Map ref: 5, NX89
Directions: In town centre off A76
Rooms: 6 en suite (2 GF), **S** from £45 **D** from £65
Notes: ⊗ on premises ⛄ under 8yrs
Parking: 8

Once the home of a wealthy Edinburgh merchant, Gillbank is a charming late Victorian house located in a quiet street close to the centre of the picturesque town of Thornhill. The house is easily accessible from the A76 (Dumfries bypass) or off the M74 at Elvanfoot through the scenic Dalveen Pass, and has its own private car park. The shops, pubs and restaurants are two minutes' walk away, and the town is surrounded by beautiful countryside, in which you'll find sculptures and other work by Andy Goldsworthy. The area is ideal for a relaxing drive amid unique scenery or for a wide variety of outdoor sports and activities. If you are planning to cycle, bicycle storage is available at Gillbank, and if you are a keen angler the River Nith, famous for sea trout and salmon fishing, is just half a mile away. Bedrooms, including two on the ground floor, are comfortable, spacious and well presented, with smart en suite shower rooms and tea- and coffee-making facilities. Breakfast is served at individual tables in the bright, airy dining room, which is next to the comfortable lounge.

Recommended in the area

Drumlanrig Castle Gardens and Country Park; Thornhill Golf Course; Morton Castle

Allison House

★★★★ GUEST ACCOMMODATION
Address: 17 Mayfield Gardens, EDINBURGH EH9 2AX
Tel: 0131 667 8049
Fax: 0131 667 5001
Email: info@allisonhousehotel.com
Website: www.allisonhousehotel.com
Map ref: 10, NT27
Rooms: 11 (10 en suite) (1 pri facs) (2 GF), **S** £47.50–£65
D £60–£120 **Notes:** ⊗ on premises **Parking:** 6

A good choice for both business travellers and those simply on holiday, Allison House offers a range of modern comforts within a splendid Georgian building. Located on the south side of Edinburgh in a residential area, this family-run establishment is on the main bus route and is convenient for the city centre and its host of amenities. Valuable off-road parking is available for those with cars. Inside, the attractive and elegant bedrooms, all with en suite shower room, have been tastefully refurbished to include Black Watch and Lindsey tartan fabrics. The rooms are generally spacious here and very well equipped, offering TV, writing desk, wireless internet connection, trouser-press, ironing facilities, hairdryer, refreshment tray and a complimentary drink from the decanters of whisky and sherry. For special occasions, you can arrange to have champagne, chocolates or flowers in your room on arrival. Breakfast is served at individual tables in the ground floor dining room and provides a range of options, including a traditional full cooked Scottish plate, or an extensive continental buffet, with fruit juices, fresh fruit, cereals, croissants, pastries and cheeses. Allison House specialises in organising a selection of golf, shopping, city, sporting and theatre breaks.

Recommended in the area
Dynamic Earth; Edinburgh Zoo; The Museum of Scotland

Eilean Donan Castle, Loch Duich

Bonnington Guest House

★★★★ GUEST HOUSE

Address: 202 Ferry Road, EDINBURGH EH6 4NW
Tel: 0131 554 7640
Fax: 0131 554 7610
Email: booking@thebonningtonguesthouse.com
Website: www.thebonningtonguesthouse.com
Map ref: 10, NT27
Directions: On A902, near corner of Ferry Rd and Newhaven Rd
Rooms: 7 (5 en suite) (2 pri facs) (1 GF) **S** £45 **D** £60–£90
Notes: ⊗ on premises **Parking:** 9

An impressive three-storey property, this guest house is situated just 10 minutes from Edinburgh city centre, with its own off-road parking and good public transport links. Built in 1840, the house backs onto Victoria Park and is close to Leith and the Botanical Gardens The individually furnished bedrooms are located on two floors. All are equipped with fridges, bottled water, a decanter of sherry, tea- and coffee-making facilities and TVs with Freeview; Wi-fi access is also available. A substantial breakfast is served in the dining room.

Recommended in the area

Edinburgh Castle; Dynamic Earth; Museum of Scotland

Ellesmere House

★★★★ GUEST HOUSE

Address: 11 Glengyle Terrace, EDINBURGH
EH3 9LN
Tel: 0131 229 4823
Email: ruth@edinburghbandb.co.uk
Website: www.edinburghbandb.co.uk
Map ref: 10, NT27
Directions: S of city centre off A702
Rooms: 4 en suite, **S** £45–£70 **D** £90–£140
Notes: ⊗ on premises

This Victorian terraced town house overlooks the famous Bruntsfield Links golf course, reputed to be the oldest golf course in the world, and is close to the Golf Tavern, dating from 1456. The terrace on which this delightful establishment stands was built in 1869 by William and Duncan McGregor, and the name 'Glengyle' has associations with the Clan McGregor. Ellesmere House is within walking distance of Edinburgh city centre and all of its attractions and, as such, makes an ideal base for visiting Scotland's capital city, whether for business, a weekend break or a longer holiday. Edinburgh has excellent shopping facilities and offers no shortage of entertainment. Guests are treated to an exceptional level of comfort here, in a clean and friendly environment. The attractive and individually decorated en suite bedrooms vary in size and have many thoughtful touches, such as flat-screen TV, Wi-fi internet connection and tea- and coffee-making facilities. There is a family room available and one of the bedrooms boasts a four-poster bed. A superb breakfast, featuring the best of local produce and all freshly prepared, is served in the elegant lounge-dining room, from a menu full of delicious choices. In the evening, there are many excellent and varied restaurants from which you can choose, all within easy walking distance.

Recommended in the area

Edinburgh Castle; Princes Street; Holyrood Palace

Elmview

★★★★★ ☗ GUEST ACCOMMODATION
Address: 15 Glengyle Terrace, EDINBURGH EH3 9LN
Tel: 0131 228 1973
Email: nici@elmview.co.uk
Website: www.elmview.co.uk
Map ref: 10, NT27
Directions: 0.5m S of city centre. Off A702 Leven St onto Valley Field St, one-way to Glengyle Ter
Rooms: 3 en suite (3 GF), **S** £75–£100 **D** £95–£120
Notes: ⊗ on premises ⩗ under 15yrs **Closed:** Dec–Feb

Elmview is situated in the heart of Edinburgh in a delightful Victorian terrace within easy walking distance of Edinburgh Castle and Princes Street. The spacious and quiet en suite bedrooms have been furnished to include everything a guest could want. Fresh flowers, complimentary sherry and elegant furnishings all add to the feeling of a personal home. Elmview overlooks a large urban park, which includes a free, 36-hole, pitch and putt golf course. The highlight of a stay is the excellent breakfast taken at one large table.
Recommended in the area
Edinburgh Castle; Edinburgh Old Town; Museum of Scotland

The International Guest House

★★★★ GUEST HOUSE
Address: 37 Mayfield Gardens, EDINBURGH
EH9 2BX
Tel: 0131 667 2511
Fax: 0131 667 1112
Email: intergh1@yahoo.co.uk
Website: www.accommodation-edinburgh.com
Map ref: 10, NT27
Directions: On A701 1.5m S of Princes St
Rooms: 9 en suite (1 GF), **S** £35–£75 **D** £60–£130
Notes: ⊗ on premises **Parking:** 3

This attractive Victorian terrace house, on the south side of the city, 1.5 miles from Edinburgh Castle, is on a main bus route to the city centre. All the bedrooms, decorated and fitted in matching period floral prints, have fresh flowers and modern en suites. Some rooms have magnificent views across to the extinct volcano known as Arthur's Seat. A hearty Scottish breakfast is served on fine bone china at separate tables in the dining room which features a lovely marble fireplace.
Recommended in the area
Edinburgh Castle; Palace of Holyroodhouse; University of Edinburgh

Kew House

★★★★★ GUEST ACCOMMODATION

Address: 1 Kew Terrace, Murrayfield, EDINBURGH
EH12 5JE
Tel: 0131 313 0700
Fax: 0131 313 0747
Email: info@kewhouse.com
Website: www.kewhouse.com
Map ref: 10, NT27
Directions: 1m W of city centre A8
Rooms: 6 en suite (2 GF), **S** £75–£90 **D** £90–£180
Parking: 6

Kew House forms part of a listed Victorian terrace dating from 1860, located a mile west of the city centre, convenient for Murrayfield Rugby Stadium, and just a 15-minute walk from Princes Street. Regular bus services from Princes Street pass the door. The house is ideal for both business travellers and holidaymakers, with secure private parking. While many period features have been retained, the interior design is contemporary, and the standards of housekeeping are superb. Expect complimentary sherry and chocolates on arrival, and you can order supper in the lounge. Full Scottish breakfast with an alternative vegetarian choice is included in the room tariff, and light snacks, with room service, are available all day. Bedrooms, including some on the ground floor, are en suite and well equipped with remote control TV with digital channels, direct-dial telephones, modem points, hairdryers, trouser presses, fresh flowers and tea and coffee facilities. The superior rooms also have thier own fridge. Kew House also offers two very comfortable serviced apartments accommodating up to three people.

Recommended in the area

Edinburgh Castle; Edinburgh International Conference Centre; Murrayfield Rugby Stadium

Ruins of Cathedral of St. Andrews

23 Mayfield

★★★★ ≦ GUEST ACCOMMODATION

Address: 23 Mayfield Gardens, EDINBURGH
EH9 2BX
Tel: 0131 667 5806
Fax: 0131 667 6833
Email: info@23mayfield.co.uk
Website: www.23mayfield.co.uk
Map ref: 10, NT27
Directions: A720 bypass S, follow city centre signs.
Left at Craigmillar Park, 0.5m on right
Rooms: 9 en suite (2 GF), **S** £45–£80 **D** £65–£125 **Notes:** ✸ under 5yrs **Parking:** 10

A great location just a mile from the city centre, adds to the charms of this family-run guest house. It occupies a detached Victorian villa that retains many original features, and has spacious rooms. Individual decor in each room is colour-coordinated. The Four Poster Room boasts a huge, hand-carved mahogany bed, Egyptian cottons, flat-screen TV and Bose sound system. Other amenities include free Wi-fi, an elegant lounge and an exceptional breakfast menu, which includes Scottish smoked salmon.

Recommended in the area

Edinburgh Castle; Holyrood Palace; Princes Street

Southside

★ ★ ★ ★ 🏠 GUEST HOUSE

Address: 8 Newington Road, EDINBURGH EH9 1QS
Tel: 0131 668 4422
Fax: 0131 667 7771
Email: info@southsideguesthouse.co.uk
Website: www.southsideguesthouse.co.uk
Map ref: 10, NT27
Directions: E end of Princes St onto North Bridge to Royal Mile, continue S 0.5m, house on right
Rooms: 8 en suite (1 GF), S £55–£80 D £70–£160
Notes: ⊗ on premises 🧒 under 10yrs

Built in 1865, Southside Guest House is an elegant Victorian sandstone terraced house in the centre of Edinburgh, only a few minutes from Holyrood Park. The owners Lynne and Franco have been involved in the hospitality trade for many years and have happily made their home in the capital. Lynne is from the Highlands, and Franco hails from Florence. They offer individually designed, stylish, well-equipped bedrooms, with direct-dial telephones, DVD players, free wireless internet access, and many other comforts including quality mattresses and crisp fine linen. Two of the rooms have four-poster beds and comfortable sofas, and the remaining rooms come in a variety of colour schemes and bed sizes. Breakfast at Southside is guaranteed to satisfy with its great choice of traditional freshly cooked Scottish dishes, cheeses, oatcakes, fresh fruit and real coffee. Guests sit at separate tables in the attractive dining room. Southside Guest House has recently enhanced its facilities with a new self-contained apartment.

Recommended in the area

Edinburgh Castle; Edinburgh Festival Theatre; The Palace of Holyroodhouse; Old Town; Holyrood Park; Princes shops and gardens

The Witchery by the Castle

★★★★★ ◎ ☷ RESTAURANT WITH ROOMS

Address: 352 Castlehill, The Royal Mile,
EDINBURGH EH1 2NF
Tel: 0131 225 5613
Fax: 0131 220 4392
Email: mail@thewitchery.com
Website: www.thewitchery.com
Map ref: 10, NT27
Directions: Top of Royal Mile at gates of
Edinburgh Castle

Rooms: 7 en suite (1 GF), **S** £295 **D** £295 **Notes:** ⊗ on premises ⛄ under 12yrs **Closed:** 25–26 Dec

A-list celebrities often choose to stay in this quirky, luxurious, romantic little place that is tucked away in a group of historic buildings right at the gates of Edinburgh Castle. And it's not just the perfect central location that appeals to guests, they are drawn by the fantastic – in the truest sense of the word – suites that could easily be the lavish set of some big-budget medieval movie. Massive four-poster beds, rich red and gold fabrics, oak-panelling and tapestries set the scene, and each of the rooms has its own individuality, such as the military uniforms in The Guardroom. The bathrooms are simply stunning. The one belonging to The Library is lined with bookshelves; the Old Rectory's bathroom is in the style of a Gothic chapel; that of the Inner Sanctum is in red laquer, with a huge antique bathtub; Sempill's bathroom has oak-panelling and Vestry's is a riot of red trompe-l'oeil drapery. The food served in the Witchery restaurant and the elegant Secret Garden is equally renowned – hardly surprising since the establishment was the brainchild of Scotland's most famous restaurateur, James Thomson. The room rates include a continental breakfast and a bottle of champagne; absolutely free is the chance of being neighbour to some member of the Hollywood elite.

Recommended in the area

Edinburgh Castle; the Royal Mile; Museum of Scotland; National Gallery of Scotland

Urquhart Castle, Loch Ness

The Spindrift

★ ★ ★ ★ 🏛 GUEST HOUSE

Address: Pittenweem Road, ANSTRUTHER
KY10 3DT
Tel: 01333 310573
Fax: 01333 310573
Email: info@thespindrift.co.uk
Website: www.thespindrift.co.uk
Map ref: 10, NO50
Directions: Enter town from W on A917,
1st building on left
Rooms: 8 (7 en suite) (1 pri facs), **S** £45–£55 **D** £64–£76 **Notes:** 🐾 under 10yrs **Parking:** 12
Closed: Xmas–late Jan

A unique feature of this house is the top-floor Captain's Room, made to resemble a shipmaster's cabin by the original owner – the east-facing window looks towards Anstruther harbour. All the individually furnished, spacious bedrooms are brightly decorated and have a wide range of extras. The lounge has an honesty bar for a pre-dinner drink, and enjoyable, home-cooked fare is served in the dining room.
Recommended in the area
Scottish Fisheries Museum; St Andrews; East Neuk coastal villages

The Roods

★ ★ ★ ★ B&B

Address: 16 Bannerman Avenue, INVERKEITHING
KY11 1NG
Tel: 01383 415049
Fax: 01383 415049
Email: isobelmarley@hotmail.com
Website: www.the-roods.co.uk
Map ref: 10, NT18
Directions: N of town centre off B981
Church St-Chapel Pl
Rooms: 2 en suite (2 GF), **S** £26–£30 **D** £50–£60 **Notes:** ⊗ on premises **Parking:** 4

In a secluded setting, this delightful house is within easy reach of both the railway station and the town centre. The individually furnished bedrooms are on the ground floor and have smart new bathrooms. Thoughtful touches bring a personal feel to the rooms, which have direct-dial telephones, central heating and tea and coffee facilities. The lounge has an inviting open fire and breakfast is served at individual tables in the pretty conservatory. Evening meals by arrangement. No dogs please.
Recommended in the area
Culross Palace, Town House and The Study; Pittencrieff House Museum; Aberdour Castle

Dunclutha Guest House

★★★★ GUEST HOUSE

Address: 16 Victoria Road, LEVEN KY8 4EX
Tel: 01333 425515
Fax: 01333 422311
Email: pam.leven@blueyonder.co.uk
Website: www.dunclutha.myby.co.uk
Map ref: 10, NO30
Directions: A915, B933 Glenlyon Rd into Leven, rdbt left onto Commercial Rd & Victoria Rd, Dunclutha opp church on right
Rooms: 4 (3 en suite) (1 pri facs), **S** £35–£45 **D** £60–£70 **Notes:** ⊗ on premises **Parking:** 3 **Closed:** 2 wks Jan

The original splendour of this former Victorian rectory sits well with modern trappings, making this an impressive place to stay. All of the bedrooms are smartly decorated. The lounge is filled with interesting items as well as a piano, and is a sociable place in the evenings. The adjoining dining room is the setting for hearty breakfasts, which include delicious home-made preserves and bread.

Recommended in the area

St Andrews; Levens Links golf course; Fife Coastal Path

The Peat Inn

★★★★★ ◉◉ RESTAURANT WITH ROOMS

Address: PEAT INN KY15 5LH
Tel: 01334 840206
Fax: 01334 840530
Email: stay@thepeatinn.co.uk
Website: www.thepeatinn.co.uk
Map ref: 10, NO40
Directions: At junct of B940 & B941, 5m SW of St Andrews
Rooms: 8 en suite (8 GF), **S** £95–£125 **D** £145–£175 **Parking:** 24 **Closed:** 25–26 Dec & 1–3 Jan

The Peat Inn is consistently one of the best restaurants in Scotland, holder of two AA Rosettes and renowned for its use of fresh, Scottish produce for over 30 years. Chef Geoffrey Smeddle ensures it remains a real haven for food lovers. Set in a 300-year-old former coaching inn, this restaurant with rooms enjoys a rural location yet is close to St Andrews. With three intimate dining areas and luxurious and spacious suite accommodation – this is the perfect blend of cuisine and comfort.

Recommended in the area

Falkland Palace; St Andrews Cathedral; Scotland's Secret Bunker

Glenderran

★ ★ ★ ★ GUEST HOUSE

Address: 9 Murray Park, ST ANDREWS KY16 9AW
Tel: 01334 477951
Fax: 01334 477908
Email: info@glenderran.com
Website: www.glenderran.com
Map ref: 10, NO51
Directions: In town centre. Off North St onto Murray
Place & Murray Park
Rooms: 5 (4 en suite) (1 pri facs), **S** £35–£45
D £70–£100 **Notes:** ⊗ on premises ⋬ under 12yrs

This immaculately presented guest house is centrally located in St Andrews. All the bedrooms have been fully refurbished, offering contemporary comforts while maintaining all the character of this beautiful Victorian house. All bedrooms have flat-screen TVs, hospitality trays and a full range of quality bathroom accessories. The house has free Wi-fi internet throughout and a laptop computer for guests' use. The excellent breakfasts are freshly cooked and use locally-sourced fresh produce.
Recommended in the area
University of St Andrews; St Andrew's Links; Cathedral

The Inn at Lathones

★★★★ ◉◉ INN

Address: Largoward, ST ANDREWS KY9 1JE
Tel: 01334 840494
Fax: 01334 840694
Email: lathones@theinn.co.uk
Website: www.theinn.co.uk
Map ref: 10, NO51
Directions: 5m S of St Andrews on A915, 0.5m
before village of Largoward on left just after
hidden dip
Rooms: 13 en suite (11 GF), **S** £120 **D** £180 **Parking:** 35 **Closed:** 26 Dec & 3–16 Jan

The Inn dates back to 1603 and over the last 10 years it has been sympathetically restored to provide comfortable light, cosy bedrooms. Facilities include a hospitality tray, satellite TV, radio, direct-dial telephone and computer access. The restaurant is widely acclaimed and the Inn welcomes the return of the former chef Marc Guilbert after a short break, during which he has further honed his special skills. Marc's style of cooking is clean and modern European with slight Asian influences.
Recommended in the area
St Andrews Old Course, British Golf Museum; Castle and Visitor Centre; St Andrews

Castle Stalker on Loch Laich

The Kelvingrove

★ ★ ★ ★ GUEST ACCOMMODATION

Address: 944 Sauchiehall Street, GLASGOW
G3 7TH

Tel: 0141 339 5011

Fax: 0141 339 6566

Email: info@kelvingrovehotel.com

Website: www.kelvingrove-hotel.co.uk

Map ref: 9, NS56

Directions: M8 junct 18, 0.5m along road signed
Kelvingrove Museum, on left

Rooms: 22 en suite (3 GF), **S** £40–£70 **D** £70–£100

This friendly terraced establishment is in Glasgow's lively West End and close to the town centre. Run by three generations of the same family it is very well maintained. All of the bedrooms, including triples and several good family rooms, are well equipped for guest comfort and convenience. The en suite bathrooms have power showers and luxuriously soft towels. Free wireless internet connection is also available. Breakfast is served in the bright breakfast room and the reception lounge is always open.

Recommended in the area

Kelvingrove Museum and Art Gallery; Botanic Gardens; SECC

Dell Druie Guest House

★★★★ B&B

Address: Inverdruie, Rothiemurchus AVIEMORE
PH22 1QH
Tel: 01479 810934
Email: general@delldruieguesthouse.com
Website: www.delldruieguesthouse.com
Map ref: 12, NH81
Directions: 0.75m S of Aviemore. Off B9152 onto
B970 to Coylumbridge and Cairngorm Mountain,
sharp left after Rothiemurchus Vistor Centre, last
house in cul-de-sac
Rooms: 3 (2 en suite) (1 pri facs) (1 GF), **S** £70–£90 **D** £80–£110
Notes: ⊗ on premises ⚲ under 14yrs **Parking:** 6

Dell Druie is an impressive modern house set in a riverside location in the heart of the Cairngorm
National Park. Less than a mile from the centre of Aviemore and three minutes' walk from The
Rothiemurchus Visitor Centre, Dell Druie offers easy access to the abundance of activities that make
The Cairngorms and Aviemore so special. This guest house offers immaculate, stylish, contemporary
bedrooms with tea and coffee making facilities, Sky TV, DVD player, and free broadband wireless
internet connection in all rooms. The fresh flowers, white cotton bed linen, fluffy white towels and
bathrobes along with many other thoughtful extra comforts such as Arran Aromatics bath products all
help make your stay relaxing and memorable. Full cooked breakfasts are served including free-range
farm eggs and other local produce including Rothiemurchus Honey with Whisky, and Scottish salmon.
There is a spacious lounge where you can watch red squirrels, pheasants and many other species of
local birds in the garden, or relax by the river in the private picnic paradise.

Recommended in the area

Cairngorm National Park; RSPB Nature Reserve

The Old Minister's House

★★★★★ GUEST HOUSE

Address: Rothiemurchus, AVIEMORE PH22 1QH
Tel: 01479 812181
Fax: 0871 661 9324
Email: kate@theoldministershouse.co.uk
Website: www.theoldministershouse.co.uk
Map ref: 12, NH81
Directions: B970 from Aviemore signed Glenmore & Coylumbridge, establishment 0.75m at Inverdruie
Rooms: 4 en suite, S £45–£65 D £90–£96
Notes: ⊗ on premises 👶 under 12yrs **Parking:** 4

This fine old manse is in the heart of the Cairngorm National Park and offers an excellent standard of accommodation. Stylish rooms come with Wi-fi access, en suite bathrooms, bathrobes and Arran Aromatic toiletries. Breakfast features a comprehensive choice, including fresh home-made bread and jams, and a host of local artisan produce. Various cooked options include smoked salmon with scrambled egg with dill sauce, while the continental breakfast includes local cheeses and Parma ham.
Recommended in the area
The Cairngorms; Strathspey Steam Railway; RSPB Nature Reserve and Rothiemurchus Estate

Glenaveron

★★★★★ B&B

Address: Golf Road, BRORA KW9 6QS
Tel: 01408 621601
Email: alistair@glenaveron.co.uk
Website: www.glenaveron.co.uk
Map ref: 12, NC90
Directions: A9 NE into Brora, right onto Golf Rd, 2nd house on right
Rooms: 3 en suite (1 GF), S £45–£55 D £66–£72
Notes: ⊗ on premises **Parking:** 6
Closed: 8–23 Oct, Xmas & New Year

This beautiful Edwardian house, set amid extensive mature gardens, is a delightful family home where guests are welcomed into a friendly and relaxing atmosphere. The bedrooms are spacious and well-equipped, with a ground floor bedroom available for easier access. Breakfast is served in the elegant dining room, house-party style. Glenaveron is an ideal base for touring the northern Highlands and for crossing to Orkney; the world famous Royal Dornoch golf club is just 20 minutes' drive away.
Recommended in the area
Royal Dornoch Golf Club; Orkney Islands

Inveraray Castle Park

Mansefield Guest House

★★★★ GUEST HOUSE

Address: Corpach, FORT WILLIAM PH33 7LT
Tel: 01397 772262
Email: mansefield@btinternet.com
Website: www.fortwilliamaccommodation.com
Map ref: 12, NN17
Directions: 2m N of Fort William A82 onto A830,
house 2m on A830 in Corpach
Rooms: 6 en suite (1 GF), **S** £25–£35 **D** £50–£80
Notes: ⊗ on premises ⛷ under 12yrs **Parking:** 7

Mansefield Guest House is a former manse set in mature gardens overlooking Loch Linnhe, with great mountain views. The friendly, family-run guest house provides bedrooms with country-style decor plus complimentary toiletries and hospitality trays. You can even request blankets if you prefer them to duvets. The cosy sitting room overlooks the garden, and a roaring coal fire burns on cold evenings as you browse the many books, magazines and tourist brochures.

Recommended in the area

Treasures of the Earth Exhibition, Corpach; Ben Nevis; boat trips to Seal Island, Loch Linnhe

Foyers Bay Country House

★ ★ ★ GUEST HOUSE

Address: Lochness, FOYERS
IV2 6YB
Tel: 01456 486624
Email: enquiries@foyersbay.co.uk
Website: www.foyersbay.co.uk
Map ref: 12, NH42
Directions: Off B852 into Lower Foyers
Rooms: 6 en suite (1 GF), **S** £55–£65 **D** £80–£90
Notes: ⊗ on premises ⬩⬩ under 16yrs
Parking: 6

Set on the quiet, undeveloped side of Loch Ness, midway between Inverness and Fort Augustus, among hillside woodlands with a colourful abundance of rhododendrons, this delightful house offers stunning views as well as forest walks and nature trails. It makes a perfect choice for a relaxing break away from it all. Foyers Bay Country House was originally built as a family home in the late 1890s and today it still offers many of the delights of a Victorian villa, though it has been thoughtfully and comfortably refurbished. There is a comfortable residents' bar and lounge adjacent to an airy, plant-filled conservatory restaurant, where traditional Scottish breakfasts and delicious evening meals are served against a backdrop of magnificent, unspoilt views of the loch. The attractive bedrooms, which vary in size and one of which is on the ground floor, all have en suite bath or shower rooms, hairdryer, TV and tea and coffee-making facilities. Some of the rooms have loch views.

Recommended in the area

Inverness; Loch Ness; Glen Affric

An Cala

★★★★★ GUEST HOUSE

Address: Woodlands Terrace,
GRANTOWN-ON-SPEY PH26 3JU
Tel: 01479 873293
Fax: 01479 873610
Email: ancala@globalnet.co.uk
Website: www.ancala.info
Map ref: 12, NJ02
Directions: From Aviemore on A95 turn left B9102
at rdbt outside Grantown. After 400yds, 1st left
Rooms: 4 en suite, **S** £55–£65 **D** £70–£84 **Notes:** ⊗ ✿ under 3yrs **Parking:** 6 **Closed:** Xmas

A large Victorian house set in well-tended gardens and overlooking woods that makes an attractive setting in which to relax, and yet is just a 12-minute walk from the town centre. The house is in the Cairngorms National Park and has on-site parking. Beautifully decorated bedrooms with king or super king-size double beds – one room has a lovely king-size four-poster bed from Castle Grant. All rooms have smart en suites and antique furniture. Freeview television and free Wi-fi are also available.
Recommended in the area
The Malt Whisky Trail; Ballindalloch Castle; Osprey Centre at Abernethy

The Ghillies Lodge

★★★★ 🛏 B&B

Address: 16 Island Bank Road, INVERNESS IV2 4QS
Tel: 01463 232137
Fax: 01463 713744
Email: info@ghillieslodge.com
Website: www.ghillieslodge.com
Map ref: 12, NH64
Directions: 1m SW from town centre on B862, pink house facing the river
Rooms: 3 en suite (1 GF), **S** £40–£50 **D** £60–£70 **Parking:** 3

Built in 1847 as a fisherman's lodge, the Ghillies Lodge lies on the River Ness with fine views over the Ness Islands and just a mile from Inverness centre, making it an ideal base for touring the Highlands. The attractive and peaceful en suite bedrooms, (including one on the ground floor) are individually styled, well equipped and wireless internet connection is available. There is a comfortable lounge-dining room and a conservatory over looks the river.
Recommended in the area
Loch Ness; Speyside distilleries; Isle of Skye

Moyness House

★ ★ ★ ★ GUEST ACCOMMODATION
Address: 6 Bruce Gardens, INVERNESS IV3 5EN
Tel: 01463 233836
Fax: 01463 233836
Email: stay@moyness.co.uk
Website: www.moyness.co.uk
Map ref: 12, NH64
Directions: Off A82 Fort William road, almost opp Highland
Regional Council headquarters
Rooms: 6 en suite (2 GF), **S** £55–£75 **D** £68–£100
Parking: 10

Built in 1880 this gracious villa, once the home of acclaimed
Scottish author Neil Gunn, has been sympathetically restored to its full Victorian charm by Jenny and
Richard Jones, and has many fine period details. The six stylish en suite bedrooms, named after Gunn's
novels, are enhanced by contemporary amenities and thoughtful extra touches. Breakfasts served in
the elegant dining room include a wide range of delicious Scottish choices, as well as vegetarian and
healthy options, using fresh local produce. The inviting sitting room overlooks the garden to the front,
and a pretty walled garden to the rear is a peaceful retreat in warm weather. Free wireless internet
connection is available throughout the house. Moyness House has ample parking within the grounds,
and is well located in a quiet residential street, less than 10 minutes' walk from the city centre where
there are several highly recommended restaurants, the Eden Court Theatre and delightful riverside
walks. Jenny and Richard are happy to advise on local eateries and to make dinner reservations for
their guests. They will also be glad to provide touring advice and help guests make the most of their
stay in the beautiful Highlands.

Recommended in the area

Culloden Battlefield; Loch Ness and the Caledonian Canal; Urquhart Castle and Cawdor Castle

Trafford Bank

★ ★ ★ ★ ★ 🏨 GUEST HOUSE

Address: 96 Fairfield Road, INVERNESS IV3 5LL
Tel: 01463 241414
Email: enquiries@invernesshotelaccommodation.co.uk
Website: www.traffordbank.co.uk
Map ref: 12, NH64
Directions: Off A82 at Kenneth St, Fairfield Rd 2nd left, 600yds on right
Rooms: 5 en suite, **S** £60–£85 **D** £80–£115
Notes: ⊗ on premises **Parking:** 10

Luxurious accommodation and Highland hospitality go hand-in-hand at this guest house, run by Lorraine Freel and Koshal Pun. This multilingual pair can welcome you in Italian, French, Hindi and Swahili. Located within walking distance of the city centre and the Caledonian Canal, Trafford Bank, built in 1873, was once the local bishop's home. Lorraine's flair for interior design has produced a pleasing mix of antique and contemporary wherever you come from furnishings, some of which she has designed herself; the dining-room chairs are a special feature, and there is unusual lighting and original art throughout the house. The bright bedrooms are individually themed; all are en suite and have enticing extras like Arran aromatic products and organic soap from the Strathpeffer Spa soap company. Each bedroom is superbly decorated with fine bed linen, hairdryers, Fairtrade tea and coffee, flat-screen digital TVs, DVD players, CD/radio alarms, iPod docking stations and silent fridges. Breakfast is prepared using the best Highland produce and served on Anta pottery in the stunning conservatory. There are two spacious lounges and the house is surrounded by mature gardens that you are welcome to enjoy. Wi-fi is available throughout the house.

Recommended in the area

Cawdor Castle; Culloden Battlefield (NTS); Loch Ness; Moniack Castle (Highland Winery)

Westbourne

★★★★ GUEST ACCOMMODATION
Address: 50 Huntly Street, INVERNESS IV3 5HS
Tel: 01463 220700
Fax: 01463 220700
Email: richard@westbourne.org.uk
Website: www.westbourne.org.uk
Map ref: 12, NH64
Directions: A9 onto A82 at football stadium over 3
rdbts, at 4th rdbt 1st left onto Wells St & Huntly St
Rooms: 9 en suite, **S** £45–£55 **D** £70–£85
Parking: 6 **Closed:** Xmas & New Year

This splendid guest house, overlooking the River Ness to the city centre, is Scottish through and through, with a tartan-theme decor in all the bedrooms and good old Scottish family names given to all rooms. The best traditions of Scottish hospitality are maintained, and the proprietors were finalists in the AA's Landlady of the Year award 2006. Deceptively spacious, the guesthouse was built in 1998 to provide the highest standards of comfort and convenience and includes two particularly large bedrooms sleeping four and three adults respectively. The lounge has a range of books, games and puzzles, plus internet access. The thoughtful approach of owners Richard and Nan Paxton includes an impressive range of facilities in the bedrooms, all designed to ensure entertainment and every comfort and convenience. Some rooms also have a safe. A full Highlanders breakfast would suit anyone preparing for a day tramping over the mountains, and the kitchen can also cater for vegetarian and other special diets.

Recommended in the area

Loch Ness; Inverness Castle; Culloden Battlefield

Craiglinnhe House

★★★★ GUEST HOUSE

Address: Lettermore, BALLACHULISH PH49 4JD
Tel: 01855 811270
Email: info@craiglinnhe.co.uk
Website: www.craiglinnhe.co.uk
Map ref: 9, NN05
Directions: From village A82 onto A828, Craiglinnhe
1.50m on left
Rooms: 5 en suite, **S** £42–£60 **D** £56–£80
Notes: ⊗ on premises 🚸 under 13yrs **Parking:** 5
Closed: 24–26 Dec

Craiglinnhe House was built in 1885 by the owner of the local slate quarry and, though it retains all of its Victorian style and character, it has been modernised to provide the utmost comfort: a perfect base for walking, climbing, skiing and exploring the West Highlands. The elegant lounge has stunning views of the loch and is a lovely place to relax, while the dining room provides a fine setting for the superb meals cooked by owner David Hughes. The stylish en suite bedrooms are attractive and well equipped.

Recommended in the area

Glencoe; Fort William; Whisky distillery

Lyn-Leven

★★★★ GUEST HOUSE

Address: West Laroch, BALLACHULISH PH49 4JP
Tel: 01855 811392
Fax: 01855 811600
Email: macleodcilla@aol.com
Website: www.lynleven.co.uk
Map ref: 9, NN05
Directions: Off A82 signed on left West Laroch
Rooms: 12 en suite (12 GF), **S** £30–£50 **D** £50–£64
Parking: 12 **Closed:** Xmas

Beautifully situated, this guest house maintains high standards in all areas. Highland hospitality puts guests at their ease, and the spectacular views of Loch Leven guarantee plenty to talk about. Bedrooms vary in size, are prettily decorated, and have showers and some thoughtful extras. The spacious lounge and smart dining room make the most of the scenic outlook, and the lounge has Sky TV. Delicious home-cooked evening meals (£9 per person) and breakfasts are served at separate tables. There is ample parking.

Recommended in the area

Ballachulish Country House Golf Course; Glencoe Visitor Centre and Museum

Corriechoille Lodge

★ ★ ★ ★ 🛟 GUEST HOUSE

Address: SPEAN BRIDGE PH34 4EY
Tel: 01397 712002
Website: www.corriechoille.com
Map ref: 12, NN28
Directions: Off A82 signed Corriechoille, continue 2.25m, left at road fork (10mph sign). At end of tarmac, turn right up hill & left
Rooms: 4 en suite (1 GF), **S** £40–£46 **D** £72–£60
Notes: ⊗ on premises 👶 under 7yrs **Parking:** 7
Closed: Nov–Mar

Standing above the River Spean, Corriechoille Lodge is an extensively renovated former fishing lodge near Spean Bridge. There are magnificent views of the Nevis range and surrounding mountains from the comfortable first-floor lounge and some of the bedrooms. Guest rooms are spacious and well-appointed, with en suite facilities, TVs and tea and coffee facilities. Enjoy traditional breakfasts, with evening meals available by arrangement. The house is licensed and stocks many single malt whiskies.
Recommended in the area
Glenfinnan Monument; Viaduct & Station Museum; Ben Nevis footpath/Glen Nevis; Creag Meagaidh

The Smiddy House

★ ★ ★ ★ ❀❀ RESTAURANT WITH ROOMS

Address: Roy Bridge Road, SPEAN BRIDGE
          PH34 4EU
Tel: 01397 712335
Fax: 01397 712043
Email: enquiry@smiddyhouse.co.uk
Website: www.smiddyhouse.co.uk
Map ref: 12, NN28
Directions: In village centre, A82 onto A86
Rooms: 4 en suite, **S** £60–£75 **D** £60–£80
Parking: 15

Ideally located for exploring the Highlands, Smiddy House offers genuine Scottish hospitality in luxurious surroundings. The guest rooms are well appointed with luxury linen and towels. The restaurant, Russell's, is awarded two AA Rosettes and provides fine Scottish cuisine in a relaxed and informal setting; there is a garden room where guests can enjoy a pre-dinner drink whilst perusing the evening's menu.
Recommended in the area
Ben Nevis and the Nevis range; Loch Ness; Glenfinnan Monument

Glenan Lodge

★ ★ ★ GUEST HOUSE
Address: TOMATIN IV13 7YT
Tel: 01808 511217
Email: enquiries@glenanlodge.co.uk
Website: www.glenanlodge.co.uk
Map ref: 12, NH82
Directions: Off A9 to Tomatin, signed to Lodge
Rooms: 7 en suite, **S** £27 **D** £54
Notes: ⊗ on premises ⚲ under 5yrs
Parking: 7

A jewel of the Highlands, Glenan Lodge is situated on the edge of the village of Tomatin just two miles from the Caingorms National Park and only 15 miles from Inverness to the north or Aviemore to the south. The house provides the perfect base from which to explore the Highlands or visit the many malt whisky distilleries in the area. For the fly fisher, the guest house has a two-mile beat on the River Finhorn for salmon and wild brown trout fishing. The Finhorn Valley is a haven for wildlife; red deer, mountain goats, golden eagles, red kites and many more birds of prey are regularly spotted, and red squirrels are daily visitors to the garden. The location is ideal for golf, cycling, walking or even skiing on Cairngorm. All the bedrooms are decorated to a high standard with en suite facilities (bath or shower), televisions and tea and coffee making equipment. There is also a guests' lounge with an open fire, piano and a selection of games and puzzles to while away the winter nights. The premises are licensed so you can enjoy a drink as you sit and relax. Home-cooked evening meals are available by prior arrangement.

Recommended in the area

Culloden; Strathspey Steam Railway; Cawdor Castle

The Old Man of Hoy, Orkney Isles

Tigh Na Leigh Guesthouse

★★★★★ 🛏 GUEST ACCOMMODATION

Address: 22–24 Airlie Street, ALYTH PH11 8AJ
Tel: 01828 632372
Fax: 01828 632279
Email: bandcblack@yahoo.co.uk
Website: www.tighnaleigh.co.uk
Map ref: 10, NO24
Directions: In town centre on B952
Rooms: 5 en suite (1 GF), **S** £45 **D** £95–£110
Notes: ⚏ under 12yrs **Parking:** 5 **Closed:** Jan

Winner of the AA Guest Accommodation of the Year for Scotland 2006/2007 award, this guest house in the heart of the country town of Alyth is an absolute delight. Tigh Na Leigh is Gaelic for 'The house of the Doctor or Physician', and although it may look rather sombre from the outside, the property is superbly modernised and furnished with an eclectic mix of modern and antique furniture. The large, luxurious and individually decorated bedrooms, one of which is on the ground floor, are very well equipped, and most rooms have spa baths. All rooms have TV/DVD player, tea and coffee-making facilities, hairdryer and bathrobes. For extra luxury, one room has a grand four-poster, while the suite has its own lounge with very comfortable sofa. The public rooms comprise three entirely different lounges, one of which has a log fire for cooler evenings and another of which provides broadband internet connection. Delicious home-cooked dinners have an international flavour, and these, as well as the hearty breakfasts, are all made from the best of Scottish produce – vegetables come from the kitchen garden or surrounding (organic) farms where possible. Meals are served in the huge conservatory/dining room overlooking the spectacular landscaped garden.

Recommended in the area

Scone Palace; Glamis Castle; Dunkeld Cathedral

Gilmore House

★ ★ ★ ★ B&B

Address: Perth Road, BLAIRGOWRIE PH10 6EJ
Tel: 01250 872791
Email: jill@gilmorehouse.co.uk
Website: www.gilmorehouse.co.uk
Map ref: 10, NO14
Directions: On A93 S
Rooms: 3 en suite, D £60–£65
Parking: 3
Closed: Xmas

Built in 1899, this deceptively spacious late-Victorian detached house is the perfect base from which to explore all that Perthshire has to offer, being conveniently located for Glamis Castle, Scone Palace and Dunkeld. The three comfortable en suite rooms include a cosy king, a twin and a very spacious superking. There are two beautiful lounges for guests' use, with plenty of reading material to plan your activities. A full Scottish breakfast or something lighter is served in the elegant dining room overlooking the front garden, and the owners pride themselves on the relaxed, warm and friendly ambience.

Recommended in the area

Glamis Castle; Blair Castle; Perth races

Merlindale

★ ★ ★ ★ B&B

Address: Perth Road, CRIEFF PH7 3EQ
Tel: 01764 655205
Fax: 01764 655205
Email: merlin.dale@virgin.net
Website: www.merlindale.co.uk
Map ref: 10, NN82
Directions: On A85 350yds from E end of High St
Rooms: 3 en suite **Notes:** ⊗ on premises
Parking: 3 **Closed:** 9 Dec–10 Jan

First impressions of this stylish detached house and its neat garden are pleasing indeed and, once through the door, this is reinforced at every turn. There is a spacious lounge, an impressive library and an elegant dining room where delicious evening meals are available (with 24 hours' notice) in addition to the traditional Scottish breakfasts. Bedrooms are pretty and comfortable. In a quiet residential area, Merlindale is within walking distance of the town centre.

Recommended in the area

Drummond Castle; Perth; Scone

Stirling Castle

An Lochan Tormaukin

★★★★ ◉ INN

Address: GLENDEVON FK14 7JY
Tel: 0845 371 1414
Email: info@anlochan.co.uk
Website: www.anlochan.co.uk
Map ref: 10, NN90
Rooms: 13 en suite, **S** £95 **D** £120 **Parking:** 50

This delightful and stylish coaching inn, dating from the 17th century and set in the lovely Perthshire hills, is just five minutes away from Gleneagles, with its famous championship golf courses. It is perfectly located for getting away from it all, yet only an hour from Glasgow and Edinburgh. Great attention is paid to guests' comfort by the welcoming team. Open log fires and stone walls add to the character and comfort of the interior. Each of the en suite bedrooms is individually furnished and decorated. Food is taken seriously at An Lochan, with the emphasis on delicious meals made from locally sourced ingredients, including Highland beef, Perthshire lamb, wild boar, venison and shellfish. Breakfast is equally varied and impressive. There is plenty to do in the area, with some good walking nearby.

Recommended in the area

Stirling Castle; Scone Palace; Crieff

Crailing Old School

★★★★ ▤ ≋ GUEST HOUSE

Address: CRAILING, Nr Jedburgh, TD8 6TL
Tel: 01835 850382
Email: jean.player@virgin.net
Website: www.crailingoldschool.co.uk
Map ref: 10, NT62
Directions: A698 onto B6400 signed Nisbet, Crailing Old School also signed
Rooms: 4 (2 en suite) (1 GF), **S** £38.50 **D** £65–£85
Notes: ⚹ under 9yrs **Parking:** 6
Closed: 24 Dec–2 Jan, 1 wk Feb & 2wks autumn

This delightful Victorian village school has been imaginatively renovated to combine original features with modern comforts. Jean Leach-Player was a runner-up in the AA's Landlady of the Year award on three occasions. This is a good area for outdoor pursuits including fishing, walking and golf. Breakfasts (and dinner by arrangement) are served in the stylish lounge/dining room and the best local ingredients are used. The lodge annexe, 10 metres from the house, offers ground floor access. Wi-fi is available.

Recommended in the area

St Cuthbert's Way; The Teviot and Tweed Rivers; Roxburghe Championship Golf Course

The Horseshoe Inn

★ ★ ★ ★ ◉◉◉ RESTAURANT WITH ROOMS
Address: EDDLESTON, Peebles EH45 8QP
Tel: 01721 730225
Fax: 01721 730268
Email: reservations@horseshoeinn.co.uk
Website: www.horseshoeinn.co.uk
Map ref: 10, NT24
Directions: A703, 5m N of Peebles
Rooms: 8 en suite (6 GF), **S** £70 **D** £100
Parking: 20
Closed: 25 Dec & Mon

Originally a blacksmith's smiddy, located just 30 minutes from Edinburgh, the inn underwent a complete transformation in 2005. Vivienne Steele has stamped her identity throughout the place, creating an informal and relaxed bistro area, a warm and cosy lounge and the impressive, award-winning Bardoulet's Restaurant. The following year the adjacent Horseshoe Lodge was refurbished, providing high quality accommodation in a Victorian former primary school. Each room is individually decorated and equipped with en suite facilities and either double or twin beds. Guests at the lodge are on hand to enjoy all the delights of the inn, and while the decor sets the mood it is the food that leaves customers wanting to return time and time again. Patrick Bardoulet revels in having his own restaurant and uses his French flair to combine his native cuisine with local ingredients to provide a host of unique dishes that blend the modern and the traditional. The front of house team, headed by Vivienne, provide friendly service, advice on dishes and wines, and cater for your every need, so you can sit back, relax and enjoy the company, the food and the surroundings.

Recommended in the area

Dawyck Botanic Gardens; Robert Smail's Printing Works; Traquair House

Fauhope House

★ ★ ★ ★ ★ ⌂ GUEST HOUSE

Address: Gattonside, MELROSE TD6 9LU
Tel: 01896 823184
Fax: 01896 823184
Email: info@fauhopehouse.com
Website: www.fauhopehouse.com
Map ref: 10, NT53
Directions: 0.7m N of Melrose over River Tweed.
N off B6360 at Gattonside 30mph sign (E) up
long driveway

Rooms: 3 en suite, **S** from £60 **D** £80–£110 **Notes:** ⊗ on premises **Parking:** 10

Fauhope House is a fine example of the Arts and Crafts style of architecture of the 1890s, designed by Sidney Mitchell, who was also responsible for Edinburgh's much-admired Ramsey Gardens property. It is perched high on a hillside on the north-east edge of the village of Gattonside, and provides the kind of breathtaking views of the River Tweed and the Eildon Hills that have inspired artists and writers down the years. It offers discerning guests comfortable seclusion and the space to relax, yet is just a ten-minute walk from the Borders town of Melrose, with its shops, restaurant and small theatre. A short drive will take you to Abbotsford, home of Sir Walter Scott, and the Robert Adam-designed Mellerstain House. The hospitality provided by experienced host Sheila Robson is first class, and the delightful country house boasts a splendid interior, furnished and decorated to the highest possible standard. Stunning floral displays enhance the overall interior design, and lavish drapes and fine furniture grace the drawing room and the magnificent dining room, where full Scottish or a continental breakfast is served. The generously sized bedrooms are luxurious and superbly equipped, each with individual furnishings and thoughtful extras.

Recommended in the area

Melrose Abbey; Roxburghe Golf Course; River Tweed; Fantastic walks

The Crescent

★★★★★ GUEST HOUSE
Address: 26 Bellevue Crescent, AYR KA7 2DR
Tel: 01292 287329
Email: joyce&mike@26crescent.co.uk
Website: www.26crescent.co.uk
Map ref: 9, NS32
Directions: Leave A79 onto rdbt, 3rd exit onto King St. Left onto Bellevue Crescent
Rooms: 5 en suite, **S** £50 **D** £70–£80
Notes: ⊗ on premises

The Cresent, built in 1898, forms part of an imposing terrace of houses in a quiet residential area of Ayr. Despite its peaceful location, the seafront, town centre and racecourse are all near. The guest house offers a traditional warm welcome and accommodation in comfortable and well appointed bedrooms with en suite facilities of a high standard. Single, double and twin rooms are available, with a four-poster suite for special occasions. Tea- and coffee-making equipment is provided along with other thoughtful extras. Breakfasts are served in the charming dining room and a lounge is available.

Recommended in the area

Culzean Castle & Country Park; Souter Johnnie's Cottage (Burns Museum); Heads of Ayr Farm Park

Ladyburn

★★★★★ ⓖ ⓓ GUEST ACCOMMODATION
Address: MAYBOLE KA19 7SG
Tel: 01655 740585
Fax: 01655 740580
Email: jh@ladyburn.co.uk
Website: www.ladyburn.co.uk
Map ref: 9, NS20
Directions: A77 (Glasgow/Stranraer) at Maybole turn to B7023 to Crosshill and right at War Memorial. In 2m turn left for approx 1m, on right
Rooms: 5 en suite, **S** £65 **D** £100 **Notes:** ⊗ on premises 12

This charming country house dates back to the early 1600s and is the home of the Hepburn family. There are antiques throughout this lovely home and the classically styled bedrooms are individually designed. Two of the bedrooms have four-poster beds and all are full of character with luxurious fabrics and pictures. Guests can relax in the gracious drawing room. Dinner is by prior arrangement and served in the candlelit dining room. Ladyburn sits in 5 acres of beautiful gardens.

Recommended in the area

Alloway, birthplace of Robert Burns; Culzean Castle (NTS); Croy Brae (Electric Brae)

Edzell Castle, Angus

Annfield Guest House

★★★★ GUEST HOUSE

Address: 18 North Church Street, CALLANDER
FK17 8EG
Tel: 01877 330204
Fax: 01877 330674
Email: reservations@annfieldguesthouse.co.uk
Website: www.annfieldguesthouse.co.uk
Map ref: 9, NN60
Directions: Off A84 Main St onto North Church St,
at top on right
Rooms: 7 (4 en suite) (1 pri facs), **S** £30–£40 **D** £55–£65 **Notes:** ⊗ on premises 🛇 under 6yrs
Parking: 7 **Closed:** Xmas & New Year

Quietly situated just two minutes' walk from Callander's bustling main street, this is a beautiful Victorian villa. Recently fully renovated to the highest standards, Annfield retains all the charm of a bygone age. The owners pride themselves on their attention to detail, from fresh flowers and goose-down duvets to silver cutlery and soft fluffy towels. Breakfast is a highlight, all prepared with local ingredients.

Recommended in the area

Falkirk Wheel; Loch Lomond and Trossachs National Park; Stirling Castle; Loch Katrine

---

Arden House

★★★★ 🛏 GUEST ACCOMMODATION

Address: Bracklinn Road, CALLANDER FK17 8EQ
Tel: 01877 330235
Email: ardenhouse@onetel.com
Website: www.ardenhouse.org.uk
Map ref: 9, NN60
Directions: Off A84 Main St onto Bracklinn Rd,
house 200yds on left
Rooms: 6 en suite (2 GF), **S** £37.50 **D** £70–£80
Notes: ⊗ on premises 🛇 under 14yrs **Parking:** 10
Closed: Nov–Mar

The fictional home of Doctors Finlay and Cameron, in a peaceful area of the town, is now owned by Ian and William, who offer a genuine welcome with tea and home-made cake on arrival. The comfortable en suite bedrooms have been refurbished and provided with thoughtful extras. A stylish lounge and bright dining room are inviting, and traditional Scottish breakfasts are a definite high spot of any visit. Runners-up in the AA Friendliest Landlady of the Year award 2008–9.

Recommended in the area

Loch Lomond and Trossachs National Park; Stirling Castle; Loch Katrine; Falkirk Wheel

Fort William, sheltered by Ben Nevis, Highlands

Bomains Farm

★★★★ GUEST HOUSE

Address: Bo'Ness, LINLITHGOW EH49 7RQ
Tel: 01506 822188
Fax: 01506 824433
Email: bunty.kirk@onetel.net
Website: www.bomains.co.uk
Map ref: 10, NS97
Directions: A706 1.5m N towards Bo Ness, left at golf course x-rds, 1st farm on right
Rooms: 5 (4 en suite) (1 pri facs), **S** £35–£40
D £50–£70 **Parking:** 12

This friendly farmhouse has stunning views of the Firth of Forth, Linlithgow and the hills beyond. The warmth of the Kirks' welcome is apparent from the moment you step into the hallway with its impressive galleried staircase. The beautifully decorated bedrooms are enhanced by quality fabrics and modern hand-painted furniture. The traditional Scottish breakfast is served at a mahogany table. The working farm is next to a golf course with fishing nearby, and is convenient for Edinburgh Airport.

Recommended in the area

Falkirk Wheel; Linlithgow Palace; Bo'ness Steam Railway

Caerlaverock Castle's triangular moat

Shorefield House

★★★★ GUEST HOUSE

Address: Edinbane, PORTREE, Isle of Skye,
IV51 9PW
Tel: 01470 582444
Fax: 01470 582414
Email: stay@shorefield-house.com
Website: www.shorefield-house.com
Map ref: 11, NG35
Directions: 12m from Portree & 8m from Dunvegan,
off A850 into Edinbane, 1st on right
Rooms: 4 en suite (3 GF), **D** £74–£90 **Notes:** ⊗ on premises **Parking:** 10 **Closed:** Nov–Etr

Peacefully situated looking across loch and sea, Shorefield House enables easy exploration of all parts of Skye by its location midway between Portree and Dunvegan. Spacious, high quality accommodation and hearty traditional breakfasts are accompanied by a continental buffet. Customer care and comfort are priority here. With excellent local restaurants for evening meals, this is the place to appreciate Skye's rich culture, landscapes and sunsets.

Recommended in the area

Dunvegan Castle and seal colony; The Three Chimneys Restaurant; Talisker Whisky Distillery

Glen Orchy House

★★★★ GUEST HOUSE

Address: 20 Knab Road, LERWICK ZE1 0AX
Tel: 01595 692031
Fax: 01595 692031
Email: glenorchy.house@virgin.net
Website: www.guesthouselerwick.com
Map ref: 13,
Directions: Next to coastguard station
Rooms: 24 en suite (4 GF) **Parking:** 10

Built as an Episcopalian convent in 1904, Glen Orchy House has subsequently been a rectory and a private residence, and was acquired by current owner Trevor Howarth in 1991, since when the house has been carefully renovated and extended. It stands above Lerwick, with views over the Knab, within easy walking distance of the town centre. A choice of double, single, twin and family rooms is offered, all en suite, including one ground-floor room with disabled facilities. There is an honesty bar in the ground-floor lounge, along with a selection of games and books. Substantial breakfasts are served, and the restaurant offers a delicious Thai menu.

Recommended in the area

Mousa Broch; Jarshof; Shetland Museum

WALES

Caerphilly Castle

Wern Farm

★ ★ ★ ★ ★ ≣ FARMHOUSE

Address: Pentraeth Road, MENAI BRIDGE,
Isle of Anglesey LL59 5RR
Tel: 01248 712421
Fax: 01248 715421
Email: wernfarmanglesey@onetel.com
Website: www.angleseyfarms.com/wern.htm
Map ref: 5, SH57
Directions: A55 junct 8 over Britannia Bridge onto
A5025, over rdbt & pass large garage, farm on right

Rooms: 3 (2 en suite), **D** £75–£80 **Notes:** ⊗ ⛔ under 12yrs **Parking:** 10 **Closed:** Nov–Feb

Peter and Linda Brayshaw's lovely 18th-century home is set in 160 acres of grazing pasture and woodland with views of Snowdonia. Spacious bedrooms are furnished with style and feature whirlpool bathrooms. A wealth of thoughtful extras add to guests' comfort, and memorable breakfasts are served in the conservatory dining room, which overlooks the gardens and pond. Other facilities include an all-weather tennis court, a games room with an antique 3/4 size billiard table, and a comfortable lounge.

Recommended in the area

Historic Beaumaris; Plas Newydd & Penrhyn Castle (NT); Newburgh Warren National Nature Reserve

Capel Dewi Uchaf Country House

★ ★ ★ ★ ≣ B&B

Address: Capel Dewi, CARMARTHEN SA32 8AY
Tel: 01267 290799
Email: uchaffarm@aol.com
Website: www.walescottageholidays.uk.com
Map ref: 1, SN42
Directions: On B4300 between Capel Dewi
& junct B4310
Rooms: 3 en suite, **S** £55 **D** £80
Notes: ⊗ on premises **Parking:** 10 **Closed:** Xmas

This beautiful Grade II listed farmhouse stands in 34 acres of lush grazing meadow by the River Towy where salmon fishing is available. A welcoming fire and period decor enhance the property's original features and breakfasts are served on the terrace on fine mornings. Fresh local produce, including home-grown vegetables and fruit, home baking and home-made preserves, is a feature of the memorable dinners and generous Welsh breakfasts. Dinner parties are catered for.

Recommended in the area

National Botanic Garden of Wales; Aberglasney Gardens; Newton House (NT)

Marloes Sands, Pembrokeshire Coast National Park

Sarnau Mansion

★★★★ GUEST ACCOMMODATION

Address: Llysonnen Road, CARMARTHEN SA33 5DZ
Tel: 01267 211404
Fax: 01267 211404
Email: fernihough@so1405.force9.co.uk
Website: www.sarnaumansion.co.uk
Map ref: 1, SN42
Directions: 5m W of Carmarthen. Off A40 onto B4298 & Bancyfelin road, Sarnau on right
Rooms: 3 en suite, **S** £45 **D** £65–£70
Notes: ⊗ on premises ⚑ under 5yrs **Parking:** 10

This fine Grade II listed Georgian mansion is set in the heart of the Carmarthen countryside, in 16 acres of grounds, which include a tennis court. It's not far from here to the many attractions and beaches of south and west Wales, and it is a delightful place to return to each evening. Many original features have been retained and the public areas are both comfortable and elegant. Bedrooms are large and nicely decorated, and all of the rooms have stunning rural views.

Recommended in the area

National Botanic Garden of Wales; Aberglasney Gardens; Dylan Thomas Boathouse, Laugharne

Allt Y Golau Farmhouse

★ ★ ★ ★ 🏠 FARMHOUSE

Address: Allt Y Golau Uchaf, FELINGWM UCHAF
SA32 7BB
Tel: 01267 290455
Fax: 01267 290743
Email: alltygolau@btinternet.com
Website: www.alltygolau.com
Map ref: 1, SN52
Directions: A40 onto B4310, N for 2m. 1st on left
after Felin Gwm Uchaf

Rooms: 3 (2 en suite) (1 pri facs) (2 GF), **S** £45 **D** £65 **Notes:** ⊗ on premises **Parking:** 3
Closed: 20 Dec–2 Jan

Beautifully renovated by owners Colin and Jacquie Rouse, this Georgian stone farmhouse offers the epitome of gracious country living and a welcome that earned Jacquie a place in the finals of the AA Friendliest Landlady of the Year Awards in 2008. The owners are knowledgeable about the heritage and nature of the area, and are always happy to advise their guests on how to get the best out of their visit. The setting of the farmhouse, with views over the Tywi Valley towards the Black Mountain, is glorious, and the 2 acres of gardens include a fine orchard. Snowdrops, daffodils and bluebells successively carpet the ground in spring, and ducks, geese, turkeys, and the hens that provide the breakfast eggs roam free here. Inside the house there are cosy sofas and easy chairs around the lovely old fireplace in the lounge. The traditional dining room features one big elm table and an eclectic display of antiques, including a stately grandfather clock. Breakfast here is a real highlight, with home baking and the finest local produce accompanying those fresh eggs. The bright, comfortable bedrooms are in traditional style, with pine furniture and patchwork quilts.

Recommended in the area

National Botanic Garden of Wales; Aberglasney Gardens; Dynefwr Castle and Park

Coedllys Country House

★ ★ ★ ★ ★ B&B

Address: Llangynin, ST CLEARS SA33 4JY
Tel: 01994 231455
Fax: 01994 231441
Email: coedllys@btinternet.com
Website: www.coedllyscountryhouse.co.uk
Map ref: 1, SN21
Rooms: 3 en suite, S £52.50–£62.50 D £80–£95
Notes: ⋈ no children under 12yrs
Parking: 6
Closed: Xmas

Set in 11 acres of grounds, Coedllys is the ultimate country hideaway, tucked away in a tranquil spot and surrounded by farmland with far-reaching views and a pretty woodland dell. Guests are invited to amble around and enjoy the abundant wildlife. Owners Valerie and Keith Harber are serious about conservation and nature and they provide a refuge for countless animals, including sheep, donkeys and goats. Inside, this large, beautiful house has been tastefully restored to provide elegant bedrooms with antique furniture and luxurious fabrics, as well as a host of thoughtful extras such as chocolates, fruit, flowers and magazines alongside soft bathrobes, slippers, flat-screen TV/DVD, free Wi-fi, comfortable sofas and large, inviting antique beds – all of which combine to make a stay here truly memorable. Energetic guests are welcome to make use of the fitness suite, or you can simply relax in the Hydro swimming pool (available April–September only) and sauna. An extensive breakfast menu, from lighter choices through to a full breakfast, uses the finest local produce, including free-range eggs from Coedllys's own chickens.

Recommended in the area

Dylan Thomas Boathouse, Laugharne; Millennium Coastal Path; National Botanical Gardens

Yr Hafod

★★★★ GUEST HOUSE

Address: 1 South Marine Terrace, ABERYSTWYTH
SY23 1JX
Tel: 01970 617579
Fax: 01970 636835
Email: johnyrhafod@aol.com
Website: www.yrhafod.co.uk
Map ref: 2, SN58
Directions: On south promenade between harbour & castle

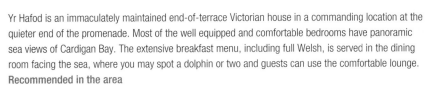

Rooms: 7 (3 en suite), **S** £28–£45 **D** £56–£74 **Notes:** ⊗ on premises **Closed:** Xmas & New Year

Yr Hafod is an immaculately maintained end-of-terrace Victorian house in a commanding location at the quieter end of the promenade. Most of the well equipped and comfortable bedrooms have panoramic sea views of Cardigan Bay. The extensive breakfast menu, including full Welsh, is served in the dining room facing the sea, where you may spot a dolphin or two and guests can use the comfortable lounge.

Recommended in the area

Devil's Bridge Steam Train; Ceredigion Museum; Constitution Hill

Afon View Guest House

★★★★ GUEST HOUSE

Address: Holyhead Road, BETWS-Y-COED
LL24 0AN
Tel: 01690 710726
Fax: 01690 710726
Email: welcome@afon-view.co.uk
Website: www.afon-view.co.uk
Map ref: 5, SH75
Directions: On A5 150yds E of HSBC bank
Rooms: 7 en suite, **S** £40–£45 **D** £60–£85

Notes: ⊗ on premises 🚼 under 4yrs **Parking:** 7 **Closed:** 23–26 Dec

Open countryside stretches away at the back of this charming stone house towards the thick woodland cresting Mount Garmon, but it is also convenient for the shops, restaurants, pubs and the station in one of the loveliest villages in North Wales. Inside, there are lots of original Victorian features, including beautiful fireplaces. This is a very cosy place to return to after a day exploring, and as well as plenty of books, maps and friendly advice, there's safe undercover storage for bicycles and a drying room.

Recommended in the area

Snowdon Mountain Railway; Swallow Falls; Conwy Castle

Cwmanog Isaf Farm

★★★★ FARMHOUSE

Address: Fairy Glen, BETWS-Y-COED LL24 0SL
Tel: 01690 710225 & 078 0842 1634
Email: heather.hughes3@tesco.net
Website: www.cwmanogisaffarmholidays.co.uk
Map ref: 5, SH75
Directions: 1m S of Betws-y-Coed off A470 by Fairy Glen Hotel, 500yds on farm lane
Rooms: 3 (2 en suite) (1 pri facs) (1 GF), **S** £45–£60 **D** £60–£70 **Notes:** ⊗ on premises ✵ under 15yrs **Parking:** 4 **Closed:** 15 Dec–7 Feb

Hidden away, yet only a 20-minute stroll from the Victorian village of Betws-y-Coed, Cwmanog Isaf, a 200-year-old house on a working livestock farm, is set in 30 acres of undulating land, including the renowned Fairy Glen, and has stunning views of the surrounding countryside. It provides comfortably furnished and well equipped bedrooms (one on the ground floor). and serves wholesome Welsh farmhouse cuisine using home-reared and local organic produce, home-made bread and preserves.

Recommended in the area

Bodnant Gardens; Fairy Glen; Portmeirion

Park Hill

★★★★ GUEST HOUSE

Address: Llanrwst Road, BETWS-Y-COED LL24 0HD
Tel: 01690 710540
Fax: 01690 710540
Email: welcome@park-hill.co.uk
Website: www.park-hill.co.uk
Map ref: 5, SH75
Directions: 0.5m N of Betws-y-Coed on A470
Rooms: 9 en suite, **S** £55–£80 **D** £60–£84
Notes: ⊗ on premises ✵ under 8yrs **Parking:** 11

The Park Hill, a fine Victorian building, is situated in the Snowdonia National Park, and has breathtaking views over the River Conwy. It makes an ideal base for walkers. You will find teddy bears here, there and everywhere, as the owners have a collection of 200. Guests can enjoy a swim in the splendid indoor heated swimming pool, relax in the whirlpool bath or take a sauna, before retiring to the bar or the comfortable and well-equipped en suite bedrooms. Breakfasts and dinners are freshly made from local produce.

Recommended in the area

Mount Snowdon; Tree Top Adventure, Snowdonia; Conwy Castle

Penmachno Hall

★★★★★ ⊜ GUEST ACCOMMODATION

Address: Penmachno, BETWS-Y-COED LL24 0PU
Tel: 01690 760410
Fax: 01690 760410
Email: stay@penmachnohall.co.uk
Website: www.penmachnohall.co.uk
Map ref: 5, SH75
Directions: 4m S of Betws-y-Coed. A5 onto B4406 to Penmachno, over bridge, right at Eagles pub signed Ty Mawr
Rooms: 3 en suite, S £75–£90 D £75–£90
Notes: ⊗ on premises **Parking:** 3 **Closed:** Xmas & New Year

Penmachno Hall, a lovingly restored Victorian rectory, is situated in over 2 acres of mature grounds in the secluded Glasgwm Valley in Snowdonia National Park. With its breathtaking views and quiet forest tracks leading to secluded waterfalls, the valley is a haven of tranquillity within easy reach of bustling Betws-y-Coed. This is an establishment that prides itself on catering for the visitor's every need. Stylish decor and quality furnishings highlight the many original features throughout the ground-floor areas, while the bedrooms come with a wealth of thoughtful extras, and each benefits from panoramic views. The spacious Morning Room has comfortable sofas and large bay windows overlooking the garden; it houses a large collection of books, maps, walking guides and tourist information, as well as games and puzzles. The slightly more formal dining room is the venue for evening meals, served dinner-party style round a central dining table. The set five-course menu is prepared daily, based on the preferences of that night's diners and using only the finest, fresh local produce. An extensive wine list complements the meal, and expert advice is available to help guests select the most appropriate wine for their tastes and the food being served.

Recommended in the area

Snowdon; Bodnant Garden (NT); Portmeirion

Tan-y-Foel Country House

★ ★ ★ ★ ★ ◉◉◉ ≙ GUEST HOUSE

Address: Capel Garmon, BETWS-Y-COED LL26 0RE
Tel: 01690 710507
Fax: 01690 710681
Email: enquiries@tyfhotel.co.uk
Website: www.tyfhotel.co.uk
Map ref: 5, SH75
Directions: 1.5m E of Betws-y-Coed. Off A5 onto A470 N, 2m right for Capel Garmon, establishment signed 1.5m on left

Rooms: 5 en suite (1 GF), **S** £110–£155 **D** £149–£225
Notes: ⊗ on premises ⚘ under 12yrs **Parking:** 14 **Closed:** Christmas and New Year

The 17th-century Welsh stone exterior of this country house gives no hint of the interior, where a series of intimate and immaculately designed rooms unfold. Bold ideas fuse the traditional character of the building with contemporary style, giving it an elegant simplicity that goes hand-in-hand with luxurious facilities. Tan-y-Foel is aimed at the discerning traveller looking for a gourmet hideaway in a peaceful, location in the heart of Snowdonia National Park. The surrounding countryside is delightful, with the opportunity for some lovely walks. Independent and family-run, this place offers a highly original country-house experience, with the owners' influence clearly in evidence throughout. There is a range of options, not only in bedroom size but in the style of decor too, and many of the regular guests have their own favourites. Naturally, each bedroom has its own bathroom, and each is well decorated and furnished, with a selection of welcoming extras. A major highlight of a stay here is the food, and dinner is a memorable occasion, consisting of carefully chosen fresh ingredients, skilfully prepared.

Recommended in the area

Bodnant Garden (NT); Snowdon Mountain Railway; Conwy Castle

Ty Gwyn Inn

★ ★ ★ INN
Address: BETWS-Y-COED LL24 0SG
Tel: 01690 710383
Fax: 01690 710383
Email: mratcl1050@aol.com
Website: www.tygwynhotel.co.uk
Map ref: 5, SH75
Directions: Junct of A5 & A470, by Waterloo Bridge
Rooms: 13 (10 en suite) (1 GF), **S** £40–£65
D £72–£120 **Parking:** 14 **Closed:** Mon–Wed in Jan

Originally a coaching inn, the Ty Gwyn dates back to 1636 and is situated on the edge of the village, close to the Waterloo Bridge. The inn retains many original features and the quality and style of the furnishings and the collections of memorabilia throughout enhance its intrinsic charm. Bedrooms, some of which feature antique and four-poster beds, are equipped with thoughtful extras. The en suite rooms have now been refurbished with new bath and shower rooms, and two rooms have spa tubs. The imaginative international dishes are prepared from fresh local produce.

Recommended in the area

Portmeirion Village; Snowdon Mountain Railway; Swallow Falls

The Old Rectory Country House

★ ★ ★ ★ ★ 🏠 GUEST ACCOMMODATION
Address: Llanrwst Road, Llansanffraid Glan Conwy,
CONWY LL28 5LF
Tel: 01492 580611
Email: info@oldrectorycountryhouse.co.uk
Website: www.oldrectorycountryhouse.co.uk
Map ref: 5, SH77
Directions: 0.5m S from A470/A55 junct on left,
by 30mph sign
Rooms: 6 en suite **Notes:** ✚ under 5yrs
Parking: 10 **Closed:** 14 Dec–15 Jan

The house, situated in glorious gardens, certainly lives up to its Welsh motto 'Hardd Hafen Hedd' meaning 'Beautiful Haven of Peace'. It has stunning views over the Conwy estuary and across to the Snowdonian mountains. The bedrooms are extremely comfortable and hospitality trays, bathrobes and quality toiletries demonstrate the thoughtful attention to detail. The atmosphere is friendly and help is willingly given with touring routes and making reservations at the restaurants and inns nearby.

Recommended in the area

Bodnant Garden (NT); Conwy; Llandudno

Sychnant Pass House

★ ★ ★ ★ ★ ⊛ GUEST ACCOMMODATION

Address: Sychnant Pass Road, CONWY LL32 8BJ
Tel: 01492 585486
Fax: 01492 585486
Email: info@sychnantpasscountryhouse.co.uk
Website: www.sychnantpasscountryhouse.co.uk
Map ref: 5, SH77
Directions: 1.75m W of Conwy. Off A547 Bangor Rd
in town onto Mount Pleasant & Sychnant Pass Rd,
1.75m on right near top of hill

Rooms: 12 en suite (2 GF), **S** £75–£160 **D** £95–£180 **Parking:** 30 **Closed:** 24–26 Dec & Jan

There are fine views from this Edwardian house, set in 3 acres of luxuriant gardens with lawns, trees and a wild garden with ponds and a stream. Nestling in the foothills of the Snowdonia National Park, it was awarded the AA's Guest Accommodation of the Year for Wales in 2003–2004 and it continues to impress. Guests at this exceptional establishment, which offers country-house luxury, can unwind and enjoy the superb health and leisure facilities, with salt-treated (no chlorine) indoor pool, fitness equipment, sauna, and hot tub. The range of bedrooms are imaginative and stylish, and include four-poster rooms, suites with galleried bedrooms and two suites with their own private terrace and hot tub. They are all superbly comfortable and equipped with a range of thoughtful extras such as dressing gowns, big fluffy towels and refrigerator. Lounges, warmed by open fires in chillier months, are comfortable and inviting, and imaginative meals created from locally sourced seasonal produce by owner Graham, a trained chef who has worked at Gleneagles and Turnberry, are served in the attractive dining room. High teas are available for younger children.

Recommended in the area

Conwy; Bodnant Garden (NT); Penrhyn Castle

The Lion Inn Gwytherin

★★★★ INN

Address: GWYTHERIN, Nr Betws y Coed
LL22 8UU
Tel: 01745 860123
Fax: 01745 860556
Email: info@thelioninn.net
Website: www.thelioninn.net
Map ref: 5, SH86
Directions: Take A548 onto B5384
Rooms: 6 en suite, S £60 D £90
Notes: ⊗ on premises
Parking: 8

The Lion Inn is set in the picturesque village of Gwytherin, through which the River Cledwen flows. Quiet and off the beaten track, it makes an ideal place in which to relax and get away from the pressures of everyday life. All of the cosy en suite bedrooms have been tastefully refurbished to a high standard and complement the character of this 16th-century inn. Each room has been decorated in an individual style and includes a wealth of home comforts, including sumptuous beds with traditional colourful, hand-woven Welsh throws, DVD player, and use of an extensive collection of films, and tea and coffee making facilities. All of the rooms have a charming country outlook, and one room boasts its own balcony, from which to admire the view and the local wildlife, including red kites. Full English breakfasts include fresh eggs and a cafetiere of coffee or pot of tea. In the evening, guests can relax in front of a log fire with a glass of wine, chosen by Master of Wine Julia Harding, or try the locally brewed real ale before moving to the dining room to enjoy the freshly cooked Welsh produce, expertly and imaginatively prepared.

Recommended in the area

Bodnant Gardens; Conwy Falls; Conwy Castle

Abbey Lodge

★ ★ ★ ★ GUEST HOUSE

Address: 14 Abbey Road, LLANDUDNO LL30 2EA

Tel: 01492 878042

Fax: 01492 878042

Email: enquiries@abbeylodgeuk.com

Website: www.abbeylodgeuk.com

Map ref: 5, SH78

Directions: A546 to N end of town, onto Clement Av, right onto Abbey Rd

Rooms: 4 en suite, S £40 D £75

Notes: ⊗ on premises 👶 under 12yrs

Parking: 3 Closed: Dec–1 Feb

Built in 1840 and set on a leafy avenue within easy walking distance of the promenade, Abbey Lodge retains all the charm of a Victorian townhouse. This Grade II listed building is under the personal supervision of its owners, Dennis and Janet, who welcome guests with a complimentary pot of tea or coffee in the comfortable guest lounge or in the pretty walled garden that shelters beneath the Great Orme. The charming en suite bedrooms are well equipped with generous hospitality trays, hairdryers, TV, magazines, books, towels and bathrobes. Internet access is available throughout the house and the owners have a fine collection of local interest books and maps to help guests plan outings. The ingredients for breakfast are mostly sourced from the local farmers market, and packed lunches can be ordered. Abbey Lodge endeavours to have due regard for the environment and offers a discount to guests arriving by public transport. Abbey Road is quiet, yet only 5 minutes' walk from the pier and the Victorian High Street with a good choice of shops, cafés and a variety of restaurants.

Recommended in the area

Bodnant Gardens; Conwy Castle; Snowdonia Mountains

Can-Y-Bae

★★★★ GUEST ACCOMMODATION

Address: 10 Mostyn Crescent, Central Promenade,
LLANDUDNO LL30 1AR
Tel: 01492 874188
Fax: 01492 868376
Email: canybae@btconnect.com
Website: www.can-y-baehotel.com
Map ref: 5, SH78
Directions: located on promenade between Venue
Cymru Theatre & Band Stand
Rooms: 16 en suite (2 GF), **S** £35–£45 **D** £70–£80

Can-Y-Bae is an attractively renovated 19th-century hotel, centrally located on the promenade of this seaside resort, just 300 yards from the theatre, and five minutes' walk from the town centre and new shopping complex. Bedrooms are equipped with both practical and homely extras, including tea- and coffee-making facilities, and the upper floors are serviced by a lift. Day rooms include a lounge with sea views, a cosy bar and an attractive basement dining room where home-cooked meals are served.

Recommended in the area

Great Orme Tramway or Cable Car; Happy Valley Gardens; Festiniog and West Highland Railway

---

St Hilary Guest House

★★★★ GUEST ACCOMMODATION

Address: The Promenade, LLANDUDNO LL30 1BG
Tel: 01492 875551
Email: info@sthilaryguesthouse.co.uk
Website: www.sthilaryguesthouse.co.uk
Map ref: 5, SH78
Directions: On B5115 seafront road near North Wales Theatre
Rooms: 10 (9 en suite) (1 pri facs) (2 GF), **S** £35–£41
D £55–£75 **Notes:** ⊗ on premises **Closed:** end Nov–early Feb

This elegant Grade II listed Victorian seafront guest house has spectacular views of Llandudno's sweeping bay and the Great and Little Orme Headlands. The proprietors Anne-Marie and Howard provide you with a welcoming and friendly atmosphere, in which you can unwind and make the most of your visit. Delicious breakfasts, tastefully decorated comfortable bedrooms with digital TV, a well stocked drinks tray, free Wi-fi, and little extras make your stay special. For those attending the theatre, or for conference delegates, Venue Cymru is only a 5 minute walk along the Promenade.

Recommended in the area

The Great Orme Country Park; Conwy Castle; Snowdonia

The Stratford House

★★★★ GUEST ACCOMMODATION

Address: 8 Craig-y-Don Parade, Promenade, LLANDUDNO
LL30 1BG
Tel: 01492 877962
Email: stratfordhtl@aol.com
Website: www.stratfordguesthouse.com
Map ref: 5, SH78
Directions: A55 onto A470 to Llandudno, at rdbt 4th exit
signed Craig-y-Don, right at Promenade
Rooms: 10 en suite (2 GF), **S** £36–£40 **D** £48–£60
Notes: ⊗ on premises

As soon as you step through the door you can't help but notice
that little things matter the most at this guest house, situated on the Craig-y-Don promenade at
Llandudno. Hosts Debra and Andrew are very experienced in providing high quality accommodation
and service to ensure that your stay is both comfortable and enjoyable. All the well-equipped bedrooms
have either a bath or shower and the beds (take your choice from four-poster or Victorian style) are
made up with crisp white linen and finished with scatter cushions to give a cosy feel. Twin, double and
family rooms are available along with facilities for babies, such as cradles, cots and changing mats,
so that families can travel a little lighter. Fresh fluffy towels are placed in the room each day and there
are ample personal toiletries. Some bedrooms have sea views, as does the pleasant breakfast room.
Breakfast starts with either chilled fruit, grapefruit cocktail or cereals, followed by a traditional cooked
breakfast using free-range eggs, hand-linked sausages and best back bacon. If you prefer not to eat
meat there is fresh fruit, yoghurts, muesli or even kippers. Finish off with hot buttered toast and a
choice of jams and marmalades.

Recommended in the area

Conwy Castle; Bodnant Garden (NT); Great Orme cable car or tramway

Cadair Idris in Snowdonia National Park

Plas Rhos

★★★★★ 🛏 GUEST ACCOMMODATION

Address: Cayley Promenade, RHOS-ON-SEA
LL28 4EP
Tel: 01492 543698
Fax: 01492 540088
Email: info@plasrhos.co.uk
Website: www.plasrhos.co.uk
Map ref: 5, SH88
Directions: A55 junct 20 onto B5115 for Rhos-on-Sea, right at rdbt onto Whitehall Rd to promenade
Rooms: 8 en suite, **S** £45–£65 **D** £70–£98 **Notes:** ⊗ on premises 👶 under 12yrs **Parking:** 4
Closed: 21 Dec–Jan

A yearning to live by the sea and indulge their passion for sailing brought Susan and Colin Hazelden to the North Wales coast. Running a hotel in Derbyshire for many years was the ideal preparation for looking after guests at their renovated Victorian home. Built as a gentleman's residence in the late 19th century, Plas Rhos is situated on Cayley Promenade, where it enjoys panoramic views over the bay, beach and coast. Breakfast, a particularly memorable meal, is taken overlooking the pretty patio garden. It consists of cereals, fresh fruit, juices and yoghurt followed by free-range eggs cooked to your liking with Welsh sausage, local back bacon, tomato, mushrooms, beans and fried bread or your choice of a number of other hot options including kippers or scrambled eggs with smoked salmon. The two sumptuous lounges have spectacular sea views, comfy chairs and sofas, and interesting memorabilia, while the modest-size bedrooms are individually decorated and have plenty of thoughtful extras. One period room is furnished with a romantic half-tester and antiques, and enjoys those same stunning views. Wi-fi broadband internet access is available in all rooms – just bring your laptop.

Recommended in the area

Conwy Castle; Bodnant Garden (NT); Snowdonia National Park

Tyddyn Llan

★★★★★ ◎◎ 🍴 RESTAURANT WITH ROOMS

Address: LLANDRILLO, Corwen
LL21 0ST
Tel: 01490 440264
Fax: 01490 440414
Email: tyddynllan@compuserve.com
Website: www.tyddynllan.co.uk
Map ref: 5, SJ03
Directions: Take B4401 from Corwen to Llandrillo.
Tyddyn Llan on right leaving village
Rooms: 13 en suite (1 GF), **S** £100–£130
D £200–£340 **Parking:** 20 **Closed:** 2 wks Jan

Three acres of beautiful grounds, including shrubs, colourful borders and a croquet lawn, surround this elegant Georgian house in the Vale of Edeyrnion, and in this setting owners Bryan and Susan Webb provide their guests with tranquillity and comfort of the highest order. It's a great place for people who enjoy the available country pursuits such as fishing, walking, horse-riding, golf and water sports. Naturally in a house of this character, bedrooms come in different shapes and sizes, but all are individually decorated and stylishly furnished with period furniture. Each has a bathroom, television, CD player, direct-dial telephone and bathrobes, and everything is of the highest quality. The heart of the house, though, is the restaurant, and food remains a strong point. Bryan Webb is the chef, and he maintains an uncompromising attitude to obtaining only the finest ingredients, many of which are delivered daily by local suppliers. All the major wine-producing countries are represented on the wine list, which contains more than 250 labels, and there is an excellent selection of brandies, Armagnacs and digestives. All in all, a stay at Tyddyn Llan represents a taste of good living.

Recommended in the area

Portmeirion; Snowdon Mountain Railway; castles at Caernarfon, Beaumaris and Harlech

Pentre Mawr Country House

★★★★★ 🛏 GUEST ACCOMMODATION

Address: LLANDYROG LL16 4LA
Tel: 01824 790732
Fax: 01492 585486
Email: info@pentremawrcountryhouse.co.uk
Website: www.pentremawrcountryhouse.co.uk
Map ref: 5, SJ16
Directions: From Denbigh follow signs to Bodfari/
Llandyrnog. Left at rdbt to Bodfari, after 50yds turn
left onto country lane, follow road and Pentre Mawr
on left

Rooms: 5 en suite, S £75–£100 D £90–£120 Notes: 👶 under 13yrs Parking: 8 Closed: Nov–Feb

This property, owned by the same family for 400 years, is a unique destination, bursting with character. Tucked away in an unspoilt corner of North Wales, in an Area of Outstanding Natural Beauty, this former farmhouse is set in nearly 200 acres of meadows, park and woodland. A true Welsh country house, it features well-appointed en suite bedrooms and suites, some with hot tubs and all very spacious and thoughtfully equipped. As well as large drawing rooms, there is also a formal dining room, ideal for family gatherings and special occasions, and a less formal dining area in the conservatory by the saltwater swimming pool in the walled garden. The daily-changing menu includes carefully sourced local meats and cheeses as well as homemade breads and sorbets. Full Welsh breakfasts with Buck's fizz are served in the morning room. Influenced by a love of the outdoors and Africa, owners Bre and Graham have introduced a number of luxurious canvas safari lodges to bring guests closer to nature without compromising on comfort; all are fully heated, have super king-size beds, oak floors and decks with hot tubs plus bathrooms with free-standing baths and showers.

Recommended in the area

Snowdonia National Park; Denbigh Castle; Moel Fammau mountain walk

Pierhead building, Cardiff

Firgrove Country House B & B

★★★★★ 🛏 🍽 B&B

Address: Firgrove, Llanfwrog, RUTHIN LL15 2LL
Tel/Fax: 01824 702677
Email: meadway@firgrovecountryhouse.co.uk
Website: www.firgrovecountryhouse.co.uk
Map ref: 5, SJ15
Directions: 0.5m SW of Ruthin. A494 onto B5105, 0.25m past Llanfwrog church on right
Rooms: 3 en suite (1 GF), D £70–£100
Notes: ⊗ on premises **Parking:** 4 **Closed:** Nov–Feb

This Grade II listed building, with its inspiring views across the Vale of Clwyd, has well-equipped bedrooms and modern comforts. The well-proportioned bedrooms retain many original period features and have smart bathrooms. One of the bedrooms has an attractive four-poster bed, while another is a self-contained ground-floor suite with an open fire, small kitchen and a private sitting room. Home-made and locally sourced produce features in the splendid breakfasts; evening meals can be enjoyed by prior arrangement. The delightful garden provides a charming setting for the house.

Recommended in the area

Offa's Dyke Path; Bodnant Garden (NT); Chester

The Wynnstay Arms

★ ★ ★ ★ ◉◉ RESTAURANT WITH ROOMS

Address: Well Street, RUTHIN
LL15 1AN
Tel: 01824 703147
Email: resevations@wynnstayarms.com
Website: www.wynnstayarms.com
Map ref: 5, SJ15
Directions: In town centre
Rooms: 7 en suite, S £45–£65 D £70–£110
Parking: 12

This former coaching inn, with a history dating back to 1549, has been beautifully refurbished by three experienced hoteliers and restaurateurs to provide top-quality accommodation, a smart café-bar and an award-winning restaurant. The en suite bedrooms, including a family room, have all been stylishly decorated. Downstairs, Fusions restaurant is earning a high reputation for its modern cuisine, prepared by Jason, the head chef/owner, using fine local produce, including Welsh Black beef, locally produced cheese and local trout. Bar W serves great bar food,

Recommended in the area

Chester; Snowdonia; Caernarfon Castle

Bach-Y-Graig

★ ★ ★ ★ FARMHOUSE

Address: Tremeirchion, ST ASAPH LL17 0UH
Tel: 01745 730627
Fax: 01745 730627
Email: anwen@bachygraig.co.uk
Website: www.bachygraig.co.uk
Map ref: 5, SJ07
Directions: 3m SE of St Asaph. Off A525 at
Trefnant onto A541 to x-rds with white railings,
left down hill, over bridge & then right
Rooms: 3 (2 en suite) (1 pri facs), S £40–£55 D £70–£85 **Notes:** ⊗ on premises **Parking:** 3
Closed: Xmas & New Year

The wealth of oak beams and panelling, and Grade II listing, testify to the historic character of this farmhouse set in 200 acres with private fishing rights on the River Clwyd. Bedrooms are furnished with fine period pieces and quality soft fabrics – some rooms have antique brass beds. The ground floor has a quiet lounge and a sitting-dining room where a scrumptious breakfast is served.

Recommended in the area

Bodnant Garden (NT); The Old Gaol, Ruthin; Tweedmill Factory Outlets, St Asaph

Tan-Yr-Onnen Guest House

★★★★★ GUEST HOUSE

Address: Waen, ST ASAPH
LL17 0DU
Tel: 01745 583821
Fax: 01745 583821
Email: tanyronnenvisit@aol.com
Website: www.northwalesbreaks.co.uk
Map ref: 5, SJ07
Directions: W on A55 junct 28, turn left in 300yds
Rooms: 6 en suite (4 GF), S £60–£80 D £75–£100
Parking: 8

Set in the heart of North Wales, in the verdant Vale of Clwyd, Patrick and Sara Murphy's guest house, Tan-Yr-Onnen, is perfectly located for exploring this beautiful area and nearby Chester. Now awarded the AA's highest B&B rating, quality is the keyword here, with very high standards throughout. The house has been extensively refurbished and the separately accessed bedrooms newly constructed; all are modern and well equipped. The en suite ground-floor rooms feature king-size beds and some have French doors opening onto the patio, while those on the first floor offer suite accommodation. All provide home comforts such as bathrobes, fluffy towels, comfy beds, flat-screen TVs (with Freeview and DVD players), and tea and coffee-making facilities, plus all little touches to make your stay feel extra special. Free Wi-fi is available. The hearty breakfast table will set you up for a day's exploration and features fruit juices, fresh fruit salad, yoghurts, cereals, home-baked bread and a full Welsh breakfast. Adjacent to the dining room is the lounge and large conservatory. Here you can enjoy a cool glass of wine in the evening as you admire the grounds and gardens at the foot of the Clwydian range. Private parking is available.

Recommended in the area

St Asaph; Bodelwyddan Castle; Offa's Dyke Path

Sgwd-Y-Eira, waterfalls in the Vale of Neath, Ystradfellte, Brecon Beacons National Park

The Old Mill

★★★★ GUEST ACCOMMODATION

Address: Melin-Y-Wern, Denbigh Road NANNERCH,
Mold CH7 5RH
Tel: 01352 741542
Email: mail@old-mill.co.uk
Website: www.old-mill.co.uk
Map ref: 5, SJ16
Directions: A541 NW from Mold, 7m enter
Melin-Y-Wern, Old Mill on right
Rooms: 6 en suite (2 GF), **S** £48–£58 **D** £66–£82
Notes: ⊗ on premises **Parking:** 12 **Closed:** Nov

This converted stable block was once part of a Victorian watermill complex in the Melin-y-Wern conservation area. The site also includes a restaurant and a wine bar. Landscaped gardens surround the Old Mill, and two of the well-equipped bedrooms, all of which are en suite, are located on the ground floor. The spacious, conservatory-style dining room provides a first-class breakfast, with full English and lighter options.

Recommended in the area

Chester; Clwydian Hills Area of Outstanding Natural Beauty; Snowdonia

Llwyndu Farmhouse

★★★★ 🍽 GUEST ACCOMMODATION

Address: Llanaber BARMOUTH
LL42 1RR
Tel: 01341 280144
Email: Intouch@llwyndu-farmhouse.co.uk
Website: www.llwyndu-farmhouse.co.uk
Map ref: 5, SH16
Directions: A496 towards Harlech where street lights
end, on outskirts of Barmouth, take next right
Rooms: 7 en suite, D £80–£94 Parking: 10
Closed: 25–26 Dec

This converted 16th-century farmhouse stands overlooking Cardigan Bay in Llanaber, near Barmouth and the Mawddach Estuary, in an Area of Outstanding Natural Beauty. Noted for its fine ale and hospitality as far back as 1600, Llwyndu maintains the centuries-old tradition by providing good food, wines and local beers as well as comfortable accommodation. Many attractive elements of the original building have also survived the centuries, including inglenook fireplaces, exposed beams and timbers. Bedrooms offer all the modern comforts, with en suite facilities, televisions and tea- and coffee-making equipment, though some reflect earlier influences with their four-poster beds. Some rooms are located in the main house and four are in a converted granary, each with their own external door. There is a cosy lounge, where you might socialise with fellow guests and plan trips out. Quality Welsh produce is to the fore in the enjoyable meals served at individual tables in the character dining room. The setting for the two or three course dinners is wonderfully atmospheric by night, with candles and old lamps lighting up the exposed stone and timber. A good choice is offered for breakfast, and vegetarian and special diets can be catered for with prior notice.

Recommended in the area

RNLI Visitor Centre; Harlech Castle; Portmeirion Village

Pengwern

★ ★ ★ ★ FARMHOUSE
Address: Saron, CAERNARFON
LL54 5UH
Tel: 01286 831500
Fax: 01286 830741
Email: janepengwern@aol.com
Website: www.pengwern.net
Map ref: 5, SH46
Directions: A487 S from Caernarfon, pass
supermarket on right, right after bridge, 2m to Saron,
over x-rds, 1st driveway on right
Rooms: 3 en suite, S £45 D £70–£90 **Notes:** ⊗ on premises **Parking:** 3 **Closed:** Oct–Apr

Pengwern is a delightful farmhouse surrounded by 130 acres of beef and sheep farmland running down to Foryd Bay, noted for its bird life. There are fine views from many bedrooms over to Anglesey, and the top of Snowdon can be seen on clear days. Bedrooms are generally spacious, and all are well equipped with modern facilities. A comfortable lounge is provided and good home cooking is served.

Recommended in the area

Plas Newydd, Anglesey (NT); Caernarfon Castle; Hydro-electric Mountain

Dolgun Uchaf Guesthouse

★ ★ ★ ★ GUEST HOUSE
Address: Dolgun Uchaf, DOLGELLAU
LL40 2AB
Tel: 01341 422269
Email: dolgunuchaf@aol.com
Website: www.guesthousessnowdonia.com
Map ref: 2, SH71
Directions: Off A470 at Little Chef just S of
Dolgellau, Dolgun Uchaf 1st property on right
Rooms: 4 en suite (1 GF) **Notes:** ✿ under 5yrs
Parking: 6

Located in the heart of Snowdonia National Park, Dolgun Uchaf, a 16th-century converted farmhouse, offers contemporary comfort amid beautiful surroundings, making it an ideal place for a relaxing weekend or a base for exploring Snowdonia. Beautifully restored it retains many original features, including exposed beams and open fireplaces. Bedrooms are all en suite and equipped with thoughtful extras. Home-cooked breakfasts and pre-booked evening meals are served in the dining room.

Recommended in the area

Cader Idris Mountain; King Arthur's Labyrinth; Centre for Alternative Technology

Tyddynmawr Farmhouse

★★★★★ FARMHOUSE
Address: Cader Road, Islawrdref, DOLGELLAU
LL40 1TL
Tel: 01341 422331
Map ref: 2, SH71
Directions: From town centre left at top of square,
left at garage onto Cader Rd for 3m, 1st farm on left
after Gwernan Lake
Rooms: 3 en suite (1 GF), **S** £60 **D** £68
Notes: ⊗ on premises **Parking:** 8 **Closed:** Jan

Birdwatchers, ramblers, photographers and artists see these spectacular surroundings as a paradise, and the farmhouse accommodation appeals equally to those just happy to sit and look. Olwen Evans prides herself on her home cooking and warm hospitality. Oak beams and log fires lend character to the stone house, and bedrooms are spacious and furnished with Welsh oak furniture; one room has a balcony, and a ground-floor room benefits from a patio. The en suites are large and luxurious. This breathtaking mountain setting is about three miles from the historic market town of Dolgellau.
Recommended in the area
Walking – Cader Idris, Precipice Walk, Torrent Walk, Maddach Estuary Walk; steam railways

Penrhadw Farm

★★★★ GUEST HOUSE
Address: Pontsticill, MERTHYR TYDFIL CF48 2TU
Tel: 01685 723481
Fax: 01685 722461
Email: treghotel@aol.com
Website: www.penrhadwfarm.co.uk
Map ref: 2, SO00
Directions: Please see map on website
Rooms: 5 en suite (1 GF), **S** £48–£65 **D** £70–£95
Notes: ⊗ on premises **Parking:** 20

This former Victorian farmhouse, located in the heart of the glorious Brecon Beacons National Park and with spectacular mountain views, has been totally refurbished to provide high-quality modern accommodation. The well-equipped, spacious bedrooms include two large suites in cottages adjacent to the main building. All rooms are en suite and come with hospitality tray, TV and trouser press. There is also a comfortable guest lounge with a TV and video recorder. Separate tables are provided in the cosy breakfast room, where hearty Welsh breakfasts are served.
Recommended in the area
The Brecon Mountain Railway; Brecon Beacons National Park; Millennium Stadium, Cardiff

Ruins of Castle Dinas Bran at Llangollen

The Stonemill & Steppes Farm Cottages

★★★★ ◉◉ RESTAURANT WITH ROOMS

Address: ROCKFIELD, Monmouth NP25 5SW
Tel: 01600 775424
Fax: 01600 715257
Email: michelle@thestonemill.co.uk
Website: www.steppesfarmcottages.co.uk
Map ref: 2, SO41
Directions: A48 to Monmouth, B4233 to Rockfield. 2.6m from Monmouth town centre
Rooms: 6 en suite (6 GF) **Notes:** ⊗ on premises **Parking:** 50

Located in Rockfield, a small hamlet of Monmouth, this operation comprises well-appointed cottages with comfortable en suite rooms for self-catering or bed and breakfast. All have been architect-designed and lovingly restored with many original features remaining. In a separate, converted 16th-century barn stands the Stonemill Restaurant with oak beams, vaulted ceilings and an old cider press.

Recommended in the area

Forest of Dean; Wye Valley; The Kymin

The Crown at Whitebrook

★★★★★ ◉◉ RESTAURANT WITH ROOMS
Address: WHITEBROOK NP25 4TX
Tel: 01600 860254
Fax: 01600 860607
Email: info@crownatwhitebrook.co.uk
Website: www.crownatwhitebrook.co.uk
Map ref: 2, SO50
Directions: 4m from Monmouth on B4293, left at sign to Whitebrook, 2m on unmarked road, Crown on right
Rooms: 8 en suite, S £80–£100 D £115–£140 **Notes:** ⊗ on premises ⋈ under 12yrs **Parking:** 20 **Closed:** 22 Dec–4 Jan

In a secluded spot in the wooded valley of the River Wye, yet just five miles from the town of Monmouth, this former drover's cottage dates back to the 17th century and boasts five acres of tranquil, landscaped gardens in which guests can wander and relax. A restaurant with rooms, its refurbished and individually decorated bedrooms boast a contemporary feel and have the latest in smart facilities. The executive rooms boast the added luxury of walk-in power showers, and two rooms have double-ended baths. All have outstanding views across the rolling countryside and offer a whole host of thoughtful extras such as individually controlled heating, flat-screen TV, internet/email and tea and coffee-making facilities. In addition, the 'comfort-cool' system helps keep the rooms cool and comfortable on hot summer days. Downstairs, the lounge combines many original features with a bright, fresh look, but it is the smart, modern restaurant that lies at the heart of the whole operation. For the outstanding cooking is the thing here, with memorable cuisine featuring locally sourced ingredients skilfully prepared by head chef James Sommerin, and all accompanied by a seriously good wine list.

Recommended in the area
Brecon Beacons; Tintern Abbey; Offa's Dyke

Labuan Guest House

★★★★ GUEST HOUSE
Address: 464 Chepstow Road, NEWPORT NP19 8JF
Tel: 01633 664533
Fax: 01633 664533
Email: patricia.bees@ntlworld.com
Website: www.labuanhouse.co.uk
Map ref: 2, ST38
Directions: M4 junct 24, 1.50m on B4237
Rooms: 5 (3 en suite) (2 pri facs) (1 GF),
S £38–£45 **D** £68–£75 **Parking:** 6

John and Patricia Bees have created a warm and friendly home-from-home atmosphere at their fine Victorian house with a lovely garden. Golfers will find kindred spirits in these keen players, who will arrange tee times for their guests at any of the 45 courses within a 40-minute drive. After a day on the course or exploring the area, the high comfort levels in the stylish en suite bedrooms are very welcome indeed. Hearty breakfasts include home-made bread and preserves and evening meals can be arranged, as can lunches to go, packed in a cool bag.

Recommended in the area

Tredegar House; Caerleon Roman Site and History Museum; Newport Wetlands

Erw-Lon

★★★★★ FARMHOUSE
Address: Pontfaen, FISHGUARD SA65 9TS
Tel: 01348 881297
Email: lilwenmcallister@btinternet.com
Website: www.erw-lonfarm.co.uk
Map ref: 1, SM93
Directions: 5.50m SE of Fishguard on B4313
Rooms: 3 en suite, **S** £35–£40 **D** £60–£66 **Notes:**
⊗ ⁇ under 10yrs **Parking:** 5 **Closed:** Dec–Mar

This lovely old house is at the heart of a working sheep and cattle farm, and its landscaped gardens overlook the stunning Gwaun Valley towards Carningli, the Mountain of the Angels. Lilwen McAllister is an exceptional hostess, acknowledged by her selection as AA Landlady of the Year in 2006. There is a very homely feel to the farmhouse and the lounge is a lovely place to relax, while the bedrooms are comfortable and well equipped. Mrs McAllister's traditional farmhouse cooking uses fresh local produce and meals are served in generous portions. Erw–Lon Farm is well situated as a base to explore Pembrokeshire and Cardigan Bay.

Recommended in the area

Castell Henllys; Strumble Head; St David's Cathedral; Pembrokeshire Coastal Path

Ramsey House

★ ★ ★ ★ 🏠 🍴 GUEST HOUSE

Address: Lower Moor, ST DAVID'S, Haverfordwest SA62 6RP
Tel: 01437 720321
Email: info@ramseyhouse.co.uk
Website: www.ramseyhouse.co.uk
Map ref: 1, SM72
Directions: From Cross Sq in St Davids towards Porthclais, house 0.25m on left
Rooms: 6 (5 en suite) (1 pri facs) (3 GF), **S** £60–£95
D £90–£95 **Parking:** 10

Family-run by Suzanne and Shaun Ellison, Ramsey House is just a gentle stroll from the centre of Britain's smallest city, St David's, a place with a rich historical heritage surrounded by beautiful countryside, with the Pembrokeshire coastal path nearby. The Ellisons provide the ideal combination of professional hotel management and the warmth of a friendly guest house with a relaxed atmosphere. They are happy to advise guests on the many activities and places of interest in the locality, and there are plenty of books and leaflets in the lounge, too, to help you plan your excursions. First-floor bedrooms have views out to sea, over countryside or the world famous cathedral. Ground-floor rooms look out over over the well kept, enclosed gardens. Accommodation includes a licensed bar, next to the dining room, secure bicycle storage, a wet room, light laundry facilities and ample off-street parking. Shaun is an accomplished chef who champions quality local produce, so you can expect a real flavour of Wales from your meals. Breakfast provides a choice of home-made items including breads and preserves, and a three-course dinner is served in the restaurant. Freshly prepared picnics can also be arranged for your day out.

Recommended in the area

Pembrokeshire islands; St David's Cathedral; Pembrokeshire Coast National Park

The Waterings

★★★★ B&B

Address: Anchor Drive, High Street ST DAVID'S
SA62 6QH
Tel: 01437 720876
Fax: 01437 720876
Email: waterings@supanet.com
Website: www.waterings.co.uk
Map ref: 1, SM72
Directions: On A487 on E edge of St David's
Rooms: 5 en suite (5 GF), S £50–£80 D £75–£80
Notes: ⊗ on premises 👶 under 5yrs **Parking:** 20

The Waterings is set in 2 acres of beautiful landscaped grounds in a quiet location close to the Pembrokeshire Coast National Park Visitor Centre and only a short walk from St David's 800-year-old cathedral, which is the setting for an annual music festival at the end of May. The magnificent coastline with its abundance of birdlife is also within easy reach. The en suite bedrooms in this spacious accommodation are all on the ground floor and are set around an attractive courtyard. All the bedrooms are equipped with TV and have tea- and coffee-making facilities. The accommodation includes two family rooms with lounge, two double rooms with lounge and a double room with small sitting area. Breakfast, prepared from a good selection of local produce, is served in a smart dining room in the main house. Outside amenities at The Waterings include a picnic area with tables and benches, a barbecue and a croquet lawn. The nearest sandy beach is just a 15-minute walk away; other activities in the area include walking, boat trips to Ramsey Island, an RSPB reserve a mile offshore, sea fishing, whale and dolphin spotting boat trips, canoeing, surfing, rock climbing and abseiling.

Recommended in the area

Ramsey Island boat trips; Pembrokeshire Coast National Park; Whitesands Beach

Panorama

★ ★ ★ ★ ☐ GUEST ACCOMMODATION
Address: The Esplanade, TENBY SA70 7DU
Tel: 01834 844976
Fax: 01834 844976
Email: mail@tenby-hotel.co.uk
Website: www.tenby-hotel.co.uk
Map ref: 1, SN10
Directions: A478 follow South Beach & Town Centre
signs. Sharp left under railway arches, up Greenhill
Rd, onto South Pde then Esplanade
Rooms: 8 en suite **Notes:** ⊗ on premises ⛷ under 5yrs

Right on the Esplanade overlooking Tenby's fine South Beach and across Carmarthen Bay, the friendly, family-run Panorama is part of a handsome terrace of Victorian properties. It provides the perfect location for exploring the Pembrokeshire coastline and the ancient town with its harbour and medieval wall. The well appointed bedrooms have been decorated and furnished to the highest standard, all en suite, with tea- and coffee-making facilities. A good selection of dishes is available at breakfast.

Recommended in the area

Caldy monastic island; Tudor Merchant's House; Tenby Museum & Art Gallery

Canal Bank

★ ★ ★ ★ ★ B&B
Address: Ty Gardd, BRECON LD3 7HG
Tel: 01874 623464
Email: enquiries@accommodation-
breconbeacons.co.uk
Website: www.accommodation-breconbeacons.
co.uk
Map ref: 2, SO02
Directions: B4601 signed Brecon, left over bridge
before fuel station, turn right, continue to end of road
Rooms: 3 en suite, **S** £50–£90 **D** £65–£90
Notes: ⊗ on premises **Parking:** 5

There are colourful narrowboats on the canal right outside the front door and it's just a short walk along the towpath to Brecon's marina and town centre. There are also views of fields, hills and the River Usk. After a day sightseeing, guests can enjoy a spa bath then sink into a big, comfy bed. In the morning, a hearty Welsh breakfast is an excellent start to the day.

Recommended in the area

Carreg Cennan Castle; the Big Pit; Brecon Beacons National Park

The Coach House

★★★★★ GUEST ACCOMMODATION

Address:	Orchard Street, BRECON
	LD3 8AN
Tel:	0844 357 1304
Fax:	01874 622454
Email:	info@coachhousebrecon.com
Website:	www.coachhousebrecon.com
Map ref:	2, SO02

Directions: From town centre W over bridge onto B4601, Coach House 200yds on right
Rooms: 7 en suite, S £55–£80 D £70–£120
Notes: ⊗ on premises ⚲ under 16yrs **Parking:** 7

Coach houses were traditionally warm and welcoming places, and while a warm welcome is assured here in Brecon, this particular example is one of a new breed, offering luxurious townhouse accommodation. The private garden of the Coach House is an oasis of colour, and offers a retreat in which to relax, read a book or take a drink. Hosts Marc and Tony are proud of their local knowledge, and offer advice on the best places to visit, walk, cycle or ride. There are also opportunities for sailing or pony-trekking in the area. The strong sense of place evident in the photographs and maps of the Brecon Beacons on the walls, showing some of the most unspoilt countryside in Wales, continues through to the Welsh-speciality breakfasts – try Eggs Brychan, made with scrambled eggs, smoked salmon and laverbread for starters. Evening meals are similarly inventive and are served in the small restaurant. Much thought has gone into the contemporary design of the light, airy bedrooms, all of which are well equipped, and some of which have a DVD player and a film library. There's even a holistic therapist on hand to soothe away the stresses of the day.

Recommended in the area

Brecon Beacons National Park; Dan yr Ogof Caves; Brecon Catherdral

Cribyn from Fan-y-Big, Brecon Beacons National Park

Llanddetty Hall Farm

★★★★ FARMHOUSE
Address: Talybont-on-Usk, BRECON
LD3 7YR
Tel: 01874 676415
Fax: 01874 676415
Map ref: 2, SO12
Directions: SE of Brecon. Off B4558
Rooms: 4 (3 en suite) (1 pri facs) (1 GF), S £36
D £56–£62 **Parking:** 6 **Notes:** 🐾 under 12yrs
Closed: 16 Dec–14 Jan

This listed farmhouse is part of a sheep farm in the Brecon Beacons National Park. The Brecon and Monmouth Canal flows through the farm at the rear, while the front of the house overlooks the River Usk. Bedrooms, including one on the ground floor, feature exposed beams and polished floorboards. Three rooms are en suite and one has a private bathroom – all have radio alarms and tea and coffee facilities. There is a lounge with a television, and a dining room where breakfast is served at an oak refectory table.
Recommended in the area
Brecon Beacons National Park; Hay-on-Wye; Aberglasney

Glangrwyney Court

★★★★★ B&B

Address: CRICKHOWELL
NP8 1ES
Tel: 01873 811288
Fax: 01873 810317
Email: info@glancourt.co.uk
Website: www.glancourt.co.uk
Map ref: 2, SO21
Directions: 2m SE of Crickhowell on A40
(near county boundary)
Rooms: 10 (9 en suite) (1 pri facs) (1 GF),
S £50–£85 D £70–£95 **Parking:** 12

A privately-owned, Georgian Grade II listed country house, Glangrwyney Court offers delightful luxury accommodation. Forming part of a small country estate on the edge of the beautiful Brecon Beacons and the Black Mountains it stands in 4 acres of walled gardens and makes an ideal base for touring this lovely area. The house throughout is tastefully decorated and furnished with period pieces. Guests are encouraged to relax in the cosy sitting room in front of a roaring log fire in the winter months. Glangrwyney Court has been home to the same family for the last 17 years, during which time the main house and the cottages have been sympathetically restored to provide excellent modern comforts. The accommodation comprises eight bedrooms in the main house, one ground-floor room in the Garden Courtyard and three cottages which are available on a bed and breakfast basis or for self-catering. All rooms have TV and DVD players, hairdryers, clock radios, quality toiletries, fluffy bath towels and robes plus tea and coffee making facilities.

Recommended in the area

Brecon Beacons National Park; Dan-Yr-Ogof Caves; Big Pit National Mining Museum of Wales

Hafod-Y-Garreg

★★★★ B&B

Address: ERWOOD LD2 3TQ
Tel: 01982 560400
Email: john-annie@hafod-y.wanadoo.co.uk
Website: www.hafodygarreg.co.uk
Map ref: 2, SO04
Directions: 1m S of Erwood. Off A470 at Trericket
Mill, sharp right, up track past cream farmhouse
towards pine forest, through gate
Rooms: 2 en suite, D £65 **Parking:** 6
Closed: Xmas

This Grade II listed farmhouse, the oldest surviving house in Wales, dates from 1402 and is believed to have been built as Henry IV's hunting lodge. The house is in a superb location, has tremendous character and, combined with stunning early Welsh oak furniture and gorgeous fabrics, it is an ideal place to get away from it all. The attractive bedrooms have beautiful bed linen and modern facilities, dinner is served in the beamed dining room and breakfast includes home-laid free range eggs.

Recommended in the area

Hay-on-Wye; Brecon Beacons; Royal Welsh Showground

Guidfa House

★★★★★ GUEST ACCOMMODATION

Address: Crossgates, LLANDRINDOD WELLS
LD1 6RF
Tel: 01597 851241
Fax: 01597 851875
Email: guidfa@globalnet.co.uk
Website: www.guidfa-house.co.uk
Map ref: 2, SO06
Directions: 3m N of Llandrindod Wells,
at junct of A483 & A44

Rooms: 6 en suite (1 GF), S £60 D £75–£100 **Notes:** ⊗ on premises ⚑ under 10yrs **Parking:** 10

Expect a relaxed stay at Anne and Tony Millan's charming Georgian house, set within picturesque gardens and located in the village of Crossgates, just north of Llandrindod Wells. All rooms come well equipped with comfortable beds, fluffy towels, soft bathrobes and quality toiletries. The luxurious Coach House suite has a super-king double bed and a large, separate sitting room and spa bath. Free Wi-fi is available. The meals at Guidfa House are both delicious and imaginative, prepared from local produce.

Recommended in the area

Elan Valley RSPB Red Kite Feeding Station; Royal Welsh Showground; Builth Wells

Hay Castle

Carlton Riverside

★ ★ ★ ★ ◉◉◉ RESTAURANT WITH ROOMS

Address: Irfon Crescent, LLANWRTYD WELLS
LD5 4ST
Tel: 01591 610248
Email: info@carltonrestaurant.co.uk
Website: www.carltonrestaurant.co.uk
Map ref: 2, SN84
Directions: In town centre next to bridge
Rooms: 4 en suite, S £40–£50 D £65–£100
Closed: Dec

This delightful restaurant with rooms is in one of the town's
oldest buildings beside the old stone bridge over the River Irfon.
Llanwrtyd Wells sits at the foot of the beautiful Cambrian Mountains and is one of Wales's best kept
secrets. From here there are many wonderful walks without the necessity to drive, plus mountain biking
is very popular in this area – bikes can be hired locally. Chef Mary Ann Gilchrist is passionate about the
use of local produce and she sources as many of her ingredients as possible from nearby farmers and
growers. The stylish, intimate restaurant combines quality contemporary fabrics and furnishings with
the charm of the house and river views. There are four, individually furnished, comfortable bedrooms,
each with an en suite shower and bath with big fluffy towels and high quality toiletries. The beds have
very comfortable pocket-spring mattresses and all the rooms have flat-screen TVs, DVD players, clock
radios and hospitality trays. There are two lounges for guests to relax and enjoy a drink while perusing
the menus or reading a cookery book from the large collection on the library shelves.

Recommended in the area

National Botanic Gardens of Wales; Aberglasney House & Gardens; Llanerchaeron (National Trust)

Moors Farm B&B

★★★★★ B&B

Address: Oswestry Road, WELSHPOOL SY21 9JR
Tel: 01938 553395
Email: moorsfarm@tiscali.co.uk
Website: www.moors-farm.com
Map ref: 2, SJ20
Directions: 1.50m NE of Welshpool off A483
Rooms: 5 en suite
Notes: ⊗ on premises

Once the principal farmhouse of Powis Castle, Moors Farm remains impressive and is well situated on the main A483, between the River Severn and the Montgomery Canal. The farmhouse is still at the heart of a working farm that raises sheep and cattle. The building is full of character, with lots of exposed old beams and log-burning fires that are as warm as the welcome, and has been extensively renovated to provide accommodation that is both spacious and comfortable. Wholesome breakfasts are served in the elegant dining room around a huge family dining table, where guests all sit together in the old traditional manner. House party dinners are available by prior arrangement. The luxury Gate House barn conversion offers well-equipped spacious self-catering accommodation suitable for large families or a group of friends. Popular activities in the area include walking, cycling, golf, fishing, horse-riding, quad trekking, canoeing and canal boating. It is just a mile along the canal tow path into the heart of the bustling market town of Welshpool where you'll find cafés, restaurants and traditional pubs alongside shops selling quality local produce. The Moors Farm especially welcomes group and family bookings.

Recommended in the area

Powis Castle and Gardens (NT); Welshpool and Llanfair Light Railway; Offa's Dyke Path; Glyndwr's Way; Glansevern Hall Gardens

Little Langland

★★★★★ GUEST ACCOMMODATION

Address: 2 Rotherslade Road, Langland MUMBLES, Swansea SA3 4QN
Tel: 01792 369696
Email: enquiries@littlelangland.co.uk
Website: www.littlelangland.co.uk
Map ref: 2, SS68
Directions: Off A4067 in Mumbles onto Newton Rd, 4th left onto Langland Rd, 2nd left onto Rotherslade Rd

Rooms: 6 en suite, **S** £65–£70 **D** £85–£100 **Notes:** ⊗ on premises 🚼 under 8yrs **Parking:** 6

Little Langland has recently undergone a total refurbishment, although the lovely Victorian façade remains intact, and the proprietors Christine and Roger Johnson are justly proud of their comfortable new interior. This family-run establishment is only five miles from Swansea city centre and is within easy access of the stunning Gower Peninsula with its many coves and bays and the first area in Britain to be designated an Area of Outstanding Natural Beauty. The en suite bedrooms here are stylish, comfortable and well furnished, and all include thoughtful extras such as free broadband internet connection, as well as flat-screen LCD TV, hairdryer and tea and coffee-making facilities. Guests can also make use of the brand new café bar, which is an ideal place for a relaxing drink with friends. It offers a bar menu of freshly prepared snacks, made using locally sourced ingredients wherever possible, along with a good variety of coffees, beers and wines. Breakfast is served in the comfortable dining area. All in all, Little Langland makes a great base for visiting South Wales, whether planning a relaxing or a more energetic trip.

Recommended in the area

Rotherslade Bay; Oystermouth village; Mumbles Head

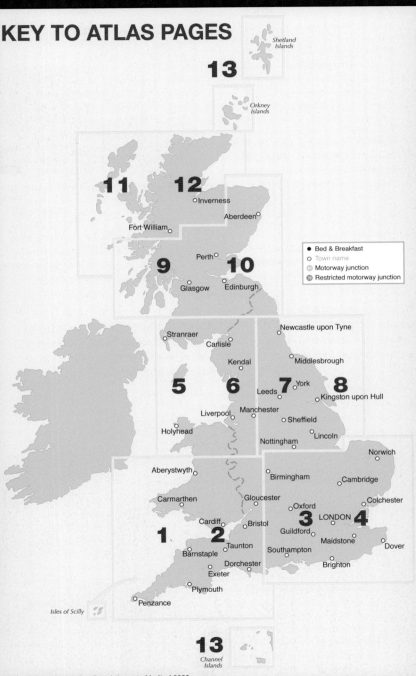

KEY TO ATLAS PAGES

Shetland Islands

13

Orkney Islands

11   **12**

○ Inverness

Aberdeen ○

Fort William ○

● Bed & Breakfast
○ Town name
Ⓜ Motorway junction
Ⓡ Restricted motorway junction

Perth ○

9   **10**

Glasgow ○   ○ Edinburgh

○ Stranraer

Newcastle upon Tyne ○

Carlisle ○

Kendal ○   Middlesbrough ○

5   **6**   **7** York ○   **8**

Leeds ○

Liverpool ○   Manchester ○   Kingston upon Hull ○

Holyhead ○   Sheffield ○

Nottingham ○   Lincoln ○

Norwich ○

Aberystwyth ○   Birmingham ○   Cambridge ○

Carmarthen ○   Gloucester ○   Colchester ○

Cardiff ○   ○ Bristol   Oxford ○   **3** LONDON   **4**

1   **2**   Guildford ○   Maidstone ○   Dover ○

Barnstaple ○   Taunton ○   Southampton ○   Brighton ○

Dorchester ○
Exeter ○
Plymouth ○

Penzance ○

Isles of Scilly

13
Channel Islands

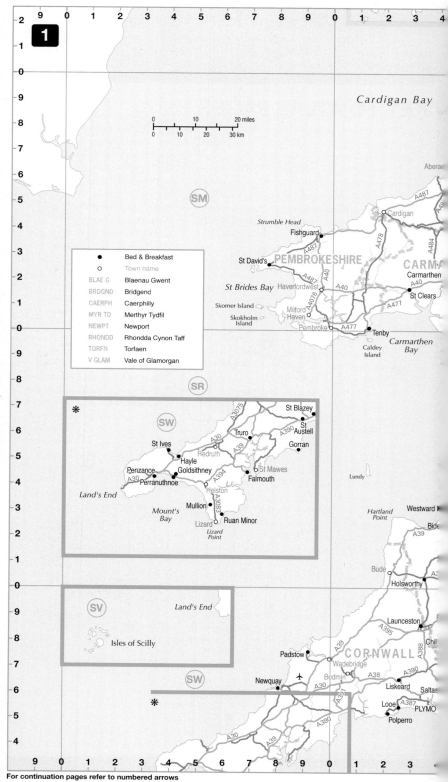

1

Cardigan Bay

0　10　20 miles
0　10　20　30 km

SM

Bed & Breakfast
Town name
BLAE G　Blaenau Gwent
BRDGND　Bridgend
CAERPH　Caerphilly
MYR TD　Merthyr Tydfil
NEWPT　Newport
RHONDD　Rhondda Cynon Taff
TORFN　Torfaen
V GLAM　Vale of Glamorgan

Strumble Head
Fishguard
St David's
PEMBROKESHIRE
CARM
St Brides Bay
Haverfordwest
Carmarthen
St Clears
Skomer Island
Skokholm
Island
Milford
Haven
Pembroke
Tenby
Caldey
Island
Carmarthen
Bay

Aberae

Cardigan

SR

SW

St Blazey
Truro
St Austell
St Ives
Gorran
Hayle
Redruth
Penzance
Goldsithney
St Mawes
Perranuthnoe
Falmouth
Land's End
Helston
Mullion
Mount's
Bay
Lizard
Ruan Minor
Lizard
Point

Lundy

Hartland
Point
Westward H
Bide

Bude
Holsworthy

Launceston
Chil

SV
Land's End

Isles of Scilly

SW

Padstow
Newquay
Wadebridge
Bodmin
CORNWALL
Liskeard
Saltas
Looe
PLYMO
Polperro

For continuation pages refer to numbered arrows

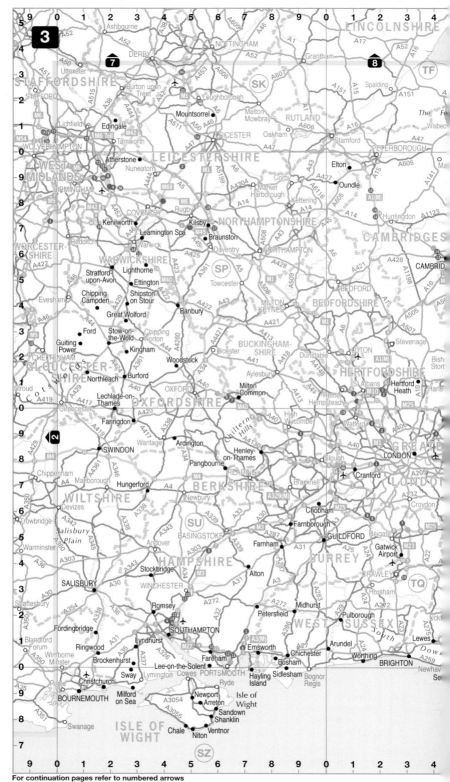

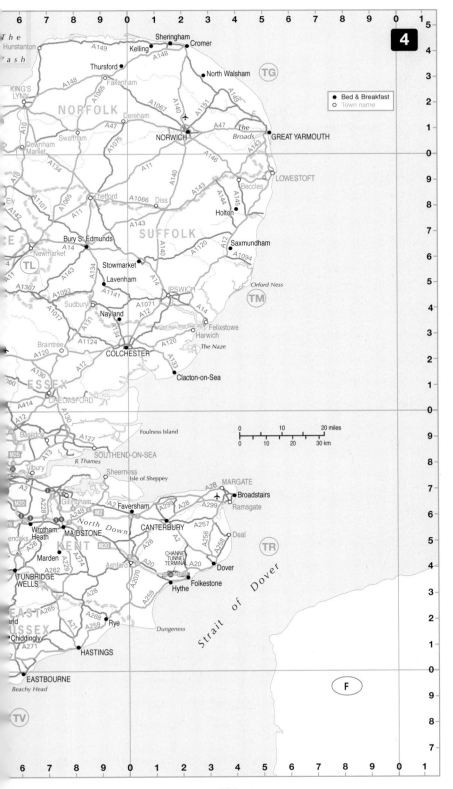

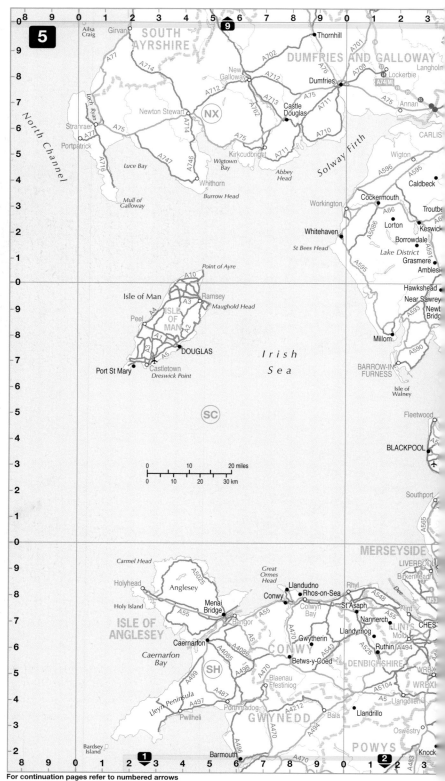

North Channel

SOUTH AYRSHIRE

Ailsa Craig
Girvan
Thornhill

DUMFRIES AND GALLOWAY
Langholm

A77
A714
A702

New Galloway
A712
A76
Lockerbie
A74(M)

NX
A712
A762
A713
Dumfries
A709
Annan

Newton Stewart
Castle Douglas
A711
A75

Stranraer
A75
A710
CARLIS

Loch Ryan
Portpatrick
A716
A75

Kirkcudbright
A711

A747
A746
Wigtown Bay
Abbey Head

Luce Bay
Whithorn
Burrow Head

Mull of Galloway

Solway Firth

Wigton
A596
A595
Caldbeck

Workington
Cockermouth
A66
Troutbe
Keswick

Whitehaven
A5086
Lorton
Borrowdale

St Bees Head
Lake District
Grasmere
Ambles

A595

Point of Ayre
A10
Hawkshead
Near Sawrey
Newt Bridg

Isle of Man
Ramsey
Maughold Head

A4
A3
ISLE OF MAN

Peel
A71
A2
A593

A1
A3
A5
DOUGLAS
Millom

Port St Mary
Castletown
Dreswick Point

Irish Sea

BARROW-IN-FURNESS

SC
Isle of Walney

Fleetwood

A5

BLACKPOOL

0   10   20 miles
0   10   20   30 km

Southport
A565

MERSEYSIDE
LIVERPOO
Birkenhead

Carmel Head
A5025
Great Ormes Head
Llandudno
Rhyl
LIVERPOOL

Holyhead
Anglesey
Conwy
Rhos-on-Sea
A548
Flint
M53

Holy Island
Menai Bridge
A55
Colwyn Bay
St Asaph
Nannerch
CHES

ISLE OF ANGLESEY
Bangor
A55
A55
Mold
FLINTS

Caernarfon
A487
Gwytherin
Llandyrnog
Ruthin
A494
WREX

Caernarfon Bay
A4085
A4086
CONWY
A543
A525
WREXI

SH
A498
A470
Betws-y-Coed
DENBIGHSHIRE
A5104

Lleyn Peninsula
A487
Blaenau Ffestiniog
A470
Llangollen

Pwllheli
A497
Porthmadog
A4212
A5
Oswestry

Bardsey Island
GWYNEDD
Bala
Llandrillo
A494

Barmouth
A496
A470
POWYS
Knock
A483

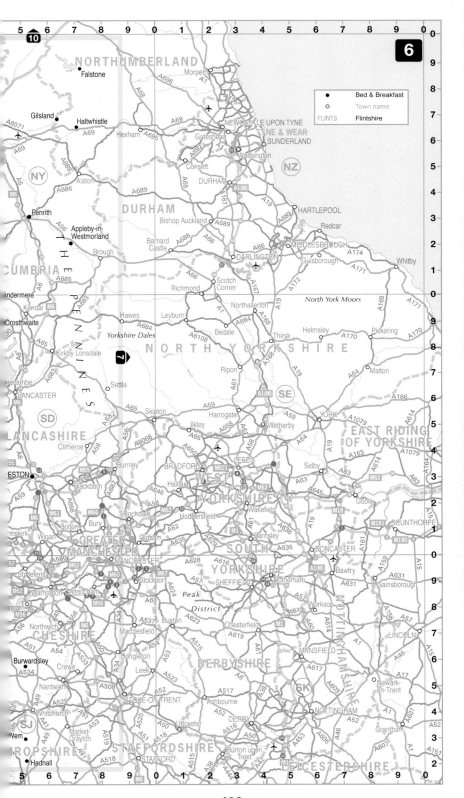

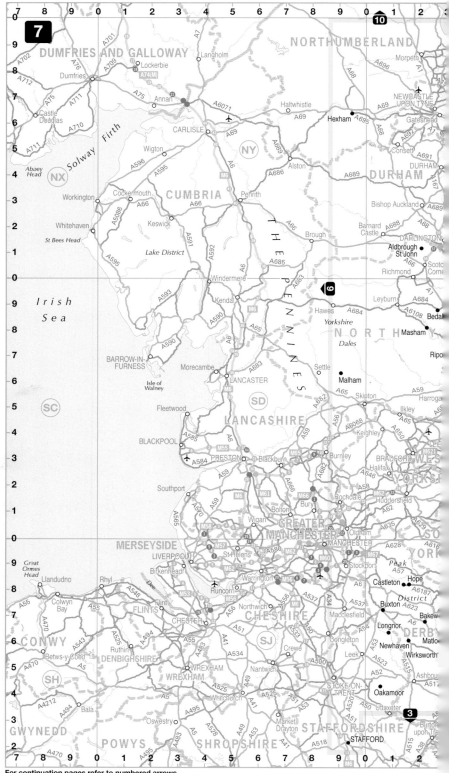

Bed & Breakfast
Town name

0   10   20 miles
0   10   20   30 km

Tynemouth
TYNE & WEAR
SUNDERLAND
ashington
NZ
HARTLEPOOL
A1(M)
A689
A19
Redcar
MIDDLESBROUGH
A174
A66
Guisborough
A171
Whitby
A172
Robin Hood's Bay
North York Moors
A169
A171
Northallerton
A168
SCARBOROUGH
Thirsk
Helmsley
A170
A170
Pickering
Flamborough Head
Ampleforth
A19
A64
Malton
A165
TA
Sutton-on-the-Forest
Westow
A614
Bridlington
Knaresborough
A59
A166
A614
Driffield
Goldsborough
YORK
A1079
A164
A165
Wetherby
EAST RIDING
A64
A19
A165
A58
SE
A163
A1079
A185
A162
Selby
A614
Beverley
A63
A63
A164
M62
A63
KINGSTON UPON HULL
Goole
R. Humber
akefield
A1077
A160
M18
A15
Immingham
Spurn Head
A635
M181
SCUNTHORPE
A180
GRIMSBY
Barnsley
M180
A18
Cleethorpes
DONCASTER
A161
Epworth
A159
A46
A1(M)
Bawtry
Gainsborough
A15
A16
Market Rasen
A1031
Mablethorpe
Rotherham
A631
A631
The Wolds
Louth
SHEFFIELD
A57
Fillingham
A46
A157
A153
A16
A52
A619
Worksop
Marton
A156
A158
Skegness
esterfield
A614
A57
A1
LINCOLN
Horncastle
A158
SK
M1
MANSFIELD
A616
A607
A15
LINCOLNSHIRE
TF
Alfreton
A617
Newark-on-Trent
A153
The Wash
Hunstanton
A149
3elper
A60
A6097
A17
Normanton
Sleaford
Boston
NOTTINGHAM
Hough-on-the-Hill
A1
A17
A52
NORFOLK
RBY Risley
A52
A607
Grantham
A52
A16
A453
A46
A606
A151
Spalding
A151
A17
KING'S LYNN
A148
LEICESTERSHIRE
A1
A15
A47

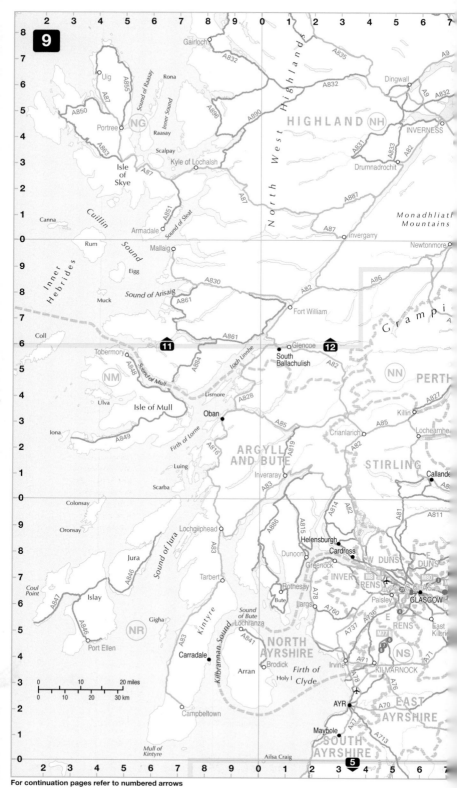

●	Bed & Breakfast
○	Town name
C EDIN	City of Edinburgh
C GLAS	City of Glasgow
CLACKS	Clackmannanshire
W DUNS	West Dunbartonshire
E DUNS	East Dunbartonshire
E RENS	East Renfrewshire
INVER	Inverclyde
N LANS	North Lanarkshire
RENS	Renfrewshire

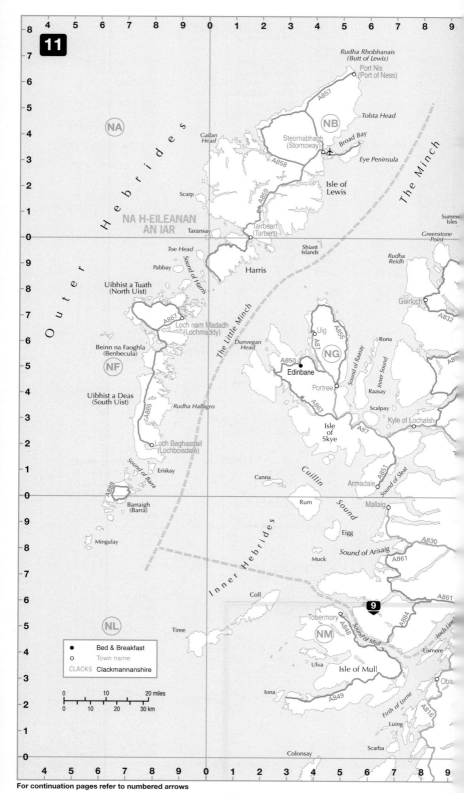

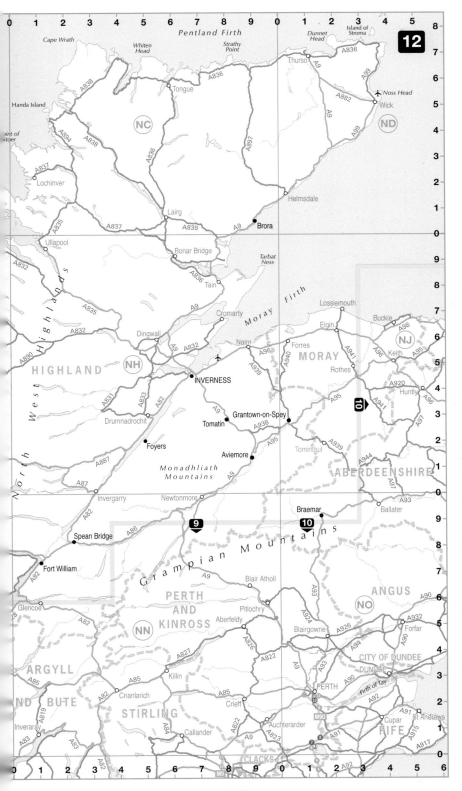

Orkney Islands

- ● Bed & Breakfast
- ○ Town name

HY

Westray

Rousay

Sanday

Eday

Stronsay

Mainland

Shapinsay

Stromness ○ Kirkwall ○

Hoy

South Ronaldsay

ND

13

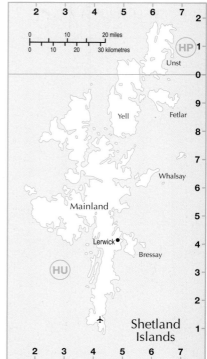

Shetland Islands

HP

Unst

Yell

Fetlar

Whalsay

Mainland

Lerwick ●

Bressay

HU

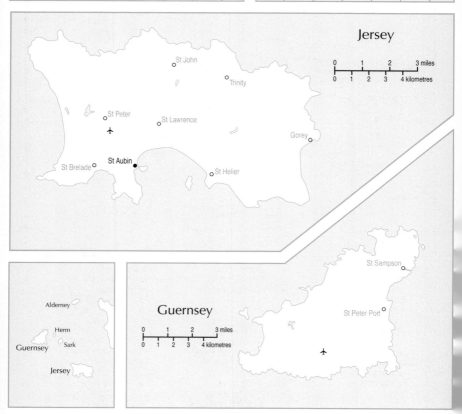

Jersey

○ St John

○ Trinity

○ St Peter

○ St Lawrence

○ Gorey

St Brelade ○

St Aubin ●

○ St Helier

Guernsey

Alderney

Herm

Guernsey Sark

Jersey

St Sampson ○

St Peter Port ○

County Map

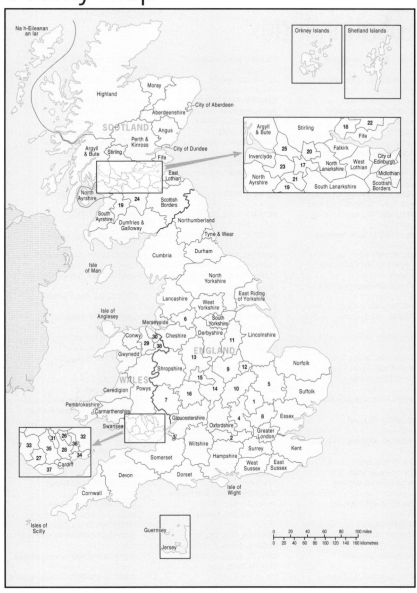

England
1 Bedfordshire
2 Berkshire
3 Bristol
4 Buckinghamshire
5 Cambridgeshire
6 Greater Manchester
7 Herefordshire
8 Hertfordshire
9 Leicestershire
10 Northamptonshire
11 Nottinghamshire
12 Rutland
13 Staffordshire
14 Warwickshire
15 West Midlands
16 Worcestershire

Scotland
17 City of Glasgow
18 Clackmannanshire
19 East Ayrshire
20 East Dunbartonshire
21 East Renfrewshire
22 Perth & Kinross
23 Renfrewshire
24 South Lanarkshire
25 West Dunbartonshire

Wales
26 Blaenau Gwent
27 Bridgend
28 Caerphilly
29 Denbighshire
30 Flintshire
31 Merthyr Tydfil
32 Monmouthshire
33 Neath Port Talbot
34 Newport
35 Rhondda Cynon Taff
36 Torfaen
37 Vale of Glamorgan
38 Wrexham

Location Index

Location Index

Location Index

444

Location Index

445

B&B Index

B&B Index

447

B&B Index

The Automobile Association would like to thank the following photographers, companies and picture libraries for their assistance in the preparation of this book.

Abbreviations for the picture credits are as follows: (t) top; (b) bottom; (l) left; (r) right; (c) centre; (AA) AA World Travel Library.

4 Royalty Free Photodisc; 6 Royalty Free Photodisc; 8 TongRo Image Stock / Alamy; 10 Royalty Free Photodisc; 11 Royalty Free Photodisc; 12 Stockbyte Royalty Free; 14 Royalty Free Photodisc; 15 Royalty Free Photodisc; 16/17 AA/M Jourdan; 18 AA/C Jones; 20t AA/W Voysey; 21 AA/S Day; 24 AA/T Mackie; 26 AA/A Tryner; 30 AA/M Moss; 33t AA/J Wood; 36t AA/R Tenison; 42t AA/R Tenison; 47t AA/R Moss; 50t AA/J Wood; 52t AA/J Wood; 56t AA/S Day; 60t AA/J Wood; 61 AA/A Mockford & N Bonetti; 64t AA/J Sparks; 71t AA/T Mackie; 75t AA/E A Bowness; 76t AA/T Mackie; 80 AA/A Mockford & N Bonetti; 84t AA/R Coulam; 86 AA/M Birkitt; 87t AA/A Midgley; 89t AA/T Mackie; 94t AA/T Mackie; 95 AA/N Hicks; 100t AA/A Lawson; 107t AA/C Jones; 110t AA/N Hicks; 113t AA/N Hicks; 118t AA/B Pearce; 121t AA/N Hicks; 122 AA/M Jourdan; 128t AA/R Ireland; 132t AA/H Ireland; 134 AA/J Miller; 136t AA/M Birkitt; 137 AA/H Palmer; 143t AA/S Day; 144 AA/H Palmer; 148t AA/S Day; 149t AA/H Palmer; 150 AA/W Voysey; 154 AA/M Moody; 156t AA/M Moody; 158t AA/W Voysey; 160 AA/M Moody; 161t AA/A Burton; 163t AA/T Souter; 167 AA/A Burton; 168 AA/C Jones; 173t AA/H Williams; 174 AA/M Moody; 175t AA/M Moody; 176 AA/N Setchfield; 182 AA/S Day; 184 AA/A Tryner; 185t AA/M Birkitt; 186 AA/T Mackie; 187t AA/M Birkitt; 192 AA/J Tims; 195t AA/R Ireland; 196 AA/T Mackie; 203 AA/T Mackie; 204 AA/M Birkitt; 207t AA/M Birkitt; 208 AA/R Coulam; 215t AA/H Williams; 216 AA/M Birkitt; 217t AA/S Day; 223 AA/M Short; 227t AA/S Day; 230t AA; 233 AA/N Hicks; 234 AA/H Williams; 238t AA; 250t AA/J Tims; 252t AA/J Tims; 253 AA/T Mackie; 255t AA/T Mackie; 256t AA/J Welsh; 257 AA/T Mackie; 259 AA/D Forss; 260t AA/M Birkitt; 263 AA/T Mackie; 264 AA/J Tims; 266t AA/M Trelawny; 267 AA/J Miller; 278t AA/S&O Mathews; 280 AA/D Forss; 286 AA/J Miller; 288 AA/M Moody; 292 AA; 295 AA/S McBride; 296t AA/S McBride; 302 AA/R Newton; 303t AA/W Voysey; 308 AA/M Moody; 310t AA/M Moody; 311 AA/D Tarn; 313t AA; 314 AA/M Kipling; 316t AA/M Kipling; 319t AA; 322t AA/M Kipling; 322t AA/M Kipling; 328t AA/M Kipling; 331t AA/M Kipling; 334t AA/M Kipling; 335 AA/W Voysey; 337 AA/W Voysey; 338 AA; 340/341 AA/R Weir; 343 AA/J Beazley; 350t AA/S Whitehorne; 354t AA/R Weir; 357 AA/J Smith; 361t AA/S Day; 364 AA/J Carnie; 373 AA/S Whitehorne; 376 AA/S Anderson; 381 AA/J Henderson; 383t AA/S Day; 384 AA/M Alexander; 386/387 AA/I Burgum; 389t AA/C Molyneux; 402 AA/S Lewis; 406t AA/N Jenkins; 409t AA/I Burgum; 414t AA/N Jenkins; 420t AA/N Jenkins; 423 AA/D Santillo

Every effort has been made to trace the copyright holders, and we apologise in advance for any accidental errors. We would be happy to apply any corrections in the following edition of this publication.

ENGLAND

Durdle Door, Dorset

Lambourn market place